T0323530

THE EXTENDED
ENERGY–GROWTH NEXUS

THE EXTENDED ENERGY–GROWTH NEXUS
Theory and Empirical Applications

Edited by

JOSÉ ALBERTO FUINHAS
NECE-UBI, CeBER and Faculty of Economics,
University of Coimbra, Coimbra, Portugal

ANTÓNIO CARDOSO MARQUES
NECE-UBI and Management and
Economics Department,
University of Beira Interior, Covilhã, Portugal

ACADEMIC PRESS

An imprint of Elsevier

Academic Press is an imprint of Elsevier
125 London Wall, London EC2Y 5AS, United Kingdom
525 B Street, Suite 1650, San Diego, CA 92101, United States
50 Hampshire Street, 5th Floor, Cambridge, MA 02139, United States
The Boulevard, Langford Lane, Kidlington, Oxford OX5 1GB, United Kingdom

Notices

Knowledge and best practice in this field are constantly changing. As new research and experience broaden our understanding, changes in research methods, professional practices, or medical treatment may become necessary.

Practitioners and researchers must always rely on their own experience and knowledge in evaluating and using any information, methods, compounds, or experiments described herein. In using such information or methods they should be mindful of their own safety and the safety of others, including parties for whom they have a professional responsibility.

To the fullest extent of the law, neither the Publisher nor the authors, contributors, or editors, assume any liability for any injury and/or damage to persons or property as a matter of products liability, negligence or otherwise, or from any use or operation of any methods, products, instructions, or ideas contained in the material herein.

British Library Cataloguing-in-Publication Data
A catalogue record for this book is available from the British Library

Library of Congress Cataloging-in-Publication Data
A catalog record for this book is available from the Library of Congress

ISBN: 978-0-12-815719-0

For Information on all Academic Press publications
visit our website at https://www.elsevier.com/books-and-journals

Publisher: Candice Janco
Acquisition Editor: J. Scott Bentley
Editorial Project Manager: Karen R. Miller
Production Project Manager: Joy Christel Neumarin
                    Honest Thangiah
Cover Designer: Mark Rogers

Typeset by MPS Limited, Chennai, India

Working together
to grow libraries in
developing countries

www.elsevier.com • www.bookaid.org

Dedications

To our students

Contents

4. The impacts of China's effect and globalization on the augmented energy—nexus: evidence in four aggregated regions   97

Luís Miguel Marques, José Alberto Fuinhas and António Cardoso Marques

5. The effect of fiscal and financial incentive policies for renewable energy on CO_2 emissions: the case for the Latin American region   141

Matheus Koengkan, José Alberto Fuinhas and António Cardoso Marques

6. Energy—growth nexus, domestic credit, and environmental sustainability: a panel causality analysis   173

Matheus Belucio, Cátia Lopes, José Alberto Fuinhas and António Cardoso Marques

List of contributors

Tiago Lopes Afonso
NECE-UBI and Management and Economics Department, University of Beira Interior, Covilhã, Portugal

Matheus Belucio
Economics Department, University of Évora, Évora, Portugal; Faculty of Economics, University of Coimbra, Coimbra, Portugal

Alexandre Magno de Melo Faria
GPDS-CNPq and Faculty of Economics, Federal University of Mato Grosso, Cuiabá, Brazil

José Alberto Fuinhas
NECE-UBI, CeBER and Faculty of Economics, University of Coimbra, Coimbra, Portugal

Hélde A.D. Hdom
The Capes Foundation, Ministry of Education of Brazil, Brasilia, Brazil

Matheus Koengkan
CEFAGE-UE and Department of Economics, University of Évora, Portugal

Cátia Lopes
Management and Economics Department, University of Beira Interior, Covilhã, Portugal

António Cardoso Marques
NECE-UBI and Management and Economics Department, University of Beira Interior, Covilhã, Portugal

Luís Miguel Marques
NECE-UBI and Management and Economics Department, University of Beira Interior, Covilhã, Portugal

Sónia Almeida Neves
NECE-UBI and Management and Economics Department, University of Beira Interior, Covilhã, Portugal

Diogo Santos Pereira
NECE-UBI and Management and Economics Department, University of Beira Interior, Covilhã, Portugal

Renato Santiago
NECE-UBI and University of Beira Interior, Management and Economics Department, Covilhã, Portugal

Acknowledgments

The financial support of the NECE—Research Unit in Business Science and Economics, sponsored by the FCT—Portuguese Foundation for the Development of Science and Technology, Ministry of Science, Technology and Higher Education, project UID/GES/04630/2019, is acknowledged.

Introduction

It is widely accepted that energy is an essential input to produce both goods and services. Due to this fact, the hypothesis on the existence of a relationship between a country's energy consumption and its economic output seems quite logical.

The connection between these two variables got stronger after the industrial revolution, which gave energy a key role in the production process. However, even with the advances in the economic growth literature, energy was still seen as an intermediate production input by mainstream economists. This derives from the fact that many economists still ground their works in the neoclassical growth model proposed by Solow (1956). According to this model, capital and labor should be considered as the only primary inputs for growth.

Despite the previous facts, there are a great number of economists (especially the ones linked with energy economics and ecological economics) who recognize energy as an important production factor and defend the idea that this variable should not be ignored in economic growth studies (e.g., Stern, 2011).

The prominence of the energy consumption—economic growth relationship increased with the occurrence of energy supply shocks (e.g., the world oil crises in 1973). This led researchers to become more aware of the role of energy in the economy. More recently, concerns regarding global warming and climate changes have reinforced the importance of this issue, and inclusively led to the rise of new study issues, such as the examination of the Environmental Kuznets Curve for example.

The seminal paper of Kraft and Kraft (1978) is usually cited as the first to investigate the causal relationship between energy consumption and economic growth. Since then, several studies have been published centered on this specific topic, but their results are far from being consensual. The differences in the studies' conclusions makes it particularly difficult to make completely reliable policy implications based on their outcomes.

Looking to the survey of Ozturk (2010), one can easily confirm that there are a host of different results in the literature regarding the energy consumption—economic growth nexus. Additionally, in this survey, four possible hypotheses concerning the causal relationship between energy and growth are also synthetized. These are:

(1) *Growth hypothesis* (unidirectional causality running from energy to growth);

(2) *Conservation hypothesis* (unidirectional causality running from growth to energy);

(3) *Feedback hypothesis* (bidirectional causality between energy and growth); and

(4) *Neutrality hypothesis* (energy and growth are neutral with respect to each other).

An additional hypothesis that could also be mentioned is the "curse hypothesis," which states that an abundance of energy sources can negatively affect a country's economic growth (e.g., Fuinhas & Marques, 2013).

In addition to the surveys, some *meta*-analytic works were produced (e.g., Chen, Chen, & Chen, 2012; Hajko, 2017) to identify the motives for the heterogeneity in the energy—growth nexus studies' results. They also tried (but failed) to find a fundamental energy—growth nexus relationship. Regarding the reasons for the contradictory results, it seems that the results are especially influenced by the estimation methods that researchers chose to use. In the Ozturk (2010) survey, and Hajko (2017) *meta*-analysis, one can see that the vector autoregressive (VAR)/vector error correction model methodology with Granger causality testing, and the Hisiao's (1981) and Toda and Yamamoto's (1995) versions of Granger causality, are the methodologies that researchers used most often. Cointegration testing is also frequently used in most of the studies.

In the literature, one can see that the energy consumption—economic growth nexus started to be studied in a bivariate specification (e.g., Kraft & Kraft, 1978). The great explanation power that energy variables seem to have on economic growth, and the feasible results produced by these bivariate models, significantly contributed to the increased use of these frameworks. However, problems such as the omitted variable bias led some researchers to extend their specifications by introducing more variables into their models. The supply and demand approaches of this nexus can be an example of this fact, with the inclusion in the models of capital and labor (e.g., Lee & Chien, 2010; Payne, 2009) and energy prices (e.g., Damette & Seghir, 2013; Fatai, Oxley, & Scrimgeour, 2004), respectively, in addition to energy consumption and economic growth.

Despite these two approaches, the study of the augmented energy consumption—growth nexus is not restricted to the inclusion of the previously mentioned variables. Examples of the inclusion of other macroeconomic (or environmental) variables on the analysis of the complexity of the nexus are, for example, financial development (e.g., Islam, Shahbaz, Ahmed, & Alam, 2013), carbon dioxide emissions (e.g., Apergis & Ozturk, 2015), trade openness (e.g., Farhani & Ozturk, 2015), and more recently, globalization (e.g., Marques, Fuinhas, & Marques, 2017). The study of the augmented energy consumption—economic growth nexus becomes especially important for researchers who want to make policy recommendations from their works, given that, in this framework, they can use a set of different macroeconomic control variables in addition to energy consumption and economic growth. Multivariate specifications permit the exploration of additional relationships and effects that are not captured in the bivariate specifications, broadening the conclusions drawn from these studies.

As we previously stressed, despite the high number of papers that have been published exploring the role of energy on growth, and scrutinizing the direction of causality between these variables, the conclusions from them are far from being consensual. However, it is widely accepted that energy has a positive role in the economic growth of countries, and the study of its effects on growth becomes increasingly important if we consider that energy consumption will probably increase in the upcoming decades, with a large contribution of that increase coming from the emerging countries (BP). In this sense, policies that grant the sustainable growth of countries are urgently needed. The results/conclusions of the energy consumption—growth nexus studies should be seen as important tools in the development of these policies. However, new viewpoints and new approaches are needed in the study of the energy consumption—economic growth nexus to surpass the conflicting results problem.

This book, which has a well-developed pedagogical strand, aims to be a facilitator for masters' students and practitioners to see how one can take advantage of a very stable econometric relationship, which is the energy consumption—economic growth nexus, to explore the contribution of other variables, and new explanatory models. This extended nexus, say augmented nexus, is an extraordinarily flexible tool that can be used to capture the impact of several variables that are essential for understanding the complexity of the nexus. In short, this book is essentially research focused. It will help researchers and practitioners to access the best econometric techniques to handle empirical approaches. This cut short the time required for students to get used to applying powerful econometric tools.

To facilitate learning the sources of data, Stata and EViews programming codes will be disclosed. The book is organized as follows.

In the first chapter, entitled "Energy-growth nexus and economic development: a quantile regression for panel data," the policy objectives of economic growth and energy sustainability are researched in a context of energy transition that is increasingly influenced by worldwide political agendas. Given that economic growth and sustainability could be two different concepts, a very pertinent question arises: how should they be measured? To cope with this query this chapter works by using two different approaches: (1) the economic growth approach, using the standard real Gross Domestic Product per capita; and (2) the sustainable development approach, using the index of economic and sustainable welfare. To operationalize the empirical approach, a database with 55 countries around the world, and with a time-span ranging from 1995 to 2014, was constructed, and a quantile regression for panel data was used to analyze the energy use, economic growth, and sustainability framework. This chapter is innovative in the sense that it analyzes and compares economic growth and sustainable development by level of income and development. Additionally, this econometric approach was able to shed light on some of the inconsistencies that are reported in the literature. Overall, it has provided empirical evidence that supports the need to devise conditional policies, whether they are focused on economic growth or sustainable development.

Moving on to the second chapter, entitled "On the augmented energy—growth nexus: electricity generation, waste, and CO_2 emissions in Latin America and Caribbean countries: a panel autoregressive distributed lag approach," it studies the impacts of the energy consumption and economic growth nexus on the environment in Latin America and the Caribbean countries. More specifically, the empirical analysis focuses on the impacts of energy use, electricity generation, Gross Domestic Product (GDP), and waste-to-energy, on carbon dioxide emissions. A database with annual data for 21 countries, from 1971 to 2013, was built, and the nexus was examined using the autoregressive distributed lag (ARDL) econometric technique.

The third chapter, entitled "Income inequality, globalization, and economic growth: a panel vector autoregressive approach for Latin American countries," points out that, currently, and despite the sizable empirical and theoretical literature, the discussion on the effects of both income inequality and globalization on economic growth remains a topic of hot debate. Although most authors view income inequality as a harmful determinant for economic growth, the opinions become much more divided when it comes to the globalization phenomenon. Given the exposure of Latin America countries to globalization, and the fact that the region is one of the most unequal regions in the world, the empirical research was focused on the analysis of the effects of these two phenomena on their economic growth. The process of generating inequalities is a dynamic one, and so, it requires the longest time span possible to research it. In accordance, an annual panel database of nine Latin American countries, from 1970 to 2015 was analyzed using the panel vector autoregressive (PVAR) econometric methodology. The conclusions of this research could contribute to help Latin American policymakers in the design of enhanced economic growth policies.

Turning to the fourth chapter, entitled "The impacts of China's effect and globalization on the augmented energy—nexus: evidence in four aggregated regions," it provides a comparative analysis of China's spillover effects and globalization impacts on the energy—growth nexus of four world regions: North America and South America; Europe and Central Asia; Pacific Asia; and Africa and the Middle East. At a huge regional level, both the aggregation of data, and the methodology used, play a meaningful role to perform comparable results. Two alternative measures of world globalization were tested, using an ARDL approach.

In the fifth chapter, entitled "The effect of fiscal and financial incentive policies for renewable energy on CO_2 emissions: the case for the Latin American region," the impact of fiscal and financial incentive policies for renewable energy on carbon dioxide emissions was examined. To achieve the goals of this chapter, a panel database for 12 Latin American countries, from 1980 to 2014, was built, and the econometric technique based on an ARDL model, in the form of UECM, was performed. To confirm the model's robustness, several shocks were included in the analysis. This research extends the literature surrounding the impacts of renewable energy policies on environmental degradation and opens the way for the development of a new research approach into the efficiency of public policies on renewable energy.

The sixth chapter is entitled "Energy—growth nexus, domestic credit, and environmental sustainability: a panel causality analysis," and its focus goes beyond the assessment of the relations between carbon dioxide emissions and economic growth. A database of 19 high income countries, based on the criterion of no breaks in the time series, was built for a time-span ranging from 2001 to 2016. Through a PVAR approach, and a bivariate analysis, the effects of domestic credit on the nexus were assessed. This research highlights the necessity to draw the attention of regulators to the integration of public policies in the financial sector and to environmental sustainability.

In the seventh chapter, entitled "The relationship between financial openness, renewable and nonrenewable energy consumption, CO_2 emissions, and economic growth in the Latin American countries: an approach with a panel vector autoregressive model," the relationship between financial openness, renewable and nonrenewable energy consumption, carbon dioxide emissions, and economic growth was apprised. A panel database was built for 12 Latin American countries, from 1980 to 2014, and the estimation was based on the PVAR model. The empirical findings of this research help to expand the literature in this field of research. Also, we hope that they contribute to attracting the policymaker's attention to the analyzed problems.

In the eighth chapter, entitled "The interactions between conventional and alternative energy sources in the transport sector: a panel of OECD countries," the aim is to assess the extended transport sector energy—growth nexus. The interactions between transport sector energy consumption, carbon dioxide emissions, economic growth, and trade openness were considered using transport energy consumption from both conventional and alternative energy sources. An annual panel database from 1971 to 2015, comprising 19 European Union countries, was used. The presence of endogeneity led to the use of the PVAR model. This research indicates that policymakers should promote changes in the energy paradigm, namely with the incorporation of alternative energy sources, such as transport sector renewable fuels and electricity. This research does not find evidence that the transport sectors' alternative sources are contributing directly to reducing carbon dioxide emissions, but it discovered that renewable fuels promote a reduction in the transport sector's fossil fuels use.

Finally, in the ninth chapter, entitled "Daily management of the electricity generation mix in France and Germany," an innovative line of study is introduced to the current literature, by assessing the electricity consumption and economic growth nexus, and the interactions between electricity sources, using high frequency data, namely daily data. The analysis was focused on French and German electricity systems and economic activity, from 1 January 2015 until 30 April 2018, through a VAR model.

This research could help with the identification of the conditions which are needed in the electricity supply for a successful transition toward renewable energies, without hampering economic activity.

References

Apergis, N., & Ozturk, I. (2015). Testing environmental Kuznets curve hypothesis in Asian countries. *Ecological Indicators, 52*, 16−22.

BP. *BP Energy Outlook.* [cited May 28, 2018]. Available from <http://www.bp.com/content/dam/bp/pdf/energy-economics/energy-outlook-2016/bp-energy-outlook-2016.pdf>.

Chen, P. Y., Chen, S. T., & Chen, C. C. (2012). Energy consumption and economic growth-new evidence from meta-analysis. *Energy Policy, 44*, 245−255.

Damette, O., & Seghir, M. (2013). Energy as a driver of growth in oil exporting countries? *Energy Economics, 37*, 193−199.

Farhani, S., & Ozturk, I. (2015). Causal relationship between CO_2 emissions, real GDP, energy consumption, financial development, trade openness, and urbanization in Tunisia. *Environmental Science and Pollution Research, 22*, 15663−15676.

Fatai, K., Oxley, L., & Scrimgeour, F. G. (2004). Modelling the causal relationship between energy consumption and GDP in New Zealand, Australia, India, Indonesia, The Philippines and Thailand. *Mathematics and Computers in Simulation, 64*(3−4), 431−445.

Fuinhas, J. A., & Marques, A. C. (2013). Rentierism, energy and economic growth: The case of Algeria and Egypt (1965−2010). *Energy Policy, 62*, 1165−1171.

Hajko, V. (2017). The failure of energy-economy nexus: A *meta*-analysis of 104 studies. *Energy, 125*, 771−787.

Hsiao, C. (1981). Autoregressive modeling and money-income causality detection. *Journal of Monetary Economics, 7*, 85−106.

Islam, F., Shahbaz, M., Ahmed, A. U., & Alam, M. M. (2013). Financial development and energy consumption nexus in Malaysia: A multivariate time series analysis. *Economic Modelling, 30*, 435−441.

Kraft, J., & Kraft, A. (1978). On the relationship between energy and GNP. *The Journal of Energy and Development, 3*, 401−403.

Lee, C. C., & Chien, M. S. (2010). Dynamic modelling of energy consumption, capital stock, and real income in G-7 countries. *Energy Economics, 32*(3), 564−581.

Marques, L. M., Fuinhas, J. A., & Marques, A. C. (2017). Augmented energy-growth nexus: Economic, political and social globalization impacts. *Energy Procedia, 136*, 97−101.

Ozturk, I. (2010). A literature survey on energy−growth nexus. *Energy Policy, 38*(1), 340−349.

Payne, J. E. (2009). On the dynamics of energy consumption and output in the United States. *Applied Energy, 86*(4), 575−577.

Solow, R. M. (1956). A contribution to the theory of economic growth. *The Quarterly Journal of Economics, 70*(1), 65.

Stern, D. I. (2011). The role of energy in economic growth. *Ecological Economics Reviews, 1219*, 26−51.

Toda, H. Y., & Yamamoto, T. (1995). Statistical inference in vector autoregressions with possibly integrated processes. *Journal of Econometrics, 66*(1−2), 225−250.

CHAPTER ONE

Energy—growth nexus and economic development: a quantile regression for panel data

Tiago Lopes Afonso[1,*], António Cardoso Marques[1,*] and José Alberto Fuinhas[2,*]

[1]NECE-UBI and, Management and Economics Department, University of Beira Interior, Covilhã, Portugal
[2]NECE-UBI, CeBER and Faculty of Economics, University of Coimbra, Coimbra, Portugal

Contents

1.1 Motivation

Energy is more than a simple input in the production process, more important than a mere utility. It constitutes a critical piece in the organizational process and in the life of society as a whole. Accordingly, when analyzing the use of energy, two main approaches could be pursued: namely, focusing on the production process and, as such, on economic growth or, instead, focusing on society as a whole, from a development

* This research was supported by NECE, R&D unit and funded by the FCT—Portuguese Foundation for the Development of Science and Technology, Ministry of Science, Technology and Higher Education, project UID/GES/04630/2019.

perspective. The former approach has thus far been largely dominant in the literature.

Indeed, economic growth, represented by the growth rate of gross domestic product (GDP), has been a core goal for policymakers. In general, GDP has been considered as a main indicator of both wealth and sustainable development. More recently, countries have started to consider larger environmental concerns when defining economic policies to promote growth, and to bear in mind the target of sustainable development. Evidence of this can be seen in the widespread participation in agreements aimed at controlling greenhouse gases emissions, such as the commitment of the COP21 assembly of the United Nations Frameworks Convention on Climate Change (UNFCCC). As a result of this concern to reduce the human ecological footprint, some authors have studied the issues around this topic. These have been mainly associated with: renewable energy policies (Marques & Fuinhas, 2012); energy efficiency (Moutinho, Madaleno, & Robaina, 2017); and the energy—growth nexus (Cai, Sam, & Chang, 2018).

However, in general, the literature about the energy—growth nexus has failed to consider the externalities of energy production. Furthermore, GDP has some limitations as a measure of well-being and environmental status, given that it does not take into account environmental damage or social costs. This chapter seeks to fill this gap in the literature. The need to distinguish economic growth and sustainable development has led to the search for an alternative measure. The Index of Sustainable Economic Welfare (ISEW) has emerged in the literature (Beça & Santos, 2010; Böhringer & Jochem, 2007; Brennan, 2008; O'Mahony, Escardó-Serra, & Dufour, 2018) as a standard indicator of sustainable development. Although it has suffered several changes since it was proposed, the goal of the ISEW remains the same: to provide a measure for social welfare without compromising future generations. Although the information included in the ISEW is complex, there are currently few alternatives, such as Ecological Footprint, City Development index, Human Development index, Environmental Sustainability index, Environmental Performance index, Environmental Vulnerability index, Well-Being Assessment, Genuine Savings, or Green National Product (Böhringer & Jochem, 2007).

Within a context of energy transitioning toward a more diversified electricity mix, the study and comparison of the (traditional) energy—growth nexus, with a new focus on sustainability, deserves even more attention.

Consequently, this study considers two approaches: (1) the Economic Growth Approach (EGA) and (2) the Sustainable Development Approach (SDA).

The main goal of the study is to analyze the consequences of the use of energy on both economic growth and sustainable development. Specifically, it aims to compare these two approaches by income level, which is a novel aspect of this study. This chapter also has a didactic objective; the econometric procedure is detailed in order to allow replicability, by presenting the software commands and the outputs obtained directly from the econometric software.

The method used also constitutes a fresh insight in the literature. To analyze the role of energy by considering income level, a quantile regression for panel data with nonaddictive fixed effects was carried out. Quantile regression permits the heterogeneous effects of explanatory variables on the dependent variable to be captured through quantiles. In order to assess the issues of interest to the current study, a comparison between GDP and ISEW was performed to evaluate the role of renewable and nonrenewable electricity production in economic growth and sustainable development.

The ISEW was computed for 63 countries around the world, from 1995 to 2014. The time span was strongly limited to the availability of data, once the ISEW computation of the ISEW requires more than a few variables.

In order to obtain a balanced panel, 55 countries were analyzed by using quantile technique. Most countries are leading the energy transition process from fossil to renewable energies, thus signaling a strong commitment to sustainable development. However, they cannot disregard economic growth. All countries follow the Paris agreement on climate change, despite the fact that the United States of America has recently withdrawn from the agreement. The deployment of renewables brings not only technical challenges, but also economic and social ones, which urgently need to be understood.

The contributions of this study to the literature are threefold: (1) it calculates a harmonized ISEW for as many countries as possible, by considering externalities; (2) it employs the very recent panel data technique of quantile regression to assess the specifics of the effects by level of both income and sustainability; and (3) it compares these two distinct approaches to the energy—growth nexus. Indeed, the findings of the study clarify a certain lack of consensus in the literature, specifically by stressing the differing effects of energy on economic growth, according to the traditional energy—growth nexus analysis. Finally, this study also contributes by highlighting the different impacts induced by natural resource rents on the EGA and SDA. The results show that ISEW is able to capture the negative externalities of energy use.

The rest of the study is structured as follows: Section 1.2 offers a literature review about electricity—growth nexus; Section 1.3 presents the ISEW construction, data used in the estimations, and the econometric procedure; Section 1.4 shows the results obtained in the study; Section 1.5 presents the discussion; and Section 1.6 provides the conclusion.

1.2 Economic growth and sustainable development: the debate

Studies of the role of energy consumption are common in the literature. Their results are not always consensual as they may vary according to sample size, time span, and methodology. Usually the sample is set up by considering a common characteristic between countries, for example, belonging to the same organization, that is, the European Union, OECD, or by income level, namely, G7 and G20, from higher to low income.

The four hypotheses tested on the energy—growth nexus are the now well known, namely: (1) the *neutrality hypothesis*, which is characterized by a noncausality between energy and growth; (2) the *conservation hypothesis*, which is supported by a unidirectional causality running from growth to energy; (3) the *growth hypothesis*, which is validated by a unidirectional causality from energy consumption to economic growth; and (4) the *feedback hypothesis*, which is supported by the bidirectional causality between growth and energy. These hypotheses have been intensively tested and the key challenges are identified in the literature, by studying different samples, methodologies, and time spans. Hajko (2017) studied 104 papers about the energy—growth nexus and pointed out the problem of omitted variables and the inappropriate use of methods.

There are many focuses and categories within the nexus. Indeed, some studies focus on the relationship between primary energy consumption and economic activity (Carmona, Congregado, Feria, & Iglesias, 2017; Liu, Zhou, & Wu, 2015), or on a specific type of energy, such as electricity (Salahuddin & Alam, 2016; Sarwar, Chen, & Waheed, 2017; Shahbaz,

Sarwar, Chen, & Malik, 2017). More recently the nexus analysis has been scrutinized by desegregating energy sources into coal (Jinke, Hualing, & Dianming, 2008), nuclear (Baek, 2015), natural gas (Destek, 2016), or renewable and nonrenewable energies (Adewuyi & Awodumi, 2017; Alvarez-Herranz, Balsalobre-Lorente, Shahbaz, & Cantos, 2017; Amri, 2017a; Kahia, Aïssa, Ben, & Lanouar, 2017; Rafindadi & Ozturk, 2017). These studies are based on a context of energy transition in which the challenges of deploying renewables and reducing carbon dioxide emissions need to be addressed without adversely affecting economic growth.

Besides the strict relationships between the input (energy) and the output (GDP), the nexus uses control variables, such as labor force or capital. Moreover there is a kind of extended nexus control for additional factors, such as the effect of globalization. Globalization could be measure in various ways: Foreign Direct Investment, Trade Openness (Chen & Lei, 2018), Terms of Trade (Kulish & Rees, 2017), and the KOF Globalization Index (Dreher, 2006). The effect of these factors seems to be positive, and these results are consistent in the literature (Amri, 2017a; Destek, 2016; Rafindadi & Ozturk, 2017).

The literature has also been focused on analyzing the consequences of energy use on output, although much less on analyzing the link and the interaction of sources according to distinct levels of output or wealth. Typically countries are grouped by their income level according to World Bank classification or geographical area (Ahmed & Azam, 2016; Amri, 2017a; Nourry, 2008), but the existence of varying income levels within the groups is not considered, except in Shahbaz, Zakaria, Shahzad, and Mahalik (2018). Indeed, studying groups of countries by income level could produce more informative results about the nature of the relationship between energy and economic growth. This grouping of countries is made in order to make the sample more homogeneous in terms of defining energy policy but does not consider the existence of heterogeneity between the countries. In this study the method used enabled the income differences within the group of countries to be examined.

Following this concern about environmental issues, a new nexus has emerged in the literature. Indeed the Energy-ISEW is arising to fill the gap in the literature by considering inequalities and externalities from a sustainable development perspective. However, literature using this approach is still extremely scarce. Some exceptions are Gaspar, dos, Marques, and Fuinhas (2017); Menegaki, Marques, and Fuinhas (2017); Menegaki and Tiwari (2017); Menegaki and Tugcu (2017, 2016a, 2016b); and

(Marques, Fuinhas, & Pais, 2018). The results for European countries (Gaspar et al., 2017) are actually different for these two approaches, namely the economic growth approach, and the sustainable approach. The neutrality hypothesis was verified in the sustainable approach, whereas the conservation hypothesis was verified in the economic approach. In the case of some American countries (Menegaki & Tiwari, 2017), the neutrality hypothesis was found in both sustainable and economic approaches by using energy consumption. Only in renewable energy sources there is a feedback hypothesis in the sustainable approach, while the growth hypothesis is found in the economic approach. The results for the G7 (Canada, France, Germany, Italy, Japan, United Kingdom, and the United States) (Menegaki & Tugcu, 2017), and for Sub-Saharan Africa countries (Menegaki & Tugcu, 2016a) were also different when economic and sustainable approaches are employed. These studies demonstrate the difference between economic growth and sustainable development.

This study aims to fill the gap in research that compares GDP and ISEW for 63 countries around the world. The use of the ISEW provides additional information for policymakers about economic growth and considers inequalities and externalities in the analyses.

1.3 Data and method

This section comprises the following items: presentation of the ISEW calculation, data and definition of variables, and the method applied.

1.3.1 The index of sustainable economic welfare calculation

Recently, the ISEW was calculated for some individual countries (Menegaki & Tsagarakis, 2015; Pulselli, Bravi, & Tiezzi, 2012). These have also recently used specific components available from national statistics services, and for groups. Table 1.1 presents the studies performed for multicountries, where the comparability between countries could be observed.

Table 1.1 Multicountries index of sustainable economic welfare studies.

Paper	Sample
Lawn and Clarke (2010)	Australia, New Zealand, Japan, India, China, Thailand, and Vietnam
Menegaki and Tugcu (2016a)	*Sub-Saharan Africa*: Angola, Benin, Botswana, Burkina Faso, Burundi, Cameroon, Central Africa, Chad, Comoros, Congo, Cote d'Ivore, Djibouti, Equatorial Guinea, Eritrea, Ethiopia, Gabon, Gambia, Guinea, Kenya, Lesotho, Liberia, Madagascar, Malawi, Mali, Mauritania, Mauritius, Mozambique, Namibia, Niger, Nigeria, Rwanda, Sao Tome & Principe, Senegal, Seychelles, Sierra Leone, South Africa, Sudan, Swaziland, Tanzania, Togo, Uganda, and Zimbabwe
Menegaki and Tugcu (2017)	*G7*: Canada, France, Germany, Italy, Japan, United Kingdom, and the United States
Menegaki et al. (2017)	*European Countries*: Austria, Belgium, Bulgaria, Croatia, Czech Republic, Denmark, Estonia, Finland, France, Germany, Greece, Hungary, Iceland, Ireland, Italy, Latvia, Lithuania, Luxembourg, Malta, Netherlands, Norway, Poland, Portugal, Romania, Russia, Serbia, Slovakia, Slovenia, Spain, Sweden, Switzerland, Ukraine, and United Kingdom
Menegaki and Tiwari (2017)	*American countries*: Argentina, Bolivia, Brazil, Canada, Chile, Colombia, Costa Rica, Cuba, Dominican Democracy, Ecuador, El Salvador, Guatemala, Haiti, Honduras, Jamaica, Mexico, Nicaragua, Panama, Panama, and the United States
Gaspar et al. (2017)	*European countries*: Austria, Belgium, Czech Republic, Denmark, Finland, France, Germany, Greece, Hungary, Ireland, Italy, the Netherlands, Norway, Poland, Portugal, Spain, Slovakia, Sweden, Switzerland, and United Kingdom.
Menegaki and Tugcu (2018)	*Asian countries*: Armenia, Bangladesh, Jordan, Kazakhstan, Kyrgyzstan, Pakistan, Republic of Korea, Singapore, Sri Lanka, and Tajikistan

The calculation of the ISEW is not uniform (Böhringer & Jochem, 2007), since the components considered are different in each study. Consequently, the comparison between indexes is far from clear.

There are a few alternative ways to calculate the ISEW. One is to calculate the ISEW with the same component for all countries, a method that follows Menegaki and Tiwari (2017). The criterion also considers data availability. Even when the ISEW calculation focuses on a single country, more often than not, the components differ from one study to another. Indeed, data availability appears to play a major role, that is, it is found to be crucial in deciding which components are included. The detailed theoretical foundations of ISEW can be seen in Brennan (2008).

The ISEW was calculated using a uniform method for all countries and using a consistent database without extrapolating data. Table 1.2 shows the components, method, and variables used in the ISEW calculation.

All variables were obtained from the World Development Indicators (WDI) published by the World Bank, except the Gini coefficient that was extracted from the Standardized World Income Inequality Database (SWIID) v6.1[1] (Solt, 2016). The Gini coefficient was used as a determinant

Table 1.2 The index of sustainable economic welfare components and calculation method.

Item	Component	Sign	Calculation method
A	Adjusted personal consumption	+	Final household consumption $\times$ (1–Gini index)
B	Education expenditure	+	Public education expenditure $\times$ 0.5
C	Health expenditure	+	Public health expenditure $\times$ 0.5
D	Net capital growth	+/–	Gross Capital Formation – Gross Capital Consumption
E	Mineral depletion	–	Mineral depletion is the ratio of the value of the stock of mineral resources to the remaining reserve lifetime (capped at 25 years). It covers tin, gold, lead, zinc, iron, copper, nickel, silver, bauxite, and phosphate
F	Energy depletion	–	Ratio of the value of the stock of energy resources to the remaining reserve lifetime (capped at 25 years). It covers coal, crude oil, and natural gas
G	Forest depletion	–	Net forest depletion is calculated as the product of unit resource rents and the excess of roundwood harvest over natural growth
H	Damage from CO_2 emissions	–	Carbon dioxide damage is estimated to be $20 per ton of carbon (the unit damage in 1995 US dollars) times the number of tons of carbon emitted

[1] See https://fsolt.org/swiid/

of economic inequality (Nikolaev, Boudreaux, & Salahodjaev, 2017). The *gini_disp* was used, that is, household disposable income (after taxes).

The B and C items were multiplied by 0.5, because half of public expenditure is defensive (Jackson & Stymne, 1996). Therefore some expenditures are available for prevention, while the other half is specific to repair damages.

Social costs are not used in this study. This component could include the cost of social problems: the cost of divorce, cost of noise pollution, cost of crime, or cost of underemployment and unpaid work. Usually, this component is calculated by using the number of unpaid workers multiplied by the minimum wage or the average wage. In the sample, some countries did not establish a minimum wage and therefore the database for average wages has a lot of missing data. Usually, the social cost items are calculated by national authorities using dissimilar methodologies or, in some cases, it is not performed at all.

1.3.2 Variables

Although the ISEW was calculated for 20 years for 63 countries, due the lack of data for some independent variables, the sample for the empirical model was reduced. The ISEW was calculated for Argentina, Armenia, Australia, Austria, Belarus, Belgium, Bolivia, Brazil, Bulgaria, Burkina Faso, Canada, Croatia, Cyprus, Czech Republic, Denmark, Dominican Republic, Ecuador, El Salvador, Finland, France, Germany, Greece, Guatemala, Honduras, Hungary, Iceland, India, Ireland, Israel, Italy, Japan, Kazakhstan, Latvia, Luxembourg, Madagascar, Malaysia, Mexico, Moldova, Morocco, Namibia, Netherlands, Norway, Pakistan, Panama, Paraguay, Peru, Philippines, Portugal, Romania, Rwanda, Singapore, South Africa, Spain, Sri Lanka, Sweden, Switzerland, Tanzania, Thailand, Turkey, Ukraine, United Kingdom, United States, and Uruguay. As such, the sample for the empirical model is composed of only 55 countries. Argentina, Belarus, Bolivia, Burkina Faso, Iceland, Madagascar, Rwanda, and Tanzania were excluded.

The analysis covers the period from 1995 to 2014 for 55 countries, that is, 1100 observations. This time span was chosen by taking into account the availability of global data, that is, data for the variables that comprise ISEW, and their respective explanatory variables at December 2017. In order to guarantee a balanced panel data, a set of variables has

Table 1.3 Variable's definitions.

		Source
LGDPPC	Gross domestic product (constant 2010 US$) per capita	WDI
LISEWPC	Index of sustainable and economic welfare (constant 2010 US$) per capita	Table 1.2
LEPC	Energy use (kg of oil equivalent per capita)	WDI
LKOFI	Globalization—KOF overall index	KOF
LGFCFPC	Gross fixed capital formation (constant 2010 US$) per capita	WDI
LRENTPC	Total natural resources rents (constant 2010 US$) per capita	WDI
LEFPC	Ecological footprint per capita	GFN
LCPI	Consumer price index (2010 = 100)	WDI

Note: All variables are in natural logarithm.

been collected from three different databases: WDI[2] database, KOF Swiss Institute[3], and Global Footprint Network (GFN)[4]. Table 1.3 shows the variables' definitions.

As previously mentioned, this work follows the trend designed for studying the energy—growth nexus. The common variables used are GDP and Energy use per capita. Both are extracted from WDI database. GDP was divided by population to compute GDP per capita. Energy use per capita was extracted directly from WDI.

Globalization, capital, natural resources rents, and ecological footprint were used as control variables. The KOF overall index of globalization was developed by Dreher (2006) and covers three dimensions: political, economic, and social. The KOF index is the most complete and comprehensive index of globalization against the alternatives. It is composed by a few components, such as trade openness, FDI, hidden imports barriers, embassies in countries, membership in international organizations, telephone main lines, daily newspapers, and so forth. For a more complete perception, see Dreher (2006) and Gygli, Haelg, and Sturm (2018).

The real gross fixed capital formation was used as a proxy for capital, as usual. Natural resources rents were extracted as a percentage of GDP and it was converted in constant 2010 US$. Inflation, denoted by the consumer price index, could also influence economic growth

[2] See http://databank.worldbank.org/data/source/world-development-indicators
[3] See https://www.ethz.ch/content/dam/ethz/special-interest/dual/kof-dam/documents/Globalization/2018/Data_2018.xlsx
[4] See https://www.footprintnetwork.org/licenses/public-data-package-free-2018/

(Ibarra & Trupkin, 2016), not only because it is able to influence investment decisions, but also the propensity for consumption. This variable was also used as proxy of energy prices. Ecological footprint measures the global hectares that are needed to produce the natural resources consumed. For an extensive methodology and framework about ecological footprint, see Borucke et al. (2013).

1.3.3 Method

Usually countries are grouped according to their income level. This classification follows the World Bank classification based on Gross National Income. As stated before, this work is focused on examining both the economic growth and sustainable development approaches, measured by GDPPC and ISEWPC, respectively. Notwithstanding the sample, including various countries around the world, *GDPPC* and *ISEWPC* reveals different levels of income and of sustainability. Accordingly, a quantile approach was used, taking into account this evidence, the sample, and the objectives of this study.

Quantile regression allows us to observe the different effects that independent variables could provoke in the conditional distribution of the dependent variable. These different effects can produce useful information that cannot be captured using the traditional regression model (Bitler, Gelbach, & Hoynes, 2006; Hübler, 2017). Indeed, the quantile regression model is based on the median, whereas traditional regression is based on the mean. Therefore quantile regression is robust in the presence of outliers (Koenker & Hallock, 2001) and can actually be more efficient than the Ordinary Least Squares (OLS) method when the residuals do not follow a normal distribution (Niu, Jia, Ye, Dai, & Li, 2016).

In order to work with quantile regression and fixed effects, Powell (2016) introduced a Quantile Regression for Panel Data (QRPD). QRDP seems to be robust with a small number of periods. The coefficients can be interpreted as in a traditional panel data regression and allows fixed effects. The command *qregpd* is available at *ssc install* Stata archive.

How to do:
** Install qregpd command **
  ssc install qregpd

The QRPD was used, and the results were compared with those from a Pooled OLS. The Pooled regression is used as a benchmark. Two regressions were estimated in order to evaluate the performance of energy using both the EGA and SDA approaches, respectively. The Wald test was made to test the global significance of the estimated models. The null hypothesis of the Wald test is that all the coefficients are equal to zero.

In order to check the normality of the residuals from the EGA (r_ega) and SDA (r_sda) from Pooled regression, the Shapiro—Wilk and Skewness—Kurtosis test were performed. The Breusch—Pagan test for heteroskedasticity was also calculated.

How to do:
** shapiro-wilk w test for normal data **
 swilk r_1 r_2

How it looks like

Shapiro-Wilk W test for normal data

Variable	Obs	W	V	z	Prob>z
r_ega	1,100	0.99087	6.277	4.567	0.00000
r_sda	1,100	0.94374	38.702	9.089	0.00000

Source: Stata

How to do:
** Skewness/Kurtosis tests for Normality**
 sktest r_ega r_sda

How it looks like

Skewness/Kurtosis tests for Normality

Variable	Obs	Pr(Skewness)	Pr(Kurtosis)	adj chi2(2)	joint Prob>chi2
r_ega	1,100	0.0846	0.0000	23.31	0.0000
r_sda	1,100	0.0000	0.0000	.	0.0000

Source: Stata

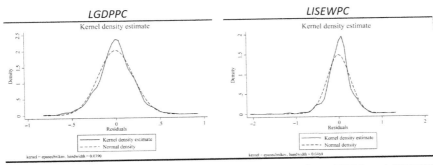

Figure 1.1 Kernel density estimated and normal density for *LGDPPC* and *LISEWPC*. Own elaboration.

The null hypothesis of normality is rejected in both EGA and SDA, at a significance level of 1%. Fig. 1.1 shows the univariate kernel density for both residual of *LGDPPC* and *LISEWPC*. This evidence constitutes additional support for the adequacy of using the quantile regression.

How to do:
** Univariate kernel density estimation **
    kdensity r_ega, kernel(epanechnikov)normal
    kdensity r_sda, kernel(epanechnikov)normal

In order to check multicollinearity among the variables, the Variance Inflation Factor (VIF) was performed. The VIF mean of 4.57 in both regressions is a sign that multicollinearity is not a problem.

How to do:
** Variance Inflation Factor **
    reg lgdppc lepc lkofi lgfcfpc lrentpc lefpc lcpi
    vif
    reg lisewpc lepc lkofi lgfcfpc lrentpc lefpc lcpi
    vif1

The output is presented as follows:

How it looks like

Variable	VIF	1/VIF
lefpc	9.21	0.108535
lepc	7.77	0.128728
lgfcfpc	6.26	0.159754
lkofi	1.74	0.575782
lcpi	1.31	0.762967
lrentpc	1.11	0.904452
Mean VIF	4.57	

Source: Stata

The results are equal for both regressions, once the explanatory variables are the same.

1.4 Results

The presence of heteroscedasticity was also tested, by performing the Breusch–Pagan test. The null hypothesis of homoscedasticity was rejected at 1% significance level.

For EGA:

How to do:

** pooled regression **
   reg lgdppc lepc lkofi lgfcfpc lrentpc lefpc lcpi
   estat hottest

How it looks like

```
Breusch-Pagan / Cook-Weisberg test for heteroskedasticity
        Ho: Constant variance
        Variables: fitted values of lgdppc

     chi2(1)     =       78.23
     Prob > chi2  =      0.0000
```

Source: Stata

For SDA:

How it looks like

```
Breusch-Pagan / Cook-Weisberg test for heteroskedasticity
        Ho: Constant variance
        Variables: fitted values of lisewpc

        chi2(1)       =      183.56
        Prob > chi2   =      0.0000
```

Source: Stata

The Pooled regression robust estimator was used as a benchmark due to the presence of heteroscedasticity. This estimator provides corrected standard errors, and consequently the correct coefficient significant level.

How to do:
** pooled regression robust**
    reg lgdppc lepc lkofi lgfcfpc lrentpc lefpc lcpi, robust
    reg lisewpc lepc lkofi lgfcfpc lrentpc lefpc lcpi, robust

---

More than three independent variables require an optimization method, such as the Markov Chain Monte Carlo (MCMC) (Powell, 2016). The adaptive MCMC optimization procedure was used with the default option in the estimation of both EGA and SDA. The default options are characterized by 1000 draws, 0 draws dropped as a burn-in period, and consequently 1,000 draws were retained. The default acceptance rate of the algorithm is 0.234. Since MCMC is an optimization algorithm with random draws, a seed of 1000 was used, in order to always obtain the same results and to allow replication of the results. The results were estimated with other seeds and, generally, the results remain stable.

Table 1.4 and Table 1.5 show the results for the EGA and SDA, respectively. The 25th, 50th, and 75th quantiles were respectively calculated in order to assess the role of energy in economic activity and sustainable development. The method used does not allow to perform causalities, it only allows to observe the effect at the quantiles.

Table 1.4 shows the estimation for using the EGA on the energy—growth nexus, that is, by using *LGDPPC*. The null of the Wald test was rejected in all estimated models, so all coefficients are different from zero.

How to do:

** qregpd EGA and Wald test**

    set seed 1000

    qregpd lgdppc lepc lkofi lgfcfpc lrentpc lefpc lcpi, id(id) fix(year) q(25) optimize (mcmc) draws(1000) burn(0) arate(0.234)

        testparm lepc lkofi lgfcfpc lrentpc lefpc lcpi

        set seed 1000

    qregpd lgdppc lepc lkofi lgfcfpc lrentpc lefpc lcpi, id(id) fix(year) q(50) optimize (mcmc) draws(1000) burn(0) arate(0.234)

        testparm lepc lkofi lgfcfpc lrentpc lefpc lcpi

        set seed 1000

    qregpd lgdppc lepc lkofi lgfcfpc lrentpc lefpc lcpi, id(id) fix(year) q(75) optimize (mcmc) draws(1000) burn(0) arate(0.234)

        testparm lepc lkofi lgfcfpc lrentpc lefpc lcpi

Table 1.4 Estimations for economic growth approach.

Dependent variable: LGDPPC	Pooled	Quantiles		
		25th	50th	75th
LEPC	0.00028	0.60262***	0.09371	− 0.07760***
LKOFI	0.04071	0.25471***	0.00176	0.02761
LGFCFPC	0.83519***	0.31341**	0.70388***	0.77213***
LRENTPC	0.00861***	− 0.04471***	0.02042***	0.02020***
LEF	0.29231***	0.54971***	0.32916***	0.39842***
LCPI	− 0.03639***	− 0.05281***	0.00172	0.01817***
Constant	2.40048***			
Obs	1100	1100	1100	1100
Wald test	8457.87***	8.2e + 06***	1.5e + 06***	3.3e + 05***

Notes: ***, **, and * represent statistic significant level for 1%, 5%, and 10%, respectively, and Wald test has χ^2 distribution.

The sample is composed by dissimilar countries in terms of energy policy, different sign over the quantile could be expected. Regarding *LGFCFPC, LEF,* and *LCPI*, they produce the expected effect in all estimated quantiles. The *CPI* has a negative sign in low income countries. Inflation is the annual percentage change on *CPI*, and in low income countries, inflation is high, sometimes uncontrolled, inhibiting economic activity. The *LCPI* is relatively stable over the period for high-income countries, meaning that the inflation ratio is low, so the Central banks

Table 1.5 Estimations for sustainable development approach.

Dependent variable: LISEWPC	Pooled	Quantiles		
		25th	50th	75th
LEPC	− 0.17680***	− 0.24070***	− 0.09872***	0.09288***
LKOFI	0.13614*	0.54480***	0.44302***	− 0.03182
LGFCFPC	0.95882***	0.98844***	0.86856***	0.79809***
LRENTPC	− 0.03022***	− 0.03022***	− 0.02334***	− 0.03367***
LEF	0.18868***	0.17115***	0.23770***	0.17296***
LCPI	0.06316***	0.1235**	0.03200***	0.06632***
Constant	1.45773***			
Obs	1100	1100	1100	1100
Wald test	4777.84***	1.0e + 06***	1.0E + 07***	2.7e + 06***

Notes: ***, **, and * represent statistic significant level for 1%, 5%, and 10%, respectively and Wald test has χ^2 distribution.

have accomplished the goal of low inflation rates and consequently, are promoting economic activity. *LKOFI* is only significant at 25th quantile.

After examining the role of energy, the conclusion is that energy use promotes growth only for the low distribution of the *LGDPPC*. Predominantly, fossil sources are the main energy source in low income countries, while the richer countries are moving to clean energies. The technological maturity of fossil sources is at a different level to that of renewable energies. In the 25th quantile the effect is positive while being negative for the 75th. This is a very relevant finding and it explains one apparent divergence found in the literature. This fact will be more thoroughly discussed in Section 1.5. With respect to the rents provided from the exploitation of natural resources, they also lead to different effects on economic activity. The observed effect is negative at 25th and positive at 50th and 75th quantiles. The Ecological Footprint contributes to economic activity over the all quantiles.

As expected, the results are similar for the 50th quantile and the Pooled estimation, which can be seen as an additional sign of robustness. In the Pooled estimation, almost all variables are significant at 1%, excluding *LEPC and LKOFI* which are not significant, as at 50th quantile. In the case of the 75th quantile, only *LKOFI* is not significant.

As far as the SDA is concerned, Table 1.5 shows the results, when *ISEWPC* is the explained variable. Regarding the global significance of the models, the nonsignificance of all coefficients' explanatory variables was rejected.

How to do:
** qregpd SDA and Wald test**

    set seed 1000

    qregpd lgdppc lepc lkofi lgfcfpc lrentpc lefpc lcpi, id(id) fix(year) q(25) optimize (mcmc) draws(1000) burn(0) arate(0.234)

      testparm lepc lkofi lgfcfpc lrentpc lefpc lcpi

      set seed 1000

    qregpd lgdppc lepc lkofi lgfcfpc lrentpc lefpc lcpi, id(id) fix(year) q(50) optimize (mcmc) draws(1000) burn(0) arate(0.234)

      testparm lepc lkofi lgfcfpc lrentpc lefpc lcpi

      set seed 1000

    qregpd lgdppc lepc lkofi lgfcfpc lrentpc lefpc lcpi, id(id) fix(year) q(75) optimize (mcmc) draws(1000) burn(0) arate(0.234)

      testparm lepc lkofi lgfcfpc lrentpc lefpc lcpi

After exploring the results among the QRDP on the SDA, one concludes that the results were different for *LEPC*, and *CPI*. Energy is negative at 25th and 50th quantiles, which constitutes an effective difference when compared to the EGA. Indeed, from the comparison between the two approaches, it should be highlighted that: globalization is nonsignificant at 50th and 75th while the effect is positive and statistically significant in the SDA. Both capital and ecological footprint have been encouraging economic growth and sustainable development. In Section 1.5, one goes further in the discussion of these findings, by highlighting the specificities of each approach and by providing guidance for policymakers.

The results for the comparison of Pooled and 50th quantile reveal that the nature of the effects remain unchanged. *LKOFI* is not significant at 75th, *LCPI* are significant at the 5% significance level, whereas the rest of the variables are significant at 1%. Therefore in the SDA, the use of the quantile technique seems to be relevant for understanding the complexity of the effect, namely by releasing additional information about the behavior of the effects that other techniques are actually unable to provide.

1.5 Discussion

When comparing both EGA and SDA, the results are markedly different. The objectives established to promote economic growth may not cause the desired effect when sustainability is taken into consideration.

This means that energy policies should take into account the externalities resulting from energy production. The use of an alternative indicator such as the ISEW would bring complementary information of the role of the standard factors used in the energy—growth nexus.

When focusing on the EGA, the role played by aggregated energy consumption is variable among the quantiles. Indeed, among high GDP levels, the effect is positive at lower and middle quantiles. However, for high GDP levels, energy seems to be constraining economic activity. Note that renewable energies are not considered in this study, since most healthier countries have a considerable share of this kind of sources. This finding seems to be of particular relevance for the literature. Indeed, it could help to justify the divergent effects documented by the empirical literature of the effect of clean energies on growth being positive (Alper & Oguz, 2016; Rafindadi & Ozturk, 2017), negative (Dogan, 2015; Ocal & Aslan, 2013), or even neutral (Amri, 2017b).

Regarding possible explanations for these findings, one should take into account that the sample is based on countries with a large distinction between income levels, and that this negative effect was detected for the wealthy countries and most advanced economies in the world. This negative effect could be a consequence of efforts to promote alternative energies, namely, feed-in tariffs. High levels of income allow more financial resources to be aimed at encouraging these programs, but at the same time this could be compromising their economic growth by transferring such extra costs to their economies as a whole.

Looking at the SDA, energy consumption is promoting sustainability at high-income level, as expected. This can be seen as a kind of growth hypothesis for the sustainability approach, or even a sustainability hypothesis. Indeed, the usage of clean energies do not cause the depletion of natural resources, or even carbon dioxide damage. As such, these findings will be helpful for policymakers seeking to justify the usefulness of promoting the deployment of clean energy to achieve sustainable development.

With reference to the lower and middle quantile, they are not promoting sustainable development, due the use of fossil energies to promote growth. Possible explanations for this are far from scarce, such as the negative contribution due the carbon dioxide damage caused by burning fossil fuels.

Regarding the control factors, namely the capital and ecological footprint, both play a significant role in creating prosperity, not only under the sustainability approach, but also according to the growth approach. This outcome is identical for both EGA and SDA, even with different identities.

The different effects observed for the rents resulting from the exploitation of natural resources on economic activity over various levels of income, deserve particular consideration. In general, it seems that the effect is negative (SDA) and is related to the gains obtained from the exploitation of mineral, forest, and energy resources, which are insufficient to cover the corresponding environmental depletion. The exception is for the lower income countries, where the added value of the goods and services resulting from the exploitation of natural resources is unsuccessful in producing wealth.

In terms of globalization the results show that it leads to a positive and significant effect for lower level of income, on the EGA. This finding supports the mainstream argument that trade deployment between counties actually constitutes a driver of the economic activity. A negative effect can be observed using the sustainability approach, which also constitutes grounds for those arguing that globalization is a lead to sustainability.

The results observed for the consumer price index are distinct when focusing on EGA and SDA. The observed effect is negative for the economic framework and positive for the sustainable framework, at lower quantile. The effect is positive at middle and upper quantiles. On the one hand, some inflation can be an incentive for investment and, as such, for growth. On the other hand, inflation compromises purchasing power and consequently the ability to satisfy individuals' needs.

Finally, it is worth highlighting that the ISEW has some limitations, namely in the components included. While GDP is always calculated in the same way, ISEW is conditioned by the data currently available. This fact makes it difficult to compare different studies. Nevertheless, the ISEW seems to provide complementary information about the role of energy use in sustainable development. Policymakers are focusing on economic policies and the target is the promotion of growth. However, this objective can influence other prominent issues, such as an increase in income inequalities or carbon dioxide damage.

1.6 Conclusions

The study focused on studying the nexus between energy use according to two different perspectives: economic growth and sustainable development, for the time span 1995—2014. In order to accomplish this objective, GDP and ISEW were used as the dependent variables for the EGA and the SDA, respectively. Due to different income and ISEW levels, the quantile regression model for panel data was applied in order to observe the effects on the dependent variables over the conditional distribution. Quantile regression for panel data can be an alternative method to the heterogeneous panel data estimator, since it allows us to detect the different impacts of the independent variables on the outcome variable across the panel. The ISEW was calculated based on data availability for the selected 63 countries around the world. This measure takes into account the income inequality and externalities caused by the depletion of natural resources.

The empirical model was performed for 55 countries, and the results are quite different when both perspectives are compared, thus justifying the appropriateness of the comparative option taken in this study. Although energy consumption inhibits economic activity for lower income countries, when the depletion of natural resources is considered, the result changes. The less wealthy countries should accelerate the energy transition programs to invert the negative effect on sustainability. Considering that energy consumption is statistically neutral for economic growth at middle income, conservation measures aimed in promoting efficient consumption of energy reducing the impact on sustainable development. Therefore carbon dioxide damage can be mitigated. However, based on the economic growth approach, the effect of energy consumption was not observed in wealthy countries. This may be due to the efforts these countries have made and the consequent costs they have had to pay to implement programs designed to increase the share of renewables.

Some control variables, such as capital and ecological footprint reveal an identical effect on both EGA and SDA. These factors seem to be important for a more sustainable and healthier future. Conversely, the consumer price index has a positive impact on ISEW and GDP, except for less wealthy countries. Rents from natural resources have a negative impact on ISEW, despite being positive for middle and high levels of income. Sustainable development should not be based on rents from natural resources. Overall, the energy transition from fossil to renewables is essential to improve sustainable development.

References

Adewuyi, A. O., & Awodumi, O. B. (2017). Renewable and non-renewable energy-growth-emissions linkages: Review of emerging trends with policy implications. *Renewable and Sustainable Energy Reviews, 69*(August 2016), 275–291. Available from: https://doi.org/10.1016/j.rser.2016.11.178.

Ahmed, M., & Azam, M. (2016). Causal nexus between energy consumption and economic growth for high, middle and low income countries using frequency domain analysis. *Renewable and Sustainable Energy Reviews, 60*, 653–678. Available from: https://doi.org/10.1016/j.rser.2015.12.174.

Alper, A., & Oguz, O. (2016). The role of renewable energy consumption in economic growth: Evidence from asymmetric causality. *Renewable and Sustainable Energy Reviews, 60*, 953–959. Available from: https://doi.org/10.1016/j.rser.2016.01.123.

Alvarez-Herranz, A., Balsalobre-Lorente, D., Shahbaz, M., & Cantos, J. M. (2017). Energy innovation and renewable energy consumption in the correction of air pollution levels. *Energy Policy, 105*(March), 386–397. Available from: https://doi.org/10.1016/j.enpol.2017.03.009.

Amri, F. (2017a). Intercourse across economic growth, trade and renewable energy consumption in developing and developed countries. *Renewable and Sustainable Energy Reviews, 69*(November 2016), 527–534. Available from: https://doi.org/10.1016/j.rser.2016.11.230.

Amri, F. (2017b). The relationship amongst energy consumption (renewable and non-renewable), and GDP in Algeria. *Renewable and Sustainable Energy Reviews, 76*(March), 62–71. Available from: https://doi.org/10.1016/j.rser.2017.03.029.

Baek, J. (2015). A panel cointegration analysis of CO 2 emissions, nuclear energy and income in major nuclear generating countries. *Applied Energy, 145*, 133–138. Available from: https://doi.org/10.1016/j.apenergy.2015.01.074.

Beça, P., & Santos, R. (2010). Measuring sustainable welfare: A new approach to the ISEW. *Ecological Economics, 69*(4), 810–819. Available from: https://doi.org/10.1016/j.ecolecon.2009.11.031.

Bitler, M. P., Gelbach, J. B., & Hoynes, H. W. (2006). What mean impacts miss: Distributional effects of welfare reform experiments. *American Economic Review, 96*(4), 988–1012. Available from: https://doi.org/10.1257/aer.96.4.988.

Böhringer, C., & Jochem, P. E. P. (2007). Measuring the immeasurable: A survey of sustainability indices. *Ecological Economics, 63*(1), 1–8. Available from: https://doi.org/10.1016/j.ecolecon.2007.03.008.

Borucke, M., Moore, D., Cranston, G., Gracey, K., Iha, K., Larson, J., & Galli, A. (2013). Accounting for demand and supply of the biosphere's regenerative capacity: The national footprint accounts' underlying methodology and framework. *Ecological Indicators, 24*, 518–533. Available from: https://doi.org/10.1016/j.ecolind.2012.08.005.

Brennan, A. J. (2008). Theoretical foundations of sustainable economic welfare indicators: ISEW and political economy of the disembedded system. *Ecological Economics, 67*(1), 1–19. Available from: https://doi.org/10.1016/j.ecolecon.2008.05.019.

Cai, Y., Sam, C. Y., & Chang, T. (2018). Nexus between clean energy consumption, economic growth and CO2 emissions. *Journal of Cleaner Production, 182*, 1001–1011. Available from: https://doi.org/10.1016/j.jclepro.2018.02.035.

Carmona, M., Congregado, E., Feria, J., & Iglesias, J. (2017). The energy-growth nexus reconsidered: Persistence and causality. *Renewable and Sustainable Energy Reviews, 71* (May 2016), 342–347. Available from: https://doi.org/10.1016/j.rser.2016.12.060.

Chen, W., & Lei, Y. (2018). The impacts of renewable energy and technological innovation on environment-energy-growth nexus: New evidence from a panel quantile regression. *Renewable Energy*, *123*, 1—14. Available from: https://doi.org/10.1016/j.renene.2018.02.026.

Destek, M. A. (2016). Natural gas consumption and economic growth: Panel evidence from OECD countries. *Energy*, *114*, 1007—1015. Available from: https://doi.org/10.1016/j.energy.2016.08.076.

Dogan, E. (2015). The relationship between economic growth and electricity consumption from renewable and non-renewable sources: A study of Turkey. *Renewable and Sustainable Energy Reviews*, *52*, 534—546. Available from: https://doi.org/10.1016/j.rser.2015.07.130.

Dreher, A. (2006). Does globalization affect growth? Evidence from a new index of globalization. *Applied Economics*, *38*(10), 1091—1110. Available from: https://doi.org/10.1080/00036840500392078.

Gaspar, J., dos, S., Marques, A. C., & Fuinhas, J. A. (2017). The traditional Energy-growth nexus: A comparison between sustainable development and economic growth approaches. *Ecological Indicators*, *75*, 286—296. Available from: https://doi.org/10.1016/j.ecolind.2016.12.048.

Gygli, S., Haelg, F., & Sturm, J.-E. (2018). *The KOF globalisation index — Revisited.* KOF Working Papers No. 439. Retrieved from https://doi.org/10.3929/ethz-b-000238666

Hajko, V. (2017). The failure of energy-economy nexus: A meta-analysis of 104 studies. *Energy*, *125*, 771—787. Available from: https://doi.org/10.1016/j.energy.2017.02.095.

Hübler, M. (2017). The inequality-emissions nexus in the context of trade and development: A quantile regression approach. *Ecological Economics*, *134*, 174—185. Available from: https://doi.org/10.1016/j.ecolecon.2016.12.015.

Ibarra, R., & Trupkin, D. R. (2016). Reexamining the relationship between inflation and growth: Do institutions matter in developing countries? *Economic Modelling*, *52*, 332—351. Available from: https://doi.org/10.1016/j.econmod.2015.09.011.

Jackson, T., & Stymne, S. (1996). *Sustainable economic welfare in Sweden: A pilot index 1950—1992.* Stockholm Environment Institute. Retrieved from http://www.sei-international.org/mediamanager/documents/Publications/SEI-Report-1996-SustainableEconomicWelfareInSweden.pdf

Jinke, L., Hualing, S., & Dianming, G. (2008). Causality relationship between coal consumption and GDP: Difference of major OECD and non-OECD countries. *Applied Energy*, *85*, 421—429. Available from: https://doi.org/10.1016/j.apenergy.2007.10.007.

Kahia, M., Aïssa, M. S., Ben., & Lanouar, C. (2017). Renewable and non-renewable energy use — economic growth nexus: The case of MENA net oil importing countries. *Renewable and Sustainable Energy Reviews*, *71*(February), 127—140. Available from: https://doi.org/10.1016/j.rser.2017.01.010.

Koenker, R., & Hallock, K. F. (2001). Quantile regression. *Journal of Economic Perspectives*, *15*(4), 143—156.

Kulish, M., & Rees, D. M. (2017). Unprecedented changes in the terms of trade. *Journal of International Economics*, *108*, 351—367. Available from: https://doi.org/10.1016/j.jinteco.2017.07.005.

Lawn, P., & Clarke, M. (2010). The end of economic growth? A contracting threshold hypothesis. *Ecological Economics*, *69*(11), 2213—2223. Available from: https://doi.org/10.1016/j.ecolecon.2010.06.007.

Liu, Y., Zhou, Y., & Wu, W. (2015). Assessing the impact of population, income and technology on energy consumption and industrial pollutant emissions in China. *Applied Energy*, *155*, 904—917. Available from: https://doi.org/10.1016/j.apenergy.2015.06.051.

Marques, A. C., & Fuinhas, J. A. (2012). Are public policies towards renewables successful? Evidence from European countries. *Renewable Energy*, *44*, 109−118. Available from: https://doi.org/10.1016/j.renene.2012.01.007.

Marques, A. C., Fuinhas, J. A., & Pais, D. F. (2018). Economic growth, sustainable development and food consumption: Evidence across different income groups of countries. *Journal of Cleaner Production*, *196*, 245−258. Available from: https://doi.org/10.1016/J.JCLEPRO.2018.06.011.

Menegaki, A. N., Marques, A. C., & Fuinhas, J. A. (2017). Redefining the energy-growth nexus with an index for sustainable economic welfare in Europe. *Energy*, *141*, 1254−1268. Available from: https://doi.org/10.1016/j.energy.2017.09.056.

Menegaki, A. N., & Tiwari, A. K. (2017). The index of sustainable economic welfare in the energy-growth nexus for American countries. *Ecological Indicators*, *72*, 494−509. Available from: https://doi.org/10.1016/j.ecolind.2016.08.036.

Menegaki, A. N., & Tsagarakis, K. P. (2015). More indebted than we know? Informing fiscal policy with an index of sustainable welfare for Greece. *Ecological Indicators*, *57*, 159−163. Available from: https://doi.org/10.1016/j.ecolind.2015.04.037.

Menegaki, A. N., & Tugcu, C. T. (2016a). Rethinking the energy-growth nexus: Proposing an index of sustainable economic welfare for Sub-SaharanAfrica. *Energy Research and Social Science*, *17*, 147−159. Available from: https://doi.org/10.1016/j.erss.2016.04.009.

Menegaki, A. N., & Tugcu, C. T. (2016b). The sensitivity of growth, conservation, feedback & neutrality hypotheses to sustainability accounting. *Energy for Sustainable Development*, *34*, 77−87. Available from: https://doi.org/10.1016/j.esd.2016.09.001.

Menegaki, A. N., & Tugcu, C. T. (2017). Energy consumption and sustainable economic welfare in G7 countries: A comparison with the conventional nexus. *Renewable and Sustainable Energy Reviews*, *69*(December 2016), 892−901. Available from: https://doi.org/10.1016/j.rser.2016.11.133.

Menegaki, A. N., & Tugcu, C. T. (2018). Two versions of the index of sustainable economic welfare (ISEW) in the energy-growth nexus for selected Asian countries. *Sustainable Production and Consumption*, *14*(December 2017), 21−35. Available from: https://doi.org/10.1016/j.spc.2017.12.005.

Moutinho, V., Madaleno, M., & Robaina, M. (2017). The economic and environmental efficiency assessment in EU cross-country: Evidence from DEA and quantile regression approach. *Ecological Indicators*, *78*, 85−97. Available from: https://doi.org/10.1016/j.ecolind.2017.02.042.

Nikolaev, B., Boudreaux, C., & Salahodjaev, R. (2017). Are individualistic societies less equal? Evidence from the parasite stress theory of values. *Journal of Economic Behavior and Organization*, *138*, 30−49. Available from: https://doi.org/10.1016/j.jebo.2017.04.001.

Niu, S., Jia, Y., Ye, L., Dai, R., & Li, N. (2016). Does electricity consumption improve residential living status in less developed regions? An empirical analysis using the quantile regression approach. *Energy*, *95*, 550−560. Available from: https://doi.org/10.1016/j.energy.2015.12.029.

Nourry, M. (2008). Measuring sustainable development: Some empirical evidence for France from eight alternative indicators. *Ecological Economics*, *67*(3), 441−456. Available from: https://doi.org/10.1016/j.ecolecon.2007.12.019.

Ocal, O., & Aslan, A. (2013). Renewable energy consumption−economic growth nexus in Turkey. *Renewable and Sustainable Energy Reviews*, *28*, 494−499. Available from: https://doi.org/10.1016/j.rser.2013.08.036.

O'Mahony, T., Escardó-Serra, P., & Dufour, J. (2018). Revisiting ISEW valuation approaches: The case of Spain including the costs of energy depletion and of climate change. *Ecological Economics*, *144*(May 2017), 292–303. Available from: https://doi.org/10.1016/j.ecolecon.2017.07.024.

Powell, D. (2016). *Quantile regression with nonadditive fixed effects*. RAND Working Paper. Retrieved from http://works.bepress.com/david_powell/14

Pulselli, F. M., Bravi, M., & Tiezzi, E. (2012). Application and use of the ISEW for assessing the sustainability of a regional system: A case study in Italy. *Journal of Economic Behavior and Organization*, *81*(3), 766–778. Available from: https://doi.org/10.1016/j.jebo.2010.12.021.

Rafindadi, A. A., & Ozturk, I. (2017). Impacts of renewable energy consumption on the German economic growth: Evidence from combined cointegration test. *Renewable and Sustainable Energy Reviews*, *75*(November 2016), 1130–1141. Available from: https://doi.org/10.1016/j.rser.2016.11.093.

Salahuddin, M., & Alam, K. (2016). Information and communication technology, electricity consumption and economic growth in OECD countries: A panel data analysis. *International Journal of Electrical Power and Energy Systems*, *76*, 185–193. Available from: https://doi.org/10.1016/j.ijepes.2015.11.005.

Sarwar, S., Chen, W., & Waheed, R. (2017). Electricity consumption, oil price and economic growth: Global perspective. *Renewable and Sustainable Energy Reviews*, *76*, 9–18. Available from: https://doi.org/10.1016/j.rser.2017.03.063.

Shahbaz, M., Sarwar, S., Chen, W., & Malik, M. N. (2017). Dynamics of electricity consumption, oil price and economic growth: Global perspective. *Energy Policy*, *108*, 256–270. Available from: https://doi.org/10.1016/j.enpol.2017.06.006.

Shahbaz, M., Zakaria, M., Shahzad, S. J. H., & Mahalik, M. K. (2018). The energy consumption and economic growth nexus in top ten energy-consuming countries: Fresh evidence from using the quantile-on-quantile approach. *Energy Economics*, *71*, 282–301. Available from: https://doi.org/10.1016/j.eneco.2018.02.023.

Solt, F. (2016). The standardized world income inequality database*. *Social Science Quarterly*, *97*(5), 1267–1281. Available from: https://doi.org/10.1111/ssqu.12295.

CHAPTER TWO

The electricity generation, waste, and CO_2 emissions in Latin America and the Caribbean countries: a panel autoregressive distributed lag approach

Hélde A.D. Hdom[1,a], José Alberto Fuinhas[2,b],
António Cardoso Marques[3,b] and Alexandre Magno de Melo Faria[4,c]

[1]The Capes Foundation, Ministry of Education of Brazil, Brasilia, Brazil
[2]NECE-UBI, CeBER and Faculty of Economics, University of Coimbra, Coimbra, Portugal
[3]NECE-UBI and Management and Economics Department, University of Beira Interior, Covilhã, Portugal
[4]GPDS-CNPq and Faculty of Economics, Federal University of Mato Grosso, Cuiabá, Brazil

Contents

[a] The Capes Foundation, Ministry of Education of Brazil. Post Code 250, Brasilia. DF 70.040-020, Brazil.
[b] The Research was supported by the Capes Foundation of the Ministry of Education of Brazil, project BEX/0013/13-7/2013 and NECE, R&D unit and funded by the FCT—Portuguese Foundation for the Development of Science and Technology, Ministry of Science, Technology and Higher Education, project UID/GES/04630/2019.
[c] Research Group on Socio-Environmental Development, National Council for Scientific and Technological Development, Brazil.

The Extended Energy–Growth Nexus.
DOI: https://doi.org/10.1016/B978-0-12-815719-0.00002-4

2.1 Introduction

Emissions of greenhouse gases (GHG) have received considerable attention from economic and environmental researchers during the last decade. Waste produced by economic activity has been increasing, and this fact has favored the high concentration of GHG in the Earth's atmosphere. These emissions have given rise to the high concentrations of carbon dioxide (CO2), methane (CH4), and nitrous oxide (N2O) gases in the atmosphere leading to an increased absorption of energy by the climate system (IPCC, 2014a).

In global terms economic growth and energy consumption continue to be the main contributors to the increase of carbon dioxide emissions, which further enhance the high concentration of pollutants in the atmosphere (IPCC, 2014b). Methane gas is the second most important GHG, with its emissions coming from a wide range of anthropogenic activities, for example, the production and transportation of fossil fuels, agricultural production, and the disposal of solid waste (organic and inorganic). The third most important GHG is nitrous oxide. Agricultural and industrial activities, as well as combustion and waste disposal, are the main sources of this gas. Estimates suggest that 40% of total N2O emissions are anthropogenic (IPCC, 2014b).

Solid waste generated worldwide is around 2.2 kg/capita/day, with the most recent projections pointing to a waste management cost expected to reach approximately 375.5 billion US$ by 2025. In addition, it is anticipated that the least developed countries (LDCs) will use most of their budgetary resources for the basic management of the waste generated, that is, garbage collection, with only a small fraction of that budget being effectively applied to its disposal. The scenario for LDCs contrasts with the one from the developed countries, with high incomes, where most expenditure is spent on the disposal and reuse of waste, mainly for energy generation (Hoornweg & Bhada-Tata, 2012).

A prominent idea that can lead to improvements in the quality of the environment, while reducing the climatic risks associated with pollutants emissions, is based on the transition from the current energy mix, based on fossil fuels, to other sources of cleaner (renewable) energy. However, there are few known scientific investigations that have examined the emissions produced from other energy sources, whether they are fossil or renewable (Bölük & Mert, 2014). In the renewable energy context, the financial support for new investments has increased by 17% (reference from 2013 to 2014), with all regions of the globe increasing their investments in renewable energy production. The total value of these investments was 270 billion US$ worldwide, 131.3 billion US$ in the case of developing countries, and 138.9 billion US$ in the case of developed economies (REN21, 2015).

In economic and environmental literature, the conflictive relationship between the economy and the environment has been demonstrated by researchers, who are far from being consensual. In fact, there is a dichotomy in this relationship. The environmental perspective denotes that economic activity has a negative impact on the environment. On the other hand, the economic perspective states that environmental protection measures produce negative impacts on a country's economic output and well-being (Andre Grimaud, 1999; Grimaud & Tournemaine, 2007; Ligthart & Van der Ploeg, 1994). Although, there are also researchers who have argued that improvements in environmental conditions can be achieved at the same time as high levels of growth (Hart, 2004; Lans Bovenberg & Smulders, 1995; Porter & Van der Linde, 1995). If this last hypothesis is verified, countries would not need to apply efforts to reduce the negative impacts of economic activity on the environment, since economic development would raise environmental quality levels (Bölük & Mert, 2014).

The truth is that in the historical context there is some parallelism between the environment in the past and the current situation. During the past two centuries, especially during the last 50 years of the 20th century, the global economy has grown so dramatically that it has even transformed the thinking of the researchers who have devoted themselves to the study of planetary resources and their exhaustion (Mebratu, 1998). At a certain stage in this process, the depletion of natural resources proved to be a serious problem for the accelerated development process of several industrialized nations, a fact that was widely discussed and which motivated the report "The limits to Growth" (Meadows, Meadows, Randers, & Behrens, 1972). Especially concerned with the lack of raw materials to feed the productive structure, this report aimed to analyze the world situation while at the same time making some predictions giving some solutions for the future

However, another report has been behind most of the current economy-environment debates. The Brundtland report from 1987, by The World Commission on Environment and Development (WCED) (1987) entitled "Our Common Future," guided the debate on sustainable development and contributed to the creation of institutional mechanisms, national and international, aimed at the promotion of economic development along with the protection of the environment and well-being of people (Mebratu, 1998; Sneddon, Howarth, & Norgaard, 2006; Zaccai, 2012). The term "sustainable development" emerged institutionally within the framework of the United Nations (UN) and served as a turning point in the way of thinking about the relationship between the economy and the environment. This fact led researchers to be more aware of the failures of growth and economic development, especially when related to equity, the decline of environmental quality and the inability to contain the explosion of unsustainable (human and economic) activities (Sneddon et al., 2006).

An important historical contribution, which criticized the dominant development model adopted by a majority of the economists, was the one from Georgescu-Roegen (1971). In his work, based on the second law of thermodynamics, the law of entropy, he points to the inevitable degradation of natural resources with the course of human activities. The author also criticized the economists who defended a boundless material economic growth and developed an opposing and extremely daring theory for the time, the economic decay theory. The author argued that developed countries should accept a lower standard of living in order that the LDCs could escape poverty. Underlying this idea was the evidence that the exploitation of nature resulted in natural resources depletion and environmental degradation, since the material and energy resources in the production structure produced emissions of waste that polluted the environment. Cechin (2010) argued that pollution from waste emission would become the main problem for society even before natural resources became scarce.

Sneddon et al. (2006) argued that increasing scientific understanding regarding climate change and other biophysical transformations, and their implications for mankind, dictated the great collapse of the philosophical foundations of the dominant market paradigm, which has led countries to consider the need for adaptation to the new concept of sustainable development. Global consumption of natural resources and the levels of greenhouse gas emissions have been strongly driven by the development of industrialization in developing countries (IPCC, 2014b; Krausmann et al., 2009). Despite the complexity of this debate, it seems that there is a certain consensus among researchers and public decision-makers that global climate change is a real issue in environmental economics. As the literature has stated there are several factors that could lead to global warming and/or climate change, either by the use of energy, which is indispensable to the functioning of the industrial process and of the whole economy, by the use of land and forest, or by the accumulation of generated urban solid waste (USW), as well as the postconsumption of economic goods (IPCC, 2007).

The relationship between physical and economic growth on a global scale, and the increase in the resource intensity in the economy, has shown that the average growing income of the population and the use of nonrenewable and other natural resources are both closely linked to economic growth (IPCC, 2014b; Krausmann et al., 2009). In this sense the objective of this chapter is to examine the interaction among economic growth indicators, waste consumption in the generation of renewable fuels, electricity production, primary energy use, and carbon dioxide emissions in Latin American and the Caribbean (LAC) countries. It is believed that exploring these relationships, and more precisely, the impacts of economic growth, and USW produced by society, on the pollutants emissions is essential for designing adequate public policies and to delineate better strategies for the achievement of sustainable development by the developing countries.

2.2 The waste sector's framework in Latin America and the Caribbean

Although the recycling rate in Latin America is unknown, it is estimated that "waste pickers" in the region exceed 100,000 small enterprises, involved in waste collection (UNHABITAT, 2010). This aspect is very relevant because a selective collection system operated by public agents in Latin America is limited to the few more advanced cities. However, the identification of "waste-pickers" means zero cost for municipal administrations (IPEA, 2010). In turn, the recycling market, despite its importance and relevance in Latin America, is limited to the reuse of the materials collected, since the commercialization of recyclable material depends on other intermediary markets (UNHABITAT, 2010).

In this context, given the structural, economic, cultural, and social reality of each country, the commercialization of the material collected by the waste collectors is carried out mainly by middlemen orbiting in the recycling market "satellite companies." These commercial relationships are based not only on the informal market, but also on very precarious conditions. In this sense, understanding the structure of the USW market is crucial to strengthening the efficiency of this market. Thus, the strengthening of the market would lead to less dependence on the waste collectors.

Fig. 2.1 shows an expanded picture of the phases involved in the waste sector, from the garbage produced until the commercialization of the recycled raw material.

Furthermore, the GHG emissions come from more than a few sources such as household consumption, companies, cities, and countries (Peters, 2010). As a result of this, global GHG emissions from waste worldwide went up 1.45 GtCO$_2$ eq. in 2010. LAC were responsible for 0.14 GtCO$_2$ eq. (IPCC, 2014b). Conversely one of the biggest challenges facing developing countries is how to promote economic growth without jeopardizing an environment abundant in primary natural resources. These countries are faced with scarce financial resources but an abundance of natural resources. Even without the economic capacity and the income levels necessary for the basic improvement of life quality, as well as the urgent need for technological conversion, these countries are adopting and practicing policy measures for energy efficiency (Domingos, 2017).

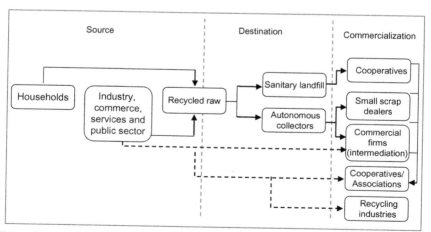

Figure 2.1 Generation, destination, and trade of urban solid waste for Latin America and the Caribbean. Source: *Adapted from Domingos, H. A. (2011). Economia dos Reciclados: uma análise do Mercado de Resíduos Sólidos no Aglomerado Urbano Cuiabá e Várzea Grande.* Universidade Federal de Mato Grosso, UFMT, Cuiabá, Mato Grosso, Brasil. *Domingos (2011).*

Moreover the usage of USW could be an opportunity for developing countries to produce energy. The problems related to municipal and industrial solid waste are in fact an opportunity that could eliminate the risk of exposure to the environment and climate change. In addition, global consumption of material resources continues to grow and with them, the environmental degradation associated with resource extraction and global GHG emissions continues to intensify, despite the increase in productivity and efficiency achieved by technological development and eco-efficiency. Therefore energy production by USW processing and gas capture in landfills is the great challenge of USW management in Latin American cities.

Fig. 2.2 shows the consumption of renewable waste fuel (CrenW), production of energy (EnergyUse), electricity (ElectrPower), and CO2 emissions (PCO2 emissions) in LAC countries.

There is a wide variation in energy production, renewable fuel consumption of waste, and CO2 emissions between countries. The level of renewable fuel consumption in Guatemala, Honduras, Nicaragua, Paraguay, and Uruguay exceeds the consumption level of countries such as Brazil, Argentina, and Chile. Regarding primary energy production, the exceptions are Trinidad and Tobago, where the values related to the consumption of waste for fuel generation are much lower than the other Latin American countries. The decisive option in the actions of conversion of energy from waste is the understanding that other blocking forces exist and could be used as an alternative source of energy production, as is the case of the use of waste for the generation of renewable fuels and electricity consumption.

2.3 Literature review

The relationship between energy consumption, economic growth, and the environment has been thoroughly examined in the field of primary energies. For example, Lotfalipour, Falahi, and Ashena (2010) found empirical evidence of a causal relationship between economic growth and CO2 emissions for Iran for the period between 1967 and 2007. A similar result was found by Apergis and Payne (2009) for several Central American countries (Soytas, Sari, & Ewing, 2007). Additionally, Menyah and Wolde-Rufael (2010a) also found empirical evidence on the existence

Figure 2.2 Production of energy and carbon dioxide emissions in 2013. Source: *Author's computations using Data from World Development Indicators "World Bank-WDI" (2017)*.

of a causal relationship between energy consumption and CO2 emissions during the periods ranging from 1960 to 2004 and 1960 to 2007 in the United States. The same result was also found by Zhang and Cheng (2009) for China, and by Niu, Ding, Niu, Li, and Luo (2011) for the Asia Pacific countries. Alam, Ara Begum, Buysse, and Van Huylenbroeck (2012) confirmed the presence of these same relationships for Bangladesh in the period from 1972 to 2006.

Ghosh (2010) found evidence of a causal relationship between economic growth and CO2 emissions and between energy consumption and CO2 emissions for the period between 1971 and 2006 in India. Wang, Zhou, Zhou, and Wang (2011) also found empirical evidence of a causal relationship between energy consumption and CO2 emissions in China. In this same study evidence was found that both energy consumption and long-term economic growth caused CO2 emissions. The same relationship was found by Bloch et al. (2012), and by Chang (2010), with both coal consumption and economic growth causing pollutant emissions in China. Other studies that showed evidence of a causal relationship between energy consumption and CO2 emissions were: Chandran Govindaraju and Tang (2013) for India and China; Al-Mulali (2011) for the countries of the Middle East and North Africa or MENA (Middle East and North Africa); Dinda and Coondoo (2006) for 88 countries (data for the 1960−90 period); and Pao and Tsai (2010) for the BRIC's—Brazil, Russia, India, and China—using statistical data for the period between 1971 and 2005.

Pao and Tsai (2011a, 2011b) also obtained similar results for Brazil, confirming the presence of an inverted U shape relationship and the EKC hypothesis, with data for the 1980−2007 period. In turn Pao, Yu, and Yang (2011) identified a causal link between economic growth and CO2 emissions for Russia based on data from 1990 to 2007. Menyah and Wolde-Rufael (2010b) found empirical evidence in favor of a causal link between CO2 emissions and economic growth and between energy and CO2 emissions for the South African economy. A study by Bella, Massidda, and Mattana (2014) concluded that, among three groups of OECD countries, there is one group that causes great concern, because in the long run an increase in its environmental degradation is expected. This group is composed of Australia, Canada, Ireland, New Zealand, the United Kingdom, and the United States. In addition, according to the authors, the absence of any causal link between electricity consumption and CO_2 emissions undermines the effectiveness of energy conservation policies since the implementation of policies against environmental degradation is hardly justified by economic reasons. Moreover, the authors state that a change of perspective, oriented toward public action, is needed in order to provide solid economic reasons for public intervention against environmental degradation, where the causal link can contribute to intensify this pessimistic point of view (Bella et al., 2014).

In a more recent study, Domingos, Faria, Fuinhas, and Marques (2017) analyzed the impact of waste consumption on the production of biogas and electricity for the European Union (EU) member States, finding evidence that biogas reduces CO_2 emissions, while electricity increases the emissions of pollutants. The authors suggest that the EU should increase the influence of renewable energy in its energy mix in order to ensure compliance with the 2020 targets. Jebli and Youssef (2015) and Jebli (2016) analyzed the energy−growth−environment nexus, using renewable waste fuels, for the countries of North Africa and for the specific case of Tunisia, respectively. In the first study the authors found evidence that both CO_2 emissions and the consumption of renewable waste fuels had a positive impact on economic growth. In the second study, causal relationships were found between the same decomposing variables both in the short and long term. The author suggested that public policy makers from Tunisia should carry out the exploration of waste as a strategy to mitigate its emissions and benefit the health and well-being of the country's population.

2.4 Methodology

This chapter studies a panel data of LAC countries, to assess the interactions between: (1) economic growth; (2) renewable waste fuels consumption; (3) electricity production, (4) primary energy use; and (5) carbon dioxide emissions. An autoregressive distributed lag (ARDL) approach is employed to analyze the short- and long-run relationships. Furthermore, the ARDL approach has the advantage of being robust in the presence of mixed integration order variables, that is, I(1), I(0), and borderline (I(0)/I(1)) (Attiaoui, Toumi, Ammouri, & Gargouri, 2017).

2.4.1 Data

This research examines a balanced panel data from 1971 until 2013, with 21 LAC countries (Argentina, Bolivia, Brazil, Chile, Colombia, Costa Rica, Cuba, Dominican Republic, Ecuador, El Salvador, Guatemala, Honduras, Jamaica, Mexico, Nicaragua, Panama, Paraguay, Peru, Trinidad and Tobago, Uruguay, and Venezuela). The data used in this research has been retrieved from the World Development Indicators (WDI)[1], namely:

- *Ypc*—Gross domestic product (GDP), in local currency units;
- *CrenW*—Share of renewables from solid biomass, liquid biomass, industrial wastes, and municipal wastes, in percentage;
- *PCO$_2$pc*—Carbon dioxide emissions per capita, in thousands of tones;
- *ElectrPower*—Electricity produced per capita, in Kilowatts per hour; and
- *EnergyUse*—Primary energy used, per capita, in kilograms of oil equivalent.

All variables except *CrenW* have been divided by the population, converting the series in per capita series.

2.4.2 Methodology

The ARDL methodology apportioned the effects into short and the long run, where the short term characterizes the dynamics adjustments, and the long run the equilibrium (Pesaran & Shin, 1999). In fact, when studying a long time-span, it is expected that the variables react differently on both the short and long run. Thus this chapter could provide helpful insights into the augmented energy—growth—environment nexus, especially, in the analysis of the effects of biomass/wastes, electricity production, and primary energy use on both the economic growth and development of well-being. This research is also useful to disclose the technological and environmental progress of LAC countries.

To comply with these research objectives two models were estimated, namely:

- Model 1—Pollution (*PCO2* was the dependent variables); and
- Model 2—Economic Growth (*Ypc* was the dependent variable).

---

[1] See http://databank.worldbank.org/data/reports.aspx?source = world-development-indicators

Eqs. (2.1) and (2.3) reveals the short-run of models 1 and 2, respectively, and Eqs. (2.2) and (2.4) disclose the long-run models 1 and 2. The "L" prefix denotes the natural logarithms of variables in levels, and the "D" prefix represents the first differences of variables.

$$LPCO2_{it} = f(LYpc_{it}; LCrenW_{it}; LEnergyUse_{it}) \qquad (2.1)$$

$$DLPCO2_{it} = f(DLYpc_{it}; DLCrenW_{it}; DLEnergyUse_{it}) \qquad (2.2)$$

$$LYpc_{it} = f(LPCO2_{it}; LCrenW_{it}; LElectrPow_{it}) \qquad (2.3)$$

$$DLYpc_{it} = f(DLPCO2_{it}; DLCrenW_{it}; DLElectrPow_{it}) \qquad (2.4)$$

The LAC countries have strong economic factors, mainly because of the abundance of natural resources exported to the rest of the world (Apergis & Payne, 2010). Accordingly, a higher income is associated with a higher level of production and consumption. So, these activities increase energy consumption, which in turn increases greenhouse gas emissions (Calbick & Gunton, 2014). Many countries in the region under analysis are developing countries. Thus it is expected that these countries have specificities while sharing a common level of development. The general ARDL models for Pollution model and for Economic Growth model are specified in the Eqs. (2.5a) and (2.5b), respectively.

$$LPCO2_{it} = \alpha_{1i} + \delta_{1i}T_t + \sum_{j=1}^{k}\beta_{11ij}LPCO2_{it-j} + \sum_{j=0}^{k}\beta_{12ij}LYpc_{it-j}$$
$$+ \sum_{j=0}^{k}\beta_{13ij}LCrenW_{it-j} + \sum_{j=0}^{k}\beta_{14ij}LEnergyUse_{it-j} + \varepsilon_{1it} \qquad (2.5a)$$

$$LYpc_{it} = \alpha_{2i} + \delta_{2i}T_t + \sum_{j=1}^{k}\beta_{21ij}LYpc_{it-j} + \sum_{j=0}^{k}\beta_{22ij}LPCO2_{it-j}$$
$$+ \sum_{j=0}^{k}\beta_{23ij}LCrenW_{it-j} + \sum_{j=0}^{k}\beta_{24ij}LElectrPower_{it-j} + \varepsilon_{2it} \qquad (2.5b)$$

The dynamic effects of the countries are decomposed into short and long term, the unrestricted error correction mechanism (UECM) makes the necessary adjustments (Fuinhas, Marques, & Couto, 2015). Thus

Eqs. (2.5a) and (2.5b) are reparametrized in the general UECM form to perform the decomposition of the short and long run relationship as follows:

$$DLPCO2_{it} = \alpha_{3i} + \delta_{3i}T_t + \sum_{j=1}^{k}\beta_{31ij}DLPCO2_{it-j}$$

$$+ \sum_{j=0}^{k}\beta_{32ij}DLYpc_{it-j} + \sum_{j=0}^{k}\beta_{33ij}DLCrenW_{it-j}$$

$$+ \sum_{j=0}^{k}\beta_{34ij}DLEnergyUse_{it-j} + \gamma_{11i}LPCO2_{it-1} + \gamma_{12i}LYpc_{it-1}$$

$$+ \gamma_{13i}LCrenW_{it-1} + \gamma_{14i}LEnergyUse_{it-1} + \varepsilon_{3it}$$

$$(2.6a)$$

$$DLYpc_{it} = \alpha_{4i} + \delta_{4i}T_t + \sum_{j=1}^{k}\beta_{41ij}DLYpc_{it-j} + \sum_{j=0}^{k}\beta_{42ij}DLPCO2_{it-j}$$

$$+ \sum_{j=0}^{k}\beta_{43ij}DLCrenW_{it-j} + \sum_{j=0}^{k}\beta_{44ij}DLElectrPower_{it-j} \qquad (2.6b)$$

$$+ \gamma_{41i}LYpc_{it-1} + \gamma_{42i}LPCO2_{it-1} + \gamma_{43i}LCrenW_{it-1}$$

$$+ \gamma_{44i}LEnergyPower_{it-1} + \varepsilon_{4it}$$

where α_{ki} denotes the intercept for each country i ($i = 1,2,...,8$), δ_{ki}, β_{ki}, and Υ_{ki}, the coefficients of the parameters, and ε_{ki} are the error term, respectively.

To guarantee that the estimations are not affected by violations of the basic hypothesis, which could strongly compromise the conclusions that would be disclosed by the models results, a battery of test were made. The Pesaran test (Pesaran, 2004) to identify the cross-sectional correlation; the Wooldridge test (Woodridge, 2002) to test the serial correlation of the models; the Modified Wald test (Greene, 2002) to reveal the presence of homoscedastic or heteroscedastic errors; and the Breusch–Pagan LM (BP) test (Breusch and Pagan, 1980) to test the contemporaneous correlation in models. Besides, the Westerlund cointegration test (Westerlund, 2007) was employed to reveal the cointegration between the series.

2.5 Empirical results and discussion

The existence of the cross-section dependence in the variables was verified through the CD test. The null hypothesis of this test predicts the cross-section independence and it was used to analyze if the memory of the variables shares common impacts. The results showed in Table 2.1 supports that all the variables present cross-section dependence (rejects the H0 at 1% level of significance). This means that the public policies adopted in the different countries share common impacts, usually inherent to the long memory of the variables (Fuinhas et al., 2015).

How to do:

```
** Stata command xtcd **
    xtcd lypc_lcu lpco2pc lcren_waste lenergy_use lelectr_prod
    xtcd dlypc_lcu dlpco2pc dlcren_waste dlenergy_use dlelectr_prod
```

How it looks like

Variable	CD-test	p-value	corr	abs(corr)
lypc_lcu	55.16	0.000	0.580	0.642
lpco2pc	38.96	0.000	0.410	0.486
lcren_waste	46.51	0.000	0.489	0.588
lenergy_use	33.41	0.000	0.352	0.517
lelectr_prod	83.97	0.000	0.884	0.884

Source: Author's computations using Stata Software

As the first-generation unit root test could not be robust in presence of the cross-section dependence, the second-generation unit root (CIPS) test was performed for the variables in their levels and in the first differences (see Table 2.2). Regarding the variables in levels, the results show that the production of renewable waste fuels (CrenW), GDP (LYpc), CO2 emissions (LPCO2), and primary energy use (LEnergyUse) are stationary when there is no trend. Meanwhile, electricity generation

Table 2.1 Cross-sectional dependence.

Variable	Cross-sectional dependence			Variable	Cross-sectional dependence		
Level	CD-test	Corr	Abs (corr)	First difference	CD-test	Corr	Abs (corr)
LYpc	55.16***	0.580	0.642	*DLYpc*	20.59***	0.219	0.255
LPCO₂	38.96***	0.410	0.486	*DLPCO₂*	5.71***	0.061	0.144
LCrenW	46.51***	0.489	0.588	*DLCrenW*	2.70***	0.029	0.128
LElectrPower	83.97***	0.884	0.884	*DLElectrPower*	6.20***	0.066	0.155
LEnergyUse	33.41***	0.352	0.517	*DLEnergyUse*	4.38***	0.047	0.132

Notes: CD test has $N \sim (0,1)$, under the H0: cross-sectional independence; ***, **, and * denote statistical significance levels at 1%, 5%, and 10%, respectively; and the Stata command xtcd was used to achieve the results for cross-sectional dependence (CSD).

Table 2.2 Unit root test.

Variable	Second generation		Variable	Second generation	
Level	CIPS (Zt-bar)		First difference	CIPS (Zt-bar)	
	Without trend	With trend		Without trend	With trend
LYpc	−2.867***	−2.380***	*DLYpc*	−10.236***	−8.201***
LPCO₂	−2.917***	0.115	*DLPCO₂*	−15.269***	−13.819***
LCrenW	−1.285*	0.511	*DLCrenW*	−12.857***	−11.635***
LElectrPower	−1253	1.372	*DLElectrPower*	−10.089***	−8.644***
LEnergyUse	−2.525***	0.068	*DLEnergyUse*	−11.495***	−10.323***

Notes: ***, **, and * denotes statistical significance levels at 1%, 5% and 10%, respectively; Panel Unit Root test (CIPS) null hypothesis: series are I(1); and the Stata command multipurt was used to compute CIPS.

(*LElectrPower*) shows a unit root. Only the *LYpc* is stationary in levels with and without trend. Concerning the results of the variables in the first differences, all of them are stationary with and without trend, that is, the variables are I(1).

How to do:

** Stata command multipurt **

    multipurt lypc_lcu lpco2pc lcren_waste lenergy_use lelectr_prod, lags(1)

    multipurt dlypc_lcu dlpco2pc dlcren_waste dlenergy_use dlelectr_prod, lags(1)

How it looks like

(B) Pesaran (2007) Panel Unit Root test (CIPS)

Variable	lags	Specification without trend		
		Zt-bar	p-value	t-bar
lypc_lcu	0	-0.406	0.342	.
lypc_lcu	1	-2.867	0.002	.
lpco2pc	0	-3.283	0.001	.
lpco2pc	1	-2.917	0.002	.

Source: Author's computations using Stata Software

The waste sector is extremely complex in the world. However, in the developed countries, such as the EU Member states, public policies have contributed to overcoming some challenges that this sector has faced (Domingos et al., 2017). Regarding Latin American countries, the waste sector is still faced with several challenges. For instance, there are not enough public policies taking, for example, measurement of the waste produced by the cities. When compared to developed countries, in Latin American the investment in the treatment plants related to the new technologies and/or innovative management techniques is low.

However, there is a promising future for waste treatment, namely in their potential for energy production—WTE. In the LAC countries, in 1 year about 341 kg of the solid waste per capita is produced. In 2013, the contribution of the WTE (renewable and nonrenewable) for the total energy demand was 0.4% (OECD & IEA, 2015). Additionally, electricity production is based on renewable sources, having hydroelectric power as the largest share of the total electricity production in the Latin America countries. The reduction of the dependence upon fossil fuels has been promoted since the 1960s with the construction of large hydroelectric plants to take advantage of the natural resources.

The Westerlund (2007) cointegration test was applied to ascertain the existence of cointegration between the variables under the null hypothesis of the noncointegration. The presence of the cointegration supports the equilibrium between the variables in the long-term. The results of the Westerlund test shown in Table 2.3 are presenting four statistics.

Table 2.3 Westerlund cointegration test.

Statistics	Value	z-value	P-value	P-value robust
Gt	−3.215	−1.776	.038	.014
Ga	−17.094	0.144	.557	.018
Pt	−15.061	−3.023	.001	.005
Pa	−16.076	−1.164	.122	.021

Notes: Westerlund cointegration test (2007) has a null hypothesis (H0) of noncointegration; for controlling CSD, robust values through 800 simulations with bootstrapping regression was generated; the Gt and Ga parameters test for cointegration on an individual basis for each country and Pt and Pa test the cointegration with effects on the panel (Westerlund & Edgerton, 2007); and the four tests were obtained by using the xtwest command in Stata (with the option constant trend lags(1) lrwindow(3) bootstrap(800)).

At the individual level, that is, for each country the statistics of Gt and Ga were shown. At the panel level, the statistics of Pt and Pa were provided. Considering the statistics of the P-value, only for the Gt and Pt, there is a rejection of the null hypothesis at the 5% and 1% level of significance, respectively. However, considering that there is cross-section dependence for all the variables, the statistics of the P-value could be biased. Therefore it proceeded the statistics for the P-value robust by using 800 simulations in bootstrapping regression. In this case there is evidence for the existence of the cointegration at 5% level of significance at both individual and panel level (see Table 2.3).

How to do:
** Stata command xtwest **
    set matsize 800
    xtwest lpco2pc lypc_lcu lcren_waste lenergy_use lelectr_prod, constant trend lags (1) lrwindow(3) bootstrap(800)

How it looks like

```
Results for H0: no cointegration
With 21 series and 5 covariates
```

Statistic	Value	Z-value	P-value	Robust P-value
Gt	−3.215	−0.999	0.159	0.014
Ga	−15.043	2.095	0.982	0.018
Pt	−14.129	−1.368	0.086	0.005
Pa	−14.146	0.780	0.782	0.021

Source: Author's computations using Stata Software

2.6 Panels autoregressive distributed lag results

To test if the panel has fixed effects (FE) or random effects (RE), the panel (Pollution) and (Growth) using the Stata command xtreg followed by the command Hausman were estimated. The Hausman test was revealed to be statistically highly significant (chi-square values 67.16 and 34.25, respectively), indicating for both estimations that the FE model is more appropriate to perform the analyses. A battery of tests to assessing possible violations of the models is presented in Table 2.4. For all four tests used for this study (Pesaran, Woodridge, Wald, and Breusch–Pagan), the null hypotheses (H0) were rejected, thus demonstrating that both models present correlated residuals, serial correlation of first order, and are heteroscedastic.

How to do:

** Breusch–Pagan LM test **
     xtreg dlpco2pc dlypc_lcu dlcren_waste dlenergy_use l_lypc_lcu l_lpco2pc l_lcren_waste l_lenergy_use, fe
     xtcsd, pesaran abs
** Wooldridge test **
     xtserial dlpco2pc dlypc_lcu dlcren_waste dlenergy_use l_lypc_lcu l_lpco2pc l_lcren_waste l_lenergy_use, output
     ** Modified Wald test **
     xtreg dlpco2pc dlypc_lcu dlcren_waste dlenergy_use l_lypc_lcu l_lpco2pc l_lcren_waste l_lenergy_use, fe
     xttest3
     ** Breusch–Pagan LM test **
     xtreg dlpco2pc dlypc_lcu dlcren_waste dlenergy_use l_lypc_lcu l_lpco2pc l_lcren_waste l_lenergy_use, fe
     xttest2

Table 2.4 Specification test.

	Pollution	Growth
	DLPCO$_2$	DLYpc
Pesaran test	2.216**	13.443***
Woodridge test	$F(1,20) = 101.654***$	$F(1,20) = 208.572***$
Modified Wald test	$\chi^2_{21} = 6114.98***$	$\chi^2_{21} = 461.26***$
Breusch-Pagan LM test	$\chi^2_{210} = 313.257***$	$\chi^2_{210} = 455.27***$

Note: ***, **, and * denote statistically significant values at the levels of 1%, 5%, and 10%, respectively.

Table 2.5 Estimate results and diagnostic test.

Dependent variables	Pollution (DLPCO$_2$)	Growth (DLYpc)
Variables	**FE D-K**	**FE D-K**
Constant	-1.004***	0.494**
Trend	—	-0.001***
Short-run impacts		
DLYpc	0.369***	—
DLPCO$_2$	—	0.118***
DLCrenW	-0.061*	-0.038**
DLEnergyUse	0.631***	—
DLElectrPower	—	0.167***
Variables lagged once		
LYpc (-1)	0.044**	-0.033*
LPCO2(-1)	-0.200***	0.023*
LCrenW(-1)	-0.032***	—
LEnergyUse(-1)	0.109***	—
LElectrPower(-1)	—	-0.027***
Elasticities (long run)		
Lypc	0.221***	—
LPCO$_2$	—	0.705***
LcrenW	-0.161***	—
LenergyUse	0.545***	—
LElectrPower	—	-0.843
Speed of adjustment		
Error correction mechanism (ECM)	-0.200***	-0.033*

Notes: ***, **, and * denote significant values at the levels of 1%, 5%, and 10%, respectively; to obtain Table 2.4, we applied the command xtscc in the Stata program with lag (1); and the long-run elasticities were calculated by dividing the coefficient of the dependence variable with a lag by the coefficients for each explanatory variable with a lag and multiplied by the ratio -1 (Fuinhas et. al., 2015).

These results were estimated using the Driscoll and Kraay (1998) estimator with fixed effects. This estimator calibrates the standard error that occurs in sample errors (Fuinhas et al., 2015), being robust to handle the first order autocorrelation, and heteroscedasticity present in our models. Finally, the ARDL panel results are shown in Table 2.5.

The GDP has a positive impact on CO_2 emissions in LAC countries at a statistically significance level of 1%, in the pollution model; the short-run impact showed that if the GDP increases by 1%, then carbon dioxide emissions increase by about 0.37% in the short-run. A positive elasticity of 0.22% proves that the values of the coefficients of CO_2 emissions are elastic in relation to the positive GDP variation in the long run. Primary energy consumption (Energy Use) has a positive impact of 0.63% on CO_2

emissions at the level of significance of 1% in the short run, while the long-run elasticity is 0.54% with a statistical significance level of 1%, revealing that pollution is elastic to the positive changes of primary energy. On the other hand, renewable waste fuels (CrenW) cause negative impacts on CO_2 emissions at the level of statistical significance of 10%, in the short-run. The long-run elasticity is 0.16% at 1% statistical significance level. If waste consumption is increased by 1%, CO_2 emissions contract by 0.16%, proving that the values of the coefficient of CO_2 emissions is inelastic to positive changes in the waste consumption when generating renewable energy (WTE). The lagged CO_2 emission has a statistically significant negative sign, and the model's imbalance is corrected by about 20% in the following period, as is demonstrated by the coefficient value of (ECM).

How to do:

** Stata command xtscc **

    xtscc dlpco2pc dlypc_lcu dlcren_waste dlenergy_use l_lypc_lcu l_lpco2pc l_lcren_waste l_lenergy_use, fe lag(1)

        nlcom (ratio1: -_b[l_lcren_waste]/_b[l_lpco2pc])

        nlcom (ratio1: -_b[l_lypc_lcu]/_b[l_lpco2pc])

        nlcom (ratio1: -_b[l_lenergy_use]/_b[l_lpco2pc])

How it looks like

```
Regression with Driscoll-Kraay standard errors    Number of obs    =      882
Method: Fixed-effects regression                  Number of groups =       21
Group variable (i): countries                     F( 7,     41)    =    37.24
maximum lag: 1                                     Prob > F         =   0.0000
                                                  within R-squared =   0.3111
```

dlpco2pc	Coef.	Drisc/Kraay Std. Err.	t	P>|t|	[95% Conf. Interval]	
dlypc_lcu	.3691628	.1007441	3.66	0.001	.1657059	.5726196
dlcren_waste	-.0608	.0312563	-1.95	0.059	-.1239234	.0023234
dlenergy_use	.6313656	.0571841	11.04	0.000	.5158799	.7468513
l_lypc_lcu	.0442618	.0167424	2.64	0.012	.0104498	.0780739
l_lpco2pc	-.2001696	.0352895	-5.67	0.000	-.2714381	-.1289011
l_lcren_waste	-.0321995	.009174	-3.51	0.001	-.0507267	-.0136723
l_lenergy_use	.1092306	.0304823	3.58	0.001	.0476703	.1707908
_cons	-1.004257	.251316	-4.00	0.000	-1.5118	-.4967142

ratio1: -_b[l_lcren_waste]/_b[l_lpco2pc]

dlpco2pc	Coef.	Std. Err.	z	P>|z|	[95% Conf. Interval]	
ratio1	-.1608609	.0516231	-3.12	0.002	-.2620403	-.0596814

Source: Author's computations using Stata Software

In the Growth model, the short-run impact demonstrates that CO_2 emissions have a positive impact on GDP at the significance level of 1% in the short-run. In the long run the CO_2 emissions has a positive impact on growth at a significance level of 1%. Indeed, if the level of pollution increases by 1%, GDP has growth by about 0.70%. Electricity generation has a positive impact on GDP at the 1% level of significance in the short-run. Actually, if electricity generation increases by 1%, the GDP increases by about 0.16% in the short-run. An unusual result is detected in electricity generation, that is, both the lagged *LElectrPower*, and the elasticity present negative coefficients. The value of the elasticity is -0.84%, in the long run, indicating that GDP, in the long run, presented an inelasticity to the generation of electricity. Generally speaking, this type of relationship is like in the case where energy consumption negatively impacts economic growth. In fact, electricity generation is based on renewable energy, mainly using hydro-electric power plants, which are the largest source of electric energy in these countries.

Renewable waste fuels have a negative impact on GDP growth at the significance level of 5%. Indeed, if there is a 1% increase in the consumption of waste to generate energy, the GDP contracts by approximately 0.04%. Thus, economic growth is inelastic to the changes in consumption of WTE, in the short-run. These results differ from those found by Jebli and Youssef (2015) for MENA countries who analyzed the impact of waste consumption in economic growth. However, similar results were found in relation to the impacts of the exploitation of waste as a strategy to reduce pollution having a positive effect on population welfare. The ECM reveals that the model's imbalance is corrected by about 0.03%, in the following period.

2.7 Conclusion

Throughout the last decade there has been a global trend to explore public policies which encourage the substitution of conventional energy sources into renewable ones. Following this trend, this study aims to analyze the impacts of waste-to-energy on environmental pollution and economic growth for LAC countries between the period 1971 and 2013.

The analysis was made by using two models. The first model examines both the short- and long-run impacts of GDP per capita, waste-to-energy, and primary energy consumption on CO_2 emissions. The second model studies both the short- and long-run impacts of energy consumption, CO_2 emissions, renewable fuel production of waste, and electricity production in economic growth.

Regarding the empirical results, the presence of cross-sectional dependence (CSD) and cointegration is observed. The *Pollution* model provides empirical evidence on waste consumption in energy production in LAC countries, revealing a negative causality on CO2 emissions, while GDP and primary energy consumption causes an increase in pollution levels. The *Growth* model provides empirical evidence on CO_2 emissions impacts on economic growth, revealing the existence of a positive causality both in the short and long run. Additionally, it is proved that electricity production positively causes economic growth in the short-run, while in the long-run electricity production causes negative economic growth. Finally, the waste-to-energy also has negative impacts on economic growth in the short-run.

The complexity of the waste sector in Latin America is relevant to the achieved results. In fact, there are two important factors in this approach. The first concerns the process of management by public agents. For example, in most countries, solid waste policies do not cover the whole country because services are decentralized and administered at the municipal level. Therefore, countries such as Brazil, Mexico, Costa Rica, Colombia, and Chile still need to overcome many obstacles to implement national policies. Other policies and strategies such as the improvement of urban sanitation quality, community education on waste management, the promotion of residual waste recovery at source, and technical assistance in municipalities were announced but not executed (UNHABITAT, 2010). For the Brazil case, a National Police on Solid Waste (PNRS) came into force in 2010 and after 8 years only a small number of municipalities have endeavored to comply with the law. Furthermore, in 2014 in Brazil the closure of all open dumps was brought into force. However, four years after the deadline, the number of open dumps in activity is still relatively high.

The second factor considers the exploitation of waste-to-energy plants by the private sector. This sector is interested in waste management due to new business opportunities generated by the advancement of technology. However, poor people who survive from waste collection in landfills should not be forgotten. In this case, it is recommended that public policies investigate an appropriate transition between the waste recovery and recycling sector and the energy extraction sector. There are several families, in Latin America, carrying out an informal role in reverse logistic in waste management (the collection of homogenous recyclable materials such as paper, cardboards, bottles, plastics, and metals for resale) which have no access to social public policies that ensures their survival. These economically vulnerable families should have help to get them back into the job market, especially the younger ones who can receive training to work in the power plants. With regard to the older ones, governments must ensure a guaranteed minimum income.

Therefore, the transition from the traditional solid waste treatment methods such as open dumps into bioenergy production methods has relevant impacts on peoples' wellness, the environment, and the economy. Accordingly, to deal with this transition new challenges are expected through the next few years, namely for developing countries in LAC.

References

Al-mulali, U. (2011). Oil consumption, CO_2 emission and economic growth in MENA countries. *Energy*, *36*(10), 6165−6171. Available from: https://doi.org/10.1016/j.energy.2011.07.048.

Apergis, N., & Payne, J. E. (2009). CO_2 emissions, energy usage, and output in Central America. *Energy Policy*, *37*(8), 3282−3286. Available from: https://doi.org/10.1016/j.enpol.2009.03.048.

Apergis, N., & Payne, J. E. (2010). Energy consumption and growth in South America: Evidence from a panel error correction model. *Energy Economics*, *32*(6), 1421−1426. Available from: https://doi.org/10.1016/j.eneco.2010.04.006.

Attiaoui, I., Toumi, H., Ammouri, B., & Gargouri, I. (2017). Causality links among renewable energy consumption, CO_2 emissions, and economic growth in Africa: Evidence from a panel ARDL-PMG approach. *Environmental Science and Pollution Research*, *24*(14), 13036−13048 <https://doi.org/10.1007/s11356-017-8850-7>.

Bella, G., Massidda, C., & Mattana, P. (2014). The relationship among CO_2 emissions, electricity power consumption and GDP in OECD countries. *Journal of Policy Modeling*, *36*(6), 970−985. Available from: https://doi.org/10.1016/j.jpolmod.2014.08.006.

Bloch, H., Rafiq, S., & Salim, R. (2012). Coal consumption, CO2 emission and economic growth in China: Empirical evidence and policy responses. *Energy Economics*, *34*(2), 518−528. Available from: https://doi.org/10.1016/j.eneco.2011.07.014.

Bölük, G., & Mert, M. (2014). Fossil & renewable energy consumption, GHGs (greenhouse gases) and economic growth: Evidence from a panel of EU (European Union) countries. *Energy*, *74*. Available from: https://doi.org/10.1016/j.energy.2014.07.008.

Breusch, T. S., & Pagan, A. R. (1980). The Lagrange Multiplier Test and its Applications to Model Specification in Econometrics. *The Review of Economic Studies, Volume 47* (Issue 1), 239−253. Available from: https://doi.org/10.2307/2297111.

Calbick, K. S., & Gunton, T. (2014). Differences among OECD countries' GHG emissions: Causes and policy implications. *Energy Policy*, *67*, 895–902. Available from: https://doi.org/10.1016/j.enpol.2013.12.030.

Cechin, A. (2010). *A natureza como limite da economia: A contribuição de Nicholas Georgescu-Roegen*. Ed. SENAC. São Paulo: Edusp.

Chandran Govindaraju, V. G. R., & Tang, C. F. (2013). The dynamic links between CO_2 emissions, economic growth and coal consumption in China and India. *Applied Energy*, *104*, 310–318. Available from: https://doi.org/10.1016/j.apenergy.2012.10.042.

Chang, C.-C. (2010). A multivariate causality test of carbon dioxide emissions, energy consumption and economic growth in China. *Applied Energy*, *87*(11), 3533–3537. Available from: https://doi.org/10.1016/j.apenergy.2010.05.004.

Dinda, S., & Coondoo, D. (2006). Income and emission: A panel data-based cointegration analysis. *Ecological Economics*, *57*, 167–181. Available from: https://doi.org/10.1016/j.ecolecon.2005.03.028.

Domingos, H.A. (2011). *Economia dos Reciclados: uma análise do Mercado de Resíduos Sólidos no Aglomerado Urbano Cuiabá e Várzea Grande*. Universidade Federal de Mato Grosso, UFMT, Cuiabá, Mato Grosso, Brasil.

Domingos, H.A. (2017). *Ensaios sobre o Impacto do Consumo de Energias de Origem Fóssil e Renovável, o Crescimento Económico e a Tecnologia Sobre o Ambiente — Uma Abordagem com Modelação ARDL e com Dados de Painel Hélde Araujo Domingos*. University of Beira Interior, UBI, Covilhã, Portugal.

Domingos, H.A., Faria, A.M.M., Fuinhas, J.A., & Marques, A.C. (2017). Renewable energy and greenhouse gas emissions from the waste sectors of European Union member states: A panel data analysis. *Environmental Science and Pollution Research*, *24*(23), 18770–18781 <https://doi.org/10.1007/s11356-017-9324-7>.

Driscoll, J. C., & Kraay, A. C. (1998). Consistent covariance matrix estimation with spatially dependent panel data. *Review of Economics and Statistics*, *80*(4), 549–560. Available from: https://doi.org/10.1162/003465398557825.

Fuinhas, J. A., Marques, A. C., & Couto, A. P. (2015). Oil rents and economic growth in oil producing countries: Evidence from a macro panel. *Economic Change and Restructuring*, *48*(3–4), 257–279. Available from: https://doi.org/10.1007/s10644-015-9170-x.

Georgescu-Roegen, N. (1971). *The entropy law and the economic process*. Cambridge, MA: Harvard University Press.

Ghosh, S. (2010). Examining carbon emissions economic growth nexus for India: A multivariate cointegration approach. *Energy Policy*, *38*(6), 3008–3014. Available from: https://doi.org/10.1016/j.enpol.2010.01.040.

Greene, W. (2002). *Econometric analysis*. Upper Saddle River, NJ: Prentice-Hall.

Grimaud, A. (1999). Pollution permits and sustainable growth in a Schumpeterian model. *Journal of Environmental Economics and Management*, *38*(3), 249–266. Available from: https://doi.org/10.1006/jeem.1999.1088.

Grimaud, A., & Tournemaine, F. (2007). Why can an environmental policy tax promote growth through the channel of education? *Ecological Economics*, *62*(1), 27–36. Available from: https://doi.org/10.1016/j.ecolecon.2006.11.006.

Hart, R. (2004). Growth, environment and innovation: A model with production vintages and environmentally oriented research. *Journal of Environmental Economics and Management*, *48*(3), 1078–1098. Available from: https://doi.org/10.1016/j.jeem.2004.02.001.

Hoornweg, D., & Bhada-Tata, P. (2012). What a waste: A global review of solid waste management. Retrieved December 1, 2014, from <http://www.mswmanagement.com/MSW/Articles/20536.aspx?format=2>.

IPEA. (2010). *Pesquisa sobre Pagamento por Serviços Ambientais Urbanos para Gestão de Resíduos Sólidos*. Brasília - DF. Avalaible in http://www.ipea.gov.br/portal/index.php? option = com_content&view = article&id = 8858.

Jebli, M. Ben. (2016). On the causal links between health indicator, output, combustible renewables and waste consumption, rail transport, and CO_2 emissions: The case of Tunisia. *Environmental Science and Pollution Research International*, 16699−16715. <https://doi.org/10.1007/s11356-016-6850-7>.

Jebli, M. Ben, & Youssef, S. Ben. (2015). Economic growth, combustible renewables and waste consumption, and CO_2 emissions in North Africa. *Environmental Science and Pollution Research*, 16022−16030. <https://doi.org/10.1007/s11356-015-4792-0>.

Krausmann, F., Gingrich, S., Eisenmenger, N., Erb, K.-H., Haberl, H., & Fischer-Kowalski, M. (2009). Growth in global materials use, GDP and population during the 20th century. *Ecological Economics*, *68*(10), 2696−2705. Available from: https://doi.org/10.1016/j.ecolecon.2009.05.007.

Lans Bovenberg, A., & Smulders, S. (1995). Environmental quality and pollution-augmenting technological change in a two-sector endogenous growth model. *Journal of Public Economics*, *57*(3), 369−391. Available from: https://doi.org/10.1016/0047-2727(95)80002-Q.

Ligthart, J. E., & van der Ploeg, F. (1994). Sustainable growth and renewable resources in the global economy. *Trade, Innovation, Environment*, *2*, 259−280. Retrieved from: http://link.springer.com/chapter/10.1007%2F978-94-011-0948-2_11#.

Lotfalipour, M. R., Falahi, M. A., & Ashena, M. (2010). Economic growth, CO2 emissions, and fossil fuels consumption in Iran. *Energy*, *35*(12), 5115−5120. Available from: https://doi.org/10.1016/j.energy.2010.08.004.

Meadows, D. H., Meadows, D. L., Randers, J., & Behrens, W. W. (1972). *The limits to growth: A report for the club of Rome's project on the predicament of mankind*. New York, NY: Universe Books. Retrieved from: http://www.donellameadows.org/wp-content/userfiles/Limits-to-Growth-digital-scan-version.pdf.

Mebratu, D. (1998). Sustainability and sustainable development. *Environmental Impact Assessment Review*, *18*(6), 493−520. Available from: https://doi.org/10.1016/S0195-9255(98)00019-5.

Menyah, K., & Wolde-Rufael, Y. (2010a). CO_2 emissions, nuclear energy, renewable energy and economic growth in the US. *Energy Policy*, *38*(6), 2911−2915. Available from: https://doi.org/10.1016/j.enpol.2010.01.024.

Menyah, K., & Wolde-Rufael, Y. (2010b). Energy consumption, pollutant emissions and economic growth in South Africa. *Energy Economics*, *32*(6), 1374−1382. Available from: https://doi.org/10.1016/j.eneco.2010.08.002.

Niu, S., Ding, Y., Niu, Y., Li, Y., & Luo, G. (2011). Economic growth, energy conservation and emissions reduction: A comparative analysis based on panel data for 8 Asian-Pacific countries. *Energy Policy*, *39*(4), 2121−2131. Available from: https://doi.org/10.1016/j.enpol.2011.02.003.

OECD; IEA. (2015). Annex I: Municipal solid waste potential in cities, 1−9.

Pao, H.-T., & Tsai, C.-M. (2010). CO2 emissions, energy consumption and economic growth in BRIC countries. *Energy Policy*, *38*(12), 7850−7860. Available from: https://doi.org/10.1016/j.enpol.2010.08.045.

Pao, H.-T., & Tsai, C.-M. (2011a). Modeling and forecasting the CO2 emissions, energy consumption, and economic growth in Brazil. *Energy*, *36*(5), 2450−2458. Available from: https://doi.org/10.1016/j.energy.2011.01.032.

Pao, H. T., & Tsai, C. M. (2011b). Multivariate Granger causality between CO2 emissions, energy consumption, FDI (foreign direct investment) and GDP (gross domestic product): Evidence from a panel of BRIC (Brazil, Russian Federation, India, and

China) countries. *Energy*, *36*(1), 685–693. Available from: https://doi.org/10.1016/j.energy.2010.09.041.

Pao, H.-T., Yu, H.-C., & Yang, Y.-H. (2011). Modeling the CO2 emissions, energy use, and economic growth in Russia. *Energy*, *36*(8), 5094–5100. Available from: https://doi.org/10.1016/j.energy.2011.06.004.

Pesaran, M.H. (2004) *General diagnostic tests for cross section dependence in panels*. Cambridge Working Papers in Economics, No. 0435. University of Cambridge, Faculty of Economics.

Pesaran, M. H., & Shin, Y. (1999). An autoregressive distributed lag modelling approach to cointegration analysis. In S. Storm (Ed.), *Econometrics and economic theory in the 20th century: The Ragnar Frisch centennial symposium* (pp. 1–31). Cambridge: Cambridge University Press.

Peters, G. (2010). Carbon footprints and embodied carbon at multiple scales. *Current Opinion in Environmental Sustainability*, *2*(4), 245–250. Available from: https://doi.org/10.1016/j.cosust.2010.05.004.

Porter, M., & Van der Linde, C. (1995). Toward a conception of the environment-competitiveness relationship. *Journal of Economic Perspectives*, *9*(4), 97. Available from: https://doi.org/10.1257/jep.9.4.97.

REN21 (Renewable Energy Policy Network for the 21st Century). (2015). *Renewable 2015 global status report. REN21*. Paris: REN21 Secretariat. Retrieved from <http://www.ren21.net/status-of-renewables/regional-status-reports/>.

Sneddon, C., Howarth, R. B., & Norgaard, R. B. (2006). Sustainable development in a post-Brundtland world. *Ecological Economics*, *57*(2), 253–268. Available from: https://doi.org/10.1016/j.ecolecon.2005.04.013.

Soytas, U., Sari, R., & Ewing, B. T. (2007). Energy consumption, income, and carbon emissions in the United States. *Ecological Economics*, *62*, 482–489. Available from: https://doi.org/10.1016/j.ecolecon.2006.07.009.

StataCorp. (2015). *Stata Statistical Software: Release 14*. College Station, TX: StataCorp LP.

IPCC (The Intergovernmental Panel on Climate Change). (2007). Climate change 2007: Synthesis report. In Core Writing Team, R. K. Pachauri, & A. Reisinger (Eds.), *Contribution of working groups I, II and III to the fourth assessment report of the intergovernmental panel on climate change*. Geneva, Switzerland. Retrieved from <http://www.ipcc.ch/publications_and_data/ar4/syr/en/contents.html>.

IPCC (The Intergovernmental Panel on Climate Change). (2014a). Climate change 2014: Synthesis report. In Core Writing Team, R. K. Pachauri & L. A. Meyer (Eds.), *Contribution of working groups I, II and III to the Fifth Assessment Report of the Intergovernmental Panel on Climate Change*. Geneva, Switzerland. Retrieved from <http://www.ipcc.ch/report/ar5/syr/>.

IPCC (The Intergovernmental Panel on Climate Change). (2014b). Climate change 2014: Mitigation of climate change. In *Working group III contribution to the fifth assessment report of the intergovernmental panel on climate change*. New York, USA. Retrieved from <http://www.ipcc.ch/report/ar5/wg3/>.

The United Nations agency for human settlements and sustainable urban development (Unhabitat). (2010). *WTE industry in Latin America*. Retrieved from <http://mirror.unhabitat.org/downloads/docs/10740_1_594319.pdf>.

Wang, S. S., Zhou, D. Q., Zhou, P., & Wang, Q. W. (2011). CO_2 emissions, energy consumption and economic growth in China: A panel data analysis. *Energy Policy*, *39*(9), 4870–4875. Available from: https://doi.org/10.1016/j.enpol.2011.06.032.

Westerlund, J. (2007). Testing for Error Correction in Panel Data. *Oxford Bulletin of Economics and Statistics*, *69*(6), 709–748. Available from: https://doi.org/10.1111/j.1468-0084.2007.00477.x.

Westerlund, J., & Edgerton, D. L. (2007). A panel bootstrap cointegration test. *Economics Letters*, 97(3), 185−190. Available from: https://doi.org/10.1016/j.econlet.2007.03.003.

World Commission on Environment and Development (WCED). (1987). *Report of the world commission on environment and development: Our common future*. Retrieved from <http://www.un-documents.net/our-common-future.pdf>.

Wooldridge, J. M. (2002). *Econometric analysis of cross section and panel data*. Cambridge, MA: The MIT Press.

World Development Indicators − WDI" from the World Bank are available at http://databank.worldbank.org. (2017).

Zaccai, E. (2012). Over two decades in pursuit of sustainable development: Influence, transformations, limits. *Environmental Development*, 1(1), 79−90. Available from: https://doi.org/10.1016/j.envdev.2011.11.002.

Zhang, X.-P., & Cheng, X.-M. (2009). Energy consumption, carbon emissions, and economic growth in China. *Ecological Economics*, 68(10), 2706−2712. Available from: https://doi.org/10.1016/j.ecolecon.2009.05.011.

Further reading

Al-mulali, U., & Binti Che Sab, C. N. (2012). The impact of energy consumption and CO_2 emission on the economic growth and financial development in the Sub-Saharan African countries. *Energy*, 39(1), 180−186. Available from: https://doi.org/10.1016/j.energy.2012.01.032.

Ang, J. B. (2007). CO_2 emissions, energy consumption, and output in France. *Energy Policy*, 35, 4772−4778. Available from: https://doi.org/10.1016/j.enpol.2007.03.032.

Assadourian, E. (2010). Transforming cultures: From consumerism to sustainability. *Journal of Macromarketing*, 30(2), 186−191. Available from: https://doi.org/10.1177/0276146710361932.

Behmiri, N. B., & Pires Manso, J. R. (2012). Crude oil conservation policy hypothesis in OECD (organisation for economic cooperation and development) countries: A multivariate panel Granger causality test. *Energy*, 43(1), 253−260. Available from: https://doi.org/10.1016/j.energy.2012.04.032.

Behmiri, N. B., & Pires Manso, J. R. (2014). The linkage between crude oil consumption and economic growth in Latin America: The panel framework investigations for multiple regions. *Energy*, 72, 233−241. Available from: https://doi.org/10.1016/j.energy.2014.05.028.

Cheng, B. S. (1997). Energy consumption and economic growth in Brazil, Mexico and Venezuela: A time series analysis. *Applied Economics Letters*, 4(11), 671−674. Available from: https://doi.org/10.1080/758530646.

Chontanawat, J., Hunt, L. C., & Pierse, R. (2008). Does energy consumption cause economic growth? Evidence from a systematic study of over 100 countries. *Journal of Policy Modeling*, 30(2), 209−220. Available from: https://doi.org/10.1016/j.jpolmod.2006.10.003.

Costantini, V., & Martini, C. (2010). The causality between energy consumption and economic growth: A multi-sectoral analysis using non-stationary cointegrated panel data. *Energy Economics*, 32(3), 591−603. Available from: https://doi.org/10.1016/j.eneco.2009.09.013.

Fallahi, F. (2011). Causal relationship between energy consumption (EC) and GDP: A Markov-switching (MS) causality. *Energy*, 36(7), 4165−4170. Available from: https://doi.org/10.1016/j.energy.2011.04.027.

Fuinhas, J. A., & Marques, A. C. (2012). Energy consumption and economic growth nexus in Portugal, Italy, Greece, Spain and Turkey: An ARDL bounds test approach

(1965–2009). *Energy Economics*, *34*(2), 511–517. Available from: https://doi.org/10.1016/j.eneco.2011.10.003.

Halicioglu, F. (2009). An econometric study of CO_2 emissions, energy consumption, income and foreign trade in Turkey. *Energy Policy*, *37*, 1156–1164. Available from: https://doi.org/10.1016/j.enpol.2008.11.012.

Hamit-Haggar, M. (2012). Greenhouse gas emissions, energy consumption and economic growth: A panel cointegration analysis from Canadian industrial sector perspective. *Energy Economics*, *34*(1), 358–364. Available from: https://doi.org/10.1016/j.eneco.2011.06.005.

Alam, M. J., Ara Begum, I., Buysse, J., & Van Huylenbroeck, G. (2012). Energy consumption, carbon emissions and economic growth nexus in Bangladesh: Cointegration and dynamic causality analysis. *Energy Policy*, *45*, 217–225. Available from: https://doi.org/10.1016/j.enpol.2012.02.022.

Jinke, L., Hualing, S., & Dianming, G. (2008). Causality relationship between coal consumption and GDP: Difference of major OECD and non-OECD countries. *Applied Energy*, *85*(6), 421–429. Available from: https://doi.org/10.1016/j.apenergy.2007.10.007.

Kraft, J., & Kraft, A. (1978). On the relationship between energy and GNP. *Journal of Energy Development*, *3*, 401–403.

Lai, T. M., To, W. M., Lo, W. C., Choy, Y. S., & Lam, K. H. (2011). The causal relationship between electricity consumption and economic growth in a gaming and tourism center: The case of Macao SAR, the People's Republic of China. *Energy*, *36*(2), 1134–1142. Available from: https://doi.org/10.1016/j.energy.2010.11.036.

Lean, H. H., & Smyth, R. (2010). CO2 emissions, electricity consumption and output in ASEAN. *Applied Energy*, *87*(6), 1858–1864. Available from: https://doi.org/10.1016/j.apenergy.2010.02.003.

Lee, C.-C., & Chang, C.-P. (2007). The impact of energy consumption on economic growth: Evidence from linear and nonlinear models in Taiwan. *Energy*, *32*(12), 2282–2294. Available from: https://doi.org/10.1016/j.energy.2006.01.017.

Lee, C.-C., & Chang, C.-P. (2008). Energy consumption and economic growth in Asian economies: A more comprehensive analysis using panel data. *Resource and Energy Economics*, *30*(1), 50–65. Available from: https://doi.org/10.1016/j.reseneeco.2007.03.003.

Lee, C. C., Chang, C. P., & Chen, P. F. (2008). Energy-income causality in OECD countries revisited: The key role of capital stock. *Energy Economics*, *30*(5), 2359–2373. Available from: https://doi.org/10.1016/j.eneco.2008.01.005.

Mehrara, M. (2007). Energy consumption and economic growth: The case of oil exporting countries. *Energy Policy*, *35*(5), 2939–2945. Available from: https://doi.org/10.1016/j.enpol.2006.10.018.

Murray, D. A., & Nan, G. D. (1996). A definition of the gross domestic product-electrification interrelationship. *Journal of Energy and Development*, *19*, 275–283.

Nachane, D. M., Nadkarni, R. M., & Karnik, A. V. (1988). Co-integration and causality testing of the energy–GDP relationship: A cross-country study. *Applied Economics*, *20*(11), 1511–1531. Available from: https://doi.org/10.1080/00036848800000083.

Narayan, P. K., & Smyth, R. (2008). Energy consumption and real GDP in G7 countries: New evidence from panel cointegration with structural breaks. *Energy Economics*, *30*(5), 2331–2341. Available from: https://doi.org/10.1016/j.eneco.2007.10.006.

Odhiambo, N. M. (2009). Energy consumption and economic growth nexus in Tanzania: An ARDL bounds testing approach. *Energy Policy*, *37*(2), 617–622. Available from: https://doi.org/10.1016/j.enpol.2008.09.077.

Ozturk, I., & Acaravci, A. (2013). The long-run and causal analysis of energy, growth, openness and financial development on carbon emissions in Turkey. *Energy Economics*, *36*, 262–267. Available from: https://doi.org/10.1016/j.eneco.2012.08.025.

Saboori, B., & Sulaiman, J. (2013). CO_2 emissions, energy consumption and economic growth in Association of Southeast Asian Nations (ASEAN) countries: A cointegration approach. *Energy*, *55*, 813–822. Available from: https://doi.org/10.1016/j.energy.2013.04.038.

Soytas, U., & Sari, R. (2003). Energy consumption and GDP: Causality relationship in G-7 countries and emerging markets. *Energy Economics*, *25*(1), 33–37. Available from: https://doi.org/10.1016/S0140-9883(02)00009-9.

Squalli, J. (2007). Electricity consumption and economic growth: Bounds and causality analyses of OPEC members. *Energy Economics*, *29*(6), 1192–1205. Available from: https://doi.org/10.1016/j.eneco.2006.10.001.

Stern, D. I. (1993). Energy and economic growth in the USA. *Energy Economics*, *15*(2), 137–150. Available from: https://doi.org/10.1016/0140-9883(93)90033-N.

Ucan, O., Aricioglu, E., & Yucel, F. (2014). Energy consumption and economic growth nexus: Evidence from developed countries in Europe. *International Journal of Energy Economics and Policy*, *4*(3), 411–419. Available from: https://doi.org/10.1016/j.enpol.2013.05.115.

Warr, B. S., & Ayres, R. U. (2010). Evidence of causality between the quantity and quality of energy consumption and economic growth. *Energy*, *35*(4), 1688–1693. Available from: https://doi.org/10.1016/j.energy.2009.12.017.

Wooldridge, J. M. (2002). *Econometric analysis of cross section and panel data*. Cambridge, MA: The MIT Press.

Yu, E. S. H., & Jin, J. C. (1992). Cointegration tests of energy consumption, income, and employment. *Resources and Energy*, *14*(3), 259–266. Available from: https://doi.org/10.1016/0165-0572(92)90010-E.

CHAPTER THREE

Income inequality, globalization, and economic growth: a panel vector autoregressive approach for Latin American countries

Renato Santiago[1,*], José Alberto Fuinhas[2,*] and António Cardoso Marques[1,*]

[1]NECE-UBI and Management and Economics Department, University of Beira Interior, Covilhã, Portugal
[2]NECE-UBI, CeBER and Faculty of Economics, University of Coimbra, Coimbra, Portugal

Contents

3.1 Introduction

In an increasingly globalized world, and where the struggle against inequality is seen as a global priority, the studies surrounding the impacts of both globalization and inequality on economic growth saw their importance increase, helping policymakers in the development of growth-promoting policies in their respective countries or regions.

* This research was supported by NECE, R&D unit and funded by the FCT — Portuguese Foundation for the Development of Science and Technology, Ministry of Science, Technology and Higher Education, project UID/GES/04630/2019.

The Extended Energy—Growth Nexus.
DOI: https://doi.org/10.1016/B978-0-12-815719-0.00003-6

Regarding the inequality spectrum income inequality is the one which has had its relationship with growth most intensively analyzed. However, the theories around the effects that it produces on growth are far from being entirely consensual.

While some economists defend the view that inequality has adverse effects on growth (e.g., Piketty & Goldhammer, 2014; Stiglitz, 2012), others state that the literature on the inequality—growth relationship is so extensive that it is impossible to respond with confidence if it has a negative or positive effect on growth, or even if it has a significant effect (e.g., Klasen, Scholl, Lahoti, Ochmann, & Vollmer, 2016).

Regarding this last statement the majority of empirical literature favors the hypotheses of a negative impact of inequality on growth, and even studies from international organizations like the OECD (Cingano, 2014) and the IMF (Grigoli, Paredes, & Bella, 2016; Ostry, Berg, & Tsangarides, 2014) seem to point to this same result. Nevertheless the possible existence of both positive and negative effects cannot be ruled out (e.g., Castells-Quintana & Royuela, 2017). These results can be linked with the possible existence of nonlinearities in this relationship (Barro, 2000). The development stage of the countries (e.g., Khalifa & El Hag, 2010), their income levels (Lin, Huang, & Weng, 2006), and the dynamics that researchers choose to analyze (short or long run) (e.g., Halter, Oechslin, & Zweimüller, 2014), can be stressed as some of the reasons for this to happen.

In the particular case of Latin America, inequality is a characteristic which is often linked to the region's idiosyncrasies (Gasparini & Lustig, 2011), and so, it is not strange that researchers who study its effects on growth, use this region as the sample for their works. Delbianco, Dabús, and Caraballo (2014), for example, studied the effects of income inequality on growth for 20 countries from the Latin American to the Caribbean region, with a time span ranging from 1980 to 2010. The results from this study highlighted that in general, inequality produces a negative effect on growth but the relationship greatly depends on the income level of the country. Indeed in the richest countries the relationship turned out positive.

Regarding the econometric methods that researchers used to inquire about this subject we can describe two different research waves. In the first wave cross-country and time-series methods (e.g., Alesina & Rodrik, 1994) were the preferred methods. In the second wave the panel data analysis became more usual and the negative effects of inequality on growth started to be contested empirically (e.g., Li & Zou, 1998). Nowadays a majority of studies still use panel data techniques in the analysis of the inequality—growth nexus (e.g., Dabla-Norris, Kochhar, Suphaphiphat, Ricka, & Tsounta, 2015; Halter et al., 2014; Ostry et al., 2014), but even with the advance in econometrics, and with increased data availability, the discussion about the results remains blurred.

Turning to the other subject of analysis, we can start by referring to the last few decades where, as we have already stressed, there was a generalized increase in the world's globalization levels, which led to an increase in the research of this same subject. One relationship that has been intensively studied is the one that globalization has with economic growth. However, despite the studies that have been produced, there is still no consensus in this matter.

Theoretically there are several ways in which globalization may affect growth (see Grossman & Helpman, 2015), but empirically, even with the number of studies that point to its positive effect on growth (e.g., Dreher, 2006; Gurgul & Lach, 2014; Marques, Fuinhas, & Marques, 2017), it is still not possible to say with certainty that this process is beneficial in all situations, which nourishes the view that globalization can produce both winners and losers. Some economists highlight that nations should know how to manage the globalization process if they want to take advantages from it (e.g., Stiglitz, 2004), which means that the studies linked with the globalization effects on various macroeconomic variables are extremely important. Indeed they should assist policymakers in the development of growth-promoting policies.

The main reasons for the lack of consensus on the effects of globalization on growth are the difficulties that researchers find in defining and measuring globalization. With regard to its definition, Dreher (2006, p. 1092) says that globalization is "the process of creating networks of connections among actors at intra or multi-continental distances, mediated through a variety of flows including people, information and ideas, capital, and goods." This definition implies that globalization has a multidimensional characteristic, which means that researchers should analyze more than its economic dimension.

If we look into the recent literature (e.g., Marques et al., 2017; Lee, Lee, & Chang, 2015), we can see that, contrary to the primordial works, where globalization was proxied by "economic-only variables" as trade openness, and foreign direct investment (e.g., Dollar & Kraay, 2001; Frankel & Romer, 1999; Sachs & Warner, 1995), nowadays, researchers are increasingly aware of the process multidimensions.

A widely accepted version is that globalization has, at least, three main dimensions (economic, political, and social) that we should take into consideration (Keohane & Nye, 2000). This idea is present in the globalization indicators that are generally used in the recent literature, as in the Konjunkturforschungsstelle (KOF) Index of Globalization (Gygli, Haelg, & Sturm, 2018), for example.

The diversity that is seen in the results of globalization-growth studies has already been analyzed. Some reasons for its occurrence can be the econometric techniques used, the period and sample that researchers choose, the country specific effects, the dimensions of globalization that researchers choose to include in their estimations, and whether they choose to use levels or growth rates (see Potrafke, 2015). Additionally, some studies point out that the globalization—growth relationship can also be possibly influenced by the country's income levels (e.g., Majidi, 2017).

Regarding the empirical techniques that were used in the globalization—economic growth studies, we see that the use of panel data techniques to address this issue is becoming more usual, given the fact that it has a vast number of advantages over the cross-sectional, and time-series analysis (see Hsiao, 2007). Also the use of dynamic estimators has started to increase, with researchers considering globalization as a dynamic phenomenon, and treating it as an endogenous variable (e.g., Rao & Vadlamannati, 2011).

With all this in mind, the objective of this chapter is to examine whether income inequality and globalization has promoted or depressed the Latin American countries' growth. The reason to choose this region is linked with the fact that, despite the various government's efforts, inequality levels in the region are still considered high and can be a part of the explanation why Latin American countries struggle to achieve sustainable economic growth. The analysis of the globalization effects on these countries' growth is also suitable because the region has a historically linkage to this process, with the arrival of the Portuguese and Spanish empires. Since then, these countries' economies are mainly characterized by the exploration and exportation of natural resources, and by low levels of diversification of activities. With this in mind, and despite the possible existence of the natural resource curse (Sachs & Warner, 2001) these countries do not seem to be willing to make big changes in their economic structure. Additionally, in more recent times, developed countries (and some developing countries like China) have increased their investments and influence in Latin America, taking advantage of their outward orientation. Taking into account all of these facts, it becomes especially important to know if this phenomenon is really an advantage or disadvantage in terms of their own economic output.

To reach our purpose, we used the gross domestic product (GDP), as a proxy for economic growth, the KOF Index of Globalization (Gygli et al., 2018) to measure globalization, and Gini index data from the Standardized World Income Inequality Database to measure income inequality. A panel of nine Latin American countries was analyzed, with annual data from 1970 to 2015, recurring to the panel vector autoregressive (PVAR) which allow us to inquire about the effects that these variables have on economic growth as well as the effects that economic growth has on these variables. Additionally, the PVAR methodology also permits the analysis of the relationships that income inequality, globalization, and secondary energy consumption have with each other, which, given the aim of our study, comes in a secondary plan.

Before we proceed, it is important to stress that this chapter has pedagogy as one of its main objectives. In this sense, the reader is expected to be able to replicate the processes described here and perhaps gain or increase his / her taste for research work.

The rest of the chapter is organized as follows: Section 3.2 describes the data, methodology, and the preliminary analysis. Section 3.3 presents the results and their discussion, and Section 3.4 concludes.

3.2 Data and methodology

The main purpose of this study is to evaluate the effects of income inequality and globalization upon the economic growth of a group of Latin American countries. To reach this purpose, we will use annual data from 1970 to 2015 for a panel of nine countries: Argentina, Brazil, Chile, Colombia, Costa Rica, Mexico, Panama, Peru, and Venezuela. Given that the process of generating inequalities is a dynamic one, we tried to use the longest time span possible. The econometric analysis was performed using STATA 14.0. In Table 3.1 the name, definition, and source of the raw variables are presented.

Our dependent variable, and our proxy for economic growth, will be the GDP in constant local currency unit *per capita* (YPC). To achieve this variable, we divide the GDP in constant local currency unit (Y) by the

Table 3.1 Variables description.

Variable	Definition	Source
Y	Gross domestic product in constant local currency unit	World Bank
P	Total population in total number of persons	World Bank
GI	Gini (disposable income)	SWIID
G	Globalization overall	KOF Index of Globalization
SEC	Secondary energy consumption in thousands BOE	CEPALSTAT

total population (P), both from World Bank.[2] The use of *per capita* values is used due to the fact that they are capable of removing distortions produced by population changes. The use of local currency aims to avoid the influence of exchange rates.

Income inequality will be measured by the Gini index of disposable income (GI) from the Standardized World Income Inequality Database (SWIID). For more information about the Standardized World Income Inequality Database, see Solt (2016).

To measure globalization, we are going to use the KOF Index of Globalization (G)[3] (Gygli et al., 2018), primarily because it corresponds to the economic, social, and political spectrums of globalization. To see a good review of the studies that used this index, see Potrafke (2015).

Secondary energy consumption in kg of oil equivalent *per capita* (SECPC), will be our control variable, mainly because the economies have developed and shifted to a structure where energy has a clear role in the explanation of their economic growth (Ucan, Aricioglu, & Yucel, 2014). Secondary energy sources are made from primary energy sources such as natural gas, coal, petroleum among others, and include electricity and hydrogen. We also choose this variable because the energy use of a country, electricity in particular, has proven to be related to its economic output (e.g., Abdoli, Farahani, & Dastan, 2015; Aslan, 2014). Several studies have been produced which investigate the relationship between energy consumption and economic growth, which has led to an increase and diversification of the energy—growth nexus literature. Today we can distinguish four hypotheses regarding the results obtained in the study of the relationship between energy consumption and growth (Ozturk, 2010),

---

[2] Available at: http://databank.worldbank.org/data/source/world-development-indicators
[3] Available at: https://www.kof.ethz.ch/en/forecasts-and-indicators/indicators/kof-globalisation-index.html

which are the: (1) Growth hypothesis (unidirectional causality running from energy to growth); (2) Conservation hypothesis (unidirectional causality running from growth to energy); (3) Feedback hypothesis (bidirectional causality between energy and growth); and (4) Neutrality hypothesis (energy and growth are neutral with respect to each other). An additional hypothesis that can also be referred to is the one which states that there is a causality, with a negative signal, running from energy consumption to economic growth, also known as the "curse" hypothesis, which says that the abundance of energy sources can negatively affect the economic output of a country (see e.g., Fuinhas & Marques, 2013). To achieve the secondary energy consumption *per capita* (SECPC), we transformed the variable secondary energy consumption in thousands BOE (barrels of oil equivalent) (SE) from the CEPALSTAT[4] into kilogram of oil equivalent (SEKG) and then we divide it by the total population (P).

How to do:
Declare data as panel data
   xtset country year

How to do:
Generating/transform variables
   gen ypc = y/p
   gen sekg = se* 140000
   gen secpc = sekg/p

To accomplish our goals the PVAR method was used, mainly due to the possible presence of endogenous variables in our model. In this sense, Love and Zicchino (2006) proposed an estimator that allows the presence of stationary endogenous variables, and unobserved individual heterogeneity. The specification of the PVAR model used in this empirical analysis follows the specification of the Eq. (3.1):

$$Z_{it} = T_0 + T_1 Z_{it-1} + f_i + d_{c,t} + \varepsilon_t, \tag{3.1}$$

---

[4] Available at: http://estadisticas.cepal.org/cepalstat/WEB_CEPALSTAT/estadisticasIndicadores.asp? idioma = e

where Z_{it} represents the vector of the variables in our analysis (i.e., DLYPC, DLGI, DLG, and DLSECPC), T_0 denotes the vector of constants, $T_1 Z_{it-1}$ denotes the polynomial matrix, f_i denotes the fixed effects, $d_{c,t}$ denotes the time-fixed effects, and ε_t is the random errors term. Moreover the prefixes (L) and (D) denote natural logarithms, and first differences, respectively.

How to do:

Generating logarithms

gen lypc = ln(ypc)
gen lg = ln(g)
gen lgi = ln(gi)
gen lsecpc = ln(secpc)

How to do:

Generating first differences

gen dlypc = d.lypc
gen dlg = d.lg
gen dlgi = d.lgi
gen dlsecpc = d.lsecpc

To understand the characteristics of the series and of the cross sections, the descriptive statistics, the presence of cross-sectional dependence, and the order of integration of our variables have to be analyzed. The descriptive statistics of the variables are presented in Table 3.2.

Table 3.2 Descriptive statistics and cross-sectional dependence.

Variables	Descriptive statistics				
	Obs	Mean	Std. Dev.	Min.	Max.
LYPC	413	11.1826	3.088364	7.228553	16.21481
LGI	411	3.843822	0.1053273	3.526361	3.998201
LG	414	3.975525	0.1683927	3.593742	4.328353
LSECPC	414	6.305875	0.4222473	5.430905	7.219495
DLYPC	404	0.0164171	0.0445857	− 0.1650963	0.1503634
DLGI	402	− 0.0015143	0.0087252	− 0.0363677	0.0270288
DLG	405	0.0093766	0.0232191	− 0.0648866	0.087141
DLSECPC	405	0.0156502	0.052622	− 0.2161102	0.2198987

Notes: To achieve the results of descriptive statistics, the Stata commands *sum* was used.

How to do:

Descriptive statistics
sum lypc lgi lg lsecpc
sum dlypc dlgi dlg dlsecpc

How it looks like

. sum lypc lgi lg lsecpc

Variable	Obs	Mean	Std. Dev.	Min	Max
lypc	413	11.1826	3.088364	7.228553	16.21481
lgi	411	3.843822	.1053273	3.526361	3.998201
lg	414	3.975525	.1683927	3.593742	4.328353
lsecpc	414	6.305875	.4222473	5.430905	7.219495

. sum dlypc dlgi dlg dlsecpc

Variable	Obs	Mean	Std. Dev.	Min	Max
dlypc	404	.0164171	.0445857	-.1650963	.1503634
dlgi	402	-.0015143	.0087252	-.0363677	.0270288
dlg	405	.0093766	.0232191	-.0648866	.087141
dlsecpc	405	.0156502	.052622	-.2161102	.2198987

Source: StataCorp. 2015.

We should mention that the variables LYPC, LGI, DLYPC, and DLGI have fewer observations than the other variables due to the lack of data for GDP in the case of Venezuela in 2015, and for the Gini index in the cases of Mexico in 2015, and Peru in 1970–71. Despite this fact the STATA 14 still assumes our panel as a "strongly balanced" panel.

In order to analyze the presence of cross-section dependence and the order of integration of our variables, the Pesaran cross-sectional dependence (CD) test (Pesaran, 2004), and the cross-sectionally augmented IPS (CIPS) test (Pesaran, 2007) were performed. Table 3.3 gives us the results of both tests.

How to do:

Pesaran CD test
xtcd lypc lgi lg lsecpc
xtcd dlypc dlgi dlg dlsecpc

Table 3.3 Cross-sectional dependence test and second-generation unit root test (cross-sectionally augmented IPS).

Variables	Cross-sectional dependence (CD)			CIPS (Zt-bar)	
	CD test	Corr	Abs(corr)	Without trend	With trend
LYPC	25.71***	0.636	0.683	− 0.174	− 1.612*
LGI	9.99***	0.248	0.494	1.426	1.828
LG	36.47***	0.905	0.905	− 2.111**	− 1.570*
LSECPC	23.99***	0.594	0.607	− 0.116	0.948
DLYPC	11.35***	0.285	0.285	− 7.507***	− 6.435***
DLGI	12.20***	0.306	0.386	− 3.229***	− 2.983***
DLG	4.50***	0.113	0.136	− 9.953***	− 8.994***
DLSECPC	3.41***	0.085	0.146	− 7.547***	− 7.069***

Notes: CD test was performed according to the null hypothesis of the cross-sectional independence; the second-generation unit root test was performed under the null hypothesis wherein the variables are I(1); ***, **, and * denote statistical significance level at 1%, 5%, and 10%, respectively; and to compute these tests, the commands *xtcd* and *multipurt* were used, respectively.

How it looks like

```
. xtcd lypc lgi lg lsecpc


Average correlation coefficients & Pesaran (2004) CD test

Variables series tested: lypc lgi lg lsecpc
                              Group variable: id
                           Number of groups: 9
                  Average # of observations: 50.83
                               Panel is: unbalanced
```

Variable	CD-test	p-value	corr	abs(corr)
lypc	25.71	0.000	0.636	0.683
lgi	9.99	0.000	0.248	0.494
lg	36.47	0.000	0.905	0.905
lsecpc	23.99	0.000	0.594	0.607

```
Notes: Under the null hypothesis of cross-section
       independence CD ~ N(0,1)
```

. xtcd dlypc dlgi dlg dlsecpc

Average correlation coefficients & Pesaran (2004) CD test

Variables series tested: dlypc dlgi dlg dlsecpc
                              Group variable: id
                           Number of groups: 9
                 Average # of observations: 49.71
                                 Panel is: unbalanced

Variable	CD-test	p-value	corr	abs(corr)
dlypc	11.35	0.000	0.285	0.285
dlgi	12.20	0.000	0.306	0.386
dlg	4.50	0.000	0.113	0.136
dlsecpc	3.41	0.001	0.085	0.146

Notes: Under the null hypothesis of cross-section
       independence CD ~ N(0,1)

Source: StataCorp. 2015.

Given the results of the Pesaran CD test (Pesaran, 2004), we conclude that cross-sectional dependence is present in all variables, both in natural logarithms and in first differences. This means that a correlation exists between our series across countries. This phenomenon happens due to the common shocks that our crosses share, and if we ignore it, it can produce inconsistent and incorrect conclusions in the econometric approach (Eberhardt & Teal, 2011). However, as the PVAR estimator controls for the unobserved individual heterogeneity, including time-fixed effects, the presence of cross-section dependence is not a motive of concern.

Due to the fact that the presence of cross-sectional dependence was verified in all the variables, we only executed the second-generation unit root test, the CIPS test by Pesaran (2007), this because first-generation unit root tests are not trustworthy when this phenomenon is present.

How to do:
CIPS test
  multipurt lypc lgi lg lsecpc, lags(3)
  multipurt dlypc dlgi dlg dlsecpc, lags(3)

How it looks like

(B) Pesaran (2007) Panel Unit Root test (CIPS)

Variable		Specification without trend		
	lags	Zt-bar	p-value	t-bar
lypc	0	-0.100	0.460	.
lypc	1	-0.174	0.431	.
lypc	2	1.263	0.897	.
lypc	3	1.710	0.956	.
lgi	0	3.673	1.000	.
lgi	1	1.426	0.923	.
lgi	2	2.036	0.979	.
lgi	3	1.107	0.866	.
lg	0	-2.594	0.005	.
lg	1	-2.111	0.017	.
lg	2	-1.989	0.023	.
lg	3	-1.949	0.026	.
lsecpc	0	-0.064	0.475	.
lsecpc	1	-0.116	0.454	.
lsecpc	2	0.288	0.613	.
lsecpc	3	0.680	0.752	.

Variable		Specification with trend		
	lags	Zt-bar	p-value	t-bar
lypc	0	0.099	0.540	.
lypc	1	-1.612	0.054	.
lypc	2	0.594	0.724	.
lypc	3	0.980	0.836	.
lgi	0	6.018	1.000	.
lgi	1	1.828	0.966	.
lgi	2	3.596	1.000	.
lgi	3	3.639	1.000	.
lg	0	-1.807	0.035	.
lg	1	-1.570	0.058	.
lg	2	-1.630	0.052	.
lg	3	-1.926	0.027	.
lsecpc	0	1.131	0.871	.
lsecpc	1	0.948	0.829	.
lsecpc	2	1.065	0.857	.
lsecpc	3	0.931	0.824	.

Null for MW and CIPS tests: series is I(1).
MW test assumes cross-section independence.
CIPS test assumes cross-section dependence is in
   form of a single unobserved common factor.

(B) Pesaran (2007) Panel Unit Root test (CIPS)

| Variable | lags | Specification without trend | | |
		Zt-bar	p-value	t-bar
dlypc	0	-9.821	0.000	.
dlypc	1	-7.507	0.000	.
dlypc	2	-5.532	0.000	.
dlypc	3	-4.270	0.000	.
dlgi	0	-3.800	0.000	.
dlgi	1	-3.229	0.001	.
dlgi	2	-2.913	0.002	.
dlgi	3	-2.800	0.003	.
dlg	0	-13.787	0.000	.
dlg	1	-9.953	0.000	.
dlg	2	-7.273	0.000	.
dlg	3	-5.294	0.000	.
dlsecpc	0	-12.446	0.000	.
dlsecpc	1	-7.547	0.000	.
dlsecpc	2	-5.193	0.000	.
dlsecpc	3	-3.323	0.000	.

| Variable | lags | Specification with trend | | |
		Zt-bar	p-value	t-bar
dlypc	0	-9.093	0.000	.
dlypc	1	-6.435	0.000	.
dlypc	2	-4.257	0.000	.
dlypc	3	-2.880	0.002	.
dlgi	0	-3.613	0.000	.
dlgi	1	-2.983	0.001	.
dlgi	2	-2.883	0.002	.
dlgi	3	-3.689	0.000	.
dlg	0	-13.153	0.000	.
dlg	1	-8.994	0.000	.
dlg	2	-6.224	0.000	.
dlg	3	-4.156	0.000	.
dlsecpc	0	-12.512	0.000	.
dlsecpc	1	-7.069	0.000	.
dlsecpc	2	-4.678	0.000	.
dlsecpc	3	-2.724	0.003	.

Null for MW and CIPS tests: series is I(1).
MW test assumes cross-section independence.
CIPS test assumes cross-section dependence is in
form of a single unobserved common factor.

Source: StataCorp. 2015.

Looking at the results, we see that some of the variables are on the borderline between the orders of integration $I(0)/I(1)$, but that in first differences, all variables are stationary with and without trend, meaning that we can continue with the PVAR estimation.

To check if collinearity and multicollinearity are not a problem for our estimation, the correlation matrix and the variance inflation factor (VIF) had to be analyzed. Given the low correlation values and the lower VIF and mean VIF values, we can conclude that collinearity and multicollinearity are not a concern. The correlation matrix and the VIF statistics can be seen in Table 3.4.

How to do:
Correlation Matrix
    corr lypc lgi lg lsecpc
    corr dlypc dlgi dlg dlsecpc

How it looks like

```
. corr lypc lgi lg lsecpc
(obs=410)
```

	lypc	lgi	lg	lsecpc
lypc	1.0000			
lgi	0.1453	1.0000		
lg	0.0162	-0.2158	1.0000	
lsecpc	-0.2355	-0.5229	0.5114	1.0000

```
. corr dlypc dlgi dlg dlsecpc
(obs=401)
```

	dlypc	dlgi	dlg	dlsecpc
dlypc	1.0000			
dlgi	-0.1698	1.0000		
dlg	0.0483	0.1086	1.0000	
dlsecpc	0.5821	-0.1109	-0.0143	1.0000

Source: StataCorp. 2015.

Table 3.4 Correlation matrices and variance inflation factor statistics.

	LYPC	LGI	LG	LSECPC	DLYPC	DLGI	DLG	DLSECPC
LYPC	1.0000							
LGI	0.1453	1.0000						
LG	0.0162	−0.2158	1.0000					
LSECPC	−0.2355	−0.5229	0.5114	1.0000				
VIF		1.38	1.36	1.79				
Mean VIF	1.51							
DLYPC					1.0000			
DLGI					−0.1698	1.0000		
DLG					0.0483	0.1086	1.0000	
DLSECPC					0.5821	−0.1109	−0.0143	1.0000
VIF					1.02	1.02	1.01	1.01
Mean VIF					1.02			

How to do:

VIF test

    corr lypc lgi lg lsecpc
    corr dlypc dlgi dlg dlsecpc

How it looks like

```
. qui:regress lypc lgi lg lsecpc

. estat vif
```

Variable	VIF	1/VIF
lsecpc	1.79	0.559987
lgi	1.38	0.723016
lg	1.36	0.734782
Mean VIF	1.51	

```
. qui:regress dlypc dlgi dlg dlsecpc

. estat vif
```

Variable	VIF	1/VIF
dlgi	1.02	0.976232
dlsecpc	1.01	0.987690
dlg	1.01	0.988192
Mean VIF	1.02	

Source: StataCorp. 2015.

The following estimation step was the execution of the Hausman test to determine if fixed or random effects were present in the panel. The null hypothesis of this test is that the difference in coefficients is not systematic or that the random effects estimator is the most appropriated. In our framework, we applied the Hausman test to four specifications, each one with a different dependent variable (DLYPC, DLGI, DLG, and DLSECPC).

How to do:

Hausman test

```
qui: xtreg dlypc dlgi dlg dlsecpc, fe
estimate store fixed
qui: xtreg dlypc dlgi dlg dlsecpc, re
estimate store random
hausman fixed random
hausman fixed random, sigmamore

qui: xtreg dlgi dlypc dlg dlsecpc, fe
estimate store fixed
qui: xtreg dlgi dlypc dlg dlsecpc, re
estimate store random
hausman fixed random
hausman fixed random, sigmamore

qui: xtreg dlg dlgi dlypc dlsecpc, fe
estimate store fixed
qui: xtreg dlg dlgi dlypc dlsecpc, re
estimate store random
hausman fixed random

qui: xtreg dlsecpc dlgi dlg dlypc, fe
estimate store fixed
qui: xtreg dlsecpc dlgi dlg dlypc, re
estimate store random
hausman fixed random
hausman fixed random, sigmamore
```

How it looks like

| | ── Coefficients ── | | | |
| | (b) | (B) | (b-B) | sqrt(diag(V_b-V_B)) |
	fixed	random	Difference	S.E.
dlgi	-.7043876	-.5840995	-.120288	.0485124
dlg	.1142447	.1330837	-.0188389	.0086034
dlsecpc	.4897638	.4916803	-.0019164	.0053734

```
                     b = consistent under Ho and Ha; obtained from xtreg
          B = inconsistent under Ha, efficient under Ho; obtained from xtreg

   Test:  Ho:  difference in coefficients not systematic

              chi2(3) = (b-B)'[(V_b-V_B)^(-1)](b-B)
                      =        16.69
              Prob>chi2 =      0.0008
```

| | —— Coefficients —— | | | |
	(b) fixed	(B) random	(b-B) Difference	sqrt(diag(V_b-V_B)) S.E.
dlypc	-.0393062	-.0342942	-.005012	.0021097
dlg	.044797	.0441861	.0006109	.0015643
dlsecpc	.0013723	-.0011585	.0025308	.0015493

b = consistent under Ho and Ha; obtained from xtreg
B = inconsistent under Ha, efficient under Ho; obtained from xtreg

Test: Ho: difference in coefficients not systematic

$$chi2(3) = (b-B)'[(V\_b-V\_B)^\wedge(-1)](b-B)$$
$$= 13.95$$
$$Prob>chi2 = 0.0030$$

| | —— Coefficients —— | | | |
	(b) fixed	(B) random	(b-B) Difference	sqrt(diag(V_b-V_B)) S.E.
dlgi	.3394973	.316957	.0225402	.0359782
dlypc	.0483139	.0541816	-.0058677	.0079394
dlsecpc	-.0243055	-.0276453	.0033398	.0054936

b = consistent under Ho and Ha; obtained from xtreg
B = inconsistent under Ha, efficient under Ho; obtained from xtreg

Test: Ho: difference in coefficients not systematic

$$chi2(3) = (b-B)'[(V\_b-V\_B)^\wedge(-1)](b-B)$$
$$= 2.27$$
$$Prob>chi2 = 0.5191$$

| | —— Coefficients —— | | | |
	(b) fixed	(B) random	(b-B) Difference	sqrt(diag(V_b-V_B)) S.E.
dlgi	.0344807	-.0441956	.0786763	.0621347
dlg	-.0805816	-.0933933	.0128118	.0096452
dlypc	.6866792	.6762459	.0104333	.0100272

b = consistent under Ho and Ha; obtained from xtreg
B = inconsistent under Ha, efficient under Ho; obtained from xtreg

Test: Ho: difference in coefficients not systematic

$$chi2(3) = (b-B)'[(V\_b-V\_B)^\wedge(-1)](b-B)$$
$$= 7.67$$
$$Prob>chi2 = 0.0534$$

Source: StataCorp. 2015.

Table 3.5 Lag order selection criteria.

Lag	CD	J	J—P value	MBIC	MAIC	MQIC
1	0.6463969	42.40725	0.1032625	− 146.3895	− 21.59275	− 71.18859
2	0.6947982	8.006647	0.9486682	− 86.39171	− 23.99335	− 48.79127
3	0.7184107					

Notes: Stata's command *pvarsoc* was used; this procedure gives us the coefficient of determination (CD), the Hansen's J statistic (J), and its P-value (J-P value) (Hansen, 1982), and the Bayesian information criterion (MBIC), the Akaike information criterion (MAIC), and the Quinn information criterion (MQIC) introduced by Andrews and Lu (2001).

The presence of fixed effects was detected in two of the four specifications, namely with DLYPC and DLGI as the dependent variables. As a note we should highlight that the option *sigmamore* was used in the cases where the covariance matrix was not positive definite. Also, in the specification where the DLSECPC was the dependent variable, the chi-squared (χ^2) turned out negative which following the *Hausman specification test*, from the Stata Manual, can be interpreted "*as strong evidence that we cannot reject the null hypothesis.*"[5]

Given that fixed effects are present in our panel, correlation problems between the regressors can arise. To overcome this issue the "*Hermelet procedure*" (Arellano & Bover, 1995) was used in order to remove the fixed effects. The system was then estimated by the Generalized Method of Moments (GMM), with the lags of the regressors as instrumental variables.

Before the PVAR estimation the last preliminary test that we had to compute was the lag order selection statistics. The results can be seen in Table 3.5.

How to do:
Lag order selection criteria
    pvarsoc dlypc dlgi dlg dlsecpc, maxlag(3) pvaropts (instl(1/3))

5 Available at: www.stata.com/manuals/rhausman.pdf (p. 9)

How it looks like

```
Selection order criteria
Sample:  1974 - 2014                          No. of obs      =        365
                                              No. of panels   =          9
                                              Ave. no. of T   =     40.556
```

lag	CD	J	J pvalue	MBIC	MAIC	MQIC
1	.6463969	42.40725	.1032625	−146.3895	−21.59275	−71.18859
2	.6947982	8.006647	.9486682	−86.39171	−23.99335	−48.79127
3	.7184107	.	.	.	.	.

Source: StataCorp. 2015.

After passing the Hansen's J test, which is a statistical test used for testing over-identifying restrictions, the optimal lag length should be the one that minimizes the MBIC, MAIC, and MQIC information criterions. In our case, the MBIC and the MQIC criterions are lower when we select one lag, although the MAIC criteria are lower when we select two lags. Despite these mixed results, we based our decision on the MAIC criteria, following Serena and Perron (2001), and thus, we will estimate a second-order PVAR. Although, generally, the VAR estimator is more suitable for highly frequency data, we used a panel with annual observations because data were only available in annual frequency. With this type of data—annual—the optimal lag length usually has a low value.

3.3 Results and discussion

The PVAR was estimated using two lags and with the *gmmstyle* option (Holtz-Eakin, Newey, & Rosen, 1988), which replaces the missing values with zeroes and is capable of producing more efficient estimates. The second-order PVAR results are listed in Table 3.6. The stability of the PVAR was checked and confirmed once the eigenvalues are inside the unit circle. This also indicates that our variables are stationary (Lütkepohl, 2005). The eigenvalue stability condition is displayed in Table 3.7.

Table 3.6 The panel vector autoregressive model results.

Variables		DLYPC	DLGI	DLG	DLSECPC
DLYPC	L1.	0.3102215***	0.0098551	0.0559808	0.3101445***
	L2.	− 0.0853452	− 0.0261405**	− 0.0569501	− 0.151762**
DLGI	L1.	− 1.506673***	0.8317427***	− 0.3321133	− 0.8756496*
	L2.	0.3880947	− 0.0144618	0.384005	0.054567
DLG	L1.	0.2138133*	0.0109281	− 0.0059621	0.1110493
	L2.	0.0618823	0.038701**	0.0388531	0.1962791**
DLSECPC	L1.	0.0129578	− 0.0003492	0.0225059	− 0.095534
	L2.	− 0.0440691	0.0163243***	0.0613468**	0.1687598***

Notes: ***, **, and * denote statistical significance of 1%, 5%, and 10% level, respectively; the Stata command *pvar* with the option GMM, with one 2 lags, was used.

Table 3.7 Eigenvalue stability condition.

Eigenvalue			Graph
Real	**Imaginary**	**Modulus**	
0.8228496	0	0.8228496	
− 0.5412739	0	0.5412739	
0.4658435	0	0.4658435	
0.1345605	0.3285776	0.355063	
0.1345605	− 0.3285776	0.355063	
− 0.1052671	0	0.1052671	
0.0645975	− 0.0816826	0.1041387	
0.0645975	0.0816826	0.1041387	

Roots of the companion matrix

Notes: All the eigenvalues are inside the unit circle meaning PVAR satisfies stability condition; Stata command *pvarstable* was used.

How to do:

Second-order PVAR estimation

    pvar dlypc dlgi dlg dlsecpc, lags(2) instl(1/3) gmmst

How it looks like

```
Panel vector autoregresssion


GMM Estimation

Final GMM Criterion Q(b) =        .019
Initial weight matrix: Identity
GMM weight matrix:      Robust
                                          No. of obs      =       374
                                          No. of panels   =         9
                                          Ave. no. of T   =    41.556
```

	Coef.	Std. Err.	z	P>|z|	[95% Conf.	Interval]
dlypc						
dlypc						
L1.	.3102215	.0772931	4.01	0.000	.1587298	.4617131
L2.	-.0853452	.0672403	-1.27	0.204	-.2171338	.0464434
dlgi						
L1.	-1.506673	.4340462	-3.47	0.001	-2.357388	-.6559583
L2.	.3880947	.4467379	0.87	0.385	-.4874955	1.263685
dlg						
L1.	.2138133	.1103395	1.94	0.053	-.002448	.4300747
L2.	.0618823	.0972016	0.64	0.524	-.1286293	.2523938
dlsecpc						
L1.	.0129578	.048725	0.27	0.790	-.0825414	.1084571
L2.	-.0440691	.043881	-1.00	0.315	-.1300743	.0419361
dlgi						
dlypc						
L1.	.0098551	.0083353	1.18	0.237	-.0064818	.026192
L2.	-.0261405	.0103574	-2.52	0.012	-.0464407	-.0058403
dlgi						
L1.	.8317427	.0605612	13.73	0.000	.713045	.9504405
L2.	-.0144618	.0536852	-0.27	0.788	-.1196829	.0907593
dlg						
L1.	.0109281	.0128811	0.85	0.396	-.0143183	.0361745
L2.	.038701	.0153518	2.52	0.012	.0086121	.0687899
dlsecpc						
L1.	-.0003492	.0061965	-0.06	0.955	-.0124941	.0117958
L2.	.0163243	.0062538	2.61	0.009	.0040669	.0285816

dlg						
dlypc						
L1.	.0559808	.0412548	1.36	0.175	-.0248772	.1368388
L2.	-.0569501	.038339	-1.49	0.137	-.1320931	.018193
dlgi						
L1.	-.3321133	.2532699	-1.31	0.190	-.8285132	.1642866
L2.	.384005	.280613	1.37	0.171	-.1659864	.9339965
dlg						
L1.	-.0059621	.071498	-0.08	0.934	-.1460956	.1341715
L2.	.0388531	.0645151	0.60	0.547	-.0875941	.1653004
dlsecpc						
L1.	.0225059	.0302123	0.74	0.456	-.0367091	.0817209
L2.	.0613468	.0268513	2.28	0.022	.0087193	.1139743
dlsecpc						
dlypc						
L1.	.3101445	.0877475	3.53	0.000	.1381626	.4821264
L2.	-.151762	.0756826	-2.01	0.045	-.3000971	-.0034268
dlgi						
L1.	-.8756496	.4503326	-1.94	0.052	-1.758285	.0069862
L2.	.054567	.4189187	0.13	0.896	-.7664986	.8756326
dlg						
L1.	.1110493	.1252942	0.89	0.375	-.1345228	.3566215
L2.	.1962791	.0943159	2.08	0.037	.0114233	.381135
dlsecpc						
L1.	-.095534	.0721953	-1.32	0.186	-.2370341	.0459661
L2.	.1687598	.0634879	2.66	0.008	.0443257	.2931939

Instruments : l(1/3).(dlypc dlgi dlg dlsecpc)

Source: StataCorp. 2015.

How to do:
Eigenvalue stability condition
pvarstable, graph

How it looks like

Eigenvalue stability condition

Eigenvalue		Modulus
Real	Imaginary	
.8228496	0	.8228496
-.5412739	0	.5412739
.4658435	0	.4658435
.1345605	-.3285776	.355063
.1345605	.3285776	.355063
-.1052671	0	.1052671
.0645975	-.0816826	.1041387
.0645975	.0816826	.1041387

All the eigenvalues lie inside the unit circle. pVAR satisfies stability condition.

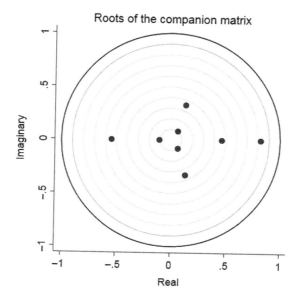

Roots of the companion matrix

Source: StataCorp. 2015.

After the second-order PVAR estimation and its stability check, we performed the Granger causality test (Abrigo & Love, 2015), based on the Wald test. The null hypothesis is the absence of causality. Moreover the presence of endogeneity is confirmed by the blocks of exogeneity analysis (ALL). The results of the Granger causality test are exhibited in Table 3.8.

How to do:
Granger causality test
    pvargranger

How it looks like

```
panel VAR-Granger causality Wald test
  Ho: Excluded variable does not Granger-cause Equation variable
  Ha: Excluded variable Granger-causes Equation variable
```

Equation \ Excluded	chi2	df	Prob > chi2
dlypc			
dlgi	15.560	2	0.000
dlg	4.679	2	0.096
dlsecpc	1.415	2	0.493
ALL	22.407	6	0.001
dlgi			
dlypc	8.722	2	0.013
dlg	6.503	2	0.039
dlsecpc	7.788	2	0.020
ALL	17.173	6	0.009
dlg			
dlypc	3.691	2	0.158
dlgi	2.015	2	0.365
dlsecpc	5.220	2	0.074
ALL	15.151	6	0.019
dlsecpc			
dlypc	15.256	2	0.000
dlgi	4.632	2	0.099
dlg	4.700	2	0.095
ALL	27.725	6	0.000

Source: StataCorp. 2015.

Table 3.8 Granger causality test.

	DLYPC	DLGI	DLG	DLSECPC
DLYPC does not cause	–	8.722**	3.691	15.256***
DLGI does not cause	15.560***	–	2.015	4.632*
DLG does not cause	4.679*	6.503**	–	4.700*
DLSECPC does not cause	1.415	7.788**	5.220*	–
ALL	22.407***	17.173***	15.151**	27.725***

Notes: ***, **, and * denote statistical significance of 1%, 5%, and 10% level, respectively; the Stata command *pvargranger* was used.

Looking at the Granger causality test results, we found:

- A bidirectional causality between income inequality and economic growth, with a negative signal in both directions. However, the causality seems to be stronger from income inequality to economic growth. These results indicate that not only can the economic growth of the countries of our sample be affected by changes in income inequality, but also, income inequality can be affected by their economic performance. More specifically an increase in these countries' economic growth seems to lead to a decrease in their income inequality levels, while an increase in their income inequality levels seems to cause a reduction in their economic output.

- A unidirectional causality running from economic growth to secondary energy consumption. This result supports the conservation hypothesis of the energy—growth nexus, which means that an increase or decrease in secondary energy consumption does not affect the economic growth of the countries from the sample. The positive sign of this relationship tells us that economic growth is still capable of promoting secondary energy consumption.

- A unidirectional causality running from globalization to income inequality, that is, the changes in globalization levels in these Latin American countries seems to affect their income inequality levels. Furthermore the positive signal that we found in this relationship indicates that globalization seems to foster their income inequality problems.

- A causality running from secondary energy consumption to income inequality, with a positive signal, which as in the case of globalization, shows that secondary energy consumption can exacerbate their income inequality.

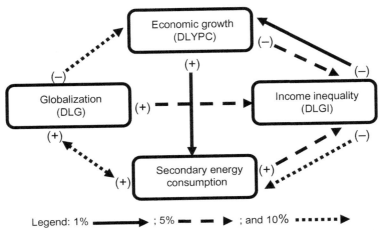

Figure 3.1 Summary of the causalities. *Notes: The causality signals were based on the sum of the lagged variables coefficients of the PVAR estimations (Table 3.6).*

- Lastly, concerning other causalities that were found—from globalization to economic growth; from globalization to secondary energy consumption; from secondary energy consumption to globalization; and from income inequality to secondary energy consumption—we should state that all of them were found only at the 10% level of significance. This fact makes it very difficult to make strong inferences about these relationships. These results also raise doubts on the globalization endogeneity.

In Fig. 3.1 the signal and the direction of the causal relationships that were found between the variables are presented in order to simplify the interpretation of the results.

Discussing the results we should note that the existing literature already defined some causes for the detrimental effect that income inequality can possibly have on economic growth. If we look to the Latin American region characteristics, these can be perfectly applied to our case. Rent-seeking activities (e.g., Alesina & Perotti, 1994), social and political instability (e.g., Alesina & Perotti, 1996), and credit market imperfections (e.g., Galor & Zeira, 1993) can be some of the reasons that could explain our results. Moreover our findings indicate that the causality also runs in the opposite direction and that economic growth may have been able to reduce income inequality. The fact that income inequality has been decreasing in Latin America led Tsounta and Osueke (2014) to investigate its causes. Their conclusions tell us that, after policies, economic growth was the main reason for this decreasing trend.

We also found evidence that economic growth does not depend on secondary energy consumption *per capita*, but that economic growth can lead to an increase in secondary energy consumption *per capita*. This result, as we have already stated, supports the conservation hypothesis of the energy—growth nexus. Along the same lines, Pablo-Romero and De Jesús (2016) also found evidences that the energy demand on Latin American and Caribbean countries seems to increase as they experience more growth. Given that secondary energy is composed mainly of electricity, it makes sense that, as a country grows, it increases the consumption of this type of energy. Additionally, the fact that the causality does not go in the opposite direction possibly means that measures, which lead to secondary energy conservation are not going to hurt these countries growth.

Relative to the causality that seems to run from globalization to income inequality, our findings indicate that globalization could have led to an increase in income inequality in these countries. The relationship between globalization and income inequality has been extensively studied given the importance of this issue to the current economic debate, but the conclusions are far from being consensual. In our specific case, that is, Latin America, the fact that globalization may foster income inequality is not a surprise, and that is why the criticism toward this process is particularly strong in this region (Edwards, 2008). As stressed by Stiglitz (2002), globalization is not an evil phenomenon but if countries want to succeed, they have to know how to manage this process properly, which in Stiglitz's opinion, did not happen in most cases. The Washington Consensus, that is, a group of reforms specially designed to increase globalization and economic freedom levels in the Latin American region, is usually cited as an example of poor liberalization and globalization policies due to their consequences for the region (low growth rates and increased social problems). In their study on how globalization has affected income inequality in developing countries, Goldberg and Pavcnik (2007) stress the increase in capital flows and the skill-biased technological change as some of the channels through which globalization can increase income inequality.

The results also pointed out that secondary energy consumption *per capita* may have also increased the income inequality levels of the region. This result was derived from the fact that, although the energy subsidies given by many Latin American (and Caribbean) countries were developed to help the poor, some evidence shows that the major share of the money spent to keep energy prices low ends up in the hands of the wealthier population (Beylis & Barbara, 2017).

For now we will not expand the discussion relatively to the Granger causality that runs from globalization to economic growth, from globalization to secondary energy consumption *per capita*, from secondary energy consumption *per capita* to globalization, and from income inequality to secondary energy consumption *per capita*, because the evidences regarding the existence of these causalities are far from being robust.

Before we continue, and given the aim of this chapter, we should highlight that, by the Granger causality test, only income inequality seems to have been able to directly influence the Latin American countries' growth. However, globalization and secondary energy consumption *per capita* could also have contributed to indirectly hamper the economic growth of these countries through their contribution to the income inequality increase.

Although the importance of the Granger causality test is to perceive the relationships between the variables, this test does not give us all the information. In this sense, additionally to the Granger causality test, the forecast error variance decomposition (FEVD) and the impulse response functions (IRFs) were also computed.

The outputs of the FEVD allow us to know the forecast error variance percentage that a variable explains of another variable that has been faced with a shock/innovation, the time that a variable need to achieve equilibrium and the contribution of each variable for such purpose. The FEVD followed the Cholesky decomposition and were performed using 1000 Monte Carlo simulations for 10 periods.

Turning to the results from the IRFs, they reveal the behavior of one variable faced with a shock or innovation in another variable. Also they are capable of revealing the time that the variable needs to return to equilibrium after the shock/innovation occurred. A Gaussian approximation based on 1000 Monte Carlo simulations was used to estimate the IRFs which, as in the case of the FEVD, also followed the Cholesky decomposition.

Additionally, we should indicate that the results of the eigenvalue stability condition (Table 3.7.) lead us to believe that the IRFs and the FEVD have a known interpretation (Abrigo & Love, 2015). The results from the FEVD, and from the IRFs, are presented in Table 3.9 and Fig. 3.2, respectively.

Table 3.9 Forecast error variance decomposition.

Response variables	Forecast horizon	Impulse variables			
		DLYPC	**DLGI**	**DLG**	**DLSECPC**
DLYPC	1	1	0	0	0
	2	0.9577677	0.0299076	0.0121857	0.0001391
	5	0.9052997	0.076268	0.0166957	0.0017367
	10	0.8914427	0.0880925	0.0177904	0.0026745
DLGI	1	0.0080864	0.9919136	0	0
	2	0.0047717	0.9939322	0.001292	4.01e-06
	5	0.0088008	0.9459323	0.031236	0.0140309
	10	0.0088918	0.9327161	0.0377249	0.0206673
DLG	1	0.0005197	0.0070495	0.9924308	0
	2	0.0176617	0.0124862	0.9683497	0.0015024
	5	0.0175345	0.0124642	0.9570289	0.0129724
	10	0.0175357	0.0124756	0.9569139	0.0130748
DLSECPC	1	0.3094463	0.001649	0.003012	0.6858926
	2	0.334852	0.0102198	0.0059554	0.6489727
	5	0.3176622	0.031597	0.0155062	0.6352347
	10	0.3147112	0.0393516	0.0161313	0.6298059

Notes: Stata command *pvarfevd* was used.

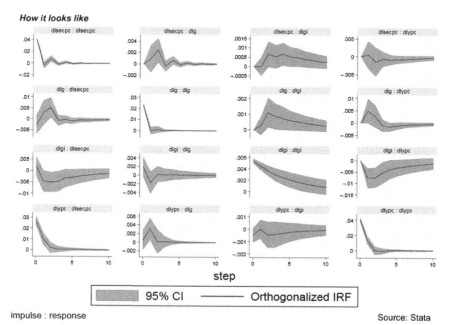

Figure 3.2 Impulse response functions.

How to do:
Forecast error variance decomposition
    pvarfevd, mc(1000) st(10)

How it looks like

Forecast-error variance decomposition

Response variable and Forecast horizon	Impulse variable			
	dlypc	dlgi	dlg	dlsecpc
dlypc				
0	0	0	0	0
1	1	0	0	0
2	.9577677	.0299076	.0121857	.0001391
3	.927098	.0564104	.015321	.0011705
4	.9134805	.0695656	.0155895	.0013644
5	.9052997	.076268	.0166957	.0017367
6	.9001778	.0805957	.0171923	.0020343
7	.8966207	.0836436	.0174348	.002301
8	.8942025	.0857353	.0175912	.0024709
9	.8925524	.0871452	.0177088	.0025936
10	.8914427	.0880925	.0177904	.0026745

dlgi				
0	0	0	0	0
1	.0080864	.9919136	0	0
2	.0047717	.9939322	.001292	4.01e-06
3	.0066186	.9668176	.0197758	.006788
4	.0082406	.9552838	.0269919	.0094837
5	.0088008	.9459323	.031236	.0140309
6	.008903	.9412611	.0335757	.0162601
7	.0089086	.9375755	.0353262	.0181898
8	.0089031	.9353369	.0364512	.0193087
9	.0088971	.9337369	.0372235	.0201424
10	.0088918	.9327161	.0377249	.0206673

dlg				
0	0	0	0	0
1	.0005197	.0070495	.9924308	0
2	.0176617	.0124862	.9683497	.0015024
3	.0174879	.0124399	.9580764	.0119959
4	.0175419	.0124405	.9577599	.0122576
5	.0175345	.0124642	.9570289	.0129724
6	.0175372	.0124663	.9569876	.013009
7	.0175359	.0124713	.9569265	.0130663
8	.0175359	.0124729	.9569219	.0130694
9	.0175357	.0124748	.9569148	.0130746
10	.0175357	.0124756	.9569139	.0130748

dlsecpc				
0	0	0	0	0
1	.3094463	.001649	.003012	.6858926
2	.334852	.0102198	.0059554	.6489727
3	.3223829	.0194557	.0154672	.6426942
4	.319165	.0277098	.0155497	.6375754
5	.3176622	.031597	.0155062	.6352347
6	.3164485	.0345472	.0158504	.633154
7	.3158264	.0364421	.0159041	.6318274
8	.3152787	.0378218	.0160227	.6308767
9	.3149561	.0387266	.0160758	.6302415
10	.3147112	.0393516	.0161313	.6298059

FEVD standard errors and confidence intervals are not saved. Use option save.

Source: StataCorp. 2015.

Regarding DLYPC, the results show that its forecast error variance is mainly explained by shocks to itself (95.8% in the second year, 90% in the 10th year). Although, we also observe that shocks to DLGI explain around 8.8% of the forecast error variance in the 10th year, which reinforce the idea that income inequality is capable of an influence on these Latin American countries' growth. Contrariwise, shocks to DLG and DLSECPC reveal to have small influence on the explanation of the DLYPC forecast error variance, that is, about 1.7% and 0.3%, respectively at the end of the 10th year. In this case, we can conclude that both globalization and secondary energy consumption *per capita* do not influence these countries' growth.

As in the previous case the forecast error variance of DLGI starts for being largely explained by itself—around 99% in the first and second years—but the impact of this shock loses some of its strength as we move forward in time. At the 10th year, shocks to DLGI and DLG explain around 93% and 4%, respectively, of the DLGI forecast error variance. This means that changes in globalization levels affect the income inequality levels of these Latin American countries. In the same line, we see that DLSECPC is also important for the convergence of DLGI to equilibrium, meaning that secondary energy consumption *per capita* (as in the case of globalization) can, in fact, influence income inequality in these countries. In an opposite sense the shock to DLYPC did not shown to be relevant to the explanation of the DLGI forecast error variance.

Relatively to the DLG forecast error variance, we see that globalization continues to show signs of not being an endogenous variable, with its variance being explained almost exclusively by itself.

Lastly, considering DLSECPC, we see that the shock to DLYPC explains a great part of the forecast error variance of DLSECPC (about 33% in the second year; 32% in the fifth year; and 31% in the 10th year), which indicates that economic growth largely contributes to secondary energy consumption *per capita*. Additionally, we see that a shock to DLGI explains around 4% of the forecast error variance of DLSECPC in the 10th period, meaning that income inequality is also able to influence secondary energy consumption *per capita*. Given this result, some inferences can be drawn on the Granger causality that runs from DLGI to DLSECPC that was found at a 10% level of significance. This negative effect can possibly be related to the decrease in the purchasing power that can be generated by an income inequality increase and which can probably lower the consumption of secondary energy (mainly electricity).

Rodriguez-Oreggia and Yepez-Garcia (2014) studied the relationship between income and energy consumption for Mexico, and according to their findings, in general, *"there is an increasing relation between income levels and energy demand"* (Rodriguez-Oreggia & Yepez-Garcia, 2014; p. 28). This means that if a majority of the population (poor and middle class) lower their income level, it is likely that energy consumption suffers a break.

Looking at the differences in the Granger causality test and FEVD results, we should state that although these tests are interconnected, they are not the same thing. One variable may Granger cause another variable without showing a large impact on the adjustment of the "caused" variable.

How to do:
Impulse response functions
        pvarirf, mc(1000) oirf byopt(yrescale) st(10)

Turning to the IRFs we see that, after a shock, all variables seem to converge to equilibrium, which is a signal of their stationarity. By Fig. 3.2, and in line with the FEVD results, we can see that a shock to DLGI causes a negative response by DLYPC and by DLSECPC, a shock to DLG and to DLSECPC seem to trigger a positive response by DLGI, a shock to DLYPC leads to a positive response by DLSECPC, and a shock in DLGI leads to a negative response by DLSECPC. Additionally, we observe that the shocks of the variables on their own seem to be those with the greatest magnitudes, which supports the fact of the major part of the variables being autoregressive. Another additional fact that could be stated is that income inequality appears to be highly persistent, and for that reason, shocks to this variable produce long lasting effects on the other variables.

Given the results of the Granger causality test, the response of economic growth to a globalization impulse, of globalization to a secondary energy consumption *per capita* impulse, and of income inequality to an impulse on economic growth, should also be mentioned. Although the responses of the variables seem to be in line with the Granger causality test results, the combined magnitude and persistence of these shocks effects leads us to believe that these are relatively insignificant and that is why the causal relationships between these variables was not shown to be relevant in the FEVD analysis.

Summing up, and given the aim of this chapter, by the Granger causality test, the FEVD, and by the IRF's, we found evidence of a negative impact of income inequality on these Latin American countries' growth. Still, evidences for the hypothesis that economic growth could decrease income inequality were not so strong.

Although we also found a causal relationship running from globalization to economic growth, its significance raised doubts about the strength of such relationship, and by both the FEVD and the IRF's results we verified that globalization did not show signs of directly influencing these countries' economic growth. However, globalization could affect economic growth indirectly given that, by our estimations, it could have contributed to an increase in income inequality, and consequently, could have hampered growth through this channel. The same can be said relatively to secondary energy consumption *per capita*, which also showed signs of being related to increases in income inequality, as also the opposite, that is, income inequality seems to have negatively affected secondary energy consumption *per capita*.

Furthermore, even though the results demonstrated that changes in secondary energy consumption *per capita* were not capable of influencing economic growth in these countries, they also showed that economic growth Granger caused secondary energy consumption *per capita* (supporting the conservation hypothesis of the energy—growth nexus). In addition, the FEVD showed that economic growth plays a determinant role on the secondary energy consumption *per capita*. Lastly, the FEVD and the IRF's estimations also increased our doubts regarding the presence of bidirectional causality between globalization and secondary energy consumption *per capita* (found at a 10% level of significance) in these Latin American countries.

3.4 Conclusion

This chapter applied a panel VAR for nine Latin American countries from 1970 to 2015, in order to assess the effects of income inequality and globalization on economic growth. Moreover the PVAR methodology also enabled us to explore additional relationships between the variables in the study.

The preliminary tests confirmed that multicollinearity was not a problem to our estimation, that cross-section dependence was present in all variables (in logarithms and in first differences), and that all of our variables were stationary in first differences. The preliminary tests also confirmed the presence of fixed effects in our PVAR model.

The PVAR was estimated using two lags, following the lag order selection criteria. The Granger causalities, the FEVD, and the IRFs were then computed.

The results from our estimations showed strong evidences that income inequality had a depressing effect on the economic growth of these nine Latin American countries. Regarding the relationship between globalization and growth, the results are not so clear. Although, evidences on the existence of a causal relationship running from globalization to growth, with a negative signal, were also found, even so only at the 10% significance level. Additionally, globalization showed few signs of being endogenous.

Relatively to secondary energy consumption *per capita*, the results from our estimations indicate that this variable did not directly influenced the economic growth of these countries, but also indicated that economic growth is able to positively influence secondary energy consumption *per capita*. This means that the conservation hypothesis is confirmed for these Latin American countries in the case of secondary energy consumption. This means that these countries' governments can possibly adopt public policies oriented to the limitation of consumption, centered on efficiency measures, for example, without neglecting their economic growth.

Although both globalization and secondary energy consumption *per capita* did not shown robust signs of having a direct effect on economic growth, our outcomes suggest that they can possibly have contributed to hampering economic growth indirectly, given the fact that both variables seem to have enhanced the income inequality levels of these Latin American countries. Additionally, the results also indicated that the increase in income inequality levels also appears to be capable of causing a decrease in secondary energy consumption *per capita*. Although the idea that an increase in secondary energy consumption *per capita* seems to lead to an increase in these countries' inequality levels, and an increase in their inequality levels seem to lead to a decrease in their secondary energy consumption *per capita* seems to be slight contradictory, we should note that these effects are probably not contemporaneous, with one occurring after the other. Moreover, they can also have different dynamics (short run vs long run), which turns the question about the existence of a contradiction a lot less problematic.

The results support the branch of the literature which states that inequality has adverse effects on growth. This conclusion indicates that Latin American policymakers should focus their attention on the reduction of the income inequality levels of their respective countries with the development of measures that lead to a more efficient redistribution of income. We also think that the region's governments should strengthen the fight against rent-seeking activities, given that this can be one of the major sources for income inequality, especially in the Latin American case.

The development of solutions to face this problem gets more complicated and challenging when we see that both globalization and secondary energy consumption *per capita* can directly contribute to the increase of the income inequality levels, and indirectly, to a decrease in economic growth. These facts widen the fields of action where policymakers must intervene, drawing attention to the way in which these countries have been conducting their globalization process and their energy policies. Given the previous discussion of the results, we suggest that the governments from the region should restructure their economies in order to change the way in which they participate in the global integration process and develop measures which will ensure that all their populations can benefit from globalization. They also should change the scheme of their energy subsidies, given that they seem to have regressive effects, which mean that they benefit the richer groups, and thus contribute to the increase of inequality. Additionally, the results suggest that energy conservation policies can be applied in these countries to the case of secondary energy consumption *per capita*, because the decrease in its consumption does not seems to affect the economic output of these countries.

References

Abdoli, G., Farahani, Y. G., & Dastan, S. (2015). Electricity consumption and economic growth in OPEC countries: A cointegrated panel analysis. *OPEC Energy Review*(3), 1−17.

Abrigo, M.R.M., Love, I., *Estimation of panel vector autoregression in stata: A package of programs*, p. 28, 2015.

Alesina, A., & Perotti, R. (1994). The political economy of growth: A critical survey of the recent literature. *The World Bank Economic Review*, 8(3), 351−371.

Alesina, A., & Perotti, R. (1996). Income distribution, political instability, and investment. *European Economic Review*, 40(6), 1203−1228.

Alesina, A., & Rodrik, D. (1994). Distributive politics and economic growth. *The Quarterly Journal of Economics, 109*(2), 465−490.

Andrews, D. W. K., & Lu, B. (2001). Consistent model and moment selection procedures for GMM estimation with application to dynamic panel data models. *Journal of Econometrics, 101*(1), 123−164.

Arellano, M., & Bover, O. (1995). Another look at the instrumental variable estimation of error-components models. *Journal of Econometrics, 68*(1), 29−51.

Aslan, A. (2014). Causality between electricity consumption and economic growth in Turkey: An ARDL bounds testing approach. *Energy Sources, Part B: Economics, Planning and Policy, 9*(1), 25−31.

Barro, R. J. (2000). Inequality and growth in a panel of countries. *Journal of Economic Growth, 5*, 5−32.

Beylis, G., & Barbara, C. (2017). *Energy pricing policies for inclusive growth in Latin America and the Caribbean. Directions in Development.* Washington, DC: World Bank.

Castells-Quintana, D., & Royuela, V. (2017). Tracking positive and negative effects of inequality on long-run growth. *Empirical Economics, 53*(4), 1349−1378.

Cingano, F., *Trends in income inequality and its impact on economic growth*, OECD Social, Employment and Migration Working Papers, No. 163, OECD Publishing, 2014.

Dabla-Norris, E., Kochhar, K., Suphaphiphat, N., Ricka, F., Tsounta, E., *Causes and consequences of income inequality: A global perspective*, No 15/13, IMF Staff Discussion Notes, International Monetary Fund, 2015.

Delbianco, F., Dabús, C., & Caraballo, M. Á. (2014). Income inequality and economic growth: New evidence from Latin America. *Cuadernos de Economía, 33*(63), 381−398.

Dollar, D., Kraay, A., *Trade, growth, and poverty*, World Bank Policy Research Working Paper No. 2615, 2001.

Dreher, A. (2006). Does globalization affect growth? Evidence from a new index of globalization. *Applied Economics, 38*(10), 1091−1110.

Eberhardt, M., & Teal, F. (2011). Econometrics for grumblers: A new look at the literature on cross-country growth empirics. *Journal of Economic Surveys, 25*(1), 109−155.

Edwards, S. (2008). Globalisation, growth and crises: The view from Latin America. *Australian Economic Review, 41*, 123−140.

Frankel, J. A., & Romer, D. (1999). Does trade cause growth? *American Economic Review, 89*(3), 379−399.

Fuinhas, J. A., & Marques, A. C. (2013). Rentierism, energy and economic growth: The case of Algeria and Egypt (1965−2010). *Energy Policy, 62*, 1165−1171.

Galor, O., & Zeira, J. (1993). Income distribution and macroeconomics. *Review of Economic Studies, 60*(1), 35−52.

Gasparini, L., Lustig, N., *The rise and fall of income inequality in Latin America*, Working Papers No. 213, ECINEQ, Society for the Study of Economic Inequality, 2011.

Goldberg, P., Pavcnik, N., *Distributional effects of globalization in developing countries*, NBER Working Paper No. w12885, 2007.

Grigoli, F., Paredes, E., Di Bella, G., *Inequality and growth: A heterogeneous approach*, IMF Working Papers 16/244, International Monetary Fund, 2016.

Grossman, G. M., & Helpman, E. (2015). Globalization and growth. *American Economic Review, 105*(5), 100−104.

Gurgul, H., & Lach, è. (2014). Globalization and economic growth: Evidence from two decades of transition in CEE. *Economic Modelling, 36*, 99−107.

Gygli, S., Haelg, F., Sturm, J., *The KOF globalisation index − Revisited*, KOF Working Papers, 2018.

Halter, D., Oechslin, M., & Zweimüller, J. (2014). Inequality and growth: The neglected time dimension. *Journal of Economic Growth, 19*(1), 81−104.

Hansen, L. P. (1982). Large sample properties of generalized method of moments estimators. *Econometrica*, *50*(4), 1029−1054.

Holtz-Eakin, D., Newey, W., & Rosen, H. S. (1988). Estimating vector autoregressions with panel data. *Econometrica*, *56*(6), 1371−1395.

Hsiao, C. (2007). Panel data analysis-advantages and challenges. *Test*, *16*(1), 1−22.

Keohane, R., & Nye, J. (2000). *Globalization: What's new? What's not? (and so what?)*. *Foreign Policy*(118), 104−119.

Khalifa, S., & El Hag, S. (2010). Income disparities, economic growth, and development as a threshold. *Journal of Economic Development*, *35*(2), 23−36.

Klasen, S., Scholl, N., Lahoti, R., Ochmann, S., Vollmer, S., *Inequality − Worldwide trends and current debates*. Courant Research Centre: Poverty, Equity and Growth - Discussion Papers 209, Courant Research Centre PEG, 2016.

Lee, C.-C., Lee, C.-C., & Chang, C.-P. (2015). Globalization, economic growth and institutional development in China. *Global Economic Review*, *44*(1), 31−63.

Li, H., & Zou, H. (1998). Income inequality is not harmful for growth: Theory and evidence. *Review of Development Economics*, *2*(3), 318−334.

Lin, S. C., Huang, H. C., & Weng, H. W. (2006). A semiparametric partially linear investigation of the Kuznets' hypothesis. *Journal of Comparative Economics*, *34*(3), 634−647.

Love, I., & Zicchino, L. (2006). Financial development and dynamic investment behavior: Evidence from panel VAR. *Quarterly Review of Economics and Finance*, *46*(2), 190−210.

Lütkepohl, H. (2005). *New introduction to multiple time series analysis*. Berlin: Springer.

Majidi, A. F. (2017). Globalization and economic growth: The case study of developing countries. *Asian Economic and Financial Review*, *7*(6), 589−599.

Marques, L. M., Fuinhas, J. A., & Marques, A. C. (2017). Augmented energy-growth nexus: Economic, political and social globalization impacts. *Energy Procedia*, *136*, 97−101.

Ostry, J., Berg, A., & Tsangarides, C. (2014). Redistribution, inequality, and growth. *IMF Staff Discussion Note*, *14*(2), 1.

Ozturk, I. (2010). A literature survey on energy−growth nexus. *Energy Policy*, *38*(1), 340−349.

Pablo-Romero, M. D. P., & De Jesús, J. (2016). Economic growth and energy consumption: The energy-environmental Kuznets curve for Latin America and the Caribbean. *Renewable and Sustainable Energy Reviews*, *60*, 1343−1350.

Pesaran, M.H., *General diagnostic tests for cross section dependence in panels*, CESifo Working Paper Series 1229, CESifo Group Munich, 2004.

Pesaran, M. H. (2007). A simple panel unit root test in the presence of cross-section dependence. *Journal of Applied Econometrics*, *22*(2), 265−312.

Piketty, T., & Goldhammer, A. (2014). *Capital in the twenty-first century*. Cambridge, MA: The Belknap Press of Harvard University Press.

Potrafke, N. (2015). The evidence on globalisation. *The World Economy*, *38*(3), 509−552.

Rao, B. B., & Vadlamannati, K. C. (2011). Globalization and growth in the low income African countries with the extreme bounds analysis. *Economic Modelling*, *28*(3), 795−805.

Rodriguez-Oreggia, E., Yepez-Garcia, R.A., *Income and energy consumption in Mexican households*, World Bank Policy Research Working Paper No. 6864, 2014.

Sachs, J.D., Warner, A.M., *Natural resource abundance and economic growth*, NBER Working Paper No. w5398, 1995.

Sachs, J. D., & Warner, A. M. (2001). The curse of natural resources. *European Economic Review*, *45*(4−6), 827−838.

Serena, N., & Perron, P. (2001). Lag length selection and the construction of unit root tests with good size and power. *Econometrica*, *69*(6), 1519−1554.

Solt, F. (2016). The standardized world income inequality database. *Social Science Quarterly*, *97*, 1267−1281.

StataCorp. (2015). *Stata Statistical Software: Release 14*. College Station, TX: StataCorp LP.

Stiglitz, J. E. (2002). *Globalization and its discontents*. New York, NY: W. W. Norton.

Stiglitz, J. E. (2004). Globalization and growth in emerging markets. *Journal of Policy Modeling*, *26*(4), 465−484.

Stiglitz, J. E. (2012). *The price of inequality: How today's divided society endangers our future*. New York, NY: W.W. Norton & Co.

Tsounta, E., Osueke, A., *What is behind Latin America's declining income inequality?*, IMF Working Paper No. 14/124, 2014.

Ucan, O., Aricioglu, E., & Yucel, F. (2014). Energy consumption and economic growth nexus: Evidence from developed countries in Europe. *International Journal of Energy Economics and Policy*, *4*(3), 411−419.

Further reading

Dreher, A., & Gaston, N. (2008). Has globalization increased inequality? *Review of International Economics*, *16*(3), 516−536.

Kaldor, N. (1957). A model of economic growth. *The Economic Journal*, *67*(268)), 591−624.

Lazear, E., & Rosen, S. (1981). Rank-order tournaments as optimum labor contracts. *Journal of Political Economy*, *89*.

Okun, A. M. (2015). *Equality and efficiency: The big tradeoff*. Washington, DC: Brookings Institution Press.

Sadorsky, P. (2012). Energy consumption, output and trade in South America. *Energy Economics*, *34*, 476−488.

CHAPTER FOUR

The impacts of China's effect and globalization on the augmented energy—nexus: evidence in four aggregated regions

Luís Miguel Marques[1,*], José Alberto Fuinhas[2,*] and António Cardoso Marques[1,*]

[1]NECE-UBI and Management and Economics Department, University of Beira Interior, Covilhã, Portugal
[2]NECE-UBI, CeBER and Faculty of Economics, University of Coimbra, Coimbra, Portugal

Contents

4.1 Introduction

From the early 2000s, China's economic growth, energy consumption (E), and globalization levels increased exponentially. In fact, China's gross domestic product (GDP) increased by more than 300% from 2000

* This research was supported by NECE, R&D unit and funded by the FCT — Portuguese Foundation for the Development of Science and Technology, Ministry of Science, Technology and Higher Education, project UID/GES/04630/2019.

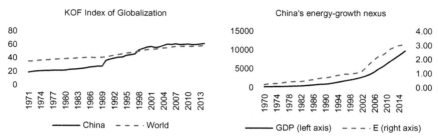

Figure 4.1 China and World Konjunkturforschungsstelle index of globalization[1] (on the left graph) and China's economic growth in billions of 2010 US\$[2] and primary energy consumption in billions of tonnes of oil equivalent[3] (on the right graph).

to 2016 and China's energy consumption increase more than 200% across the same time span (see Fig. 4.1). This fact greatly contributed to the increasing globalization level in China that went from a Konjunkturforschungsstelle (KOF) globalization index of 56.35 in 2000 to a 62.02 index in 2014. It should be noted that in 2000 the world average index was 52.56 and in 2016, it was 58.91, meaning that the world average index has increased around 6 points, since China's involvement. Those facts are consistent with China's strong contribution on a world globalization level.

A trend in increase of globalization has being observed, which should impact on energy markets. International trade promotes relationships between countries, namely the energy dependent ones and the energy producers. It is expected that this trend will continue throughout the globe in coming years. For instance, the demand for energy will keep growing in emerging economies. Strong growth in Asia will most likely drive increasing energy consumption and, to satisfy this, some oil producers will play a major role by increasing oil supply. Those facts support the possibility of China and globalization development playing major roles in the world energy—growth nexus. For those reasons, it could be important to understand the impacts of globalization, as well as China's spillover effects on different global regions. On the one hand, globalization impacts on the energy—growth nexus attracted the researchers' attention because: (1) the increasingly global energy markets and greater international cooperation, raises uncertainties about the impact of globe energy policies; and

---

[1] Available at: http://globalization.kof.ethz.ch/.

[2] Available at: http://databank.worldbank.org/data/source/world-development-indicators.

[3] Available at: https://www.bp.com/content/dam/bp/en/corporate/excel/energy-economics/statistical-review-2017/bp-statistical-review-of-world-energy-2017-underpinning-data.xlsx.

(2) the study of the augmented energy—growth nexus with globalization could help to understand the conflicting results found in literature. On the other hand, the research into China's spillover effects on world energy—growth nexus is almost inexistent.

The relationship between energy consumption and economic growth has been studied since the 1970s, when Kraft and Kraft (1978) examined this causality relationship for the United States and found that gross national product (GNP) caused increased energy consumption over the period of 1947—74. The research on the nexus evolved around the examination of Granger causality between energy and growth (and vice versa), leading to four testable relationships: (1) the *neutrality hypothesis*; (2) the *feedback hypothesis*; (3) the *conservation hypothesis*; and (4) the *growth hypothesis*. For decades, the energy—growth nexus has received considerable attention (e.g., Akarca & Long, 1980; Lee & Chang, 2007; Wang, Li, Fang, & Zhou, 2016; Yu & Jin, 1992) and by focusing on dividing the research in country-specific and multicountry studies that has led to a mix of results. Discordant results are also easy to identify. For example, Omri and Kahouli (2014) found the presence of bidirectional causality between energy and growth for a panel of high-income countries, while Ahmed and Azam (2016) by studying 24 high-income-OECD countries, found the bidirectional causality only in 5 countries, while evidence of the *growth hypothesis* and *neutrality hypothesis* was found for 4 and 15 countries, respectively. Although it is usual to relate the energy—growth pattern with income categories (Mohammadi & Amin, 2015), the cited results reveal that the income level may not be directly related with the causality direction in every outlook. However, any possible divergence in results caused by different methodologies should be taken into account.

The traditional energy—growth nexus has been extended by including variables such as financial development, population, urbanization, or industrialization. Recently, concerns about the decrease in carbon dioxide emission and globalization, among others, have led to the inclusion of even more variables in energy—growth nexus research. The globalization impacts on energy consumption, caught the researchers' attention, namely by studying developing and developed countries. The study of trade openness impacts on energy consumption, started when Cole (2006) by using the Antweiler, Copeland, and Taylor (2001) theoretical principles, observed that, for a sample of 32 developed and developing countries, trade liberalization can increase per capita energy use. Thenceforth, vast literature has been targeted at investigating the relationship between energy consumption, economic growth, and trade openness, by using individual countries or a panel of countries studies. Taking into consideration that globalization has impacts on the energy—growth nexus, and given that the markets are becoming increasingly integrated, the study of some countries' spillover effects on the globe nexus may lead to a new perspective for the policymakers. This is far from new in the literature on other subjects (e.g., Koesler, Swales, & Turner, 2016; Mensi, Hammoudeh, Nguyen, & Kang, 2016; Zhang, 2017). However, the spillover effects research is absent in what concerns the globe energy—growth nexus.

With the cited outlook in mind several questions arise:
• Are there China's spillover effects on the world energy—growth nexus?
• Has globalization homogenous impacts on the energy—growth nexus across the globe?

Answering these two questions is the main goal of this chapter. To do so, the world is divided in four regions: America, Europe and Central Asia, Asia Pacific, and Africa and the Middle East. Some methodological/econometric issues are also explored. For instance, data are rearranged to assure their comparability given that it is scarce at macrolevels. Additionally, the chapter aims to arouse interest in autoregressive models to handle heterogeneity. In consequence, an autoregressive distributed lag (ARDL) approach is followed and a step-by-step guide to EVIEWS 10^+ is provided, assuring not only the replicability of the study, but also providing the researcher with the opportunity to understand how to apply the methodology in different situations.

The best path to follow when studying world globalization impacts in the four regions raises doubts. Previous studies often used the KOF index of globalization (e.g., Ahmed, Bhattacharya, Qazi, & Long, 2016; Chang, Lee, & Hsieh, 2015; Doğan & Deger, 2016). However, the index is only provided for countries. Given that we aim to test total world globalization, two *proxies* are developed, thus allowing the authors to give clues regarding the best path to follow in future research. The first used *proxy* is the KOF index average of 146 countries and the second *proxy* is a population-weighted KOF average.

The chapter is organized as follows: Section 4.2 encompasses the aggregation of data; Sction 4.3 shows the followed methodologies; Section 4.4 presents the results divided into four subsections for each world region; and Section 4.5 discusses the results and concludes.

4.2 The aggregation of data

Studies on the world energy—growth nexus are often restricted by the lack of available data. For this reason, extra effort has to be made in order to assure data comparability. This research focuses on the study of the globe energy—growth nexus by dividing the world into four regions. It applies the gross domestic product in constant 2010$, uses population data extracted from the World Bank's Development Indicators[4], primary energy consumption in tonnes of oil equivalent extracted from the BP Statistical Review of World Energy,[5] and to measure globalization, the KOF index[6] used as a *proxy*.

The data are comprised of annual observations from 1971 to 2014. The use of homogenous variables is required to meet the goals of applying the same methodology to different regions. Unfortunately, the extracted data are not directly comparable. The GDP was extracted for America, Europe and Central Asia, Asia Pacific, and Africa and Middle East and primary energy consumption was extracted for North America, South and Central America, Europe and Eurasia, Middle East, Africa, and Asia Pacific. As a consequence, the data have been regrouped to make the variables compatible. At this point, a new restriction arises because the full composition of the primary energy consumption aggregates is not fully known. Reorganizing the data into the four aggregates previously cited (America; Europe and Central Asia; Asia Pacific; and Africa and the Middle East) gave us a high level of confidence on its comparability. Additionally, China's GDP and primary energy consumption were extracted.

With regard to the KOF index of globalization, the variable is provided year by year for 147 countries (see Table 4.1). However, a world index is not available. For this reason, two world globalization proxies were developed. In order to perform the analysis, the EViews 10[+] software was used.

The first proxy (G_1) is the average KOF index of 146 countries:

$$G_1 = \frac{\sum_{i=1}^{n} KOF_i}{n},$$ (4.1)

---

[4] Available at: http://databank.worldbank.org/data/source/world-development-indicators.
[5] Available at: https://www.bp.com/content/dam/bp/en/corporate/excel/energy-economics/statistical-review-2017/bp-statistical-review-of-world-energy-2017-underpinning-data.xlsx.
[6] Available at: http://globalization.kof.ethz.ch/.

Table 4.1 List of countries with an available Konjunkturforschungsstelle index between 1971 and 2014.

Afghanistan	Dominica	Lebanon	Puerto Rico
Albania	Dominican Republic	Lesotho	Qatar
Algeria	Ecuador	Liberia	Romania
Argentina	Egypt, Arab Rep.	Libya	Rwanda
Aruba	El Salvador	Luxembourg	Samoa
Australia	Equatorial Guinea	Macao, China	Saudi Arabia
Austria	Ethiopia	Madagascar	Senegal
Azerbaijan	Faeroe Islands	Malawi	Serbia
Bahrain	Fiji	Malaysia	Seychelles
Bangladesh	Finland	Maldives	Sierra Leone
Barbados	France	Mali	Singapore
Belgium	French Polynesia	Malta	South Africa
Benin	Gabon	Mauritania	Spain
Bermuda	Gambia, The	Mauritius	Sudan
Bhutan	Germany	Mexico	Swaziland
Bolivia	Ghana	Moldova	Sweden
Botswana	Greece	Mongolia	Switzerland
Brazil	Guatemala	Montenegro	Syrian Arab Republic
Bulgaria	Guinea	Morocco	Tanzania
Burkina Faso	Guyana	Myanmar	Thailand
Burundi	Haiti	Nepal	Togo
Cambodia	Honduras	Netherlands	Tonga
Cameroon	Hungary	New Caledonia	Trinidad and Tobago
Canada	Iceland	New Zealand	Tunisia
Cayman Islands	India	Nicaragua	Turkey
Central African Republic	Indonesia	Niger	Uganda
Chad	Iraq	Nigeria	United Arab Emirates
Chile	Ireland	Norway	United Kingdom
China	Israel	Oman	United States
Colombia	Italy	Pakistan	Uruguay
Congo, Dem. Rep.	Jamaica	Palau	Venezuela, RB
Congo, Rep.	Japan	Panama	Vietnam
Costa Rica	Jordan	Paraguay	West Bank and Gaza
Cote d'Ivoire	Kenya	Peru	Yemen, Rep.
Cuba	Korea, Rep.	Philippines	Zambia
Cyprus	Kuwait	Poland	
Denmark	Lao PDR	Portugal	

where n represents the number of countries. The second proxy (G_2) considers the weight of each country by contemplate their population, as follows:

$$G_2 = \sum_{i=1}^{n} \left(KOF_i \times \left(POP_i \Big/ \sum_{i=1}^{n} POP_i \right) \right), \qquad (4.2)$$

where n represents the number of countries and POP is the variable population. By testing the impacts of G_1 and G_2 in the models, it is expected to observe which one is the most reliable world globalization proxy. Before the model's development, the variables are evaluated. Summary statistics, including Skewness, Kurtosis, and Jarque—Bera, are provided for all variables (Table 4.2).

How to do:

summary statistics

    group a ly le lyc lec g₁ g₂

     a.stats(i)

How it looks like:

	LY	LE	LYCHN	LECHN	G_1	G_2
Mean	30.25149	21.74048	27.86425	20.53304	46.35595	0.286685
Median	30.24345	21.73563	27.83443	20.49839	44.51479	0.281805
Maximum	30.80596	21.98324	29.78180	21.82111	58.91603	0.381175
Minimum	29.57050	21.42224	26.13780	19.31233	34.94336	0.195116
Std. Dev.	0.371582	0.175592	1.141075	0.745082	8.130638	0.068432
Skewness	− 0.135990	− 0.099472	0.082657	0.218346	0.220423	0.117617
Kurtosis	1.765710	1.521228	1.745169	1.958407	1.497423	1.350277
Jarque—Bera	2.928650	4.081634	2.936869	2.338631	4.495487	5.091020
Probability	0.231234	0.129923	0.230286	0.310579	0.105637	0.078433
Sum	1331.066	956.5811	1226.027	903.4535	2039.662	12.61412
Sum Sq. Dev.	5.937139	1.325805	55.98823	23.87134	2842.612	0.201368
Observations	44	44	44	44	44	44

Source: Eviews

Table 4.2 Summary statistics.

Statistic	America		Europe and Central Asia		Asia Pacific		Africa and the Middle East		China		World	
	LY	LE	LY	LE	LY	LE	LY	LE	LYCHN	LECHN	G_1	G_2
Mean	30.251	21.740	30.322	21.768	29.602	20.886	28.408	20.024	27.864	20.533	46.356	0.287
Median	30.243	21.736	30.326	21.772	29.688	20.924	28.321	20.086	27.834	20.498	44.515	0.282
Max	30.806	21.983	30.722	21.890	30.286	21.582	29.186	20.961	29.782	21.821	58.916	0.381
Min	29.571	21.422	29.801	21.505	28.739	20.084	27.671	18.799	26.138	19.312	34.943	0.195
Std. Dev.	0.372	0.176	0.271	0.084	0.460	0.467	0.408	0.625	1.141	0.745	8.131	0.068
Skewness	−0.136	−0.099	−0.136	−1.203	−0.296	−0.103	0.401	−0.336	0.083	0.218	0.220	0.118
Kurtosis	1.766	1.521	1.881	4.642	1.836	1.629	2.096	2.066	1.745	1.958	1.497	1.350
J-B	2.929	4.082	2.431	15.550	3.129	3.525	2.678	2.429	2.937	2.339	4.495	5.091
Prob.	0.231	0.130	0.297	0.000	0.209	0.172	0.262	0.297	0.230	0.311	0.106	0.08
Obs.	44	44	44	44	44	44	44	44	44	44	44	44

Notes: Max. means maximum; Min. means minimum; Std. Dev. means standard deviation; J-B means Jarque–Bera; Prob. means probability; and Obs. means observations.

To define the best approach for the study on the dynamics between energy consumption and economic growth and China's economic growth and energy consumption, the variable's order of integration was analyzed. First of all, the graphical analysis of the level variables and their first differences was conducted (see Fig. 4.2). Second, the integration order of the variables allows to select the optimal approach and it is accessed by: (1) Augmented Dickey—Fuller (ADF); (2) Phillips—Perron (PP); and (3) Kwiatkowski—Phillips—Schmidt—Shin (KPSS). These unit root tests have been used throughout the literature (e.g., Fuinhas & Marques, 2013; Saidi, Rahman, & Amamri, 2017; Shahbaz, Loganathan, Sbia, & Afza, 2015). Additionally, a modified Dickey—Fuller (MDF) unit root test is performed. The MDF test follows Perron (1989) and allows to test for unit root in presence of a single break date. The model follows the general null hypothesis:

$$y_t = y_{t-1} + \beta t + \zeta(L)(\theta D_t(T_b) + \gamma + DU_t(T_b) + \varepsilon_t), \qquad (4.3)$$

where $D_t(T_b)$ is the one time break dummy variable, $DU_t(T_b)$ is the intercept break variable, β and θ are trend and break parameters, respectively, ε_t are the independent and identically distributed innovations, and $\zeta(L)$ is a lag polynomial representing the dynamics of stationary and invertible Autoregressive Moving Average Model (ARMA) error process. The alternative hypothesis which assumes a trend stationary model with breaks in intercept and trend is specified as follows:

$$y_t = \mu + \beta t + \zeta(L)(\theta DU_t(T_b) + \gamma DT_t(T_b) + \varepsilon_t), \qquad (4.4)$$

where $DT_t(T_b)$ represents a trend break variable. Taking the hypothesis into consideration, the general test equation is specified as follows:

$$y_t = \mu + \beta t + \theta DU_t(T_b) + \gamma DT_t(T_b) + \omega D_t(T_b) + \alpha y_{t-1}$$
$$+ \sum_{i=1}^{k} c_i \Delta y_{t-1} + \varepsilon_t \qquad (4.5)$$

From this framework four specifications should be considered: (1) non-trending data with intercept break; (2) trending data with intercept break; (3) trending data with intercept and trend breaks; and (4) trending data with trend break. To evaluate the null hypothesis, the t-statistic is used.

The graphical examinations of the variables are consistent with I(1) variables with structural breaks and even some outliers in all variables. Namely near 1980, 1990, and 2008 where the possibility of structural breaks is evident. These periods are consistent with some well-known

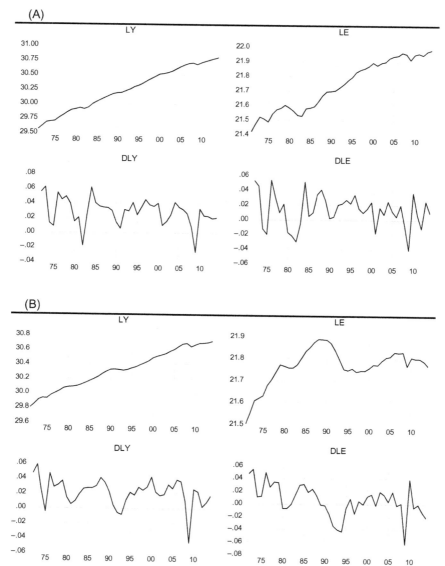

Figure 4.2 Variables in level and in its first differences. (A) America, (B) Europe and Central Asia, (C) Asia Pacific, (D) Africa and the Middle East, (E) China, and (F) World Globalization.

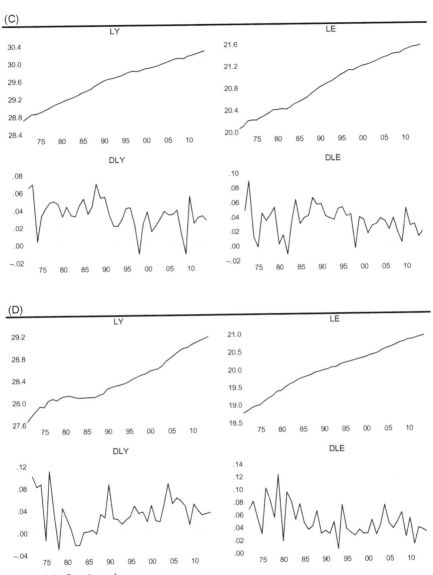

Figure 4.2 Continued.

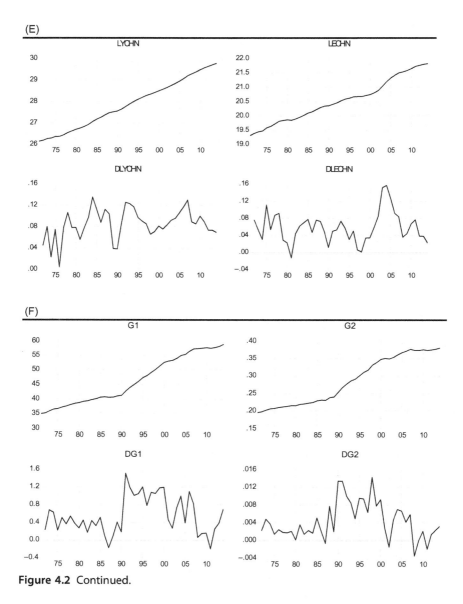

Figure 4.2 Continued.

historical periods of shocks, such as the 1980 oil glut, the 1990 oil price shock, and the 2008 great recession. The ADF, PP, and KPSS tests provide additional information on variable's order of integration. Further, the MDF test is performed providing some information on the presence of structural breaks (Table 4.3).

Table 4.3 Augmented Dickey–Fuller, Phillips–Perron, and Kwiatkowski–Phillips–Schmidt–Shin unit root tests.

Regions/variables		Augmented Dickey–Fuller (ADF)			Phillips–Perron (PP)			Kwiatkowski–Phillips–Schmidt–Shin (KPSS)	
		(a)	(b)	(c)	(a)	(b)	(c)	(a)	(b)
America	LY	−2.291	−2.125	10.428	−2.067	−2.755**	9.417	0.193**	0.892***
	LE	−1.892	−1.290	3.826	−2.074	−1.263	3.591	0.155**	0.843***
	DLY	−4.984***	−4.842***	−2.411**	−5.003***	−4.691***	−2.246**	0.097	0.397*
	DLE	−5.683***	−5.754***	−4.773***	−5.683***	−5.750***	−4.760***	0.099	0.343
Europe and Central Asia	LY	−2.935	−1.308	3.412	−2.609	−1.948	6.790	0.097	0.839***
	LE	−1.987	−2.316	1.616	−2.677	−3.635***	1.078	0.157**	0.340
	DLY	−4.790***	−4.690***	−2.852***	−4.691***	−4.609***	−2.653***	0.059	0.346
	DLE	−4.681***	−4.183***	−4.187***	−4.691***	−4.177***	−4.164***	0.122*	0.433*
Asia Pacific	LY	−1.259	−3.139**	13.085	−1.289	−3.275*	10.819	0.210**	0.837***
	LE	−0.884	−1.506	4.391	−1.069	−1.506	10.190	0.130*	0.841***
	DLY	−5.549***	−5.022***	−0.795	−5.502***	−5.001***	−1.885*	0.072**	0.661**
	DLE	−5.391***	−5.281***	−2.196**	−5.385***	−5.281***	−2.019**	0.114*	0.293
Africa and Middle East	LY	−0.933	−0.640	3.663	−1.481	−0.088	5.221	0.176**	0.826***
	LE	−2.051	−3.816***	1.346	−2.089	−3.994***	8.454	0.189**	0.834***
	DLY	−5.285***	−5.255***	−2.343**	−5.283***	−5.298***	−3.253***	0.122*	0.139
	DLE	−7.947***	−6.119***	−1.119	−7.774***	−6.530***	−1.930*	0.136*	0.538**
China	LYCHN	−3.408*	0.690	3.201	−3.388*	1.474	16.366	0.147*	0.840***
	LECHN	−2.630	−0.109	2.531	−1.773	0.111	7.283	0.137*	0.833***
	DLYCHN	−3.310*	−3.230**	−0.507	−4.056**	−4.067***	−0.678	0.121*	0.290
	DLECHN	−3.096**	−3.131**	−1.733*	−3.138	−3.170**	−1.733*	0.064	0.085
World	G_1	−1.790	−0.121	2.665	−3.345*	−3.382*	−1.715*	0.143*	0.820***
	G_2	−2.171	−0.407	2.358	−1.579	−0.228	3.886	0.120*	0.811***
	DG_1	−3.345*	−3.382**	−1.715*	−3.405*	−3.436**	−1.466	0.136*	0.167
	DG_2	−3.589**	−3.641***	−1.495	−3.665***	−3.716***	−2.111**	0.179**	0.183

Notes: (a) denotes the test statistic with trend and constant; (b) denotes the test statistic with constant; (c) denotes the test statistic without tendency and constant; and ***, **, and * denote statistical significance at 1%, 5%, and 10% level, respectively.

How to do:
single variable graphs
ly.line
dly.line
unit root tests
*** Augmented Dickey—Fuller***
ly.uroot(exog = trend)
ly.uroot
ly.uroot(exog = none)
ly.uroot(exog = trend, dif = 1)
ly.uroot(dif = 1)
ly.uroot(exog = none, dif = 1)
*** Phillips—Perron***
ly.uroot(exog = trend, pp)
ly.uroot(exog = trend, dif = 1, pp)
Kwiatkowski—Phillips—Schmidt—Shin
ly.uroot(exog = trend, kpss)
ly.uroot(exog = trend, dif = 1, kpss)
Breakpoint unit root test
ly.buroot
ly.buroot(exog = trend, break = both)
ly.buroot(exog = trend)
ly.buroot(exog = trend, break = trend)
ly.buroot(dif = 1)
ly.buroot(dif = 1, exog = trend, break = both)
ly.buroot(dif = 1, exog = trend)
ly.buroot(dif = 1, exog = trend, break = trend)

How it looks like:
single variable graphs

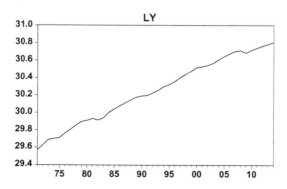

unit root tests

Null hypothesis: LY has a unit root
Exogenous: Constant
Lag length: 0 (Automatic—based on SIC, maxlag = 9)

		t-statistic	**Prob.**
Augmented Dickey—Fuller test statistic		− 2.125322	0.2361
Test critical values	1% level	− 3.592462	
	5% level	− 2.931404	
	10% level	− 2.603944	

*MacKinnon (1996) one-sided *P*-values.

Augmented Dickey—Fuller test equation
Dependent variable: D(LY)
Method: Least squares
Date: 04/26/18; Time: 14:37
Sample (adjusted): 1972 2014
Included observations: 43 after adjustments

Variable	Coefficient	Std. error	*t*-statistic	**Prob.**
LY(-1)	− 0.015422	0.007256	− 2.125322	0.0396
C	0.495063	0.219432	2.256106	0.0295
R-squared	0.099238	Mean dependent var		0.028732
Adjusted R-squared	0.077268	S.D. dependent var		0.017912
SE of regression	0.017206	Akaike info criterion		− 5.241744
Sum squared resid	0.012138	Schwarz criterion		− 5.159828
Log likelihood	114.6975	Hannan—Quinn criter.		− 5.211536
F-statistic	4.516995	Durbin—Watson stat		1.499393
Prob(*F*-statistic)	0.039632			

Source: Eviews

The ADF, PP, and KPSS tests raises doubts on some variables' integration order, such as Asia Pacific growth, Africa and Middle East energy consumption, and even the globalization proxy. Given that some variables may not be I(1) but only near I(1), the ARDL model is the best choice to handle with possible variables with different integration order (Table 4.4).

The MDF test confirms that all variables are at the most I(1), as expected. Additionally, it reveals that the 1980 energy crisis, together with

Table 4.4 Modified Dickey–Fuller unit root tests.

Regions		LY	LE	DLY	DLE
America	T-statistic	−4.940*	−3.111	−5.093***	−6.824***
	Specification	(1)	(3)	(2)	(1)
	Break	2003	1992	2007	1983
Europe and Central Asia	T-statistic	−4.124	−3.647	−5.862***	−5.569***
	Specification	(1)	(1)	(4)	(3)
	Break	2003	1991	2009	1999
Asia Pacific	T-statistic	−5.473**	−3.707	−6.449***	−6.902***
	Specification	(1)	(3)	(3)	(3)
	Break	1989	1987	2009	1982
Africa and Middle East	T-statistic	−5.313**	−4.585**	−7.170***	−9.942***
	Specification	(3)	(2)	(1)	(4)
	Break	1981	1984	1985	1985
		LYCHN	**LECHN**	**DLYCHN**	**DLECHN**
China	T-statistic	−6.514	−4.170	−5.134***	−6.553***
	Specification	(1)	(1)	(4)	(1)
	Break	1991	1996	1976	2002
		G_1	G_2	DG_1	DG_2
World—Globalization	T-statistic	−6.600***	−6.393***	−6.725***	−5.725***
	Specification	(4)	(4)	(3)	(3)
	Break	1990	1989	1990	1987

Notes: Trend specification/break Specification: (1) trend and intercept/trend and intercept; (2) trend and intercept/trend only; (3) trend and intercept/intercept only; (4) intercept only/intercept only; and *** and ** denote statistical significance at 1% and 5% level, respectively.

the 2008 financial crisis, had impacts in all globe regions. These results are in accordance with the MDF tests of previous chapter.

4.3 Methodology

As stated before, the ARDL methodology is applied to the analyses of both short-run and long-run globe energy–growth nexus. The use of the ARDL approach is far from new in energy–growth nexus literature (e.g., Farhani & Ozturk, 2015; Mirza & Kanwal, 2017; Shahbaz, Mallick, Mahalik, & Sadorsky, 2016). The ARDL methodology has the advantage to: (1) allow work upon all variables with an integration order lower than 2; (2) permit to obtain robust results by correcting outliers and structural breaks; and (3) allow the estimation of the long-run elasticities. The basic form of an ARDL regression could be represented as follows:

$$Y_t = \gamma_0 + \gamma_1 t + \sum_{i=1}^{k} \gamma_{2i} Y_{t-i} + \sum_{i=0}^{k} \gamma_{3i} X_{t-i} + \dots + \varepsilon_{4t}, \qquad (4.6)$$

where Y is the explained variable, X one of the explanatory variables, t is the trend variable, ε_{4t} is the error disturbance term, and k represents the number of lags. If the variables are cointegrated, the ARDL could be transformed into an unrestricted error correction model (UECM) in its equivalent ARDL bounds test:

$$\Delta Y_t = \delta_0 + \delta_1 t + \sum_{i=1}^{k} \delta_{2i} \Delta Y_{t-i} + \sum_{i=0}^{k} \delta_{3i} \Delta X_{t-i} + \dots + \delta_4 \Delta Y_{t-1}$$
$$+ \delta_5 \Delta X_{t-1} + \dots + \varepsilon_{5t}, \qquad (4.7)$$

By following the same steps, it is possible to develop a panel ARDL approach and its equation could be represented as follows:

$$\Delta Y_{it} = \alpha_{1i} + \delta_{1i} t + \sum_{j=1}^{k} \beta_{21ij} \Delta Y_{it-j} + \sum_{i=0}^{k} \beta_{22ij} \Delta X_{it-i} + \dots$$
$$+ \gamma_{21i} \Delta Y_{it-1} + \gamma_{22i} \Delta X_{it-1} + \dots + \varepsilon_{1it}, \qquad (4.8)$$

where Y is the explained variable, X one of the explanatory variables, t is the trend variable, ε_{1it} denotes the error term and k represents the number of lags.

To identify the structural breaks that need to be controlled, once more the four-method approach was followed: (1) visually inspection of the model's residuals; (2) inspection of the CUSUM and CUSUM of squares test. The validity of the time-series models is evaluated through a usually battery of diagnostic tests (e.g., Ahmed, 2017; Fuinhas & Marques, 2012; Shahbaz et al., 2016): (1) Jarque–Bera normality test; (2) Breusch–Godfrey serial correlation Lagrange Multiplier (LM) test; (3) Autoregressive conditional heteroskedasticity (ARCH) test for heteroskedasticity; (4) Ramsey Regression Equation Specification Error Test (RESET) test for model specification. The following table identifies all the estimated models (Table 4.5).

The models' results are shown through Section 4.4. Section 4.4.1 shows the North and South America results. The Europe and Central Asia results are presented in Section 4.4.2, while Section 4.4.3 brings up the Africa and the Middle East results. Finally, the Asia Pacific results are provided in Section 4.4.4.

Table 4.5 Estimated models.

Independent variables:

Dependent variables/regions	LY					LE				
	LE, LYCHN, LECHN	LE, G₁	LE,G₂	LE, LYCHN, LECHN, G₁	LE, LYCHN, LECHN, G₂	LY, LYCHN, LECHN	LY, G₁	LE, G₂	LY, LYCHN, LECHN, G₁	LY, LYCHN, LECHN, G₂
North and South America	(1)	(2)	(3)	(4)	(5)	(6)	(7)	(8)	(9)	(10)
Europe and Central Asia	(11)	(12)	(13)	(14)	(15)	(16)	(17)	(18)	(19)	(20)
Africa and the Middle East	(21)	(22)	(23)	(24)	(25)	(26)	(27)	(28)	(29)	(30)
Asia Pacific	(31)	(32)	(33)	(34)	(35)	(36)	(37)	(38)	(39)	(40)

4.4 Results

The ARDL approach is suitable because the variables are I(0) and I
(1). As stated before, the advantages of using the ARDL to handle variables with I(1) or near I(1) and structural breaks were extensively discussed
in previous chapters. Let YCHN mean China's economic growth,
ECHN mean China's energy consumption, and DLY and DLE mean the
economic growth and energy consumption, respectively, of the aggregates
to be studied. The new general UECM in its equivalent ARDL bounds
test are:

$$
DLY_t = \alpha_0 + \alpha_1 t + \sum_{i=1}^{k} \alpha_{2i} DLY_{t-i} + \sum_{i=0}^{k} \alpha_{3i} DLE_{t-i} + \sum_{i=1}^{k} \alpha_{4i} DLYCHN_{t-i}
$$
$$
+ \sum_{i=0}^{k} \alpha_{5i} DLECHN_{t-i} + \alpha_6 LY_{t-1} + \alpha_7 LE_{t-1} + \alpha_8 LYCHN_{t-1}
$$
$$
+ \alpha_9 LECHN_{t-1} + \mu_{10t},
$$

$$(4.9)$$

where, k represents the number of lags defined by empirical knowledge of
the variables and μ represents the disturbance terms assuming white noise
and normal distribution. The expected signs of parameters are $\alpha_0 \neq 0$,
$\alpha_1 \neq 0$, $\alpha_{2i} \neq 0$, $\alpha_{3i} \neq 0$, $\alpha_{4i} \neq 0$, $\alpha_{5i} \neq 0$, $\alpha_6 < 0$, $\alpha_7 > 0$, $\alpha_8 \neq 0$,
$\alpha_9 \neq 0$. The parameters α_{2i}, α_{3i}, α_{4i}, and α_{5i} explain the short-run
dynamic coefficients, while α_6, α_7, α_8, and α_9 explain the long-run multipliers. On one hand, a negative α_4 is expected because it would be consistent with the presence of cointegration. On the other hand, a positive
α_5 is expected, given that a negative coefficient would be consistent with
a globe *curse hypothesis* where energy consumption most likely drives to
less economic growth which is highly unlikely.

$$
DLE_t = \beta_0 + \beta_1 t + \sum_{i=1}^{k} \beta_{2i} DLE_{t-i} + \sum_{i=0}^{k} \beta_{3i} DLY_{t-i}
$$
$$
+ \sum_{i=0}^{k} \beta_{4i} DLYCHN_{t-i} + \sum_{i=0}^{k} \beta_{5i} DLECHN_{t-i} + \beta_6 LE_{t-1}
$$
$$
+ \beta_7 LY_{t-1} + \beta_8 LYCHN_{t-1} + \beta_9 LECHN_{t-1} + \mu_{10t},
$$

$$(4.10)$$

where the expected signs of parameters are $\beta_0 \neq 0$, $\beta_1 \neq 0$, $\beta_{2i} \neq 0$, $\beta_{3i} \neq 0$, $\beta_{4i} \neq 0$, $\beta_{5i} \neq 0$, $\beta_6 < 0$, $\beta_7 > 0$, $\beta_8 \neq 0$, and $\beta_9 \neq 0$. The parameters β_{2i}, β_{3i}, β_{4i}, and β_{5i} explain the short-run dynamic coefficients, while β_6, β_7, β_8, and β_9 explain the long-run multipliers. β_4 is expected to be negative revealing consistence with the presence of cointegration, and β_5 is expected to be positive because globe economic growth is a likely drive for the development of productive and nonproductive activities increasing the energy consumption.

How to do:

```
**Estimate models**
    equation a
    a.ardl(deplags = 1, reglags = 1, trend = uconst) ly le lychn lechn g1 @
sd_1987 sd_1983
    **Bounds test and elasticities**
    a.cointrep
```

How it looks like:

ARDL long run form and bounds test
Dependent variable: D(LY)
Selected model: ARDL(1, 1, 0, 0, 0)
Case 3: Unrestricted constant and no trend
Conditional error correction regression

Variable	Coefficient	Std. error	t-statistic	Prob.
C	− 3.011069	1.404046	− 2.144565	0.0392
LY(−1)[a]	− 0.140069	0.054964	− 2.548359	0.0155
LE(−1)	0.325250	0.078622	4.136882	0.0002
LYCHN[b]	0.001430	0.020185	0.070868	0.9439
LECHN[b]	0.011195	0.018360	0.609751	0.5461
G1[b]	− 0.001527	0.001759	− 0.868563	0.3912
D(LE)	0.743575	0.073309	10.14308	0.0000
SD_1987	− 0.033508	0.008523	− 3.931394	0.0004
SD_1983	0.025870	0.007499	3.449812	0.0015

[a]P-value incompatible with t-bounds distribution.
[b]Variable interpreted as $Z = Z(-1) + D(Z)$.

Levels equation
Case 3: Unrestricted constant and no trend

Variable	Coefficient	Std. error	t-statistic	Prob.
LE	2.322073	0.727600	3.191416	0.0030
LYCHN	0.010213	0.143026	0.071404	0.9435
LECHN	0.079926	0.124915	0.639847	0.5266
G	− 0.010905	0.013237	− 0.823838	0.4158

EC = LY − (2.3221*LE + 0.0102*LYC +
0.0799*LEC − 0.0109*G)

F-Bounds test		Null hypothesis: no levels relationship		
Test statistic	Value	Signif.	I(0)	I(1)
F-statistic	4.731274	10%	2.45	3.52
k	4	5%	2.86	4.01
		2.5%	3.25	4.49
		1%	3.74	5.06

t-Bounds test		Null hypothesis: no levels relationship		
Test statistic	Value	Signif.	I(0)	I(1)
t-statistic	− 2.548359	10%	− 2.57	− 3.66
		5%	− 2.86	− 3.99
		2.5%	− 3.13	− 4.26
		1%	− 3.43	− 4.6

Source: Eviews

4.4.1 North and South America

For the American aggregate, some structural breaks were expected. Some periods such as the 1980s oil crisis, the 1987 stock market crash or even the 2008 financial crisis may have had some impacts on the American energy—growth nexus. In fact, the MDF unit root test (see Table 4.4) shows the presence of possible structural breaks in the variables. For this reason, a first assessment on the model's structural breaks was made by examining the model's residuals (see Fig. 4.3) and CUSUM and CUSUM of squares tests (not shown to preserve space).

By looking into the residuals of the initial models, possible breaks can be observed. Confirming some of the MDF unit root tests results, the beginning and the end of the 1980s reveal possible structural breaks. Additionally, 2008 appears to be another structural break. By testing the statistical significance of different shift dummies and impulse dummies

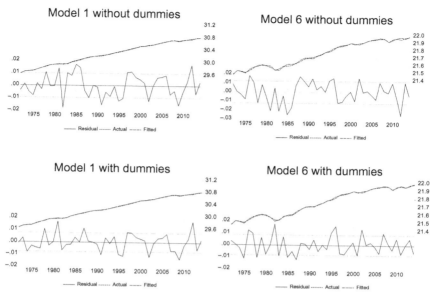

Figure 4.3 Examples of models' residuals correction with dummies.

around those years, it was observed that for the energy consumption models, two shift dummies from 1981 onwards and 1987 onwards and an impulse dummy in 2012 helped in the models' stability. Furthermore, by looking into the CUSUM and CUSUM of squares tests, no irregular behaviors were observed. The coefficients of the estimated models are presented in Table 4.6.

How to do:
Resids
 a.resids(g)
 CUSUM and CUSUM of squares
 a.rls(q) c(1) c(2) c(3) c(4) c(5) c(6) c(7) c(8) c(9)
 a.rls(v) c(1) c(2) c(3) c(4) c(5) c(6) c(7) c(8) c(9)
 Diagnostic Tests
 Jarque—Bera normality test
 a.hist
 Breusch—Godfrey serial correlation LM test
 a.auto
 ARCH test
 a.archtest
 Ramsey RESET test
 a.reset

Table 4.6 Autoregressive distributed lagmodels.

	(1)	(2)	(3)	(4)	(5)	(6)	(7)	(8)	(9)	(10)
Constant	−2.057**	−3.111**	−3.632***	−3.011**	−3.425**	3.695***	5.395***	5.509***	5.265**	6.122
Trend	—	—	—	—	—	—	—	—	—	—
DLY	0.718***	0.756***	—	—	—	0.949***	0.924***	0.924***	0.924***	0.928***
DLE	—	—	0.771***	0.744***	0.755***	—	—	—	—	−0.049
DLECHN	—	—	—	—	—	0.0114	—	—	0.0113	0.172**
LY(−1)	0.286***	0.287***	—	—	—	—	0.093**	0.113	—	—
LE(−1)	—	—	0.329***	0.325***	0.369***	—	—	—	—	0.008
LECHN(−1)	—	−0.001	−0.188	−0.002	−0.235	—	0.003**	—	0.003	—
G_1	—	—	—	—	—	—	—	0.347***	—	0.0505**
G_2	—	—	—	—	—	—	—	—	—	−0.017
LYCHN	−0.009	—	—	0.001	0.007	0.027	—	—	0.006	—
LECHN	0.016	—	—	0.011	0.005	−0.020	—	—	−0.010	—
ECM	—	—	—	—	—	−0.345***	−0.385***	−0.440***	−0.403***	−0.514***
Time dummies										
SD8714	−0.022***	−0.033***	−0.032***	−0.034***	−0.032***	0.030***	0.040***	0.035***	0.039***	—
SD8314	0.027***	−0.023***	0.024***	0.026***	0.027***	—	−0.021***	−0.024***	−0.024***	−0.027***
SD8114	—	—	—	—	—	−0.027***	−0.024***	−0.023***	−0.023***	−0.023**
ID2012	—	—	—	—	—	0.027***	—	—	—	—

Notes: ***, **, and * denote statistical significance at 1%, 5%, and 10% level, respectively.

How it looks like:

Resids

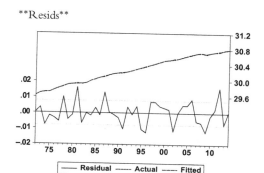

CUSUM   **CUSUM of squares**

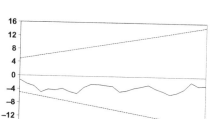
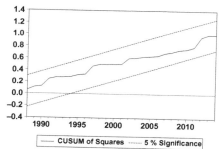

Diagnostic tests
Histogram and Jarque—Bera normality test

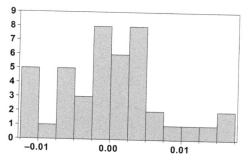

Breusch—Godfrey serial correlation LM test

Breusch—Godfrey serial correlation LM test:

F-statistic	0.338212	Prob. F(2,32)	0.7156
Obs*R-squared	0.890129	Prob. Chi-square(2)	0.6408

ARCH test

Heteroskedasticity test: ARCH

F-statistic	0.634724	Prob. F(1,40)	0.4303
Obs*R-squared	0.656050	Prob. Chi-Square(1)	0.4180

*** Ramsey RESET test***

Ramsey RESET test
Equation: A
Specification: LY LY(-1) LE LE(-1)
LYCHN LECHN G1 SD_1987 SD_1983 C
Omitted variables: squares of fitted values

	Value	df	Probability
t-statistic	0.606827	33	0.5481
F-statistic	0.368239	(1, 33)	0.5481

Source: Eviews

In general, the models revealed normally distributed errors, no serial correlation in the residuals, and no ARCH (see Table 4.7). By using the correlograms, the possibility of serial correlation in model 9 was analyzed in detail revealing no statistical significance. For this reason, serial correlation was not considered a problem. Further, the models' stability was confirmed by the Ramsey RESET test.

The results revealed that the early 1980s recession and the 1987 stock market crash permanently impacted on the American aggregate energy—growth nexus. Also, an outlier in 2012 needed to be controlled. The coefficients of China's energy consumption and economic growth on the American nexus revealed no statistical significance. Regarding globalization, impacts on energy consumption are observed at the statistical significance level of 5%. By looking into the G_1 and G_2 coefficients it is possible to observe that overall G2 has higher impacts that G_1 on energy consumption.

The ECMs are consistent with the presence of cointegration, given that the coefficients are negative and statistically significant. To confirm the presence of cointegration the ARDL bounds test was performed (see Table 4.8).

The bounds test revealed the presence of cointegration at the 5% statistical significance level for model 4 and the 5% level for the remaining models. The short-run impacts and long-run elasticities are presented in

Table 4.7 Diagnostic tests.

	(1)	(2)	(3)	(4)	(5)	(6)	(7)	(8)	(9)	(10)
ARS	0.999	0.999	0.999	0.999	0.999	0.998	0.998	0.998	0.998	0.998
SER	0.008	0.008	0.008	0.008	0.008	0.008	0.008	0.008	0.008	0.008
JB	0.686	0.584	0.479	0.663	0.455	1.988	0.751	1.105	0.775	1.821
LM	0.220	0.558	0.640	0.338	0.450	2.700[a]	2.451	1.617	2.615[a]	1.170
ARCH	0.712	0.416	0.351	0.635	0.544	0.377	0.154	0.306	0.275	0.184
RESET	1.012	0.014	0.126	0.368	0.175	0.135	0.915	0.709	0.621	0.892

Notes: Diagnostic tests results are based on *F*-statistic; ARS means adjusted R-squared; SER means standard error of regression; JB means Jarque−Bera normality test; LM means Breusch−Godfrey serial correlation LM test; ARCH means ARCH test; and Reset means Ramsey RESET test.
[a]Denotes statistical significance at 10% level.

Table 4.9. The short-run impacts correspond to the coefficient of the first differenced variable. The long-run elasticities are calculated by dividing the coefficient of the lagged independent variable by the coefficient of the lagged independent variable, multiplied by −1.

Both the short-run impacts and the long-run elasticities of energy consumption and economic growth revealed the existence of a bidirectional causality. However, it should be noted that the short-run impacts between economic growth and energy consumption had a statistical significance of 5% for model 8. Furthermore, the long-run elasticities between economic growth and energy consumption have a statistical significance at the 5% level for models 6 and 7 and a statistical significance at the 10% level for model 9. In the remaining variables, only the long-run elasticities between globalization and energy consumption reveals statistical significance at the 1% level for models 8 and 10, a 5% level for model 7, and a 10% level for model 9. Once more, it is possible to observe that G_2 has greater impacts on energy consumption than G_1. In Section 4.4.2, both short- and long-run analysis for the Europe and Central Asia case is performed. Those results will help to identify if G_2 globally has greater impacts than G_1 in the nexus.

Restrictions on energy consumption should be strongly discouraged, particularly in the case of America, which demonstrates a high elasticity. Furthermore, such impacts could persist for years, because a reduction in energy consumption will probably cause a deceleration in economic growth and thus lead to a further reduction in energy consumption, given that the results indicate the existence of endogeneity.

Table 4.8 Bounds test.

	(1)	(2)	(3)	(4)	(5)	(6)	(7)	(8)	(9)	(10)
K	3	2	2	4	4	3	2	2	4	4
F-statistic	5.766***	7.824***	8.429***	4.731**	21.974***	9.695***	14.888***	20.419***	8.540***	12.707***

Notes: For critical values, see Pesaran, Shin, and Smith (2001); *** and ** denote statistical significance at 1% and 5% level, respectively.

Table 4.9 Short-run impacts and long-run elasticities.

	(1)	(2)	(3)	(4)	(5)	(6)	(7)	(8)	(9)	(10)
Short-run										
DLY	—	—	—	—	—	0.949***	0.925***	0.913***	0.924***	0.928***
DLE	0.718***	0.756***	0.756***	0.756***	0.771***	0.771***	0.925***	0.913***	—	—
DLECHN	—	—	—	—	—	—	—	—	—	−0.049
Long-run										
LY	—	—	—	—	—	0.331**	0.242**	0.296***	0.279*	0.334***
LE	2.048***	2.850***	2.850***	2.886***	2.886***	2.886***	—	—	—	—
LYCHN	−0.066	—	—	—	—	0.078	—	—	0.015	−0.033
LECHN	0.117	—	—	—	—	−0.059	—	—	−0.026	0.016
G_1	—	−0.012	—	—	—	—	0.007**	—	0.007*	—
G_2	—	—	−0.012	−1.651	−1.651	−1.651	—	0.789***	—	0.983***

Notes: ***, **, and * denotes statistical significance at 1%, 5%, and 10% level, respectively.

4.4.2 Europe and Central Asia

Following the same steps of Section 4.4.1, the models were evaluated for the presence of structural breaks. The model's residuals and CUSUM and CUSUM of squares tests helped in confirm the presence of structural breaks. Structural breaks near the 1990 recession and the 2008 financial crisis have been identified. These are concordant results with the MDF test (see Table 4.7). Furthermore, the period from 1975 onwards revealed to have impacts on Europe and Central Asia economic growth. This is far from unexpected, given that this is a post-recession period, as well as a post-energy crisis period. The model coefficients are shown in Table 4.10.

The ECMs are consistent with the presence of cointegration for models 11−15, given that their coefficients are negative and statistically significant. For models 16, 18, and 19, the ECMs are statistically significant only at the 5% level which arises doubts about the existence of cointegration. Furthermore, the ECM in model 17 is consistent with no cointegration.

The models surpassed the relevant diagnostic tests revealing normally distributed errors, no serial correlation in the residuals, and no ARCH (see Table 4.11). The possibility of serial correlation in models 11 and 15, at the 10% level of significance, were analyzed in detail and the serial correlation was not considered a problem. The models' stability was confirmed by the Ramsey RESET test.

The bounds test (see Table 4.12) reveals the presence of cointegration in models 11−15 with a statistical significance level of 5%. In model 16, the F-statistic reveal statistical significance only at the 10% level. For this reason, it was not considered that there is cointegration. The results reveal consistency with the ECMs.

The short-run impacts and long-run elasticities are presented in Table 4.13. Both the short-run impacts and the long-run elasticities of energy consumption and economic growth revealed statistical significance at the 1% level. In the short-run, China's energy consumption has positive impacts on energy consumption. However, in the long-run it is observed that both China's energy consumption and economic growth positively impact on Europe and Central Asia economic growth.

Despite observing bidirectional causality between energy consumption and economic growth, it should be made clear that no cointegration has been proven for the models 16−20. With regard to globalization, long-run impacts on both energy consumption and economic growth were

Table 4.10 Autoregressive distributed lag models.

	(11)	(12)	(13)	(14)	(15)	(16)	(17)	(18)	(19)	(20)
Constant	2.883**	5.248***	8.607***	4.499***	5.901***	—	—	—	—	—
Trend	—	0.005***	0.005***	—	—	—	—	—	—	—
DLY	0.613**	—	—	—	—	0.807***	0.857***	0.876***	0.837***	0.844***
DLE	—	0.572***	—	0.583***	0.620***	—	—	—	—	—
DG_2	—	—	—	—	0.006	—	—	—	—	—
DLYCHN	−0.070	—	—	−0.105*	−0.115*	—	—	—	—	—
DLECHN	−0.060	—	—	−0.049	−0.0052	0.110**	—	—	0.126**	0.128**
$G_2(1)$	—	—	—	—	0.810**	—	—	—	—	—
LY(−1)	—	—	—	—	—	0.070**	0.083**	0.078**	0.097**	0.105***
LE(−1)	0.090**	0.182**	—	0.218**	0.330***	—	—	—	—	—
LYCHN(−1)	0.025	—	—	0.032*	0.029*	—	—	—	—	—
LECHN(−1)	0.055**	—	—	0.047**	0.063***	−0.007	—	—	0.002	−0.005
LE	—	—	0.360***	—	—	—	—	—	—	—
G_1	—	0.003	—	0.004	—	—	−0.002*	—	−0.002	—
G_2	—	—	1.346***	—	—	—	—	−0.232	—	−0.280
LYCHN	—	—	—	—	—	−0.009	—	—	−0.004	−0.0003
ECM	−0.218***	−0.310**	−0.557***	−0.970***	−0.507***	−0.080**	−0.112**	−0.105**	−0.128**	−0.138***

Time dummies

	(11)	(12)	(13)	(14)	(15)	(16)	(17)	(18)	(19)	(20)
SD0814	−0.040***	−0.018***	—	−0.034***	−0.028***	—	—	—	—	—
SD9114	—	—	—	—	—	—	—	—	−0.020***	0.015*
SD8914	—	—	—	—	—	−0.019***	−0.022***	−0.018**	—	—
SD7514	−0.015**	−0.024***	−0.025***	−0.019**	−0.020***	—	—	—	—	—
ID2010	—	—	—	—	—	0.035***	0.032***	0.032***	—	—
ID2009	—	—	−0.029***	—	—	—	—	—	—	—
ID1994	—	—	—	—	—	−0.029***	−0.029*	−0.029**	−0.030**	−0.030**

Notes: ***, **, and * denote statistical significance at 1%, 5%, and 10% level, respectively.

Table 4.11 Diagnostic tests.

	(11)	(12)	(13)	(14)	(15)	(16)	(17)	(18)	(19)	(20)
ARS	0.999	0.999	0.999	0.999	0.999	0.984	0.980	0.980	0.979	0.980
SER	0.008	0.009	0.008	0.008	0.007	0.009	0.010	0.010	0.011	0.011
JB	0.814	2.553	2.149	1.261	0.576	1.027	0.380	0.344	1.440	1.294
LM	3.223[a]	1.410	0.546	2.059	3.308[a]	1.711	0.119	0.133	2.115	2.376
ARCH	0.004	0.000	0.716	0.084	0.939	0.990	0.671	0.756	0.085	0.012
RESET	0.300	1.325	2.409	0.743	1.563	0.318	0.050	03842	1.296	1.314

Notes: Diagnostic tests results are based on F-statistic; ARS means adjusted R-squared; SER means standard error of regression; JB means Jarque−Bera normality test; LM means Breusch−Godfrey serial correlation LM test; ARCH means ARCH test; and Reset means Ramsey RESET test.
[a]Denotes statistical significance at 10% level.

observed. Moreover, it is possible to observe that G_2 has greater impacts than G_1 on all models, confirming the results of Section 4.4.1.

4.4.3 Asia Pacific

This section focuses on the study of the augmented energy−growth with globalization and China's energy consumption and economic growth. Once more the methodology of Section 4.3 was followed. The coefficients of the ARDL models are presented in Table 4.14. The period from 1980 onwards needed to be controlled by introducing a shift dummy. This effect is consistent with the negative impact of the 1975 energy crisis on Asia Pacific energy consumption. Moreover, the years 1974 and 2009 required the presence of impulse dummies to control for negative impacts on economic growth, as well as 1975, which required an impulse dummy to control for the impacts on energy consumption.

All the ECMs are consistent with the presence of cointegration. The models surpassed the diagnostic tests of normality, no serial correlation and no ARCH. Further, the Ramsey RESET test confirms the models' stability (Table 4.15).

The ARDL bounds test (see Table 4.16) is consistent with the presence of cointegration for all models. The models 22 and 26 are statistically significant at the 5% level, while the remaining are statistically significant at the 1% level.

The short-run semielasticities and long-run elasticities are presented in Table 4.17. Overall, the results are consistent with bidirectional causality between energy consumption and economic growth, both in the short- and long-run. Additionally, it is observed that globalization drives both energy-consumption and economic growth in the long-run. China's

Table 4.12 Bounds test.

	(11)	(12)	(13)	(14)	(15)	(16)	(17)	(18)	(19)	(20)
K	3	2	2	4	4	3	2	2	4	4
F-statistic	10.458***	5.823**	23.445***	9.126***	10.806***	3.129*	2.375	1.985	2.527	2.690

Notes: For critical values, see Pesaran et al. (2001); ***, **, and * denote statistical significance at 1%, 5%, and 10% level, respectively.

Table 4.13 Short-run impacts and long-run elasticities.

	(11)	(12)	(13)	(14)	(15)	(16)	(17)	(18)	(19)	(20)
Short-run										
DLY	—	—	—	—	—	0.807***	—	0.876***	0.837***	0.844***
DLE	0.613***	0.572***	0.647***	0.583***	0.620***	—	0.857***	—	—	—
DLYCHN	− 0.070	—	—	− 0.105*	− 0.115*	—	—	—	—	—
DLECHN	− 0.060	—	—	− 0.049	− 0.052	0.110**	—	—	0.126**	0.128**
DG_2	—	—	—	—	0.006	—	—	—	—	—
Long-run										
LY	—	—	—	—	—	0.881***	0.745***	0.739***	0.759***	0.763***
LE	0.413***	0.586***	0.647***	0.588***	0.650***	—	—	—	—	—
LYCHN	0.115*	—	—	0.086**	0.058*	− 0.112	—	—	− 0.033	− 0.002
LECHN	0.252**	—	—	0.126*	0.124***	− 0.093	—	—	0.018	− 0.039
G_1	—	0.010**	—	0.011**	—	—	− 0.017***	—	− 0.015	—
G_2	—	—	2.415***	—	1.599***	—	—	− 2.199***	—	− 2.028*

Notes: ***, **, and * denotes statistical significance at 1%, 5%, and 10% level, respectively.

Table 4.14 Autoregressive distributed lag models.

	(11)	(12)	(13)	(14)	(15)	(16)	(17)	(18)	(19)	(20)
Constant	2.487***	5.882***	5.692***	2.783***	2.799***	−2.998***	−6.655***	−4.323***	−8.607***	−7.983***
Trend	—	0.007***	0.007***	—	—	—	−0.007***	−0.003*	−0.013**	—
DLY	—	—	—	—	—	0.867***	0.877***	0.827***	0.915***	—
DLE	0.606***	0.611***	0.611***	0.602***	0.592***	—	—	—	—	—
DG_2	—	—	0.502	—	0.482	—	—	—	—	—
DLECHN	—	—	—	0.106**	0.116**	—	—	—	—	0.026
$LY(-1)$	—	—	—	—	—	0.324***	0.423***	0.399***	0.569***	—
$LE(-1)$	0.074	0.130	0.143	0.232	0.277**	—	—	—	—	—
$G_2(-1)$	—	—	−0.442*	−0.618**	—	—	—	—	—	—
$LECHN(-1)$	—	—	—	0.041**	0.027	—	—	—	—	−0.055
LY	—	—	—	−0.618**	—	—	—	—	—	0.687***
G_1	—	−0.004**	—	—	—	—	—	0.609**	—	—
G_2	—	—	—	—	—	0.077**	—	—	—	0.904***
LYCHN	−0.008	—	—	0.014	0.024	−0.092***	—	—	0.131***	—
LECHN	0.053**	—	—	—	—	—	—	—	−0.066**	0.175***
ECM	−0.165***	−0.290***	−0.294***	−0.293***	−0.326***	−0.327***	−0.283***	−0.362***	−0.506***	−0.770***

Time dummies

	(11)	(12)	(13)	(14)	(15)	(16)	(17)	(18)	(19)	(20)
SD8214	—	—	—	—	—	—	—	—	—	−0.062***
SD8114	—	—	—	—	—	−0.048***	—	—	−0.052***	—
SD8014	0.028***	0.025**	0.024**	0.033***	0.030***	—	−0.047***	−0.043***	—	—
ID1975	—	—	—	—	—	—	−0.027**	−0.027**	—	—
ID1974	—	—	—	−0.026**	−0.028***	—	—	—	—	—
ID2009	−0.029***	−0.024**	−0.023**	—	—	—	—	—	—	—

Notes: ***, **, and * denote statistical significance at 1%, 5%, and 10% level, respectively.

Table 4.15 Diagnostic tests.

	(21)	(22)	(23)	(24)	(25)	(26)	(27)	(28)	(29)	(30)
ARS	0.999	0.999	0.999	0.999	0.999	0.999	0.999	0.9999	0.999	0.999
SER	0.009	0.009	0.009	0.009	0.009	0.013	0.011	0.010	0.011	0.012
JB	1.137	0.837	2.286	0.740	1.340	3.432	3.760	2.831	2.264	1.647
LM	2.692[a]	1.353	0.983	2.478	2.013	0.123	0.866	1.219	1.732	1.079
ARCH	0.007	0.282	0.553	1.056	1.978	0.015	0.395	0.562	0.982	0.755
RESET	0.629	2.072	1.961	0.110	0.398	0.522	0.183	0.051	0.115	0.256

Notes: Diagnostic tests results are based on *F*-statistic; ARS means adjusted R-squared; SER means standard error of regression; JB means Jarque—Bera normality test; LM means Breusch—Godfrey serial correlation LM test; ARCH means ARCH test; and Reset means Ramsey RESET test.
[a]Denotes statistical significance at 10% level.

economic growth and energy consumption reveals to have long-run impacts on the Asia Pacific nexus, namely on the energy consumption side. It is interesting to note that on model 26 a positive impact of China's energy consumption on Asia Pacific energy consumption is observed. However, when globalization is added to the equation, the impact of China's energy consumption becomes negative.

The results appear to be consistent with a substitution effect between globalization and China's energy consumption given that the introduction of the G_1 and G_2 variables withdraw the LECHN statistical significance.

4.4.4 Africa and the Middle East

The last world region to be analyzed is Africa and the Middle East. This is probably the region with the greatest degree of political instability among the studied regions in this chapter. For this reason, the need to control for several historical periods was expected. Following the same approach of sections 4.4.1—4.4.3, the models revealed the need to introduce more shift and impulse dummies than previous models. The estimated ARDL models are presented in Table 4.18.

As stated above, there was the need to control for several historical periods, namely the impact of the 1970s energy crisis on energy consumption as well as the impact of the 1980s energy crisis, early 1990s recession, and the 2008 great recession on economic growth. Furthermore, a lot of impulse dummies were required to correct some year specific impacts. The ECM coefficients are consistent with the presence of cointegration for the models 31—38. It should be noted that the simultaneous introduction of globalization variables and China's energy consumption and economic growth apparently decreases the quality of the models.

Table 4.16 Bounds test.

	(21)	(22)	(23)	(24)	(25)	(26)	(27)	(28)	(29)	(30)
K	3	2	2	4	4	3	2	2	4	4
F-statistic	8.167***	5.598**	8.741***	7.569***	9.389***	5.259**	8.301***	9.504***	6.248***	15.899***

Notes: For critical values, see Pesaran et al. (2001); *** and ** denote statistical significance at 1% and 5% level, respectively.

Table 4.17 Short-run impacts and long-run elasticities.

	(21)	(22)	(23)	(24)	(25)	(26)	(27)	(28)	(29)	(30)
Short-run										
DLY	–	–	–	–	–	0.867***	0.877***	0.827***	–	–
DLE	0.606***	0.611***	0.611***	0.793***	0.592***	–	–	–	–	–
DLYCHN	–	–	–	–	–	–	–	–	–	–
DLECHN	–	–	–	0.139*	0.116**	–	–	–	–	0.026
DG_2	–	–	0.502	–	0.482	–	–	–	–	–
Long-run										
LY	–	–	–	–	–	0.992***	1.498****	1.103***	1.127***	0.893***
LE	0.446	0.610***	0.485*	0.793***	0.851***	–	–	–	–	–
LYCHN	– 0.049	–	–	0.049	0.073	0.237***	–	–	0.259***	0.227***
LECHN	0.320**	–	–	0.139*	0.082	– 0.282***	–	–	– 0.130**	– 0.072*
G_1	–	– 0.015***	–	– 0.015***	–	–	0.016***	–	0.014***	–
G_2	–	–	– 1.502***	–	– 1.897***	–	–	1.683***	–	1.362***

Notes: ***, **, and * denote statistical significance at 1%, 5%, and 10% level, respectively.

Table 4.18 Autoregressive distributed lag models.

	(21)	(22)	(23)	(24)	(25)	(26)	(27)	(28)	(29)	(30)
Constant	4.453***	11.195***	8.922***	6.751***	5.449***	—	—	—	—	—
Trend	—	0.022***	0.018***	—	—	—	—	—	—	—
DLY	—	—	—	—	—	0.278***	0.254***	0.288***	0.390***	0.412***
DLE	0.939	0.433**	0.447***	0.084	0.036	—	−0.007	—	—	—
DG^1	—	—	—	—	—	—	—	−1.010	—	−1.249
DG_2	—	—	1.691*	—	1.984***	—	—	—	—	0.364**
DLYCHN	−0.522***	—	—	−0.546***	−0.378***	0.259**	—	—	—	−0.123
DLECHN	—	—	—	—	—	—	—	—	—	0.057***
LY(−1)	—	—	—	—	—	0.055***	0.062***	0.053***	0.068***	—
LE(−1)	−0.097*	−0.201**	−0.155*	−0.147***	−0.176***	—	—	—	—	—
$G_1(-1)$	—	—	—	—	—	—	0.001*	—	0.002	0.045
$G_2(-1)$	—	—	−0.415	—	0.855***	—	—	0.061	—	0.007
LYCHN(−1)	0.065**	—	—	−0.050	−0.027	0.021	—	—	−0.010	−0.011
LECHN(−1)	—	—	—	—	—	—	—	—	−0.011	—
LY	—	—	—	0.007***	—	—	—	—	—	—
G_1	—	−0.004	—	—	—	—	—	—	−0.002	—
LYCHN	0.162***	—	—	0.256***	0.228***	−0.009	—	—	—	—
LECHN	—	—	—	—	—	—	—	—	−0.080	−0.082
ECM	−0.266***	−0.262***	−0.213***	−0.281***	−0.213***	−0.099***	−0.091***	−0.076***		

(Continued)

Table 4.18 (Continued)

	(21)	(22)	(23)	(24)	(25)	(26)	(27)	(28)	(29)	(30)
Time Dummies										
SD7614	—	—	—	—	—	0.051***	0.055***	0.054***	0.051***	0.054***
SD8114	−0.034*	−0.054**	−0.067***	—	—	—	—	—	—	—
SD9014	—	—	—	0.036***	—	—	—	—	—	—
SD0814	−0.030**	—	—	−0.049***	—	—	—	—	—	—
ID1974	—	—	0.037*	—	—	—	—	—	—	—
ID1975	—	—	—	−0.057***	−0.067***	—	—	—	—	—
ID1978	—	—	−0.056**	—	−0.058***	—	—	—	—	—
ID1979	—	—	—	—	—	0.034**	—	—	—	—
ID1980	—	—	—	—	—	—	—	—	—	—
ID1990	—	—	—	—	0.038***	−0.056***	−0.062***	−0.063	−0.068***	−0.069***
ID1993	—	—	—	—	—	−0.042***	—	—	−0.037**	−0.039**
ID1994	—	—	—	—	—	—	0.039**	0.033**	—	—
ID2009	—	—	—	—	−0.024**	—	—	—	—	—

Notes: ***, **, and * denote statistical significance at 1%, 5%, and 10% level, respectively.

Table 4.19 Diagnostic tests.

	(31)	(32)	(33)	(34)	(35)	(36)	(37)	(38)	(39)	(40)
ARS	0.998	0.997	0.998	0.999	0.999	0.999	0.999	0.999	0.999	0.999
SER	0.017	0.022	0.019	0.012	0.010	0.014	0.015	0.016	0.015	0.015
JB	1.415	0.322	0.707	0.275	1.192	1.920	0.451	0.678	0.760	0.756
LM	2.334	0.265	0.019	2.183	2.401	0.291	0.051	0.678	0.169	0.131
ARCH	0.945	0.010	0.052	0.084	0.053	1.215	0.399	0.523	0.589	0.006
RESET	0.146	1.938	2.434	0.000	0.663	0.278	0.460	0.093	0.004	0.428

Notes: Diagnostic tests results are based on *F*-statistic; ARS means adjusted R-squared; SER means standard error of regression; JB means Jarque—Bera normality test; LM means Breusch—Godfrey serial correlation LM test; ARCH means ARCH test; and Reset means Ramsey RESET test.

All the model's residuals revealed normality, no serial correlation and no ARCH (see Table 4.19). Likewise, the models surpassed the Ramsey RESET test revealing to be stable. To confirm the presence of cointegration, the ARDL bounds test was performed and is shown in Table 4.20.

The bounds test statistics are consistent with cointegration for all the models. The detailed analysis of both short- and long-run elasticities is presented in Table 4.21.

The short-run impacts are consistent with bidirectional causality between energy consumption and economic growth. With regard to the long-run, elasticities are consistent with the causality running from economic growth to energy consumption. Once more, the less restricted models appear to suffer a quality decrease in the estimations thus changing the coefficients statistical significance. Notwithstanding, China's energy consumption negatively causes economic growth in the long-run, while China's economic growth drives economic growth in the long-run. Globalization is not proven to impact on the Africa and the Middle East nexus.

4.5 Discussion on the results and policy implications

This chapter is of particular interest for several reasons. Indeed, it provides: (1) directly comparable outcomes for different regions; (2) information on globalization impacts and China's spillover effects on four world regions; (3) information on data aggregation for macro levels analysis; and (4) the results of two different approaches using KOF index of globalization to measure world globalization.

Table 4.20 Bounds test.

	(31)	(32)	(33)	(34)	(35)	(36)	(37)	(38)	(39)	(40)
K	3	2	2	4	4	3	2	2	4	4
F-statistic	20.487***	11.852***	11.422***	24.490***	45.669***	18.685***	30.150***	27.632***	12.147***	17.072***

Notes: For critical values, see Pesaran et al. (2001); *** denotes statistical significance at 1% level.

Table 4.21 Short-run impacts and long-run elasticities.

	(31)	(32)	(33)	(34)	(35)	(36)	(37)	(38)	(39)	(40)
Short-run										
DLY	—	—	—	—	—	0.278***	0.254***	0.288***	0.390***	0.412***
DLE	0.393***	0.433**	0.447***	0.084	0.036	—	—	—	—	—
DLYCHN	−0.522***	—	—	−0.546***	−0.378***	0.259**	—	—	0.361**	0.364**
DLECHN	—	—	—	—	—	—	—	—	−0.128	−0.123
DG_1	—	—	—	—	—	—	−0.007	—	−0.008	—
DG_2	—	—	1.691*	—	1.984***	—	—	−1.010	—	−1.249
Long-run										
LY	−0.365	—	—	—	—	0.554***	0.680***	0.695***	−0.418	0.699
LE	—	−0.765*	−0.727*	−0.522***	−0.826***	—	—	—	—	—
LYCHN	0.243**	—	—	−0.179	−0.128	0.209	—	—	−0.814***	0.089
LECHN	0.609***	—	—	0.913***	1.070***	−0.089	—	—	0.285	−0.138
G_1	—	−0.014	—	0.025***	—	—	0.014**	—	−0.003	—
G_2	—	—	−1.950	—	4.018***	—	—	0.804	—	0.556

Notes: ***, **, and * denotes statistical significance at 1%, 5%, and 10% level, respectively.

Using the ARDL approach with annual time series data from 1971 to 2014, the augmented energy—growth nexus with globalization and China's economic growth and energy consumption was analyzed in four world regions: America; Europe and Central Asia; Asia Pacific; and Africa and the Middle East. The methodology proved to be adequate given the presence of cointegration. Furthermore, by using the ARDL approach in four regions, the chapter proves that the use of different methodologies is not the main cause of the heterogeneous results in the literature. The use of two proxies for world globalization proved that the use of a population-weighted average version of KOF index provides improvements at the coefficient's statistical significance levels.

The heterogeneity of impacts in the four regions is evident, namely in the long-run. For instance, the results revealed how historical events had heterogeneous impacts on each region. The American and Asia Pacific aggregates revealed impacts of early the 1980s recession on nexus. In addition, the 1987 stock market crash impacted on the American aggregate nexus and the 1975 energy crisis on the Asia Pacific nexus. Regarding Europe and Central Asia, the 1990 recession as well as the 2008 financial crisis were revealed to have had permanent impacts on the nexus. Africa and the Middle East aggregate seems to be more susceptible to disturbance, given that the 1970s and 1980s energy crisis as well as the early 1990s recession and the 2008 great recession needed to be controlled for permanent impacts on the nexus. Furthermore, a lot of impulse dummies were required to control for specific years.

In the short-run, bidirectional causality between energy consumption and economic growth was generally found. However, heterogeneous results were found in the long-run (see Fig. 4.4). A long-run bidirectional causality between energy and growth was found for America and Asia Pacific. The presence of cointegration and statistically significant long-run elasticities revealed the robustness of the results. For Europe and Central Asia, and Africa and the Middle East, the direction of causality was found to be from economic growth to energy consumption. The Africa and the Middle East case seems to be consistent with the "curse hypothesis" where an increase in energy consumption tends to reduce economic growth. This is far from unexpected, given that these are poorly diversified economies and this behavior is recurrent in literature. For example, Fuinhas et al. (2015) who found the curse hypothesis for a panel of oil producers. Overall, the results are consistent with Marques, Fuinhas, and Marques (2017) who conclude for the feedback hypothesis for America

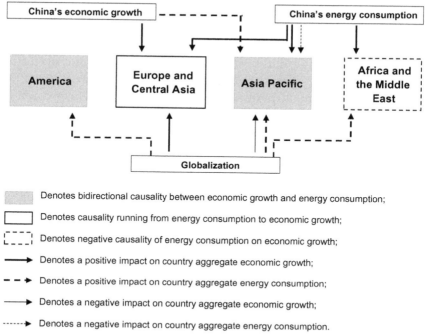

Figure 4.4 Summary of long-run behaviors (authors' elaboration).

and Asia Pacific and the growth hypothesis for Europe and Central Asia for a sample from 1968 to 2014. Furthermore, Marques et al. (2017) also asserts for the possibility of a negative impact of energy consumption on economic growth for Africa and The Middle East.

With regard to China's spillover effects, merely the American aggregate seems to be immune to any impacts. The impacts are essentially in the long-run, and results support that countries should not be indifferent to the policies that China may follow. In general China's spillover effects have positive impacts on the aggregates' nexus, except for the Asia Pacific case, where the results support a kind of substitution effect. Therefore when China's energy consumption grows, Asia Pacific energy consumption tends to reduce, most likely promoting a constriction on their economic growth. In short, a group of countries may have the power to create a globe recession, for example China's primary energy suppliers. By constricting China's energy consumption, the positive impact on Europe and Central Asia, Asia Pacific, and Africa and the Middle East may be reduced. China has energy import dependence, and if for some reason China's energy consumption and economic growth are restricted that will most likely impact at the globe nexus and consequently influence globe development. Creating internal reserves management policies may be part of the solution. Furthermore, China's policymakers should be aware that their decisions have globe impacts and every country should take into account China's impact on their own policies.

Globalization proved to have world impacts. Overall, globalization is also a long-run phenomenon promoting energy consumption which in its turn will indirectly promote economic growth in the American and Asia Pacific aggregates. However, the policymakers should be aware of the possibility that globalization may also lead to inefficient energy consumption. It should be noted that the results raise a controversial possibility that globalization drives energy consumption in Africa and the Middle East which in its turn can lead to a reduction in economic growth. In fact, this affirmation requires deeper research in future. The absence of short-term impacts should not be taken as an obstacle to take some globalization policies because the long-run result depends on the policies followed today.

Lastly, a concern regarding globe energy inefficiency arises. On one hand, restrictions on energy consumption should be strongly discouraged, particularly in the case of America, which demonstrates a high elasticity. Furthermore, such impacts could persist for years, because a reduction in energy consumption will probably cause a deceleration in economic growth and thus lead to a further reduction in energy consumption, given that the results indicate the existence of endogeneity. On the other hand, the bulk of results highlight the possibility of a growth in energy demand on nonproductive activities. Also, this could happen if globalization continues to expand. For those reasons, not only do the results suggest that reductions in energy consumption should be made by improving energy efficiency, but also that the efficiency of energy consumption should be a globe goal to prevent inefficient energy consumption caused by economic growth.

In short, by following this chapter, the researcher will be able to handle with the endogenous phenomena on the energy—growth nexus. The steps to correctly apply an autoregressive model (ARDL) with structural breaks were provided for EViews 10[+]. With regard to the overall results, the heterogeneous behaviors of the energy—growth nexus worldwide was proved, as well as the different impact responses of historical periods on each aggregated region. Furthermore, it was observed that globalization and China's energy consumption and economic growth have most likely the capacity to disturb the energy—growth nexus behaviors. Consequently, additional research on Asia Pacific is advisable where there is a possibility of China's negative impacts on energy consumption, which in its turn may lead to a hampering on economic growth, as well as negative impacts of globalization on economic growth.

References

Mackinnon, M. G. (1996). Numerical distribution functions for unit root and cointegration tests. *Journal of Applied Econometrics*, *11*(6), 601−618. Available from: https://doi.org/10.1002/(SICI)1099-1255(199611)11:6, <601::AID-JAE417>3.0.CO;2-T.

Fuinhas, J. A., Marques, A. C., & Couto, A. P. (2015). Oil rents and economic growth in oil producing countries: evidence from a macro panel. *Economic Change and Restructuring*, *48*(3), 257−279. Available from: https://doi.org/10.1007/s10644-015-9170-x.

Ahmed, K. (2017). Revisiting the role of financial development for energy-growth-trade nexus in BRICS economies. *Energy*, *128*, 487−495. Available from: https://doi.org/10.1016/j.energy.2017.04.055.

Ahmed, K., Bhattacharya, M., Qazi, A. Q., & Long, W. (2016). Energy consumption in China and underlying factors in a changing landscape: Empirical evidence since the reform period. *Renewable and Sustainable Energy Reviews*, *58*, 224−234. Available from: https://doi.org/10.1016/j.rser.2015.12.214.

Ahmed, M., & Azam, M. (2016). Causal nexus between energy consumption and economic growth for high, middle and low income countries using frequency domain analysis. *Renewable and Sustainable Energy Reviews*, *60*, 653−678. Available from: https://doi.org/10.1016/j.rser.2015.12.174.

Akarca, A. T., & Long, T. V. (1980). On the relationship between energy and GNP: A reexamination. *The Journal of Energy and Development*, *5*(2), 326−331.

Antweiler, W., Copeland, B. R., & Taylor, M. S. (2001). Is free trade good for the environment? *The American Economic Review*, *91*(4), 877−908.

Chang, C.-P., Lee, C.-C., & Hsieh, M.-C. (2015). Does globalization promote real output? Evidence from quantile cointegration regression. *Economic Modelling*, *44*, 25−36. Available from: https://doi.org/10.1016/j.econmod.2014.09.018.

Cole, M. A. (2006). Does trade liberalization increase national energy use? *Economics Letters*, *92*(1), 108−112. Available from: https://doi.org/10.1016/j.econlet.2006.01.018.

Doğan, B., & Deger, O. (2016). How globalization and economic growth affect energy consumption: Panel data analysis in the sample of Brazil, Russia, India, China countries. *International Journal of Energy Economics and Policy*, *6*(4), 806−813.

Farhani, S., & Ozturk, I. (2015). Causal relationship between CO_2 emissions, real GDP, energy consumption, financial development, trade openness, and urbanization in Tunisia. *Environmental Science and Pollution Research*, *22*(20), 15663−15676. Available from: https://doi.org/10.1007/s11356-015-4767-1.

Fuinhas, J. A., & Marques, A. C. (2012). Energy consumption and economic growth nexus in Portugal, Italy, Greece, Spain and Turkey: An ARDL bounds test approach (1965−2009). *Energy Economics*, *34*(2), 511−517. Available from: https://doi.org/10.1016/j.eneco.2011.10.003.

Fuinhas, J. A., & Marques, A. C. (2013). Rentierism, energy and economic growth: The case of Algeria and Egypt (1965−2010). *Energy Policy*, *62*, 1165−1171. Available from: https://doi.org/10.1016/j.enpol.2013.07.082.

Koesler, S., Swales, K., & Turner, K. (2016). International spillover and rebound effects from increased energy efficiency in Germany. *Energy Economics*, *54*, 444—452. Available from: https://doi.org/10.1016/j.eneco.2015.12.011.

Kraft, J., & Kraft, A. (1978). On the relationship between energy and GNP. *The Journal of Energy and Development*, *3*(2), 401—403.

Lee, C.-C., & Chang, C.-P. (2007). The impact of energy consumption on economic growth: Evidence from linear and nonlinear models in Taiwan. *Energy*, *32*(12), 2282—2294. Available from: https://doi.org/10.1016/j.energy.2006.01.017.

Marques, L. M., Fuinhas, J. A., & Marques, A. C. (2017). On the dynamics of energy-growth nexus: Evidence from a world divided into four regions. *International Journal of Energy Economics and Policy*, *7*(3), 208—215.

Mensi, W., Hammoudeh, S., Nguyen, D. K., & Kang, S. H. (2016). Global financial crisis and spillover effects among the U.S. and BRICS stock markets. *International Review of Economics & Finance*, *42*, 257—276. Available from: https://doi.org/10.1016/j.iref.2015.11.005.

Mirza, F. M., & Kanwal, A. (2017). Energy consumption, carbon emissions and economic growth in Pakistan: Dynamic causality analysis. *Renewable and Sustainable Energy Reviews*, *72*, 1233—1240. Available from: https://doi.org/10.1016/j.rser.2016.10.081.

Mohammadi, H., & Amin, M. D. (2015). Long-run relation and short-run dynamics in energy consumption—output relationship: International evidence from country panels with different growth rates. *Energy Economics*, *52*(Part A), 118—126. Available from: https://doi.org/10.1016/j.eneco.2015.09.012.

Omri, A., & Kahouli, B. (2014). Causal relationships between energy consumption, foreign direct investment and economic growth: Fresh evidence from dynamic simultaneous-equations models. *Energy Policy*, *67*, 913—922. Available from: https://doi.org/10.1016/j.enpol.2013.11.067.

Perron, P. (1989). The great crash, the oil price shock, and the unit root hypothesis. *Econometrica*, *57*(6), 1361—1401. Available from: https://doi.org/10.2307/1913712.

Pesaran, M. H., Shin, Y., & Smith, R. J. (2001). Bounds testing approaches to the analysis of level relationships. *Journal of Applied Econometrics*, *16*(3), 289—326. Available from: https://doi.org/10.1002/jae.616.

Saidi, K., Rahman, M. M., & Amamri, M. (2017). The causal nexus between economic growth and energy consumption: New evidence from global panel of 53 countries. *Sustainable Cities and Society*, *33*, 45—56. Available from: https://doi.org/10.1016/j.scs.2017.05.013.

Shahbaz, M., Loganathan, N., Sbia, R., & Afza, T. (2015). The effect of urbanization, affluence and trade openness on energy consumption: A time series analysis in Malaysia. *Renewable and Sustainable Energy Reviews*, *47*, 683—693. Available from: https://doi.org/10.1016/j.rser.2015.03.044.

Shahbaz, M., Mallick, H., Mahalik, M. K., & Sadorsky, P. (2016). The role of globalization on the recent evolution of energy demand in India: Implications for sustainable development. *Energy Economics*, *55*, 52—68. Available from: https://doi.org/10.1016/j.eneco.2016.01.013.

Wang, S., Li, Q., Fang, C., & Zhou, C. (2016). The relationship between economic growth, energy consumption, and CO_2 emissions: Empirical evidence from China. *Science of the Total Environment*, *542*, 360—371. Available from: https://doi.org/10.1016/j.scitotenv.2015.10.027.

Yu, E. S. H., & Jin, J. C. (1992). Cointegration tests of energy consumption, income, and employment. *Resources and Energy*, *14*(3), 259—266. Available from: https://doi.org/10.1016/0165-0572(92)90010-E.

Zhang, Y. (2017). Interregional carbon emission spillover—feedback effects in China. *Energy Policy*, *100*, 138—148. Available from: https://doi.org/10.1016/j.enpol.2016.10.012.

CHAPTER FIVE

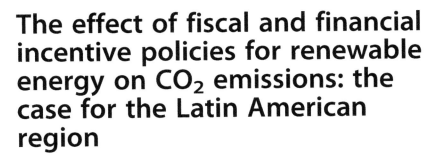

The effect of fiscal and financial incentive policies for renewable energy on CO$_2$ emissions: the case for the Latin American region

Matheus Koengkan[1], José Alberto Fuinhas[2,*] and António Cardoso Marques[3,*]

[1]CEFAGE-UE and Department of Economics, University of Évora, Portugal
[2]NECE-UBI, CeBER, and Faculty of Economics, University of Coimbra, Coimbra, Portugal
[3]NECE-UBI and Management and Economics Department, University of Beira Interior, Covilhã, Portugal

Contents

5.1 Introduction

The growth in the level of carbon dioxide emissions (CO$_2$) is one of the greatest concerns worldwide. Indeed, the consumption of fossil fuels was responsible for more than 40% of the emissions in the world in 2009 (Pérez de Arce, Sauma, & Contreras, 2016). In the Latin America

* This research was supported by NECE, R&D unit and funded by the FCT—Portuguese Foundation for the Development of Science and Technology, Ministry of Science, Technology and Higher Education, project UID/GES/04630/2019.

region CO_2 emissions have more than doubled during the last three decades and reached 451 million metric tonnes in 2008 (Boden, Marland, & Andres, 2011). Brazil accounted for 52.6% of the total of the 451 million metric tonnes of CO_2, Argentina, 52.4%, Venezuela 46.2%, Paraguay 15.6%, and Uruguay 8.5% emitted more than 10 million metric tons in 2008 (Boden et al., 2011). Despite this the region is a small contributor to the world's Global Greenhouse Gas (GHG) emissions, accounting for about 11% of GHG emissions in 2010 (Vergara, Rios, & Galindo, 2013).

To reverse this current scenario, several countries are committed to reducing CO_2 emissions to 20% (base year 1990) by 2020, 80% and 95% (base year 1990) by 2050 (Pérez de Arce et al., 2016). Certainly the integration of renewable energy into the energy mix has been essential to meet these goals. The fiscal/financial incentive policies for renewable energy have an important role in the development of alternative energy sources in the energy mix. In the Latin American countries the fiscal/financial incentive policies most often are feed-in tariffs/premiums, grants/subsidies, loans, tax relief, taxes, and user charges. Indeed, the feed-in tariffs/premiums are instruments that accelerate the investments in renewable energy technologies and energy producers. This policy is typically based on the cost of generation of each renewable energy technology (IRENA, 2017); grants/subsidies are a monetary assistance that help in reducing the initial investment in a renewable energy project to enhance it is viability and at the same time it is not required to be paid back (Thapar, Sharma, & Verma, 2016); loans are public funds based on loans designated for development and investments in alternative technologies (IRENA, 2017); tax relief is a mechanism that allows the reduction of tax outgoings on profits earned from renewable energy projects (Thapar et al., 2016); taxes are mechanisms that allow the reduction of taxes from goods imported to be used in the process of generation or production of renewable energy and conservation (IRENA, 2017); and user charges are instruments that establish the minimum purchase price of utilities that must be paid for by the renewable energy producer and by large-scale generators, and make it economically feasible for small firms, households, and farmers who have an interest in the generation of their own electricity in small scale (IRENA, 2017).

In the Latin American countries, the first fiscal/financial incentive policy appeared in Peru in 1992, with tax relief based on the Decree-Law 25844 of 1993, which defined a definitive concession for the development of renewable electricity generation (e.g., hydroelectric and other renewable resources) (IRENA, 2017). After that, feed-in tariffs began in Bolivia in 1994, where remuneration was provided for hydropower producers at subsidized price levels. At the same time in Costa Rica regulations exempted tax on renewable energy equipment purchases and provided several other tax exemptions (e.g., ad valorem tax, general sales tax, excise tax, and specific customs tax) (IRENA, 2017). From 1995 other countries in the Latin America region, such as Brazil, Colombia, and Ecuador created the same renewable energy fiscal/financial incentive policies.

These policies have encouraged a rapid growth due to the enormous abundance of renewable energy sources (RES) (e.g., hydropower, biomass, geothermal, wind, and solar) in most Latin American countries (Fuinhas, Marques, & Koengkan, 2017). This abundance stimulates the deployment of new renewable energy policies, technologies, and brings new investments. Moreover energy security concerns, high-energy prices, rapid energy demand, and the greater fossil fuels dependency in some Latin American countries are additional factors that drive the development of renewable energy fiscal/financial incentive policies in the region.

The central research question of this chapter is: What is the impact degree of fiscal/financial incentives policies for renewable energy on environmental degradation? The main aim of the chapter is to investigate the impact of fiscal/financial incentive policies for renewable energy on CO_2 emissions in the Latin American countries, as well as to share the realization of empirical investigations and allow the reapplication of it in other countries and situations. In the literature the impact of fiscal/financial incentives policies for renewable energy on environmental degradation has been little investigated, especially when addressing the Latin America region where there are very few investigations. So within these few studies some authors have been highlighted (e.g., Fuinhas et al., 2017; Jenner, Groba, & Indvik, 2013; Koengkan, 2017d; Koo, 2017; Oak, Lawson, & Champneys, 2014; Ortega, Del Rio, & Montero, 2013; Pereira Jr. et al., 2011; Pérez de Arce & Sauma, 2016; Pérez de Arce et al., 2016; Redondo & Collado, 2014; Romano, Scandurra, Carfora, & Fodor, 2017; Tabatabaei, Hadian, Marzban, & Zibaei, 2017; Thapar et al., 2016; Xin-gang, Yu-zhuo, Ling-zhi, Yi, & Zhi-gong, 2017; Butler & Neuhoff, 2008; Falconett & Nagasaka, 2010; Limpaitoon, Chen, & Oren, 2011; Menanteau, Finon, & Lamy, 2003; Rowlands, 2005).

So, although several authors have used different variables and methods to verify the impact of these policies on CO_2 emissions, what are the conclusions around the impact of fiscal/financial incentive policies for renewable energy on environmental degradation in the economic and ecological literature in the last few years? In the ecological and economic literature, there are two lines of thought or conclusion about the impact of fiscal/financial incentives policies for renewable energy on environmental degradation, where the first indicates that these policies reduce the environmental degradation, and the second does not cause any impact. For instance, Romano et al. (2017) investigated the effectiveness of renewable energy policies in developing countries, over the period of 2004–11. The standard Ordinary Least Squares (OLS) model was used as method. The authors found that the fiscal incentives have a positive effect on the increase of consumption and generation from renewable sources, and consequently decrease environmental degradation. This idea is accepted by several authors who reached the same conclusion (e.g., Falconett & Nagasaka, 2010; Fuinhas et al., 2017; Jenner et al., 2013; Koo, 2017; Menanteau et al., 2003; Oak et al., 2014; Ortega et al., 2013; Pérez de Arce & Sauma, 2016; Pérez de Arce et al., 2016; Rowlands, 2005; Tabatabaei et al., 2017; Xin-gang et al., 2017). Moreover Redondo and Collado (2014) who studied the economic valuation of renewable energy promoted by feed-in tariffs in Spain, in a period between 2010 and 2011, found that feed-in tariffs promoted renewable energy consumption, and reduced the dependency on fossil fuels and consequently environmental degradation. Butler and Neuhoff (2008) who compared the quota, auction mechanisms, and feed-in tariffs to support wind power development in the United Kingdom and Germany between 1990 and 2000, found that feed-in tariffs have the capacity to reduce the energy prices for wind energy, and create greater competition, consequently increasing the consumption of renewable energy, raising investments, and subsequently decreasing CO_2 emissions. The conclusions of Redondo and Collado (2014) and Butler and Neuhoff (2008) complement the ideas of Romano et al. (2017) and others.

On the other hand, there is a group of researchers who found that the fiscal/financial incentive policies do not cause any impact on environmental degradation. For instance, Koengkan (2017d) studied the impact of fiscal incentive policies on the installed capacity of renewable energy in the Latin America region over the period of 1980–2014 using the ARDL model. The author found that the fiscal incentive policies in the short run do not cause any impact on the installed capacity of renewable energy due to the possible inefficiency of these policies which discourage investments, and the consumption of renewable energy, and consequently the reduction of CO_2 emissions. Limpaitoon et al. (2011) complement that the carbon tax policy cannot necessarily reduce CO_2 emissions in the presence of strategic behavior of the market players. Moreover Pereira Jr. et al. (2011) used the Energy Compensation Factor (ECF) to analyze the best strategies to develop RES in Brazil's electric power generation system. The authors found that the fiscal incentives do not have any impact on the price of energy, and consequently on the consumption of renewable energy.

So, although the literature has been used in different countries and regions, with different variables and methodologies to explain the impact of fiscal and financial incentives policies for renewable energy on environmental degradation, there is no consensus about the results, by the reason of the existence of different conclusions and visions concerning this impact. So, based on the conclusions and visions of the authors in the literature review, this investigation has two hypotheses to answer the central question:

Hypothesis 1 (H1): The fiscal/financial incentive policies for renewable energy can reduce environmental degradation, where these policies stimulate investments and consumption of energy sources that are less polluting;

Hypothesis 2 (H2): The fiscal/financial incentive policies for renewable energy are not able to reduce environmental degradation due to the ineffectiveness of public policies that discourage investments, and the consumption of renewable energy.

Indeed studies that approach the impact of fiscal/financial incentive policies for renewable energy on CO_2 emissions have significant policy implications. Then, the analysis of impact of fiscal/financial incentive policies for renewable energy on environmental degradation help to develop policies more efficiently, enabling an increase in the investments in renewable energy, the consumption of this kind of source, and consequently a reduction of emissions. Finally it is considered that the empirical findings of this study will not only help to advance the existing literature, but also impact upon the policymakers in the development of new policies.

5.2 Data and model specification

The main goal of this chapter is to analyze the impact of fiscal/financial incentive policies for renewable energy on CO_2 emissions in the Latin American countries. The Latin American countries were chosen due to the rapid growth in the development of fiscal/financial incentive policies in the last two decades in this region. Additionally, the region has experienced a rapid growth in renewable energy investments and consumption, has been a pioneer in implementing the alternative sources into the energy matrix, and is an important player in innovation of RES (Fuinhas et al., 2017). The analysis of the impact of fiscal/financial incentive policies for renewable energy is a logical step for policymakers to verify whether the renewable energy policies are efficient in reducing environmental degradation, increasing investments, and the raising the consumption of renewable energy. Moreover the fiscal/financial incentive policies are the most important tools, where these policies exert a direct impact on investments and consumption of RES. So, to do a comprehensive analysis to understand the policies' impacts in the short run and long run, as well as for energy consumption, and economic growth in the emissions, the Autoregressive Distributed Lag (ARDL), in the form of Unrestricted Error Correction Model (UECM) will be applied.

The ARDL model is one of the cointegration approaches to test the existence of a long-run equilibrium within an economic system (Guan, Zhou, & Zhang, 2015). This model was first introduced by Charemza and Deadman (1992) and later improved by Pesaran, Shin, and Smith (2001). Moreover the choice to use the ARDL model is based on a flexible econometric approach that allows the decomposition of the total effects in the short- and long-run components. Indeed this model is able to study the dynamics of adjustment, controlling the impact of omitted variables, less collinearity among the independent variables, and increases the estimation efficiency, because it allows more degrees of freedom (Hsiao, 2014).

5.2.1 Data

A group of 12 Latin American countries were selected, namely: Argentina, Bolivia, Brazil, Chile, Colombia, Costa Rica, Ecuador, Mexico, Nicaragua, Paraguay, Peru, and Uruguay. The time span from 1980 to 2014 for all variables of the study was used. Then, concerning the first part of this investigation, Fig. 5.1 shows the evolution of fiscal/ financial incentive policies for renewable energy in the Latin American countries, over the period of 1980−2015.

As can be seen in Fig. 5.1, fiscal/financial incentives policies for renewable energy in the Latin American countries have more than doubled in the last two decades, confirming the necessity for study in this region and the need to identify the possible impacts on environmental degradation.

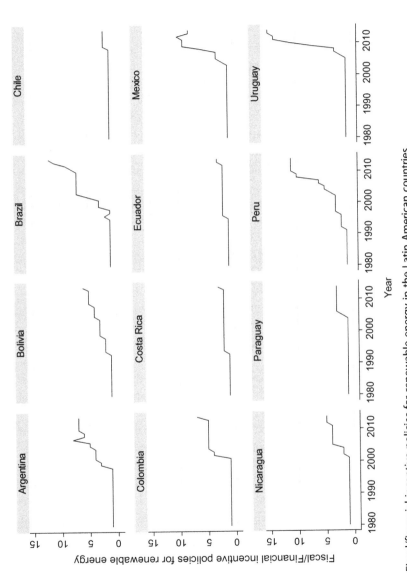

Figure 5.1 Fiscal/financial incentive policies for renewable energy in the Latin American countries.

How to do:
Panel-data line plots-Graph by
  xtline policies

The second part of this chapter is focused on the analysis of the effects of consumption of renewable energy, fossil, and economic growth on environmental degradation (CO_2 emissions). So, the variables used in this study are:

(1) Carbon dioxide emissions (CO_2) from burning fossil fuels (e.g., solid, liquid, gas fuels, and gas flaring) and the manufacture of cement (kilotons), available in World Bank Data (WDB)[1];

(2) Fiscal/Financial incentive policies (Policies), which includes the feed-in tariffs/premiums, grants, subsidies, loans, tax relief, taxes, and user charges. This variable was built in accumulated form, where each policy that was created is represented by (1) accumulated over other policies throughout its useful life or by end (e.g., 1, 1, 2, 2, 2, 3, 3), available in International Renewable Energy Agency (IRENA)[2];

(3) Gross domestic product (GDP) in constant local currency units (LCU), available from World Bank Data (WDB)[1];

(4) Renewable energy consumption (Renewable) in a Billion kilowatt-hour (kWh) from hydropower, solar, photovoltaic, wind, waste, biomass, and wave, available from the International Energy Administration (IEA)[3]; and

(5) Fossil fuels energy consumption (Fossil) in a Billion kilowatt-hour (kWh) from oil, gas, and coal, available from the International Energy Administration (IEA)[3].

Additionally, the variables CO_2 emissions, GDP, Renewable, and Fossil were transformed to *per capita* values. Indeed, the *per capita* values let us control the disparities in population growth over time and among the countries (e.g., Fuinhas et al., 2017; Koengkan, Losekann, & Fuinhas, 2018). The option for using constant GDP in LCU, instead of constant US dollars, attenuates the influence of both inflation and the changes in the exchange rates (Koengkan, 2018a). The GDP in constant (LCU) has

---

[1] See http://databank.worldbank.org/data/source/world-development-indicators
[2] See https://www.iea.org/policiesandmeasures/renewableenergy/
[3] See https://www.iea.org/statistics/?country = WORLD&year = 2015&category = Key%20indicators&indicator = TPESbySource&mode = chart&categoryBrowse = false&dataTable = BALANCES&showDataTable = false

Table 5.1 Descriptive statistics.

Variables	Descriptive statistics				
	Obs.	Mean	Std. Dev.	Min.	Max.
LCO2	420	− 6.4340	0.6155	− 7.9172	− 5.3462
LPolicies	420	0.5591	0.7510	0.0000	2.7080
LGDP	420	11.4679	2.9152	7.6628	16.1938
LRenewable	420	− 14.0829	1.0381	− 16.4111	− 11.4340
LFossil	420	− 0.6645	1.5955	− 3.6347	2.4928

Notes: Obs. denotes the number of observations; Std. Dev. denotes the standard deviation: Min. and Max. denote minimum and maximum, respectively; and L denotes variables in natural logarithms.

been used by several authors who have investigated the Latin America region (e.g., Fuinhas et al., 2017; Koengkan, 2017a, 2018b). In addition, the GDP in constant US dollars was tested previously, and this variable does not cause a significant impact. Table 5.1 shows the descriptive statistics of all variables in the study.

How to do:

Transformate the variables CO_2, GDP, Renewable, and Fossil in *per capita* values

    gen lco2 = (emissions/population)
    Transformate the variables CO_2, Policies, GDP, Renewable, and Fossil in logarithms

    gen lco2 = ln(co2)
    Descriptive statistics
    sum lco2 lpolicies lgdp lrenewable lfossil

5.2.2 Model specification

A panel ARDL in the form of UECM to decompose the total effects of explanatory variables into it is in the short- and long-run components was applied. Thus the ARDL model follows the following general equation:

$$LCO2_{it} = a_i + \sum_{j=i}^{k} \delta_{2it} LPolicies_{it-j} + \sum_{j=i}^{k} \delta_{3it} LGDP_{it-j}$$
$$+ \sum_{j=i}^{k} \delta_{4it} LRenewable_{it-j} + \sum_{j=i}^{k} \delta_{5it} LFossil_{it-j} + \sigma_{it} \tag{5.1}$$

where "L" denotes logarithms, α_i denotes intercept, $\delta_{2t}...\delta_{5it}, k = 1, ..., m$ are estimated parameters, as σ_{1it} is error term. Eq. (5.1) can be re-parameterized into the general UECM form, and Eq. (5.2) to decompose the dynamic relationships of variables in the short run and long run, as follows:

$$
\begin{aligned}
DLCO2_{it} = \; & a_i + \sum_{j=i}^{k} \gamma_{2it} DLPolicies_{it-j} + \sum_{j=i}^{k} \gamma_{3it} DLGDP_{it-j} \\
& + \sum_{j=i}^{k} \gamma_{4it} DLRenewable_{it-j} + \sum_{j=i}^{k} \gamma_{5it} DLFossil_{it-j} \quad (5.2) \\
& + \delta_{1it} LCO2_{it} + \delta_{2it} LPolicies_{it-j} + \delta_{3it} LGDP_{it-j} \\
& + \delta_{4it} LRenewable_{it-j} + \delta_{5it} LFossil_{it-j} + \sigma_{2it},
\end{aligned}
$$

where, (DLCO2 and LCO2) are the dependent variables in the first differences and logarithms, and (DLPolicies, DLGDP, DLRenewable, DLFossil, and LPolicies, LGDP, LRenewable, and LFossil) are independent variables, α_i denotes intercept, $\gamma_{2it}...\gamma_{5it}, \delta_{2it}...\delta_{5it}, k = 1,...,m$ are estimated parameters, as σ_{2it-1} is error term. Thus Eq. (5.2) is converted in Eq. (5.3) by changing σ_{2it-1} for $\omega_i + \varepsilon_{it}$:

$$
\begin{aligned}
DLCO2_{it} = \; & a_i + \sum_{j=i}^{k} \gamma_{2it} DLPolicies_{it-j} + \sum_{j=i}^{k} \gamma_{3it} DLGDP_{it-j} \\
& + \sum_{j=i}^{k} \gamma_{4it} DLRenewable_{it-j} + \sum_{j=i}^{k} \gamma_{5it} DLFossil_{it-j} \quad (5.3) \\
& + \delta_{1it} LCO2_{it} + \delta_{2it} LPolicies_{it-j} + \delta_{3it} LGDP_{it-j} \\
& + \delta_{4it} LRenewable_{it-j} + \delta_{5it} LFossil_{it-j} + \sigma_{2it},
\end{aligned}
$$

where, α_i denotes intercept, $\gamma_{2it}...\gamma_{5it}, \delta_{2it}...\delta_{5it}, k = 1,...,m$ are estimated parameters, as $\omega_i + \varepsilon_{it}$ is error term. Moreover before the realization of ARDL model, it is necessary to apply the preliminary test to check the characteristics of variables. Considering this, the following preliminary tests were applied:

(1) Variance inflation factor (VIF-test) that calculates the cantered or uncentered variance inflation factors in the linear regression model (Belsley, Kuh, & Welsch, 1980). This test verifies the presence of multicollinearity between the variables;

(2) Cross-section dependence (CSD test) to check for the existence of cross-section dependence. The null hypothesis of this test is the existence of cross-section dependence CD $\sim$ N (0,1) (Pesaran, 2004);

(3) First-generation unit root test that includes the LLC (Levin, Lin, & Chu, 2002) ADF–Fisher (Maddala & Wu, 1999), and ADF–Choi (Choi, 2001) to verify the presence of unit roots. The null hypothesis rejection of LLC is the presence of unit root (common unit root process), and in ADF–Fisher and ADF–Choi, the null hypothesis rejection is the presence of unit root (individual unit root process);

(4) Second-generation unit root test (Maddala & Wu, 1999) to check for the presence of unit roots. The null hypothesis rejection of that variable is I(1);

(5) Hausman test that determines whether the panel has Random Effects (RE) or Fixed Effects (FE). The null hypothesis of this test is that the best model is the RE;

(6) Second-generation cointegration test of Westerlund (2007) to verify the existence of cointegration in the results. The null hypothesis is the nonpresence of cointegration between the variables. Moreover the Westerlund cointegration test requires that all variables of the model be stationary, that is I(1) (Fuinhas et al., 2017); and

(7) Mean Group (MG) or Pooled Mean Group (PMG) estimators to verify the presence of heterogeneity of variables parameters in the short run and long run. Moreover the MG is an estimator that computes the average coefficients of all variables in regression (Fuinhas et al., 2017). This estimator is consistent, but in the presence of slope homogeneity, it is inefficient (Pesaran, Shin, & Smith, 1999). The PMG estimator in the presence of homogeneity of variables is more efficient than MG estimator. Moreover this estimator can make restriction among cross-section and adjustment speed term (Fuinhas et al., 2017).

So, after the preliminary tests, it is necessary to apply the specification tests with the purpose of verifying the characteristics of the ARDL model, as follows:

(1) Friedman's test to check the presence of cross-sectional dependence (Friedman, 1937). The null hypothesis rejection of this test is that the residuals are not correlated, and it follows a normal distribution;

(2) Breusch–Pagan Lagrange multiplier (LM) test to measure whether the variances across individuals are correlated (Breusch & Pagan, 1980);

(3) Wooldridge test (Wooldridge, 2002) to check the existence of serial correlation; and

(4) Modified Wald test (Greene, 2002) to check the existence of group-wise heteroscedasticity.

Section 5.3 will show the empirical results that include the results of preliminary and specification tests, estimation results of the ARDL model, impacts, elasticities, adjustment speed, and the impacts. Moreover in order to realize the econometric estimations, the EViews 9.5 and Stata 14.2 software were used.

5.3 Results

This section will show the results of preliminary tests, specification tests, estimationed results of the ARDL model, impacts, elasticities, adjustment speed, and the impacts. Considering this, Table 5.2 shows the results of VIF test and CSD test, to check the existence of multicollinearity, and the presence of cross-section dependence between the variables. Thus the null hypothesis of CSD test is the existence of cross-section dependence $CD \sim N(0,1)$.

The results of the VIF-test point to the existence of low multicollinearity between the variables in the study. So, the Mean VIF of variables in logarithms was 1.30% and in the first differences was 1.23%, both below the benchmark of 10%. Moreover with the intention of verifying

Table 5.2 Results of variance inflation factor test and cross-section dependence test.

Variance inflation factor (VIF-test)				Cross-section dependence (CSD test)			
Variables	VIF	1/VIF	Mean VIF	CD-test	P-value	Corr.	Abs. (corr)
LCO2	n.a.			24.27	.000 ***	0.505	0.541
LPolicies	1.10	0.6668		38.20	.000 ***	0.795	0.795
LGDP	1.46	0.6848		38.19	.000 ***	0.795	0.795
LRenewable	1.50	0.6668		24.15	.000 ***	0.503	0.517
LFossil	1.15	0.8720		44.19	.000 ***	0.919	0.919
			1.30				
DLCO2	n.a.			2.67	.008 ***	0.056	0.151
DLPolicies	1.00	0.9981		2.75	.006 ***	0.058	0.157
DLGDP	1.10	0.9076		17.17	.000 ***	0.362	0.362
DLRenewable	1.36	0.7364		− 0.06	.949	− 0.001	0.171
DLFossil	1.46	0.6826		5.36	.000 ***	0.113	0.192
			1.23				

Notes: L and D denote variables in natural logarithms, and the first differences; n.a. denotes "not available"; under the null hypothesis of cross-section independence, CD ∼ N(0,1); and *** denotes statistically significant at 1% levels.

the presence of cross-section dependence in the model, the CSD test was used. The results of CSD test points for nonrejection of the null hypothesis in all variables in the logarithms and the first differences, except to the variable "DLRenewable." The nonexistence of cross-section on consumption of renewable energy in the first differences is due to the shocks that affected the economic activity, and consequently the generation of renewable energy is largely country-specific and conditional on the intermittence that characterizes its generation (e.g., solar, wind, hydro, biomass, and wave) (Fuinhas et al., 2017). Then the presence of cross-section dependence in the variables means that the country of the study shares the same shocks and characteristics.

How to do:

Variance Inflation Factor:

reg lco2 lpolicies lgdp lrenewable lfossil
estat vif
reg dlco2 dlpolicies dlgdp dlrenewable dlfossil
estat vif
Cross-Section Dependence test
xtcd lco2 lpolicies lgdp lrenewable lfossil
xtcd dlco2 dlpolicies dlgdp dlrenewable dlfossil

Thus in the presence of cross-section dependence in the model, it is necessary to verify the stationary of variables with the aim of show whether the variables are I(1) or I(0), that is stationary or nonstationary. Then the first-generation unit root test that includes the LLC (Levin et al., 2002), ADF-Fisher (Maddala & Wu, 1999), and ADF-Choi (Choi, 2001) to verify the presence of unit roots. The null hypothesis rejection of LLC is the presence of unit root (common unit root process), and in ADF-Fisher and ADF-Choi, the null hypothesis rejection is the presence of unit root (individual unit root process). Moreover the second-generation unit root test (Maddala & Wu, 1999), to check the presence of unit roots. The null hypothesis rejection is that the variable is I(1). So, both tests were applied; Table 5.3 shows the outcomes of unit root test of the first generation and second generation.

The LLC, ADF-Fisher, and ADF-Choi tests with lag length (1), and individual intercept and trend were used. The results of the first-generation unit root test indicate that the variables LCO2 and LPolicies in

Table 5.3 Unit roots tests.

	First-generation unit root tests			Second-generation unit root tests	
	LLC	ADF-Fisher	ADF-Choi	Maddala and Wu (Chi_sq)	
	Individual intercept and trend			Without trend	With trend
LCO2	− 0.6640	30.3178	− 1.2148	12.411	32.276
LPolicies	− 0.0578	15.2881	0.8667	1.776	14.876
LGDP	− 3.5563 ***	61.4263 ***	− 2.4129 ***	2.071	77.746 ***
LRenewable	− 3.8550 ***	60.6989 ***	− 4.1460 ***	64.074 ***	70.606 ***
LFossil	− 1.8592 **	39.8693 **	− 2.3261 **	10.034	36.029 **
DLCO2	− 7.4484 ***	151.585 ***	− 9.4804 ***	244.448 ***	199.179 ***
DLPolicies	− 8.4512 ***	108.948 ***	− 7.6551 ***	170.414 ***	132.188 ***
DLGDP	− 6.2209 ***	103.157 ***	− 7.0754 ***	158.921 ***	213.833 ***
DLRenewable	−10.4965 ***	157.249 ***	−10.0711 ***	260.450 ***	171.085 ***
DLFossil	− 5.02570 ***	128.117 ***	− 8.1537 ***	214.158 ***	138.328 ***

Notes: L and D denote variables in natural logarithms and the first differences; the LLC has H_0: unit root (common unit root process), the test controls for individuals' effects, individual linear trends, has a lag length 1, and Newey–West automatic bandwidth selection and Bartlett kernel were used; the ADF–FISHER and ADF–Choi test has H_0: unit root (individual unit root process), the test controls for individual effects, individual linear trends, has a lag length 1; the Maddala and Wu test has H_0: series are I(1); and *** and ** denote statistically significant at 1% and 5% level, respectively.

the logarithms are I(0), and the variables LGDP, LRenewable, LFossil and all variables in the first differences are I(1). Moreover the Maddala and Wu test with lag length (1) without trend and with the trend was used. The results of this test indicate that the variables LCO2, LPolices, and LGDP without in levels are I(0), while the variables LGDP with trend, LRenewable without trend and trend, and LFossil with trend in levels are I(1), and all variables in the first differences are I(1). Then, the realization of unit root test is important because it is necessary to verify whether the panel's data is heterogeneous.

How to do:

1st generation unit root tests

  LLC (Levin et al., 2002)

  lco2.uroot(exog = trend, llc)

  lco2.uroot(exog = trend, dif = 1, llc)

  ADF-Fisher (Maddala & Wu, 1999) and ADF-Choi (Choi, 2001)

  lco2.uroot(exog = trend, adf)

  lco2.uroot(exog = trend, dif = 1, adf)

  2nd Generation unit root tests

  multipurt lco2 lpolicies lgdp lrenewable lfossil, lags(1)

  multipurt dlco2 dlpolicies dlgdp dlrenewable dlfossil, lags(1)

After, the realization of the unit root test, it is necessary to identify the presence of Random Effects (RE) or FE in the model. Thus the Hausman test of the RE against the FE specification was used. This test has as null hypothesis that the best model is the RE. The result of this test is statistically significant ($\chi_9^2 = 90.09^{***}$) at the 1% significance level, allowing us to reject the null hypothesis, and select the FE model. This model enables us to analyze the influences of variables or time, as well as removing all time-invariant features from the independent variables in the model (Fuinhas et al., 2017).

How to do:

Hausman test

  xtreg dlco2 dlpolicies dlgdp dlrenewable dlfossil l.lco2 l.lpolicies l.lgdp l.lrenewable l.lfossil, fe

  estimates store fixed

> *xtreg dlco2 dlpolicies dlgdp dlrenewable dlfossil l.lco2 l.lpolicies l.lgdp l.lrenew-*
> *able l.lfossil, re*
> *estimates store random*
> *hausman fixed random*

After the realization of the Hausman test, it is necessary to verify the existence of cointegration in the results. For this, the second-generation cointegration test of Westerlund (2007) was applied. The null hypothesis of this test is the nonpresence of cointegration between the variables. Moreover the Westerlund test requires that all variables of the model be stationary, that is I(1) (Fuinhas et al., 2017). Table 5.4 shows the results of the Westerlund cointegration tests.

The results of Westerlund test with constant indicate to a nonrejection of cointegration in the model, while a test with none and constant and trend indicates to the rejection of cointegration. Moreover the nondetection of cointegration between variables point to the use of the econometric technique that is less stringent about integration variables, that is, the ARDL models.

How to do:
Westerlund cointegration test (None)

> *xtwest lco2 lpolicies lgdp lrenewable lfossil, lags(1) lrwindow(3) bootstrap(800)*
> **Westerlund cointegration test (Constant)**
> *xtwest lco2 lpolicies lgdp lrenewable lfossil, lags(1) lrwindow(3) constant boot-strap(800)*
> **Westerlund cointegration test (Constant & trend)**
> *xtwest lco2 lpolicies lgdp lrenewable lfossil, lags(1) lrwindow(3) constant trend bootstrap(800)*

So, after the realization of the Westerlund test, it is necessary to verify whether the panel's data are heterogeneous. For this, the MG, and PMG or Dynamic Fixed Effects (DFE) estimators were tested. Table 5.5 shows the results of estimators and the outcomes of Hausman test.

The results of heterogeneous estimators indicate that the DFE estimator is appropriate, and the Hausman test indicates that the panel is homogeneous. These results also complement that all variables share the common shocks in the model.

Table 5.4 Westerlund tests.

Westerlund cointegration test

Statistics	None			Constant			Constant and trend		
	Value	Z-value	P-value robust	Value	Z-value	P-value robust	Value	Z-value	P-value robust
Gt	− 1.485	1.662	0.793	− 2.648	− 0.736	.085 *	− 2.947	− 0.317	.136
Ga	− 5.212	2.273	0.793	− 12.583	0.169	.040 **	− 11.895	2.192	.314
Pt	− 5.817	− 0.171	0.343	− 10.230	− 2.574	.011 **	− 11.421	− 2.321	.006 ***
Pt	− 5.465	0.308	0.396	− 13.457	− 1.896	.011 **	− 12.201	0.679	.116

Notes: ***, **, and *, denote statistically significant at 1%, 5%, and 10% level, respectively; Bootstrapping regression with 800 reps; H_0: No cointegration; H_1 Gt and Ga test the cointegration for each country individually; and Pt and Pa test the cointegration of the panel as a whole.

Table 5.5 Heterogeneous estimators and Hausman tests.

Variables	Dependent variable DLCO2					
	MG		PMG		DFE	
Constant	− 9.1852	***	− 5.0108	***	− 5.7603	***
DLPolicies	− 0.0007		− 0.0050		− 0.0169	
DLGDP	0.6625	***	0.6143	***	0.6319	***
DLRenewable	− 0.2382	***	− 0.2246	***	− 0.2111	***
DLFossil	0.3329	**	0.3728	***	0.2478	***
ECM	− 0.5571	***	− 0.3793	***	− 0.3978	***
LPolicies	− 0.0522		− 0.0349	**	− 0.0482	**
LGDP	0.6362	***	0.3852	***	0.3471	***
LRenewable	− 0.3408	***	− 0.2236	***	− 0.3188	***
LFossil	0.3333	**	0.5119	***	0.5903	***
	MG vs PMG		PMG vs DFE		MG vs DFE	
Hausman tests	$Chi^2(10) = -$		$Chi^2(10) = -$		$Chi^2(10) =$	
	20.57		5.62		17.40*	

Notes: L and D denote variables in natural logarithms and the first differences; ***, **, * denote statistically significant at 1%, 5%, and 10% level, respectively; Hausman results for H_0: difference in coefficients not systematic; ECM denotes error correction mechanism; and the long-run parameters are computed elasticities.

How to do:

Heterogeneous estimators and Hausman tests

> *qui: xtpmg dlco2 dlpolicies dlgdp dlrenewable dlfossil, lr (l.lco2 l.lpolicies l. lgdp l.lrenewable l.lfossil) ec(ecm) replace mg*
>
> *estimates store mg*
>
> *qui: xtpmg dlco2 dlpolicies dlgdp dlrenewable dlfossil, lr (l.lco2 l.lpolicies l. lgdp l.lrenewable l.lfossil) ec(ecm) replace pmg*
>
> *estimates store pmg*
>
> *qui: xtpmg dlco2 dlpolicies dlgdp dlrenewable dlfossil, lr (l.lco2 l.lpolicies l. lgdp l.lrenewable l.lfossil) ec(ecm) replace dfe*
>
> *estimates store dfe*
>
> *estimates table mg pmg dfe, star(.10 0.05.01) stats(N r2 r2_a) b(%7.4f)*
>
> *hausman mg pmg,alleqs constant*
>
> *hausman pmg dfe,alleqs constant*
>
> *hausman mg dfe,alleqs constant*

Considering this the specification test, such as Friedman test, Breusch and Pagan Langrarian Multiplier test, Wooldridge test, and Modified Wald test were performed to check the existence of cross-section dependence, the cross-sectional correlation in the FE model, serial correlation in

Table 5.6 Specification tests.

	Friedman test	Breusch and pagan LM test	Wooldridge's test	Modified wald test
Statistics	32.171***	n.a.	$F(1,11) = 42.673^{***}$	$\text{Chi}^2 (12) = 537.44^{***}$

Notes: *** denotes statistically significant at 1% levels; results for H_0 of Modified Wald test: sigma(i) ^2 = sigma^2 for all I; results for H_0 of Friedman test: residuals are not correlated; results for H_0 of Wooldridge test: no first-order autocorrelation; and n.a. denotes not available.

panel-data models, and groupwise heteroskedasticity in the FE model (see Table 5.6).

The outcomes of specification tests point to the presence of cross-section dependence, serial correlation in the panel-data model, and the existence of heteroskedasticity. The Breusch and Pagan LM test cannot be used due to the correlation matrix of residuals being singular.

How to do:

Friedman test

> xtreg dlco2 dlpolicies dlgdp dlrenewable dlfossil l.lco2 l.lpolicies l.lgdp l.lrenewable l.lfossil, fe

> xtcsd, friedman show abs

Breusch and Pagan LM test

> xtreg dlco2 dlpolicies dlgdp dlrenewable dlfossil l.lco2 l.lpolicies l.lgdp l.lrenewable l.lfossil, fe

> xttest2

Wooldridge's test

> xtserial dlco2 dlpolicies dlgdp dlrenewable dlfossil l_lco2 l_lpolicies l_lgdp l_lrenewable l_lfossil

Modified Wald test

> xtreg dlco2 dlpolicies dlgdp dlrenewable dlfossil l.lco2 l.lpolicies l.lgdp l.lrenewable l.lfossil, fe

> xttest3

In the existence of cross-sectional dependence, the serial correlation, and the heteroskedasticity in the model, the econometric literature recommends using the Driscoll and Kraay (DK) estimator in the ARDL regression (Fuinhas et al., 2017; Koengkan, 2017a, 2017b). The DK estimator can generate robust standard errors for several phenomena in sample errors (Fuinhas et al., 2017). Additionally, the FE, FER (Robust), DK (Driscoll and Kraay) estimators were performed in ARDL model (see Table 5.7).

Table 5.7 Estimation results of autoregressive distributed lag model.

Variables	Dependent variable DLCO2				
	FE		**FER**	**DK**	
Constant	− 5.7603	***	***	***	
DLPolicies	− 0.0169				
DLGDP	0.6319	***	***	***	
DLRenewable	− 0.2111	***	***	***	
DLFossil	0.2478	***	**	***	
LCO2	− 0.3978	***	***	***	
LPolicies	− 0.0192	**	**	**	
LGDP	0.1381	***	**	***	
LRenewable	− 0.1268	***	**	***	
LFossil	0.2348	***	***	***	
Statistics					
N	408		408	408	
R²	0.3645		0.3645		
R²_a	0.3317		0.3502		
F	24.6681		33.4469	97.8211	

Notes: L and D denote variables in natural logarithms, and the first differences; ***, and ** denote statistically significant at 1%, and 5%, respectively.

So, Table 5.7 shows the FE, FER, and DK estimators in the ARDL model. The variables estimations were performed with variables first in the model. Moreover the variables in ARDL model are statistically significant at 1% and 5%, except the variable DLPolicies in the first differences.

How to do:
Estimates store OLS

    qui: xtreg dlco2 dlpolicies dlgdp dlrenewable dlfossil l_lco2 l_lpolicies l_lgdp l_lrenewable l_lfossil, fe estimates store fe
    qui: xtreg dlco2 dlpolicies dlgdp dlrenewable dlfossil l_lco2 l_lpolicies l_lgdp l_lrenewable l_lfossil, fe robust estimates store fer
    qui: xtscc dlco2 dlpolicies dlgdp dlrenewable dlfossil l_lco2 l_lpolicies l_lgdp l_lrenewable l_lfossil,fe lag(1) estimates store dk
    estimates table fe fer dk, star (.10.05.01) stats(N r2 r2_a F) b(%7.4f)

In view of results of Table 5.7, the impacts (short run), elasticities (long run), and adjustment speed in ARDL model are presented in Table 5.8. Moreover the impacts were computed by dividing the coefficients of the variables by the coefficient of LCO2, both lagged once, and multiplying the ratio by (− 1), while the elasticities were not observed directly on estimates.

Table 5.8 Elasticities, impacts, and adjustment speed.

Variables	Dependent variable DLCO2			
	FE		**FER**	**DK**
Constant	-5.7603	***	***	***
Short run (Impacts)				
DLPolicies	-0.0169			
DLGDP	0.6319	***	***	***
DLRenewable	-0.2111	***	***	***
DLFossil	0.2478	***	**	***
Long run (Elasticities)				
LPolicies (-1)	-0.0482	**	**	***
LGDP (-1)	0.3471	***	***	***
LRenewable (-1)	-0.3188	***	***	***
LFossil (-1)	0.5903	***	***	***
Speed of adjustment				
ECM	-0.3978	***	***	***

Notes: L and D denote variables in natural logarithms, and the first differences; ***, and ** denote statistically significant at 1%, and 5% level, respectively; and ECM denotes the coefficient of the variable LCO2 lagged once.

The results of impacts (short run) and elasticities (long run) of ARDL model are statistically significant at 1% and 5% in FE, FER, and DK estimators. Indeed, the high significance of variables means that they have a great explanatory power. So, in the ARDL model the impacts (short run), and elasticities (long run) indicate that renewable energy fiscal/financial incentive policies are not able to reduce CO_2 emissions in the short run, while in the long run the policies reduce the emissions by -0.0482%. The economic growth of Latin American countries increases the emissions by 0.6319% in the short run, and 0.3471 % in the long run, respectively. Moreover the consumption of RES reduces the emissions by -0.2111% in the short run, and -0.3188% in the long run. The consumption of fossil fuels increases CO_2 emissions by 0.2478% in the short run, and 0.5903% in the long run, respectively. Additionally, the ECM of ARDL model in FE, FER, and DK are statistically significant at 1% (e.g., -0.3978 % ***) (see Table 5.8). Thus when the ECM parameter is statistically significant, it is similar when there is the realization of the Granger causality test (Fuinhas et al., 2017). Then, the ECM version of the Granger causality test and cointegration can ensure that both magnitudes of effects and causality are revealed by elasticities of themselves (see Table 5.8). The results of the economic model are consistent with the literature, where the consumption of renewable energy and renewable energy policies reduce environmental degradation, while the economic activity and consumption of fossil fuels increase it.

How to do:
Impacts in ARDL model (Fixed Effects)
> *xtreg dlco2 dlpolicies dlgdp dlrenewable dlfossil l.lco2 l.lpolicies l.lgdp l.lrenewable l.lfossil, fe*
> **Elasticities in ARDL model (Fixed Effects)**
> *xtreg dlco2 dlpolicies dlgdp dlrenewable dlfossil l.lco2 l.lpolicies l.lgdp l.lrenewable l.lfossil,fe*
> *nlcom(ratio1:-_b[l.lpolicies]/_b[l.lco2])*
> *nlcom(ratio1:-_b[l.lgdp]/_b[l.lco2])*
> *nlcom(ratio1:-_b[l.lrenewable]/_b[l.lco2])*
> *nlcom(ratio1:-_b[l.lfossil]/_b[l.lco2])*

Then, to assess the robustness of the ARDL model, dummy variables were included into the regression, by reason of the existence of shocks (economic or social/politic impacts) that occurred in some Latin American countries, such as Ecuador in 1984 when a decline in the international price of petroleum impacted on the economic activity, and by climatic changes caused by El Niño during 1982—84 that produced severe droughts, torrential rains, and coastal floods, which impacted on transportation, marketing infrastructures, and crops (Hanratty and Weil, 1991); Nicaragua between 1989 and 1991 suffered with a civil war that occurred between 1979 and 1991, together with a Nicaragua revolution. This revolution left 30,000 dead, and serious social and economic problems in Nicaragua (Fagundes, 2009); Costa Rica in 1994 and Ecuador between 1994 and 1997 were impacted by one of Mexico's economic crisis of 1994 that affected all Latin American countries with the "Tequila effect" (Mishkin, 1999); Bolivia in 2007 and Peru 2009 were affected by an international financial crisis that occurred in 2008—2009. These shocks impacted the economic growth, energy consumption, and consequently the environmental degradation in the Latin American countries. Moreover these shocks are represented by the following acronyms (e.g., IDEcuador1984 (Ecuador, year 1984), IDNicaragua1989 (Nicaragua, year 1989), IDNicaragua1990 (Nicaragua, year 1990), IDNicaragua1991 (Nicaragua, year 1991), IDCosta_Rica1994 (Costa Rica, year 1994), IDEcuador1994 (Ecuador, year 1994),

Table 5.9 Elasticities, impacts, shocks, and adjustment speed.

Variables	Dependent variable DLCO2					
	FE				FER	DK
Constant	− 3.9866	***			***	***
IDEcuador1984	0.1937	***			***	***
IDNicaragua1989	− 0.3310	***			***	***
IDNicaragua1990	0.4130	***			***	***
IDNicaragua1991	− 0.2246	***			***	***
IDCosta_Rica1994	0.2531	***			***	***
IDEcuador1994	− 0.5833	***			***	***
IDEcuador1995	0.3143	***			***	***
IDEcuador1997	− 0.3056	***			***	***
IDBolivia2007	− 0.2328	***			***	***
IDPeru2009	0.2323	***			***	***
Short run						
DLPolicies	− 0.0270				*	*
DLGDP	0.6293	***			***	***
DLRenewable	− 0.2010	***			***	***
DLFossil	0.2880	***			***	***
Long run						
LPolicies (−1)	− 0.0521	**			***	***
LGDP (−1)	0.3186	***			***	***
LRenewable (−1)	− 0.3199	***			***	***
LFossil (−1)	0.6088	***			***	***
Speed of adjustment						
ECM	− 0.2816	***			***	***

Notes: L and D denote variables in natural logarithms, and the first differences; ***, **, and *, denote statistically significant at 1%, 5%, and 10% level, respectively; and ECM denotes the coefficient of the variable LCO2 lagged once.

IDEcuador1995 (Ecuador, year 1995), IDEcuador1997 (Ecuador, 1997), IDBolivia2007 (Bolivia, year 2007), and IDPeru2009 (Peru, year 2009)). Table 5.9 presents the impacts and the elasticities with variables dummy for FE, FER, and DK estimators in the ARDL model.

The shocks (dummy variables) are significant at 1% in the ARDL model. So, as can be seen by comparing Tables 5.8 and 5.9, the ECM with shocks are less converging for long-run equilibrium whether compared to ECM without shocks. Despite the reduction of ECM in convergence for equilibrium, the model proved to be robust, even in the presence of shocks.

How to do:

Identifiy the shocks (impacts) in ARDL model

    xtreg dlco2 dlpolicies dlgdp dlrenewable dlfossil l.lco2 l.lpolicies l.lgdp l.lrenewable l.lfossil,fe

    predict double resid1, ue

    predict double resid2, u

    predict double resid3, e

    xtline resid1, overlay

    xtline resid2, overlay

    xtline resid3, overlay

    xtset country year

    **Create the dummies in ARDL model*

    gen idecuador1984 = 0.0

    replace idecuador1984 = 1 if country == 7 & year == 1984

    impacts in ARDL model (Fixed Effects)

    xtreg dlco2 idecuador1984 idecuador1994 idecuador1995 idecuador1997 idnicaragua1989 idnicaragua1990 idnicaragua1991 idcostarica1994 idbolivia2007 idperu2009 dlpolicies dlgdp dlrenewable dlfossil l.lco2 l.lpolicies l.lgdp l.lrenewable l.lfossil, fe

    Elasticities in ARDL model (Fixed Effects)

    xtreg dlco2 idecuador1984 idecuador1994 idecuador1995 idecuador1997 idnicaragua1989 idnicaragua1990 idnicaragua1991 idcostarica1994 idbolivia2007 idperu2009dlpolicies dlgdp dlrenewable dlfossil l.lco2 l.lpolicies l.lgdp l.lrenewable l.lfossil,fe

    nlcom(ratio1:-_b[l.lpolicies]/_b[l.lco2])

    nlcom(ratio1:-_b[l.lgdp]/_b[l.lco2])

    nlcom(ratio1:-_b[l.lrenewable]/_b[l.lco2])

    nlcom(ratio1:-_b[l.lfossil]/_b[l.lco2])

Section 5.4 will show the discussion of results and the answers for variables' impacts on CO_2 emissions.

5.4 Discussion

    The study of the effects of fiscal and financial incentives policies for renewable energy on CO_2 emissions in Latin American countries extends the existing literature that approaches the impact of renewable energy policies on environmental degradation. The capacity of fiscal and financial incentives policies for renewable energy in reducing the emissions in the long run is in line with several authors who have the studied this impact (e.g., Butler and Neuhoff, 2008; Falconett and Nagasaka, 2010; Fuinhas et al., 2017; Jenner et al., 2013; Menanteau et al., 2003; Oak et al., 2014; Ortega et al., 2013; Pereira Jr. et al., 2011; Pérez de Arce and Sauma, 2016; Pérez de Arce et al., 2016; Redondo and Collado, 2014; Rowlands, 2005; Thapar et al., 2016). The negative impact of fiscal/financial incentive policies on emissions in the long run is related to the possible "efficiency" of these policies, which brings new investments for alternative sources and substitutes the use of fossil fuels by renewable energy (Fuinhas et al., 2017).

The fiscal/financial policies reduce the emissions because they generate two combined effects. First the feed-in tariffs, or premium payments, reduce the price of electricity to consumers, and consequently increase energy consumption, the production of which is met, in this case, with renewable energy supplies, consequently reducing emissions. Second the subsidization of renewable energy production mitigates the market power exerted by the generation firms (Pérez de Arce and Sauma, 2016; Pérez de Arce et al., 2016). Moreover the feed-in tariffs and premium payments incentivise renewable energy technologies, and consequently alternative energy consumption in the long run (Redondo and Collado, 2014). Other authors point out that the feed-in tariffs increase the competitiveness of renewable energy technology by decreasing the production and investments costs (Jenner et al., 2013). The fiscal/financial incentive policies mechanisms provide the producers who invest in plants that emit CO_2 emissions with the option of compensating for their emissions by investing in or building plants that generate energy from alternative sources (Pereira Jr. et al., 2011). Then, the nonimpact of fiscal/financial incentive policies in the short run is related with the inefficiency of these policies to encourage investments and consumption of alternative energy in the short run. This inefficiency is associated with bureaucracy in institutions, political instability, change of governments, and political lobby that cause difficulties with the deployment of fiscal/financial incentive policies or renewable energy policies.

The positive impact of economic growth on CO_2 emissions in the short run and long run is confirmed by several researchers (e.g., Fuinhas et al., 2017; Pablo-Romero and Jésus, 2016; Paramati, Alam, & Chen, 2017; Omri, Nguyen, & Rault, 2014; Saidi and Hammami, 2015). The increase in environmental degradation by economic growth in the Latin American region is due to the development of infrastructure, trade development and economic capitalization in the Latin America countries, that has a positive impact on investments and economic growth, and consequently increases the consumption of energy (Omri et al., 2014). Moreover Saidi and Hammami (2015), complements that the increase of economic activity influences the consumption of fossil fuels, such as oil and gas. The positive influence of consumption of fossil fuels on CO_2 emissions in the short run and long run is in line with several studies (e.g., Charfeddine, 2017; Fuinhas et al., 2017; Mirza and Kanwal, 2017; Pablo-Romero and Jésus, 2016; Pao and Tsai, 2011; Shahbaz, Hye, Tiwari, & Leitão, 2013; Shahzard, Kumar, Zakaria, and Hurr, 2017; Shahbaz, Tiwari, & Nasir, 2013). According to Pablo-Romero and Jésus (2016) the high dependency on the consumption of fossil fuels is the cause of positive influence of fossil fuels consumption on environmental degradation in the Latin American countries. The reason that there is a high dependency on fossil fuels in countries of the Latin America region is due to the fact that some are major fossil energy produces, such as Argentina, Brazil, Bolivia, Colombia, Ecuador, Mexico, Peru, and Venezuela, and others are great consumers, such as Chile, Central American countries, Caribbean countries, Paraguay, and Uruguay (Fuinhas et al., 2017). Moreover environmental degradation tends to grow in the Latin American countries due to the economies tendency to use obsolete technology in the production of energy, such as fossil sources (Shahzard, Kumar, Zakaria, and Hurr, 2017).

Additionally, the capacity of consumption of RES to reduce CO_2 emissions is confirmed by several researchers (e.g., Budzianowski and Postawa, 2017; Danish, Zhang, Wang, & Wang, 2017; Dogan and Ozturk, 2017; Fuinhas et al., 2017; Jaforullah and King, 2015; Liu, Zhang, & Bae, 2017; Robalino-López, Mena-Nieto, García-Ramos, & Golpe, 2015; Wesseh and Lin, 2016; Zoundi, 2017; Özbuğday and Erbas, 2015; Qi, Zhang, & Karplus, 2014; Shafiei and Salim, 2014). The capacity of consumption of RES to reduces CO_2 emissions is due to the growth of investments in alternative energy sources resulting from the availability of an enormous abundance of renewable sources (e.g., hydropower, biomass, geothermal, wind, and solar) in most Latin American countries (Fuinhas et al., 2017). Indeed the abundance of natural resources stimulates the deployment of renewable energy technologies, and brings new investments, increases the consumption, and consequently reduces environmental degradation. Moreover the renewable energy technologies, such as hydro, geothermal, biomass, solar, and wind are less polluting and very viable, and contribute to a reduction of emissions (Gill, Viswanathan, & Hassan, 2017). Despite the consumption of RES reducing the environmental degradation, their impact is very small if compared with the positive impacts of fossil fuels and economic growth. That is, it would be necessary to triple the impact of consumption of renewable energy and public policies on emissions to compensate for the increase in environmental degradation by economic activity and fossil fuels consumption. Then this small impact of renewable energy consumption is due to the inefficiency of renewable energy public policies in the Latin American countries that are not able to promote investments in and consumption of renewable energy. The inefficiency of renewable energy public policies is confirmed by results of impacts of renewable energy fiscal/financial incentive policies on emissions, where these policies can reduce the environmental degradation just in the long run, and their impact is very small too.

5.5 Conclusions

The impact of fiscal and financial incentives policies for renewable energy on CO_2 emissions was analyzed in this chapter. This study is focused in 12 Latin American countries over a period of time from 1980 to 2014. The ARDL model in the form of UECM was computed.

The results of impacts (short run), elasticities (long run) of the ARDL model showed that the fiscal and financial incentives policies for renewable energy are not able to reduce CO_2 emissions in the short run, while in the long run these policies reduce the emissions. Moreover the economic growth of Latin American countries and consumption of fossil fuels increases the CO_2 emissions in the short and long run, while the consumption of renewable energy reduces them in the short and long run. The impact of variables in the short and long run and the ECM are statistically significant at the 1% and 5% level. Moreover the robustness test proved that the ARDL model is robust even in the presence of shocks.

Then, based on these results we can consider that the fiscal/financial incentive policies are able to reduce environmental degradation in the long run, but their impact is very small, and that the nonimpact of these same policies in the short run is related with the inefficiency of these policies, caused by bureaucracy in institutions, political instability, change of governments, and political lobbies that make more difficult the deployment of fiscal/financial incentive policies or renewable energy policies. The Latin American countries are dependenct on fossil fuels to grow. The low impact of consumption of renewable energy on CO_2 emissions is due to the inefficiency of renewable energy policies that do not promote investments in and a greater participation of alternative energy sources in the energy matrix.

Based on these considerations: What must be done to reverse this scenario in the Latin American region and what policies should be applied to improve this situation? The results of this study suggest creating renewable energy fiscal/financial incentive policies more efficiently, more subsidy policies that encourage firms and households to purchase appliances with high energy efficiency standards, and green technologies, such as solar, photovoltaic equipment or green automobiles. Other suggestions include policies that motivate private financial institutions to give special loan discounts to business firms who have an interest in investing in green energy technologies or that want to reduce their energy consumption. Moreover many reforms should be made which reduce the bureaucracy in institutions, that discourage renewable energy from foreign investments in these countries, and that target the political lobby between governments and large polluter firms or producers of fossil fuels in some countries. There needs to be a greater transparency between the private and public institutions, and also security for the investors.

Then, these policies and reforms need to be implanted in order to increase the effectiveness of fiscal/financial incentive policies and renewable energy participation in the energy mix. In turn these changes will attract alternative energy investors, promote economic growth, green development, and take advantage of the enormous abundance of renewable sources (e.g., hydropower, wind, solar, waste, biomass, and geothermal) in all Latin American countries, leading to a reduction in the dependency on fossil fuels, and environmental degradation.

This study confirmed the hypothesis that the fiscal/financial incentive policies for renewable energy decrease CO_2 emissions. Moreover this chapter extends the existing literature that approaches the impact of renewable energy policies on environmental degradation and opens the way for the development of new investigations that approach the efficiency of renewable energy public policies.

References

Belsley, D. A., Kuh, E., & Welsch, R. E. (1980). *Regression diagnostics: Identifying influential data and sources of collinearity. New York: Wiley*.

Boden, T. A., Marland, G., & Andres, R. J. (2011). Global, regional, and national fossil-fuel CO_2 emissions. *Carbon Dioxide Information Analysis Center*. Oak Ridge, Tennessee: Oak Ridge National Laboratory, U.S. Department of Energy. Available from: https://doi.org/10.3334/CDIAC/00001_V2011.

Breusch, T. S., & Pagan, A. R. (1980). The lagrange multiplier test and its applications to model specification in econometrics. *The Review of Economic Studies*, *47*(1), 239–253.

Budzianowski, W. M., & Postawa, K. (2017). Renewable energy from biogas with reduced carbon dioxide footprint: Implications of applying different plant configurations and operating pressures. *Renewable and Sustainable Energy Reviews*, *68*(2), 852–868. Available from: https://doi.org/10.1016/j.rser.2016.05.076.

Butler, L., & Neuhoff, K. (2008). Comparison of feed-in tariff, quota and auction mechanisms to support wind power development. *Renewable Energy*, *33*(8), 1854–1867. Available from: https://doi.org/10.1016/j.renene.2007.10.008.

Charemza, W. W., & Deadman, D. F. (1992). *New directions in econometric practice*. Aldershot: Edward Elgar.

Charfeddine, L. (2017). The impact of energy consumption and economic development on ecological footprint and CO_2 emissions: Evidence from a Markov switching equilibrium correction model. *Energy Economics*, *65*, 355–374. Available from: https://doi.org/10.1016/j.eneco.2017.05.009.

Choi, I. (2001). Unit root test for panel data. *Journal of International Money and Finance, 20* (1), 249–272.

Danish., Zhang, B., Wang, B., & Wang, Z. (2017). Role of renewable energy and nonrenewable energy consumption on EKC: Evidence from Pakistan. *Journal of Cleaner Production*, *156*(10), 855–864. Available from: https://doi.org/10.1016/j.jclepro.2017.03.203.

Dogan, E., & Ozturk, I. (2017). The influence of renewable and non-renewable energy consumption and real income on CO_2 emissions in the USA: Evidence from structural break tests. *Environmental Science and Pollution Research*, *24*(1), 10846–10854. Available from: https://doi.org/10.1007/s11356-017-8786-y.

Fagundes, P. E. (2009). "Patria ou muerte": os 30 anos da Revolução Sandinista. *Revista Espaço Acadêmico*, *9*(103), 1–6, ISSN:1519-6186.

Falconett, I., & Nagasaka, K. (2010). Comparative analysis of support mechanisms for renewable energy technologies using probability distributions. *Renewable Energy*, *35*(6), 1135–1144. Available from: https://doi.org/10.1016/j.renene.2009.11.019.

Friedman, M. (1937). The use of ranks to avoid the assumption of normality implicit in the analysis of variance. *Journal of the American Statistical Association*, *32*, 675–701.

Fuinhas, J. A., Marques, A. C., & Koengkan, M. (2017). Are renewable energy policies upsetting carbon dioxide emissions? The case of Latin America countries. *Environmental Science and Pollution Research*, *24*(17), 15044–15054. Available from: https://doi.org/10.1007/s11356-017-9109-z.

Gill, A. R., Viswanathan, K. K., & Hassan, S. A. (2017). Test of environmental Kuznets curve (EKC) for carbon emission and potential of renewable energy to reduce green houses gases (GHG) in Malaysia. *Environment, Development, and Sustainability*, 1–12. Available from: https://doi.org/10.1007/s10668-017-9929-5.

Greene, W. (2002). *Econometric analysis*. Upper Saddle River, NN: Prentice-Hall.

Guan, X., Zhou, M., & Zhang, M. (2015). Using the ARDL-ECM approach to explore the nexus among urbanization, energy consumption, and economic growth in Jiangsu Province, China. *Emerging Markets Finance and Trade*, *51*(2), 391–399.

Hanratty, D. C., & Weil, T. E. (1991). *Ecuador : A country study*. Washington, DC: Federal Research Division, Library of Congress.

Hsiao, C. (2014). *Analysis of panel data* (3rd edn.). New York, NY: Cambridge University Press.

International Energy Agency (IRENA) (2017). IEA/IRENA joint policies and measures database. <http://www.iea.org/policiesandmeasures/renewableenergy/>.

Jaforullah, M., & King, A. (2015). Does the use of renewable energy sources mitigate CO_2 emissions? A reassessment of the US evidence. *Energy Economics*, *49*, 711–717. Available from: https://doi.org/10.1016/j.eneco.2015.04.006.

Jenner, S., Groba, F., & Indvik, J. (2013). Assessing the strength and effectiveness of renewable electricity feed-in tariffs in European Union countries. *Energy Policy*, *52*, 385−401. Available from: https://doi.org/10.1016/j.enpol.2012.09.046.

Koengkan, M. (2017a). Is the globalization influencing the primary energy consumption? The case of Latin America and Caribbean countries. *Cadernos UniFOA, Volta Redonda*, *12*(33), 59−69, ISSN: 1809-9475.

Koengkan, M. (2017b). O nexo entre o consumo de energia primária e o crescimento econômico nos países da América do Sul: Uma análise de longo prazo. *Cadernos UniFOA, Volta Redonda*, *12*(34), 56−66, ISSN: 1809-9475.

Koengkan, M. (2017d). Do fiscal incentive policies impact the installed capacity of renewable energy? An empirical evidence from Latin American countries. *Revista de Estudos Sociais*, *20*(39). Available from: https://doi.org/10.19093/res5071.

Koengkan, M. (2018a). The decline of environmental degradation by renewable energy consumption in the MERCOSUR countries: An approach with ARDL modeling. *Environment Systems and Decisions*, *38*(3), 415−425. Available from: https://doi.org/10.1007/s10669-018-9671-z.

Koengkan, M. (2018b). The positive impact of trade openness on consumption of energy: Fresh evidence from Andean community countries. *Energy*, *158*, 936−943. Available from: https://doi.org/10.1016/j.energy.2018.06.091.

Koengkan, M., Losekann, L. D., & Fuinhas, J. A. (2018). The relationship between economic growth, consumption of energy, and environmental degradation: Renewed evidence from Andean community nations. *Environment Systems and Decisions*, 1−13. Available from: https://doi.org/10.1007/s10669-018-9698-1.

Koo, B. (2017). Examining the impacts of feed-in-tariff and the clean development mechanism on Korea's renewable energy projects through comparative investment analysis. *Energy Policy*, *104*, 144−154. Available from: https://doi.org/10.1016/j.enpol.2017.01.017.

Levin, A., Lin, C.-F., & Chu, C.-S. J. (2002). Unit root test in panel dada: Asymptotic and finite-sample properties. *Journal of Econometrics*, *108*(1), 1−24.

Limpaitoon, T., Chen, Y., & Oren, S. S. (2011). The impact of carbon cap and trade regulation on congested electricity market equilibrium. *Journal of Regulatory Economics*, *40*(3), 237−260. Available from: https://doi.org/10.1007/s11149-011-9161-4.

Liu, X., Zhang, S., & Bae, J. (2017). The impact of renewable energy and agriculture on carbon dioxide emissions: Investigating the environmental Kuznets curve in four selected ASEAN countries. *Journal of Cleaner Production*, *164*(15), 1239−1247. Available from: https://doi.org/10.1016/j.jclepro.2017.07.086.

Maddala, G. S., & Wu, S. A. (1999). Comparative study of unit root test with panel data a new simple test. *Oxford Bulletin of Economics and Statistics*, *61*(1), 631−652.

Menanteau, P., Finon, D., & Lamy, M.-L. (2003). Prices versus quantities: Choosing policies for promoting the development of renewable energy. *Energy Policy*, *31*(8), 799−812. Available from: https://doi.org/10.1016/S0301-4215(02)00133-7.

Mirza, F. M., & Kanwal, A. (2017). Energy consumption, carbon emissions and economic growth in Pakistan: Dynamic causality analysis. *Renewable and Sustainable Energy Reviews*, *72*, 1233−1240. Available from: https://doi.org/10.1016/j.rser.2016.10.081.

Mishkin, F. S. (1999). Lessons from the Tequila crisis. *Journal of Banking & Finance*, *23*, 1521−1533, PII: S 0 3 7 8 − 4266(99)00029-1.

Oak, N., Lawson, D., & Champneys, A. (2014). Performance comparison of renewable incentive schemes using optimal control. *Energy*, *64*(1), 44−57. Available from: https://doi.org/10.1016/j.energy.2013.11.038.

Omri, A., Nguyen, D. K., & Rault, C. (2014). Causal interactions between CO_2 emissions, FDI, and economic growth: Evidence from dynamic simultaneous-equation models. *Economic Modelling*, *42*, 382−389. Available from: https://doi.org/10.1016/j.econmod.2014.07.026.

Ortega, M., Del Rio, P., & Montero, E. A. (2013). Assessing the benefits and costs of renewable electricity. The Spanish case. *Renewable and Sustainable Energy Reviews, 27*, 294−304. Available from: https://doi.org/10.1016/j.rser.2013.06.012.

Özbugday, F. C., & Erbas, B. C. (2015). How effective are energy efficiency and renewable energy in curbing CO_2 emissions in the long run? A heterogeneous panel data analysis. *Energy, 82*(15), 734−745. Available from: https://doi.org/10.1016/j.energy.2015.01.084.

Pablo-Romero, M. D., & Jésus, J. D. (2016). Economic growth, and energy consumption: The energy-environmental Kuznets curve for Latin America and the Caribbean. *Renewable and Sustainable Energy Reviews, 60*, 1343−1350. Available from: https://doi.org/10.1016/j.rser.2016.03.029.

Pao, H.-T., & Tsai, C.-M. (2011). Multivariate Granger causality between CO_2 emissions, energy consumption, FDI (foreign direct investment) and GDP (gross domestic product): Evidence from a panel of BRIC (Brazil, Russian Federation, India, and China) countries. *Energy, 36*(1), 685−693. Available from: https://doi.org/10.1016/j.energy.2010.09.041.

Paramati, S. R., Alam, Md. S., & Chen, C.-F. (2017). The effects of tourism on economic growth and CO_2 emissions: A comparison between developed and developing economies. *Journal of Travel Research, 56*(6), 712−724. Available from: https://doi.org/10.1177/0047287516667848.

Pereira, A. O., Jr., Pereira, A. S., La Rovere, E., Barata, M. M. L., Villar, S. C., & Pires, S. H. (2011). Strategies to promote renewable energy in Brazil. *Renewable and Sustainable Energy Reviews, 15*(1), 681−688. Available from: https://doi.org/10.1016/j.rser.2010.09.027.

Pérez de Arce, M., & Sauma, E. (2016). Comparison of incentive policies for renewable energy in an oligopolistic market with price-responsive demand. *The Energy Journal, 37*(3), 159−179.

Pérez de Arce, M., Sauma, E., & Contreras, J. (2016). Renewable energy policy performance in reducing CO_2 emissions. *Energy Economics, 54*, 272−280. Available from: https://doi.org/10.1016/j.eneco.2015.11.024.

Pesaran, M., Shin, Y., & Smith, R. (2001). Bounds testing approaches to the analysis of level relationships. *Journal of Applied Econometrics, 16*(3), 289−326.

Pesaran, M.H. (2004). General diagnostic tests for cross section dependence in panels. *Cambridge Working Papers in Economics, No. 0435*. University of Cambridge, Faculty of Economics.

Pesaran, M. H., Shin, Y., & Smith, R. P. (1999). Pooled mean group estimation of dynamic heterogeneous panels. *Journal of American Statistical Association, 94*(446), 621−634.

Qi, T., Zhang, X., & Karplus, V. J. (2014). The energy and CO_2 emissions impact of renewable energy development in China. *Energy Policy, 64*, 60−69. Available from: https://doi.org/10.1016/j.enpol.2013.12.035.

Redondo, A. J. G., & Collado, R. R. (2014). An economic valuation of renewable electricity promoted by feed-in system in Spain. *Renewable Energy, 68*, 51−57. Available from: https://doi.org/10.1016/j.renene.2014.01.028.

Robalino-López, A., Mena-Nieto, A., García-Ramos, J. E., & Golpe, A. A. (2015). Studying the relationship between economic growth, CO_2 emissions, and the environmental Kuznets curve in Venezuela (1980−2025). *Renewable Sustainable Energy Reviews, 41*, 602−614. Available from: https://doi.org/10.1016/j.rser.2014.08.081.

Romano, A. A., Scandurra, G., Carfora, A., & Fodor, M. (2017). Renewable investments: The impact of green policies in developing and developed countries. *Renewable and Sustainable Energy Reviews, 68*(1), 738−747. Available from: https://doi.org/10.1016/j.rser.2016.10.024.

Rowlands, I. H. (2005). Envisaging feed-in tariffs for solar photovoltaic electricity: European lessons for Canada. *Renewable and Sustainable Energy Reviews, 9*(1), 51−68. Available from: https://doi.org/10.1016/j.rser.2004.01.010.

Saidi, K., & Hammami, S. (2015). The impact of CO_2 emissions and economic growth in energy consumption in 58 countries. *Energy Reports, 1,* 62−70. Available from: https://doi.org/10.1016/j.egyr.2015.01.003.

Shafiei, S., & Salim, R. A. (2014). Non-renewable and renewable energy consumption and CO_2 emissions in OECD countries: A comparative analysis. *Energy Policy, 66,* 547−556. Available from: https://doi.org/10.1016/j.enpol.2013.10.064.

Shahbaz, M., Tiwari, A. K., & Nasir, M. (2013). The effects of financial development, economic growth, coal consumption, and trade openness on CO_2 emissions in South Africa. *Energy Policy, 61,* 1452−1459. Available from: https://doi.org/10.1016/j.enpol.2013.07.006.

Shahbaz, M., Hye, Q. M. A., Tiwari, A. K., & Leitão, N. C. (2013). Economic growth, energy consumption, financial development, international trade and CO_2 emissions in Indonesia. *Renewable and Sustainable Energy Reviews, 25,* 109−121. Available from: https://doi.org/10.1016/j.rser.2013.04.009.

Shahzard, S. J. H., Kumar, R. R., Zakaria, M., & Hurr, M. (2017). Carbon emission, energy consumption, trade openness and financial development in Pakistan: A revisit. *Renewable and Sustainable Energy Reviews, 70,* 185−192. Available from: https://doi.org/10.1016/j.rser.2016.11.042.

Tabatabaei, S. M., Hadian, E., Marzban, H., & Zibaei, M. (2017). Economic, welfare and environmental impact of feed-in tariff policy: A case study in Iran. *Energy Policy, 102,* 164−169. Available from: https://doi.org/10.1016/j.enpol.2016.12.028.

Thapar, S., Sharma, S., & Verma, A. (2016). Economic and environmental effectiveness of renewable energy policy instruments: Best practices from India. *Renewable and Sustainable Energy Reviews, 66,* 487−498. Available from: https://doi.org/10.1016/j.rser.2016.08.025.

Vergara W., Rios R.R., & Galindo, L.M. (2013). *The climate and development challenge for Latin America and the Caribbean: Options for climate resilient, a low-carbon development.* Washington, DC: IDB.

Wesseh, P. H., & Lin, B. (2016). Can African countries efficiently build their economies on renewable energy? *Renewable Sustainable Energy Reviews, 54,* 161−173. Available from: https://doi.org/10.1016/j.rser.2015.09.082.

Westerlund, J. (2007). Testing for error correction in panel data. *Oxford Economics and Statistics, 31*(2), 217−224.

Wooldridge, J. M. (2002). *Econometric analysis of cross section and panel data. Massachusetts London, England: The MIT Press Cambridge.*

Xin-gang, Z., Yu-zhuo, Z., Ling-zhi, R., Yi, Z., & Zhi-gong, W. (2017). The policy effects of feed-in tariff and renewable portfolio standard: A case study of China's waste incineration power industry. *Waste Management, 68,* 711−723. Available from: https://doi.org/10.1016/j.wasman.2017.06.009.

Zoundi, Z. (2017). CO_2 emissions, renewable energy, and the environmental Kuznets curve: A panel cointegration approach. *Renewable and Sustainable Energy Reviews, 72,* 1067−1075. Available from: https://doi.org/10.1016/j.rser.2016.10.018.

Further reading

Koengkan, M. (2017c). The hydroelectricity consumption and economic growth nexus: A long time span analysis. *Revista Brasileira de Energias Renováveis, 6*(4), 678−704. Available from: https://doi.org/10.5380/rber.v6i4.49181.

CHAPTER SIX

Energy—growth nexus, domestic credit, and environmental sustainability: a panel causality analysis

Matheus Belucio[1], Cátia Lopes[2], José Alberto Fuinhas[3,*] and António Cardoso Marques[4,*]

[1]Economics Department, University of Évora, Évora, Portugal; Faculty of Economics, University of Coimbra, Coimbra, Portugal
[2]Management and Economics Department, University of Beira Interior, Covilhã, Portugal
[3]NECE-UBI, CeBER and Faculty of Economics, University of Coimbra, Coimbra, Portugal
[4]NECE-UBI and Management and Economics Department, University of Beira Interior, Covilhã, Portugal

Contents

6.1 Introduction

Since the seminal article by Kraft and Kraft (1978) studies on the relationships between economic growth and energy consumption have multiplied. At the end of the 20th century the first United Nations Conference on Climate Change placed environmental sustainability on

* This research was supported by NECE, R&D unit and funded by the FCT—Portuguese Foundation for the Development of Science and Technology, Ministry of Science, Technology and Higher Education, project UID/GES/04630/2019.

The Extended Energy–Growth Nexus.
DOI: https://doi.org/10.1016/B978-0-12-815719-0.00006-1

the agenda of the various economies. Finding ways to grow economically without harming the environment is humanity's greatest challenge.

In the energy—growth nexus literature there is also the integration of variables that refer to financial development (Chang, 2015; Destek, 2015; Islam, Shahbaz, Ahmed, & Alam, 2013; Kahouli, 2017; Saidi & Hammami, 2015). Shahbaz, Van Hoang, Mahalik, and Roubaud (2017) point out that this relationship can be very complex due to all the forms and possibilities of impacts. Details of the relationships can be seen in Fig. 6.1.

The purpose of this study was to verify the causal relationships between the variables of the energy—growth nexus (Gross Domestic Product, inflation, electricity generation, and primary energy consumption), domestic credit (domestic credit to the private sector and domestic credit provided by the financial sector), and environmental sustainability (CO_2 emissions) through a Panel Vector Autoregressive (PVAR or Panel VAR) and bivariate analysis of variables.

The panel is made up of 19 high-income countries: Australia, Austria, Belgium, Greece, France, Germany, Ireland, Israel, Italy, Japan, Netherlands, Norway, Portugal, Singapore, Spain, United States, Poland, Switzerland, and Hong Kong. The criterion used to choose was motivated for countries where there was no break in the time series during the period studied. The data comes from several databases and the built-in time horizon was from 2001 to 2016.

The energy—growth nexus literature itself has divided the studied countries into groups: European (Menegaki, Marques, & Fuinhas, 2017; Santos, Marques, & Fuinhas, 2017); Latin America and the Caribbeans

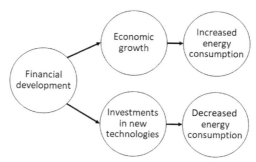

Figure 6.1 Channels of interaction. *Adapted from Shahbaz, M., Van Hoang, T.H., Mahalik, M.K., & Roubaud, D. (2017). Energy consumption, financial development and economic growth in India: New evidence from a nonlinear and asymmetric analysis.* Energy Economics, 63, 199—212.

(Chang & Carballo, 2011; Fuinhas, Marques, & Koengkan, 2017; Pablo-Romero & De Jesús, 2016); Asia-Pacific (Fang & Chang, 2016; Le & Quah, 2018); Sub-Saharan Africa (Silva, Cerqueira, & Ogbe, 2018); World (Apergis, Chang, Gupta, & Ziramba, 2016; Marques, Fuinhas, & Marques, 2017; Shahbaz, Zakaria, Shahzad, & Mahalik, 2018); OECD (Dedeoğlu & Kaya, 2013; Gozgor, Lau, & Lu, 2018); BRICS (Ahmed, 2017); BRIC (Tamazian, Chousa, & Vadlamannati, 2009); and MENA (Al-Mulali, 2011; Omri, 2013).

The bivariate analysis verifies the causal relationship between the variables. Testing them always in two directions: first the dependent variable is explained by the independent, and then the change in the position of the variables is considered. The PVAR in turn shows if the proposed model has endogeneity and reveals the causal relation that the excluded variables have in the variable of the equation.

The results of the bivariate analysis suggest that primary energy consumption is not related to the other variables. In addition, domestic credit to the private sector and domestic credit provided by the financial sector are causally related to CO_2 emissions. These same results were found in the PVAR model. The results still show that in the bivariate analysis, GDP has no impact on CO_2 emissions, but the effect behind PVAR is bidirectional, reinforcing the need for the application of more than one method to test the causal relationship between variables.

The combination of the two econometric models is beneficial for the study of the energy–growth nexus because they test the analysis between two variables. It also allows the verification of their relationship in the presence of other endogenous variables. This may be a feature that other authors who study the phenomenon can benefit from. It can also be applied in other areas where there is the possibility of endogeneity between variables.

This chapter evolves as follows: Section 6.2 covers the literature review, >Section 6.3 covers the data and methodology, Section 6.4 results and discussion and in Section 6.5 are the concluding remarks.

6.2 Literature review

Energy has become a critical issue in all modern economies, driving economic growth. In recent decades, energy has served as an important source in economies. Reflecting on energy diversity (i.e., electricity, coal, natural gas, and diesel) is not easy, despite the existence of an extensive and growing body of literature. For example, the energy consumed to produce goods and services, is consumed by vehicles, machine devices, lighting, heating, buildings, and factories, that is, it is essential in the life of economic agents (Dogan, 2015). In fact the energy sector has made economic agents dependent on energy because it is involved in each stage of the productivity process and in the well-being of people.

There are many studies that explore the determinants of economic growth and it should be noted that several theories related to economic growth have already been explored by many researchers. But none of them have included energy as an important determinant of economic growth. For example, Solow's growth model showed that technological progress is important for growth. In the AK model it was shown that a high saving rate is important for economic growth. In the same way, other models were explored, highlighting the importance of capital accumulation, innovation, research, and development. In fact studies of energy consumption and economic growth gained strength in the 1970s after the energy crisis (Shahbaz et al., 2018).

The empirical research in the energy literature has been extensive and inclusive due to the use of diverse econometric approaches. These econometric approaches go through: (1) simple regressions, (2) bivariate causality; (3) unit root tests; (4) multivariate cointegration, (5) panel cointegration, Vector Autoregressive (VAR), Vector Error Correction Model (VECM), and others (e.g., Shahbaz, Khan, & Tahir, 2013). This empirical evidence cannot help economic policies in a far-reaching energy plan to extend long-term growth (Ozturk & Acaravci, 2010; Payne, 2010).

In fact with the advancement of technologies and information it is possible to study it through different econometric approaches and techniques (e.g., Smyth & Narayan, 2015). The literature has been consistent with respect to the energy sector. In fact existing researchers seek not to understand the links between energy consumption and economic growth but rather to understand the connections with other areas of research. In general, data on energy consumption can be studied simultaneously with (1) growth variables; (2) prices; (3) demographic variables; (4) financial variables; and (5) external variables (e.g., Afonso, Marques, & Fuinhas, 2017). In other words the nexus that is currently studied not only seeks relationships between total primary energy consumption and production, but also the specific relationships between the various sources of energy and economic growth (Marques, Fuinhas, & Nunes, 2016).

In the literature different studies on the energy—growth nexus have been performed. In the energy—growth nexus analysis an aggregate energy-total approach was used (e.g., Kyophilavong, Shahbaz, Anwar, & Masood, 2015; Tang, Tan, & Ozturk, 2016). A closer focus on electricity was made at the nexus (Shahbaz & Lean, 2012a; Shahbaz, Tang, & Shabbir, 2011). The various nexus ratios, separating renewable and nonrenewable energy (e.g., Bhattacharya, Paramati, Ozturk, & Bhattacharya, 2016; Dogan, 2015) were evaluated. In addition, there has been a growing focus on each source of energy in the nexus, allowing the technological characteristics of each source to be incorporated, and its influence on economic growth analyzed (Marques, Fuinhas, & Menegaki, 2014; Ohler & Fetters, 2014).

As we delve deeper into the issue of energy consumption and economic—growth nexus, we realize that there have been several theoretical, political, and practical implications (e.g., Ghali El-Sakka, 2004; Keho, 2016; Narayan & Doytch, 2017), and these have been poorly consensual (e.g., Islam et al., 2013; Kakar, 2016). The energy—growth nexus has been characterized by contradictive conclusions and a huge and continuous debate since the appearance of the hypotheses of the Ozturk (2010). Derived from this contradiction in nexus, many researchers have introduced control variables into their models (Camarero, Forte, Garcia-Donato, Mendoza, & Ordoñez, 2015), and one could advance for new answers and conclusions. In general, and regardless of the type of study and variables used on the nexus, the authors almost always meet the four traditional hypotheses in the literature (Ozturk, 2010), illustrated in Fig. 6.2.

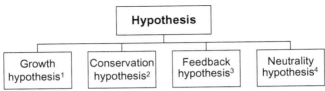

Figure 6.2 Summary the energy—growth nexus of hypotheses. *Notes*: (1) Unidirectional causality from energy to growth; (2) unidirectional causality ranging from growth to energy; (3) bidirectional causality between energy and growth; and (4) there is no causal relationship between energy and economic growth. *Adapted from Ozturk (2010). A literature survey on energy—growth nexus.* Energy Policy, 38(1), 340—349.

There is an abundance of empirical literature that focuses on energy consumption as a critical driver of economic growth. It exists to try to solve problems and to respond to existing criticisms about previous studies (Camarero et al., 2015). An underlying study in the literature combines economic growth and energy consumption incorporating financial development (e.g., Ajide, Bekoe, Yaqub, & Adeniyi, 2013; Kahouli, 2017; Komal & Abbas, 2015; Mallick & Mahalik, 2014; Sadorsky, 2010; Shahbaz & Lean, 2012b). It is known that financial development refers to a country's decision to promote and enable financial activities through increased FDI, banking activity, and stock market activity. In addition, financial development is important because it can increase the economic efficiency of a country's financial system, affecting economic activity, and energy supply. If financial development is affected by energy supply, this relationship may affect energy policy and carbon emission strategies (Sadorsky, 2011).

When analyzing the literature on financial development and energy consumption, we are faced with diverse results. There is evidence that an increase in financial development increases energy consumption (e.g., Brunnschweiler, 2010; Tang & Tan, 2014). However, it has been shown that with an increase in financial development, energy consumption decreases (e.g., Sbia, Shahbaz, & Hamdi, 2014). The analyses of three financial sectors—banking, stock market, and bond market—as well as an overall financial development index emerges in the literature, but it was concluded that there is no statistically significant relationship between financial development and energy consumption. When there is an increase in the stock market it generates only a slight decrease in energy consumption (Topcu & Payne, 2017).

The literature often faces several problems. First, in many existing studies on financial development, the authors measure it only with one or two variables linked to financial development (e.g., Islam et al., 2013; Komal & Abbas, 2015; Xu, 2012). However, financial development is a multifaceted phenomenon, that is, a proxy for financial development is not enough for a study, particularly in a set of countries (Cole, 1988). This situation occurs because countries differ: (1) in financial structures; (2) in financial institutions; (3) size of financial institutions and instruments; (4) efficiency of financial intermediaries; and (5) the effectiveness of the financial regulatory framework (Ang, 2008). Therefore the different financial development measures one includes may lead to very different conclusions (e.g., Chang, 2015; Çoban & Topcu, 2013; Kakar, 2016).

In general the demand for energy has increased significantly in the last decades, due to the high growth of the global economies. This has resulted in climate change, that is, changes in the greenhouse effect, raising new challenges for all countries (Zhang, Yu, & Chen, 2017). This has happened because energy consumption has skyrocketed, having positive effects on economic growth and financial development, but negative on pollution (Al-Mulali & Sab, 2012).

Really, by and large CO_2 emissions come from the combustion of fossil fuels, which in turn is determined by energy demand or by the level of energy intensity. However, changes in energy efficiency and fuel mix can reduce the overall level of global emissions (e.g., Bekhet, Matar, & Yasmin, 2017).

The phenomenon of economic growth should not be dissociated from the problem of environmental degradation (Marques et al., 2016). It has been demonstrated by several studies that economic growth is correlated with environmental degradation (e.g., Dinda, 2004; Saboori, Sulaiman, & Mohd, 2012). The energy sector is constantly growing, and significant changes are required in today's economic systems to address the various challenges of climate change and economic recovery (Zysman & Huberty, 2013). Sustainable development goals should be a goal for humanity. It is known that sustainability transitions are a long-term transformation processes and sustainability challenges can be observed in several areas, for example, in energy supply, water supply, sanitation systems, transport, agriculture, and the food system (e.g., Geels, 2011; Gil & Beckman, 2009).

Globally the literature incorporates energy consumption, economic growth, economic development, and CO_2 emissions. For example, Boutabba (2014) has shown that financial development has a positive long-term impact, implying that financial development retards environmental degradation. In the study by Jalil and Feridun (2011), the results revealed a negative sign for the financial development coefficient, suggesting that financial development in China did not occur to the detriment of environmental health. In sub-Saharan Africa, energy consumption played an important role in increasing economic growth and financial development but resulted in high levels of pollution (Al-Mulali & Sab, 2012). However, Tamazian et al. (2009) show that for the BRIC economies from 1992 to 2004, economic development reduces environmental degradation with higher levels of economic growth. It has also been revealed that financial development is a key factor in reducing CO_2 emissions per capita.

In short, economic growth is closely linked to energy consumption, as increasing consumption leads to greater growth (Omri, 2013). The rapid growth of the economy, industrialization, and the intensive use of natural resources have been responsible for the increase of waste that has led to the deterioration of the environment. This deterioration is responsible for damage to infrastructure, natural resources, agricultural productivity and, most importantly, the loss of human life (Shahbaz et al., 2013). In addition, Fung (2009) found that an efficient financial system creates more products, increasing the demand for energy. Thus financial development is a factor that must be considered in energy consumption economic—growth nexus.

The literature approaches the essential points on the subject under study. We realized that the lack of consensus results from the use of different econometric methodologies, countries, time horizon, and datasets. This way, our main objective is to fill the existing gaps in the literature, through new evidence for energy—growth nexus, incorporating the two types: the domestic credit and the environmental sustainability.

6.3 Data and methodology

In this section we present the data and the methodology used. The PVAR is composed by 19 high-income countries (Australia, Austria, Belgium, Greece, France, Germany, Ireland, Israel, Italy, Japan, Holland, Norway, Portugal, Singapore, Spain, United States, Poland, Switzerland, and Hong Kong), the data comprise information from 2001 to 2016. In Table 6.1 the variables description is detailed.

The econometric analysis requires several tests to be performed before estimating models. Next, in Table 6.2, we present a summary of the methodology used in the study.

Through the pairwise structure that captures the bivariate relationships between variables, we seek to obtain valuable information regarding the explanatory capacity of the PVAR model. In Eq. (6.1), we present the Granger noncausality according to Dumitrescu and Hurlin (2012):

$$y_{i,t} = c_i + A_{i,1}y_{i,t-1} + A_{i,2}y_{i,t-2} + \cdots + A_{i,p}y_{i,t-p}$$
$$+ \beta_{i,1}x_{i,t-1} + \beta_{i,2}x_{i,t-2} + \cdots + \beta_{i,p}x_{i,t-p} + u_{i,t} \quad (6.1)$$

Table 6.1 Variables definition and descriptive statistics.

Variables	Acronyms	Source	Units	Transformations
Electricity generation	DLEG	BP statistical review of world energy[a]	Terawatt-hours	Per capita, multiplied by 1 million, logarithms in first differences
Primary energy consumption	DLPEC	BP Statistical review of world energy	Million tonnes oil equivalent	Per capita, multiplied by 1 million, logarithms in first differences
CO_2 emissions	DLCO2	BP statistical review of world energy	Million tonnes carbon dioxide	Per capita, multiplied by 1 million, logarithms in first differences
Domestic credit to private sector	DLDCPS	World Bank[b]	(% of GDP)	Divided by 100, multiplied by gross domestic product, per capita, logarithms, and first differences
Domestic credit provided by financial sector	DLDCFS	World Bank	(% of GDP)	Divided by 100, multiplied by gross domestic product, per capita, logarithms, and first differences
Gross domestic product	DLGDP	World Bank	Constant LCU	Per capita, logarithms, and first differences
Inflation	INF	International Monetary Fund[c]	Percent change	

Descriptive statistics

Stats	Eg	pec	Co_2	gdp	dcps	dcfs	lft
N	304	304	304	304	304	304	304
Min.	3.769935	2.12644	4.47498	16028.16	3427.573	1332.458	− 3.545
Max.	29.86458	14.99226	39.38814	4178995	7732350	2.81e + 07	6.496
Mean	8.541495	4.726455	11.0613	286078.6	469070.5	1332305	1.723438
SD	5.036058	2.55321	6.573088	868360.7	1564626	5051956	1.542259
CV	0.5895991	0.5401955	0.5942419	3.035392	3.335588	3.791893	0.8948735
Skewness	2.766234	1.873896	2.304854	3.894638	3.950608	4.089475	−0.1126974

Note: The variable Total Population, by World Bank was used to transform the other variables into per capita.
[a]Available at: https://www.bp.com/en/global/corporate/energy-economics/statistical-review-of-world-energy.html.
[b]Available at: http://databank.worldbank.org/data/source/world-development-indicators.
[c]Available at: http://www.imf.org/external/index.htm.

Table 6.2 Summary of methodology.

Diagnostic tests/statistics	Pairwise	Model estimation	Validity
Hausman			Impulse-response function
Variance Inflation Factor (VIF)	Dumitrescu & Hurlin	PVAR−GMM	Eigenvalue stability condition
Lag order Selection	Granger Causality— Bootstrap	Granger Causality	Forecast-error variance decomposition
CD-test			

Following the method Dumitrescu and Hurlin (2012) the null hypothesis is: The independent variable does not Granger-cause the dependent variable; and the alternative hypothesis: The independent variable does Granger-cause the dependent variable for at least one panelvar (country). The command *xtgcause* is available at *ssc install* Stata archive.

How to do:
** Install xtgcause command **
   ssc install xtgcause

In addition, we used the same specification of the first-order vector auto-regressive equation by Love and Zicchino (2006). Can be seen in Eq. (6.2):

$$z_{it} = \Gamma_0 + \Gamma_1 z_{it-1} + f_i + d_{c,t} + u_t \tag{6.2}$$

where, z_{it} is a vector of variables, in first differences, except the inflation (ift) that was used at level. More details on the methodology and commands for running a PVAR can be found in Chapter 8, The interactions between conventional and alternative energy sources in the transport sector: a panel of Organization for Economic Cooperation and Development countries.

6.4 Results and discussion

For a good construction and estimation of the PVAR it is necessary that the Hausman test result be fixed effects in at least one of the possible equations. The average VIF statistic should be below 10%. Our results meet the initial requirements for panel development. Table 6.3 describes the VIF statistic, Hausman test, and cross-sectional dependence.

The CSD test indicates the presence of cross-section dependence on all variables. Therefore the unit root test Pesaran's (Pesaran, 2004) was performed. However, due to the short time horizon the test result might not be conclusive, and it was preferred to check the normality and stationary through the Eigenvalue test, presented at the most opportune moment in this chapter.

The bivariate relation between the variables was verified following the one proposed by Dumitrescu and Hurlin (2012) Granger noncausality test.

How to do:

** Stata command **

xtgcause dependent variable independent variable, lags(bic)

Then we proceed with Regress Bootstrap. As recommended by Lopez and Weber (2017) is a very useful option in the presence of cross-dependency.

How to do:

** Stata command **

xtgcause dependent variable independent variable, lags(bic) regress bootstrap breps(300)

Balance the panel and Set Matsize are necessaries (initially we use (800), and by default (300)). The results can be seen in Table 6.4.

Granger's noncausality test results reveal that there are bivariate relationships (highlighted in bold), and the relationships are statistically significant. The level of significance of the causal relationships is 1% and 5%. The only exception is the causal relationship between inflation and domestic credit provided by the financial sector to 10%. The bootstrap analysis still reveals a structure of similar results (causal relationships of 1%, 5%, and 10%). In Fig. 6.3 see the summary.

Table 6.3 VIF, Hausman and cross-sectional dependence (CSD).

Independent variables	Dependent variables						
	DLCO2	DLDCPS	DLDCFS	DLPEC	DLEG	DLGDP	IFT
DLCO2		2.23	2.23	1.2	1.83	2.24	2.25
DLDCPS	5.32		1.21	5.31	5.31	4.70	5.34
DLDCFS	5.11	1.16		5.06	5.08	4.56	5.11
DLPEC	2.38	4.42	4.40		1.92	4.30	4.47
DLEG	2.10	2.55	2.55	1.11		2.58	2.59
DLGDP	1.42	1.24	1.26	1.37	1.42		1.42
IFT	1.18	1.17	1.17	1.18	1.18	1.17	
Mean VIF	2.92	2.13	2.14	2.54	2.79	3.26	3.53
Hausman Prob > Chi^2	0.8734	0.8339	0.7455	0.3309	0.6159	0.0576	0.0008
CSD test	11.07***	8.52***	6.02***	13.57***	8.37***	28.72***	17.00***
	(0.219)	(0.168)	(0.119)	(0.268)	(0.165)	(0.567)	(0.336)
	[0.299]	[0.279]	[0.276]	[0.341]	[0.285]	[0.569]	[0.456]

Note: In () Corr; in [] Abs (corr).

Table 6.4 Bivariate relationships (Dumitrescu & Hurlin, 2012). Granger noncausality test results

Dependent variable	Independent variable	Z-bar tilde	P-value	Dependent variable	Independent variable	Z-bar tilde	P-value*	95% Critical value
dleg	dlco2	1.2981	.1943	dlco2	dleg	−0.9007	.3333	2.2973
dlco2	dleg	−0.9007	.3677	dleg	dlco2	1.2981	.1767	2.1295
dleg	dlpec	0.6226	.5335	dlpec	dleg	0.4646	.6533	2.4235
dlpec	dleg	0.4646	.6422	dleg	dlpec	0.6226	.5300	2.8888
dleg	dlgdp	1.0192	.3081	dlgdp	dleg	0.5608	.6933	2.2437
dlgdp	dleg	0.5608	.5749	dleg	dlgdp	1.0192	.3800	3.0078
dleg	dldcps	1.4934	.1353	dldcps	dleg	0.3844	.7000	2.0993
dldcps	pe	0.3844	.7007	dleg	dldcps	1.4934	**.1000**	2.0309
dleg	dldcfs	0.7318	.4643	dldcfs	dleg	0.7318	.9667	1.8945
dldcfs	dleg	−0.0383	.9695	dleg	dldcfs	−0.0383	.4700	1.9303
dleg	ift	3.0660	**.0022**	ift	dleg	−0.5821	.5267	1.9357
ift	dleg	−0.5821	.5605	dleg	ift	3.0660	**.0233**	2.2478
dlco2	dlpec	−0.5129	.6080	dlpec	dlco2	−0.4424	.7133	2.2562
dlpec	dlco2	−0.4424	.6582	dlco2	dlpec	−0.5129	.6233	2.4968
dlco2	dlgdp	0.3057	.7598	dlgdp	dlco2	0.2191	.8767	2.5042
dlgdp	dlco2	0.2191	.8266	dlco2	dlgdp	0.3057	.8367	2.8804
dlco2	dldcps	3.6197	**.0003**	dldcps	dlco2	0.2088	.8200	1.9894
dldcps	dlco2	0.2088	.8346	dlco2	dldcps	3.6197	**.0100**	1.8939
dlco2	dldcfs	2.7615	**.0058**	dldcfs	dlco2	−0.0722	.9567	1.6573
dldcfs	dlco2	−0.0722	.9424	dlco2	dldcfs	2.7615	**.0233**	1.6533
dlco2	ift	1.0757	.2821	ift	dlco2	−0.4591	.6700	2.2580
ift	dlco2	−0.4591	.6461	dlco2	ift	1.0757	.3267	2.3767

P-values computed using 300 bootstrap replications

(Continued)

Table 6.4 (Continued)
Granger noncausality test results

Dependent variable	Independent variable	Z-bar tilde	P-value	Dependent variable	Independent variable	Z-bar tilde	P-value*	95% Critical value
					P-values computed using 300 bootstrap replications			
dlpec	dlgdp	− 0.1126	.9103	dlgdp	dlpec	− 0.0212	.9867	1.9911
dlgdp	dlpec	− 0.0212	.9831	dlpec	dlgdp	− 0.1126	.9233	3.0037
dlpec	dldcps	0.7303	.4652	dldcps	dlpec	− 0.2717	.7767	1.8003
dldcps	dlpec	− 0.2717	.7858	dlpec	dldcps	0.7303	.4600	2.1966
dlpec	dldcfs	0.2378	.8120	dldcfs	dlpec	− 0.6080	.5400	1.7759
dldcfs	dlpec	− 0.6080	.5432	dlpec	dldcfs	0.2378	.8067	2.0240
dlpec	ift	0.9045	.3658	ift	dlpec	− 0.4344	.6800	2.2156
ift	dlpec	− 0.4344	.6640	dlpec	ift	0.9045	.4033	2.3598
dlgdp	dldcps	3.8789	**.0001**	dldcps	dlgdp	1.5015	.1767	2.6799
dldcps	dlgdp	1.5015	.1332	dlgdp	dldcps	3.8789	**.0500**	3.9427
dlgdp	dldcfs	0.7301	.4653	dldcfs	dlgdp	0.1441	.9067	3.1126
dldcfs	dlgdp	0.1441	.8854	dlgdp	dldcfs	0.7301	.5700	2.5748
dlgdp	ift	2.1886	**.0286**	ift	dlgdp	− 0.5572	.6700	3.6152
ift	dlgdp	− 0.5572	.5774	dlgdp	ift	2.1886	.1567	4.5005
dldcps	dldcfs	0.0525	.9581	dldcfs	dldcps	2.4982	**.0800**	3.0901
dldcfs	dldcps	2.4982	**.0125**	dldcps	dldcfs	0.0525	.9767	3.3391
dldcps	ift	− 0.1936	.8465	ift	dldcps	1.4153	.2067	2.7146
ift	dldcps	1.4153	.1570	dldcps	ift	− 0.1936	.8400	2.6191
dldcfs	ift	− 1.3775	.1684	ift	dldcfs	1.8131	**.0700**	2.0521
ift	dldcfs	1.8131	**.0698**	dldcfs	ift	− 1.3775	.2267	2.7834

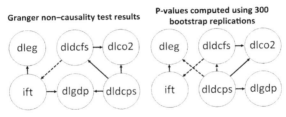

Notes: —— Causality 1% and 5%; ——— Causality 10%.

Figure 6.3 Summary of Granger causal relationships.

Table 6.5 Lag selection.

Lag	CD	J	J P value	MBIC	MAIC	MQIC
1	− 0.73175	154.7557	0.202332	− 585.075	− 127.244	− 312.705
2	0.800685	85.74185	0.663778	− 396.984	− 98.2582	− 219.268
3	0.860246	42.48051	0.493699	− 183.142	− 43.5195	− 100.078
4	0.925872	.	.	.	.	.

Table 6.6 Panel vector autoregressive—Granger causality Wald test.

Equation	Excluded						
	DLCO2	DLEG	DLPEC	DLGDP	DLDCPS	DLDCFS	IFT
DLCO2	—	0.033**	0.003***	0.007***	0.000***	0.000***	0.385
DLEG	0.000***	—	0.123	0.000***	0.000***	0.002***	0.048**
DLPEC	0.000***	0.000***	—	0.000***	0.000***	0.000***	0.015**
DLGDP	0.054*	0.526	0.000***	—	0.000***	0.001***	0.038**
DLDCPS	0.278	0.954	0.000***	0.000***	—	0.038**	0.000***
DLDCFS	0.085*	0.349	0.000***	0.000***	0.883	—	0.000***
IFT	0.192	0.006***	0.000***	0.000***	0.000***	0.000***	—

Note: ***, **, and * denote statistical significance at 1%, 5%, and 10% level, respectively.

The primary energy consumption variable does not reveal a significant statistical probability with other variables. For this reason, the variable was not shown in Fig. 6.3.

Some relationships are not captured by the Dumitrescu and Hurlin (2012) test. However, when conducting a panel analysis, where more variables begin to interact with the model, new results begin to emerge.

Next, the procedures to estimate the panel are started, in Table 6.5, the results of the checking lag order selection.

After getting the ideal number of lags (one), the PVAR estimation was performed. In Table 6.6 the results of the Granger causality Wald test are presented.

The null hypothesis of the test denotes excluded variable but does not Granger-cause the equation variable. We present some relationships that accept the null hypothesis, where (1) CO_2 does not cause DLDCPS and IFT; (2) DLEG does not cause DLGDP, DLDCPS, and DLDCFS; (3) DLPEC does not cause DLEG; (4) DLDCPS does not cause DLDCFS; and (5) INF does not cause DLCO2. The other relationships between the variables are a rejection of the null hypothesis and consequently acceptance of the alternative hypothesis, thus, excluded variable Granger-causes equation variable.

The impulse-response function reveals how a variable reacts in front of an exogenous shock. A shock can affects all endogenous variables. The graphical analysis allows verification of how much time is necessary for a variable hit by a shock to return to zero, that is, the moment of normality. Details can be seen in Fig. 6.4.

In general, most variables in 5 years are recovered from shocks. There are exceptions where variables need more time to recover from shocks, not exceeding 10 years, allowing of course that the variables are stationary. The domestic credit provided by the financial sector when it suffers shocks is the one that takes the most time to stabilize.

The Forecast-Error Variance Decomposition (FEVD) was performed based on the Cholesky decomposition. The FEVD determines how much of the variance of the prediction error of each of the variables can be explained by shocks exogenous to the other variables. For details see Table 6.7.

The forecast-error variance decomposition shows that in the first year the variations of variables mostly explain themselves and present significant values. The variables that capture the credit behavior are: DLDCPS with 45.83% (in the first year) stabilizing until the fifth year after the shock; while the DLDCFS has 13.01% in the first year and stabilizes in the second year. The IFT presents 67.71% self-explanatory.

The variable DLGDP in the first year presents self-explanation of 36.14%; electricity generation and primary energy consumption show 33.43%, and 62.02%, respectively for the first year, both stabilizing after the fifth year. The CO_2 emissions are self-explanatory in the variations in 34.32% (first year).

The last robustness check of the PVAR estimation as Abrigo and Love (2015) suggests the verification of the Eigenvalue stability condition. Details can be seen in Fig. 6.5.

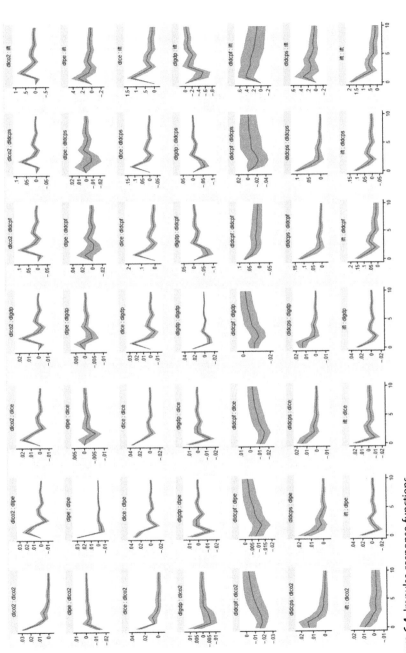

Figure 6.4 Impulse-response functions.

Table 6.7 Forecast-error variance decomposition.

Response variable and forecast horizon	Impulse variable						
	IFT	DLDCPS	DLDCFS	DLGDP	DLPEC	DLEG	DLCO2
IFT							
1	1	0	0	0	0	0	0
2	0.6771	0.0164	0.0258	0.0292	0.2388	0.0115	0.0012
5	0.5676	0.0191	0.0511	0.0529	0.2327	0.0096	0.0670
10	0.5477	0.0199	0.0618	0.0563	0.2340	0.0095	0.0708
DLDCPS							
1	0.5417	0.4583	0	0	0	0	0
2	0.3153	0.2839	0.0065	0.0820	0.3108	0.0003	0.0012
5	0.2806	0.2298	0.0211	0.0986	0.2724	0.0024	0.0951
10	0.2761	0.2253	0.0227	0.1006	0.2721	0.0025	0.1006
DLDCFS							
1	0.5237	0.3463	0.1301	0	0	0	0
2	0.3512	0.2256	0.0848	0.0677	0.2651	0.0029	0.0026
5	0.3332	0.1810	0.0744	0.0862	0.2442	0.0032	0.0778
10	0.3301	0.1738	0.0765	0.0882	0.2452	0.0034	0.0829
DLGDP							
1	0.4818	0.1166	0.0401	0.3614	0	0	0
2	0.2876	0.1384	0.0494	0.2608	0.2570	0.0027	0.0040
5	0.2466	0.1062	0.1152	0.2227	0.2129	0.0090	0.0873
10	0.2447	0.1019	0.1320	0.2159	0.2080	0.0095	0.0879
DLPEC							
1	0.1689	0.1096	0.0576	0.0436	0.6202	0	0
2	0.1391	0.1026	0.0983	0.0893	0.4581	0.0001	0.1124
5	0.1212	0.0893	0.1985	0.0763	0.3906	0.0085	0.1155
10	0.1228	0.0850	0.2229	0.0732	0.3744	0.0094	0.1122
DLEG							
1	0.1695	0.0873	0.0224	0.0216	0.3649	0.3343	0
2	0.1615	0.0652	0.0400	0.0558	0.3346	0.2313	0.1116
5	0.1467	0.0582	0.0932	0.0533	0.3189	0.1987	0.1312
10	0.1468	0.0564	0.1090	0.0524	0.3119	0.1928	0.1308
DLCO2							
1	0.0344	0.0715	0.0977	0.0175	0.3576	0.0781	0.3432
2	0.0323	0.1219	0.1751	0.0243	0.2807	0.0594	0.3062
5	0.0277	0.1068	0.2934	0.0288	0.2405	0.0523	0.2506
10	0.0330	0.1013	0.3220	0.0274	0.2285	0.0506	0.2372

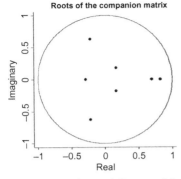

Roots of the companion matrix

Eigenvalue		
Real	Imaginary	Modulus
0.8247462	0	0.8247462
0.6939922	0	0.6939922
−0.2163355	−0.6262584	0.6625712
−0.2163355	0.6262584	0.6625712
−0.2863141	0	0.2863141
0.1636631	0.1810069	0.2440268
−0.1636631	−0.1810069	0.2440268

Figure 6.5 Eigenvalue stability condition.

To assert that there is normality and stability, the analysis of the outputs is simple; graphically the points should not exceed the limit line of the circle and the Real and Imaginary values should not be greater than 1 or less than −1.

Adding to the energy—growth nexus, variables such as credit enriches the political discussion about the need to consider financial development, as seen in the literature, for example, Kahouli (2017). Our results show that there is a unidirectional causal relationship between DLDCPS and DLEG which can be observed through bivariate analysis.

When adding other economic variables in the panel analysis, it was confirmed that the relationships of the domestic credit variables with the DLEG and the DLPEC are reinforced. In other words, high-income countries meet one of the channels of financial development according to Shahbaz et al. (2017).

As it is known, domestic credit plays an important role in economies, especially when associated with energy consumption, because together they can boost economic growth (Samarina & Bezemer, 2016). Our results show the relationships between the same variables for high-income countries. Credit-related policies need to be well planned and knowing the nature of the variables is indispensable. For example direct monetary control is useful for the control of inflationary processes (Fuinhas, 2001), but in the long-term excess domestic credit can have negative effects (Samarina & Bezemer, 2016) for the economy. Therefore regulators in high-income countries should pay attention to establishing credit policies.

In recent years, high-income countries have become more concerned about carbon dioxide emissions. Several measures to produce clean energy and reduce pollution indices have been implemented. But economic growth is still a priority, with the United States, the world's largest economic power, leaving the COP21, Paris Agreement 2015 exclusively in the face of increased economic growth.

The results of the PVAR model also show that economic growth is related to primary energy consumption and vice versa. But we still find results through bivariate analysis that suggest that there is no relationship between the two variables when studied separately. The consumption of fossil fuels damages the planet and the environment but reinforces the idea that there is room for the introduction of alternative forms of energy production, leaving public policy makers to create ways to encourage research, innovation, and the implementation of new technologies.

This chapter demonstrates through bivariate analysis the hypothesis of neutrality, between (1) GDP and PEC; and (2) GDP and GE. In addition, in the analysis of the panel, the PVAR captures the hypothesis of conservation between the GDP that drives the generation of electricity. The hypothesis of feedback between GDP and PEC was also captured.

6.5 Conclusion

In this chapter, we studied the causal relationships of energy—growth nexus, domestic credit, and environmental sustainability in two ways, namely (1) the bivariate relation between variables; and (2) the elaboration of a PVAR with the performance of the Granger causality test. Nineteen high-income countries were selected for the study. The data were comprised of annual information from 2001 to 2016.

The combination of the bivariate analysis and the PVAR allowed us to observe the relationships between variables in addition to providing more robust results. The presence of cross-section dependency indicates the need for elaboration of bootstrap replications, which was performed.

The main results of the bivariate analysis revealed that the GDP has no statistical relationship with primary energy consumption or with the generation of electricity. However, when the PVAR panel analysis is performed, and other variables were added, the results show the existence of endogeneity in the model and reveal the relationship between the variables.

Other variables that do not have a causal relationship through the bivariate model are the financial sector of domestic credit and GDP, but the relationship is seen through the endogenous PVAR model. At the same time, the domestic credit of the private sector shows to be related to GDP in both methods.

The role of credit in the economy is indispensable. It is paramount for the productive sector and for families. Our results suggest that domestic credit should be considered in future research on the energy—growth nexus. We also suggest that public policy makers should consider this variable because of their ability to capture effects on economic growth.

References

Abrigo, M. R. M., & Love, I. (2015). *Estimation of panel vector autoregression in stata: A package of programs*. Department of Economics Working Paper Series, The University of Hawai'i at Mānoa. Available in: <http://www.economics.hawaii.edu/research/workingpapers/WP_16-02.pdf>. Accessed 30.07.18.

Afonso, T. L., Marques, A. C., & Fuinhas, J. A. (2017). Strategies to make renewable energy sources compatible with economic growth. *Energy Strategy Reviews*, *18*, 121—126.

Ahmed, K. (2017). Revisiting the role of financial development for energy-growth-trade nexus in BRICS economies. *Energy*, *128*, 487—495.

Ajide, K., Bekoe, W., Yaqub, J., & Adeniyi, O. (2013). Energy consumption and financial development in Sub-Saharan Africa: A panel econometric analysis. *International Journal of Global Energy*, *36*(2-4), 225—241.

Al-Mulali, U. (2011). Oil consumption, CO_2 emission and economic growth in MENA countries. *Energy*, *36*(10), 6165—6171.

Al-Mulali, U., & Sab, C. N. B. C. (2012). The impact of energy consumption and CO_2 emission on the economic growth and financial development in the Sub Saharan African countries. *Energy*, *39*(1), 180—186.

Ang, J. B. (2008). A survey of recent developments in the literature of finance and growth. *Journal of Economic Surveys*, *22*(3), 536—576.

Apergis, N., Chang, T., Gupta, R., & Ziramba, E. (2016). Hydroelectricity consumption and economic growth nexus: Evidence from a panel of ten largest hydroelectricity consumers. *Renewable and Sustainable Energy Reviews*, *62*, 318—325.

Bekhet, H. A., Matar, A., & Yasmin, T. (2017). CO_2 emissions, energy consumption, economic growth, and financial development in GCC countries: Dynamic simultaneous equation models. *Renewable and Sustainable Energy Reviews*, *70*, 117—132.

Bhattacharya, M., Paramati, S. R., Ozturk, I., & Bhattacharya, S. (2016). The effect of renewable energy consumption on economic growth: Evidence from top 38 countries. *Applied Energy*, *162*, 733—741.

Boutabba, M. A. (2014). The impact of financial development, income, energy and trade on carbon emissions: Evidence from the Indian economy. *Economic Modelling*, *40*, 33—41.

Brunnschweiler, C. N. (2010). Finance for renewable energy: An empirical analysis of developing and transition economies. *Environment and Development Economics*, *15*(3), 241—274.

Camarero, M., Forte, A., Garcia-Donato, G., Mendoza, Y., & Ordoñez, J. (2015). Variable selection in the analysis of energy consumption–growth nexus. *Energy Economics*, *52*, 207–216.

Chang, C. C., & Carballo, C. F. S. (2011). Energy conservation and sustainable economic growth: The case of Latin America and the Caribbean. *Energy Policy*, *39*(7), 4215–4221.

Chang, S. C. (2015). Effects of financial developments and income on energy consumption. *International Review of Economics & Finance*, *35*, 28–44.

Çoban, S., & Topcu, M. (2013). The nexus between financial development and energy consumption in the EU: A dynamic panel data analysis. *Energy Economics*, *39*, 81–88.

Cole, D. C. (1988). Financial development in Asia. *Asian-Pacific Economic Literature*, *2*(2), 26–47.

Dedeoğlu, D., & Kaya, H. (2013). Energy use, exports, imports and GDP: New evidence from the OECD countries. *Energy Policy*, *57*, 469–476.

Destek, M. A. (2015). Energy consumption, economic growth, financial development and trade openness in Turkey: Maki cointegration test. *Bulletin of Energy Economics*, *3*(4), 162–168.

Dinda, S. (2004). Environmental Kuznets curve hypothesis: A survey. *Ecological economics*, *49*(4), 431–455.

Dogan, E. (2015). The relationship between economic growth and electricity consumption from renewable and non-renewable sources: A study of Turkey. *Renewable and Sustainable Energy Reviews*, *52*, 534–546.

Dumitrescu, E. I., & Hurlin, C. (2012). Testing for Granger non-causality in heterogeneous panels. *Economic Modelling*, *29*(4), 1450–1460.

Fang, Z., & Chang, Y. (2016). Energy, human capital and economic growth in Asia Pacific countries: Evidence from a panel cointegration and causality analysis. *Energy Economics*, *56*, 177–184.

Fuinhas, J. A. (2001). *O canal do crédito- admissibilidade teórica e implicações para a política monetária*. Universidade da Beira Interior. Departamento de Gestão e Economia.

Fuinhas, J. A., Marques, A. C., & Koengkan, M. (2017). Are renewable energy policies upsetting carbon dioxide emissions? The case of Latin America countries. *Environmental Science and Pollution Research*, *24*(17), 15044–15054.

Fung, M. K. (2009). Financial development and economic growth: Convergence or divergence? *Journal of International Money and Finance*, *28*(1), 56–67.

Geels, F. W. (2011). The multi-level perspective on sustainability transitions: Responses to seven criticisms. *Environmental innovation and societal transitions*, *1*(1), 24–40.

Ghali, K. H., & El-Sakka, M. I. (2004). Energy use and output growth in Canada: A multivariate cointegration analysis. *Energy Economics*, *26*(2), 225–238.

Gil, N., & Beckman, S. (2009). Introduction: Infrastructure meets business: Building new bridges, mending old ones. *California Management Review*, *51*(2), 6–29.

Gozgor, G., Lau, C. K. M., & Lu, Z. (2018). Energy consumption and economic growth: New evidence from the OECD countries. *Energy*, *153*, 27–34.

Islam, F., Shahbaz, M., Ahmed, A. U., & Alam, M. M. (2013). Financial development and energy consumption nexus in Malaysia: A multivariate time series analysis. *Economic Modelling*, *30*, 435–441.

Jalil, A., & Feridun, M. (2011). The impact of growth, energy and financial development on the environment in China: A cointegration analysis. *Energy Economics*, *33*(2), 284–291.

Kahouli, B. (2017). The short and long run causality relationship among economic growth, energy consumption and financial development: Evidence from South Mediterranean Countries (SMCs). *Energy Economics*, *68*, 19–30.

Kakar, Z. K. (2016). Financial development and energy consumption: Evidence from Pakistan and Malaysia. *Energy Sources, Part B: Economics, Planning, and Policy*, *11*(9), 868—873.

Keho, Y. (2016). What drives energy consumption in developing countries? The experience of selected African countries. *Energy Policy*, *91*, 233—246.

Komal, R., & Abbas, F. (2015). Linking financial development, economic growth and energy consumption in Pakistan. *Renewable and Sustainable Energy Reviews*, *44*, 211—220.

Kraft, J., & Kraft, A. (1978). On the relationship between energy and GNP. *The Journal of Energy and Development*, *3*, 401—403.

Kyophilavong, P., Shahbaz, M., Anwar, S., & Masood, S. (2015). The energy-growth nexus in Thailand: Does trade openness boost up energy consumption?. *Renewable and Sustainable Energy Reviews*, *46*, 265—274.

Le, T. H., & Quah, E. (2018). Income level and the emissions, energy, and growth nexus: Evidence from Asia and the Pacific. *International Economics*. (In Press).

Lopez, L., & Weber, S. (2017). Testing for Granger causality in panel data. *Stata Journal*, *17*(4), 972—984.

Love, I., & Zicchino, L. (2006). Financial development and dynamic investment behaviour: Evidence from panel VAR. *The Quarterly Review of Economics and Finance*, *46*(2), 190—210.

Mallick, H., & Mahalik, M. K. (2014). Energy consumption, economic growth and financial development: A comparative perspective on India and China. *Bulletin of Energy Economics (BEE)*, *2*(3), 72—84.

Marques, A. C., Fuinhas, J. A., & Menegaki, A. N. (2014). Interactions between electricity generation sources and economic activity in Greece: A VECM approach. *Applied Energy*, *132*, 34—46.

Marques, A. C., Fuinhas, J. A., & Nunes, A. R. (2016). Electricity generation mix and economic growth: What role is being played by nuclear sources and carbon dioxide emissions in France? *Energy Policy*, *92*, 7—19.

Marques, L. M., Fuinhas, J. A., & Marques, A. C. (2017). Augmented energy-growth nexus: Economic, political and social globalization impacts. *Energy Procedia*, *136*, 97—101.

Menegaki, A. N., Marques, A. C., & Fuinhas, J. A. (2017). Redefining the energy-growth nexus with an index for sustainable economic welfare in Europe. *Energy*, *141*, 1254—1268.

Narayan, S., & Doytch, N. (2017). An investigation of renewable and non-renewable energy consumption and economic growth nexus using industrial and residential energy consumption. *Energy Economics*, *68*, 160—176.

Ohler, A., & Fetters, I. (2014). The causal relationship between renewable electricity generation and GDP growth: A study of energy sources. *Energy economics*, *43*, 125—139.

Omri, A. (2013). CO_2 emissions, energy consumption and economic growth nexus in MENA countries: Evidence from simultaneous equations models. *Energy economics*, *40*, 657—664.

Ozturk, I. (2010). A literature survey on energy—growth nexus. *Energy policy*, *38*(1), 340—349.

Ozturk, I., & Acaravci, A. (2010). CO_2 emissions, energy consumption and economic growth in Turkey. *Renewable and Sustainable Energy Reviews*, *14*(9), 3220—3225.

Pablo-Romero, M. D. P., & De Jesús, J. (2016). Economic growth and energy consumption: The energy-environmental Kuznets curve for Latin America and the Caribbean. *Renewable and Sustainable Energy Reviews*, *60*, 1343—1350.

Payne, J. E. (2010). A survey of the electricity consumption-growth literature. *Applied energy*, *87*(3), 723—731.

Pesaran, M.H. (2004). General diagnostic tests for cross section dependence in panels. Working Paper No. CWPE;0435, Faculty of Economics, Cambridge University <https://doi.org/10.17863/CAM.5113>. Accessed 30.07.18.

Saboori, B., Sulaiman, J., & Mohd, S. (2012). Economic growth and CO_2 emissions in Malaysia: A cointegration analysis of the environmental Kuznets curve. *Energy policy*, *51*, 184−191.

Sadorsky, P. (2010). The impact of financial development on energy consumption in emerging economies. *Energy policy*, *38*(5), 2528−2535.

Sadorsky, P. (2011). Financial development and energy consumption in Central and Eastern European frontier economies. *Energy Policy*, *39*(2), 999−1006.

Saidi, K., & Hammami, S. (2015). The impact of CO_2 emissions and economic growth on energy consumption in 58 countries. *Energy Reports*, *1*, 62−70.

Samarina, A., & Bezemer, D. (2016). Do capital flows change domestic credit allocation? *Journal of International Money and Finance*, *62*, 98−121.

Santos, J. G., Marques, A. C., & Fuinhas, J. A. (2017). The traditional energy-growth nexus: A comparison between sustainable development and economic growth approaches. *Ecological Indicators*, *75*, 286−296.

Sbia, R., Shahbaz, M., & Hamdi, H. (2014). A contribution of foreign direct investment, clean energy, trade openness, carbon emissions and economic growth to energy demand in UAE. *Economic Modelling*, *36*, 191−197.

Shahbaz, M., & Lean, H. H. (2012a). The dynamics of electricity consumption and economic growth: A revisit study of their causality in Pakistan. *Energy*, *39*(1), 146−153.

Shahbaz, M., & Lean, H. H. (2012b). Does financial development increase energy consumption? The role of industrialization and urbanization in Tunisia. *Energy policy*, *40*, 473−479.

Shahbaz, M., Khan, S., & Tahir, M. I. (2013). The dynamic links between energy consumption, economic growth, financial development and trade in China: Fresh evidence from multivariate framework analysis. *Energy economics*, *40*, 8−21.

Shahbaz, M., Tang, C. F., & Shabbir, M. S. (2011). Electricity consumption and economic growth nexus in Portugal using cointegration and causality approaches. *Energy policy*, *39*(6), 3529−3536.

Shahbaz, M., Van Hoang, T. H., Mahalik, M. K., & Roubaud, D. (2017). Energy consumption, financial development and economic growth in India: New evidence from a nonlinear and asymmetric analysis. *Energy Economics*, *63*, 199−212.

Shahbaz, M., Zakaria, M., Shahzad, S. J. H., & Mahalik, M. K. (2018). The energy consumption and economic growth nexus in top ten energy-consuming countries: Fresh evidence from using the quantile-on-quantile approach. *Energy Economics*, *71*, 282−301.

Silva, P. P., Cerqueira, P. A., & Ogbe, W. (2018). Determinants of renewable energy growth in Sub-Saharan Africa: Evidence from panel ARDL. *Energy*, *156*, 45−54.

Smyth, R., & Narayan, P. K. (2015). Applied econometrics and implications for energy economics research. *Energy Economics*, *50*, 351−358.

Tamazian, A., Chousa, J. P., & Vadlamannati, K. C. (2009). Does higher economic and financial development lead to environmental degradation: Evidence from BRIC countries. *Energy Policy*, *37*(1), 246−253.

Tang, C. F., & Tan, B. W. (2014). The linkages among energy consumption, economic growth, relative price, foreign direct investment, and financial development in Malaysia. *Quality & Quantity*, *48*(2), 781−797.

Tang, C. F., Tan, B. W., & Ozturk, I. (2016). Energy consumption and economic growth in Vietnam. *Renewable and Sustainable Energy Reviews*, *54*, 1506−1514.

Topcu, M., & Payne, J. E. (2017). The financial development−energy consumption nexus revisited. *Energy Sources, Part B: Economics, Planning, and Policy*, *12*(9), 822−830.

Xu, S. J. (2012). *The impact of financial development on energy consumption in China: Based on SYS-GMM estimation*, . In Advanced Materials Research (Vol. 524, pp. 2977−2981). Trans Tech Publications.

Zhang, N., Yu, K., & Chen, Z. (2017). How does urbanization affect carbon dioxide emissions? A cross-country panel data analysis. *Energy Policy, 107*, 678−687.

Zysman, J., & Huberty, M. (2013). *Can green sustain growth?: From the religion to the reality of sustainable prosperity*. Stanford: Stanford University Press.

Further reading

Dasgupta, S., Laplante, B., & Mamingi, N. (2001). Pollution and capital markets in developing countries. *Journal of Environmental Economics and Management, 42*(3), 310−335.

Phoumin, H., & Kimura, S. (2014). Analysis on price elasticity of energy demand in East Asia: Empirical evidence and policy implications for ASEAN and East Asia. ERIA Discussion Paper Series, April 2014.

Pinzón, K. (2017). Dynamics between energy consumption and economic growth in Ecuador: A granger causality analysis. *Economic Analysis and Policy, 57*, 88−101.

Soytas, U., & Sari, R. (2003). Energy consumption and GDP: Causality relationship in G-7 countries and emerging markets. *Energy Economics, 25*(1), 33−37.

CHAPTER SEVEN

The relationship between financial openness, renewable and nonrenewable energy consumption, CO$_2$ emissions, and economic growth in the Latin American countries: an approach with a panel vector auto regression model

**Matheus Koengkan[1], José Alberto Fuinhas[2,*]
and António Cardoso Marques[3,*]**
[1]CEFAGE-UE and Department of Economics, University of Évora, Portugal
[2]NECE-UBI, CeBER, and Faculty of Economics, University of Coimbra, Coimbra, Portugal
[3]NECE-UBI and Management and Economics and Management Department, University of Beira Interior, Covilhã, Portugal

Contents

* This research was supported by NECE, R&D unit and funded by the FCT−Portuguese Foundation for the Development of Science and Technology, Ministry of Science, Technology and Higher Education, project UID/GES/04630/2019.

7.1 Introduction

The nexus between financial openness, renewable and nonrenewable consumption, CO_2 emissions, and economic growth has been receiving considerable attention from scholars, due to the impact of human activities on the environment. Consequently numerous studies have been carried out that approach the relationship between environmental degradation and human activities. In the Latin American countries, environmental degradation (CO_2 emissions) has more than doubled in the last three decades, with the region producing 451 million metric tons in 2008 (Boden, Marland, & Andres, 2011). The most polluting countries of Latin America region are Brazil and Mexico. These countries accounted for 52.6% of the 451 million metric tons of CO_2 in 2008 and both emit more than 100 million metric tons of carbon. Other countries in the region emitting more than 10 million metric tons of carbon annually are Argentina (52.4%), Venezuela (46.2%), Chile (19.9%), and Colombia (18.5%), while Paraguay (15.6%), Trinidad and Tobago (13.6%), Peru (11.1%), and Uruguay (8.5%) are the least polluting countries (Boden et al., 2011). Indeed the consumption of fossil fuels is responsible for the growth in emissions and anthropogenic climate change in the region. Beyond fossil fuel consumption, economic growth and the financial development have also influenced the growth in environmental degradation.

The central question of this chapter is: What is the directional relationship between financial openness, renewable and nonrenewable consumption, CO_2 emissions, and economic growth in the Latin American countries? The main aim of this chapter is investigate the nexus between financial openness, renewable and nonrenewable consumption, CO_2 emissions, and economic growth in 12 Latin American countries over the period of 1980—2014, using the PVAR.

In the literature this relationship has been widely explored by several authors (e.g., Ahmed, 2017; Al-Mulali, 2011; Apergis & Payne, 2012; Apergis, Payne, Menyah, & Wolde-Rufael, 2010; Asumadu-Sarkodie & Owusu, 2017; Attiaoui, Toumi, Ammouri, & Gargouri, 2017; Badeeb & Lean, 2017; Behera & Dash, 2017; Bekhet, Matar, & Yasmin, 2017; Bowden & Payne, 2010; Destek & Aslan, 2017; Jalil & Feridun, 2011; Jamel & Maktouf, 2017; Jebli & Bellouni, 2017; Kasman & Duman, 2015; Katircioğlu & Taşpinar, 2017; Khan, Yaseen, & Ali, 2017; Koengkan, Losekann, & Fuinhas, 2018; Komal & Abbas, 2015; Mirza &

Kanwal, 2017; Rafindadi & Ozturk, 2016; Sadorsky, 2010; Saidi & Mbarek, 2017; Salahuddin, Alam, Ozturk, & Sohang, 2018; Sebri & Ben-Salha, 2014; Shahbaz, Hoang, Mahalik, & Roubaud, 2017; Shahbaz, Hye, Tiwari, & Leitão, 2013; Wang, Li, & Fang, 2017).

Moreover the studies that approached the relationship between financial openness, renewable and nonrenewable consumption, CO_2 emissions, and economic growth have utilized different econometric approaches, such as Autoregressive-Distributed Lag (ARDL) (e.g., Attiaoui et al., 2017; Bekhet et al., 2017; Jalil & Feridun, 2011; Jebli & Bellouni, 2017; Mirza & Kanwal, 2017; Salahuddin et al., 2018; Sebri & Ben-Salha, 2014); Vector Error Correction Model (VECM) (e.g., Ahmed, 2017; Badeeb & Lean, 2017; Wang et al., 2017); Toda—Yamamoto causality test (e.g., Bowden & Payne, 2010); Nonlinear autoregressive-distributed lag (Shahbaz et al., 2017); Panel causality (e.g., Destek & Aslan, 2017; Kasman & Duman, 2015); Pedroni cointegration test (e.g., Apergis & Payne, 2012; Apergis et al., 2010; Behera & Dash, 2017); Granger causality test (e.g., Al-Mulali, 2011; Jamel & Maktouf, 2017; Katircioğlu & Taşpinar, 2017; Khan et al., 2017; Koengkan et al., 2018); Generalized Method of Moments estimation (GMM) (e.g., Komal & Abbas, 2015; Sadorsky, 2010; Saidi & Mbarek, 2017); and Nonlinear iterative partial least squares (NIPALS) (Asumadu-Sarkodie & Owusu, 2017). Although several authors have used different approaches to explain the nexus between financial openness, renewable and nonrenewable consumption, CO_2 emissions, and economic growth, there is not a consensus about the results, due to inconsistent conclusions about the relationship between the variables.

The studies that approach the relationship between financial openness, renewable and nonrenewable consumption, CO_2 emissions, and economic growth can have significant policy implications in the Latin America region. Moreover this chapter could help develop new policies that will increase the consumption of renewable energy, while reducing the consumption of fossil fuels, and consequently emissions, at the same time as promoting development.

This chapter is organized as follows: Section 7.2 contains the literature review, Section 7.3 presents the data and model specification, Section 7.4 presents the results and discussions, and finally Section 7.5 presents the conclusions and policy implications.

7.2 Literature review

The environment degradation—energy—economy—financial openness nexus has attracted attention from researchers in different countries over time. Indeed many of these studies have been carried out on a piecemeal basis without a comprehensive model in mind and thus ignore the potential interaction between the variables. Moreover the study of this nexus is often affected by permanent exogenous shocks which can create structural breaks and consequently can produce misleading outcomes. Thus the literature review of this chapter is divided in (1) economic growth, consumption of energy, and environmental degradation; (2) Financial openness, economic growth, and energy consumption; and (3) environmental degradation and financial openness. We discuss them in turn further.

7.2.1 Studies that approach the nexus between economic growth, consumption of energy, and environmental degradation (CO_2 emissions) nexus

In the literature several authors have approached the relationship between economic activity, energy use (renewable or fossil fuels), and environmental degradation represented by CO_2 emissions. Koengkan et al. (2018) investigated the nexus between consumption of energy, economic growth, and environmental degradation in four Andean community countries over the period of 1971—2014. The authors used the PVAR as methodology. The empirical results indicated the existence of a bidirectional relationship between economic growth to consumption of energy, CO_2 emissions to economic growth, and consumption of energy to CO_2 emissions. Attiaoui et al. (2017) studied the relationship between renewable energy consumption, CO_2 emissions, and economic activity in the Africa countries in a period from 1990 to 2011. The ARDL model was used as methodology. The authors found that there is a bidirectional relationship between economic activity, consumption of renewable energy, and CO_2 emissions. Mirza and Kanwal (2017) investigated the nexus between environmental degradation (CO_2 emissions), economic growth, and energy consumption in Pakistan, using the ARDL model and Granger causality test. The results indicated that there is a bidirectional relationship between environmental degradation, economic growth, and energy consumption.

Wang et al. (2017) examined the nexus between economic growth, emissions, energy consumption, and urbanization in different income levels countries over the period of 1980−2011. The empirical results showed the existence of a bidirectional relationship between all variables of the study. Destek and Aslan (2017) showed the existence of a bidirectional nexus between consumption of renewable energy and economic growth in Greece and South Korea, and a unidirectional nexus in Brazil, Chile, China, Egypt, India, Indonesia, Malaysia, Mexico, Philippines, Portugal, Peru, South Africa, and Turkey. Behera and Dash (2017) analyzed the relationship between consumption of energy, urbanization, emissions, and foreign direct investments (FDI) in 17 South and Southeast Asian (SSEA) countries over the period of 1980−2012. The authors found the existence of a unidirectional nexus between all variables of the model.

Jebli and Bellouni (2017) found the existence of a bidirectional nexus between the consumption of renewable energy and economic growth, and a unidirectional nexus between CO_2 emissions and the consumption of renewable energy in Tunisia over the period from 1980 to 2011. Moreover the ARDL model and the Granger causality test were applied in this study. Kasman and Duman (2015) analyzed the dynamic causality between trade openness, energy consumption, CO_2 emissions, economic activity, and urbanization, in Bulgaria, Croatia, Czech Republic, Estonia, Hungary, Iceland, Latvia, Lithuania, Macedonia, Malta, Poland, Romania, Slovak Republic, Slovenia, and Turkey over the period of 1992−2010. The results indicated that there is a unidirectional relationship between CO_2 emissions, economic growth, urbanization, energy consumption, and trade openness.

Sebri and Ben-Salha (2014) studied the nexus between consumption of renewable energy, economic growth, trade openness, and CO_2 emissions in Brazil, China, India, Russia, and South Africa, in a period of 1971−2010. The ARDL model was used as a method. The authors confirmed the presence of a bidirectional nexus between the consumption of renewable energy, economic growth, and emissions. Apergis and Payne (2012) investigated the relationship between, the consumption of renewable and nonrenewable energy and economic growth in 80 countries over the period from 1980 to 2007. The results indicated that there is a bidirectional relationship between the consumption of renewable and nonrenewable energy and economic growth.

Al-Mulali (2011) examined the relationship between the consumption of oil, CO_2 emissions, and economic growth in MENA (The Middle East and North Africa) countries. The empirical results indicated the existence of a bidirectional relationship between oil consumption, emissions, and economic activity. Apergis et al. (2010) found the existence of a bidirectional nexus between the consumption of renewable energy, environmental degradation, and economic growth in 21 countries for the period from 1984 to 2007, using a panel error correction model. Bowden and Payne (2010) examined the causal relationship between renewable, nonrenewable energy consumption, and economic growth in the United States using annual data from 1949 to 2006. The Toda—Yamamoto causality test showed the existence of a bidirectional relationship between the variables of the model.

7.2.2 Studies that approach the nexus between financial openness, economic growth, and energy consumption

Moreover the relationship between financial openness, economic growth, and energy use has been widely explored in the literature. Shahbaz et al. (2017) analyzed the relationship between energy consumption, economic growth, and financial development in India over the period of 1960—2015. In this research, the nonlinear autoregressive-distributed lag was applied to examine the asymmetric cointegration between the variables. The empirical results demonstrated that all variables of study are cointegrated in the presence of asymmetries. Moreover the asymmetric causality results highlighted the existence of negative impact of energy consumption on economic growth, the negative impact of financial development on economic growth, and a positive impact of financial development on energy consumption.

Badeeb and Lean (2017) found in the Republic of Yemen a negative relationship between oil dependence and financial development, where this impact implies that the positive impact of financial development on economic growth decreases with the increase of oil dependence. Moreover the authors found, when using the Granger causality test, the existence of a unidirectional relationship between financial development and economic growth. Ahmed (2017) studied the nexus between financial development and energy consumption in BRICS economies (Brazil, Russia, India, China, and South Africa) for the period 1991—2013. The author found the existence of a bidirectional nexus between financial development and energy consumption.

Rafindadi and Ozturk (2016) examined the nexus between financial development, economic growth, energy consumption, and export and imports in Japan in a period between 1970 and 2012. The ARDL methodology was used in this study. The authors found that financial development, economic activity, exports, and imports increased the energy used by 0.2329%, 0.5040%, 0.0921%, and 0.2193%, respectively. Moreover the authors found too the existence of a bidirectional nexus between all variables of this study. Komal and Abbas (2015) investigated the nexus between economic activity, energy consumption, and financial development in Pakistan over the period of 1972−2012. The Generalized Method of Moments estimation (GMM) was used as a methodology. The results pointed to a positive and significant impact of economic activity on energy consumption and a positive impact of financial development on energy use and economic growth.

Shahbaz et al. (2013) studied the nexus between economic growth, financial development, energy consumption, CO_2 emissions, and international trade in Indonesia over the period from 1975 to 2011. The ARDL methodology was used. The authors found the existence of a bidirectional nexus between energy consumption, CO_2 emissions, financial development, and international trade. Sadorsky (2010) examined the impact of financial development on energy consumption in 22 emerging economies over the period of 1990−2006. The results showed a positive relationship between energy consumption and financial development.

7.2.3 Studies that approach the nexus between environmental degradation and financial openness

Finally several studies have approached the relationship between CO_2 emissions and financial openness. Salahuddin et al. (2018) investigated the impact of energy consumption, economic activity, foreign direct investment, and financial development on CO_2 emissions in Kuwait using time series data for the period from 1980 to 2013. The ARDL model was used as method. The authors found that economic growth, energy consumption, foreign direct investment, and financial development stimulate environmental degradation in the short and long run. Moreover the Granger causality test indicated the existence of a bidirectional relationship between the variables.

Bekhet et al. (2017) examined the nexus between CO_2 emissions, energy consumption, economic growth, and financial development in Gulf Cooperation Council (GCC) countries from 1980 to 2011. The

ARDL model was used as methodology. The results indicated the existence of a long-run relationship between emissions, financial development, economic growth, and energy consumption in all GCC countries, except United Arab Emirates (UAE). Moreover the existence of a long-run unidirectional relationship between emissions and energy use in Saudi Arabia, UEA, and Qatar was revealed. Additionally, a unidirectional nexus between financial development and CO_2 emissions in UAE, Oman, and Kuwait was proven. Khan et al. (2017) found the existence of a bidirectional relationship between CO_2 emission and urbanization and trade openness in Europe and bidirectional causality between financial development and urbanization in Africa. Moreover a bidirectional relationship was observed between CO_2 emissions and financial development in Europe, Asia, Africa, and America. These results were found in a panel data of 2001−14 in 34 upper-middle-income countries from Asia, Europe, Africa, and America (South and North). The Granger causality test was used as methodology.

Jamel and Maktouf (2017) investigated the nexus between economic activity, financial development, trade openness, and environmental degradation in 40 European economies, during the period of study from 1985 to 2014. The authors found the existence of a bidirectional relationship between, economic growth, environmental degradation, financial development, and trade openness. Katircioğlu and Taşpinar (2017) discovered in Turkey in the period from 1960 to 2010, the existence of a long-run relationship between financial development and Environmental Kuznets curve (EKC). Saidi and Mbarek (2017) studied the impact of financial development, income, urbanization, and trade openness on environmental degradation in 19 emerging countries. The authors found that the model does not support the EKC hypothesis, which assumes an invested U-shaped nexus between income and environmental degradation. Moreover they testified that financial development has a long-run negative impact on environmental degradation.

Asumadu-Sarkodie and Owusu (2017) investigated the relationship between CO_2 emissions, energy use, economic growth, urbanization, financial development, and industrialization in Senegal during the period of 1980−2011. The empirical results pointed out that financial development, energy consumption, and industrialization increase CO_2 emissions by 0.7%, 0.4%, and 0.1% respectively, while urbanization and economic growth increase the emissions by 0.2% and 0.1%, respectively. Jalil and Feridun (2011) analyzed the impact of financial development, economic growth, and energy use on CO_2 emissions in China from 1952 to 2006 using the ARDL model. The results attest that financial development has no impact on CO_2 emissions. Moreover they found that energy consumption and economic growth increase emissions.

This section examined the literature, approaching studies which have analyzed the relationship between economic growth, consumption of energy, financial openness, and environmental degradation. Following on, Section 7.3 will be shown the database and methodology that have been used in order to bring about the realization of this investigation.

7.3 Data and model specification

The aim is to analyze the relationship between financial openness, renewable and nonrenewable consumption, CO_2 emissions, and economic growth. A group of 12 Latin American countries was selected: Argentina, Bolivia, Brazil, Chile, Colombia, Costa Rica, Ecuador, Mexico, Nicaragua, Paraguay, Peru, and Uruguay, over the period of 1980−2014. The choice of the Latin America region is due to the rapid growth in energy consumption in this part of the world, especially from renewable sources, where these sources are in their initial stage of growth. Additionally, these countries have experienced rapid economic growth and financial openness in the last two decades. The variables used in the study are:

(1) Gross domestic product (GDP) in constant local currency units (LCU), available from World Bank Data (WDB)[1];

(2) Renewable energy consumption (Renewable) in a Billion kilowatt-hour (kWh) from biomass, solar, hydropower, photovoltaic, wind, waste, and wave, available from the International Energy Administration (IEA)[2];

(3) Fossil fuels energy consumption (Fossil) in a Billion kilowatt-hour (kWh) from coal, gas, and oil, available from the International Energy Administration (IEA)[2];

---

[1] See http://databank.worldbank.org/data/source/world-development-indicators.
[2] See https://www.iea.org/statistics/?country = WORLD&year = 2015&category = Key%20indicators& indicator = TPESbySource&mode = chart&categoryBrowse = false&dataTable = BALANCES& showDataTable = false.

Table 7.1 Descriptive statistics.

Variables	Descriptive statistics				
	Obs.	Mean	Std. Dev.	Min.	Max.
LGDP	420	11.4679	2.9152	7.6628	16.1938
LRenewable	420	− 14.0829	1.0381	− 16.4111	− 11.4340
LFossil	420	− 0.6645	1.5955	− 3.6347	2.4928
LCO2	420	− 6.4340	0.6155	− 7.9172	− 5.3462
LFinancial	420	0.3624	0.2389	0.0000	0.6931

Notes: Obs. denotes the number of observations; Std. Dev. denotes the Standard Deviation; Min. and Max. denote Minimum and Maximum, respectively; and L denotes variables in the natural logarithms.

(4) Carbon dioxide emissions (CO_2) from the burning of fossil fuels (e.g., solid, liquid, gas fuels, and gas flaring) and the manufacture of cement (kilotons), available from World Bank Data (WDB)[1];

(5) Financial openness index (Financial) that measures a country's degree of capital account openness, available in The Chinn-Ito index (KAOPEN)[3].

The variables (GDP, Renewable, Fossil, and CO_2 emissions) were transformed in *per capita* values. The *per capita* values are able to reduce the effects of population disparity in the Latin American countries (Fuinhas, Marques, & Koengkan, 2017). Furthermore, the option for using the GDP in constant and in LCU, instead of GDP in constant and US dollars, reduces the effects of the inflation and the changes in the exchange rates in the countries of study. The variable (Financial) has some zeros, the research was performed transforming the raw financial openness index by adding (1) to the index of financial openness. Table 7.1 shows the descriptive statistics of all variables in the study.

How to do:

Transformate the variables GDP, Renewable, Fossil, and CO2 in *per capita* values

  gen gdp = (gdp_lcu/population)

Transformate the variables GDP, Renewable, Fossil, CO2, and Financial in logarithms

  gen lgdp = ln(gdp)

Transformate the variables GDP, Renewable, Fossil, CO2, and Financial in first-differences

---

[3] See http://web.pdx.edu/ ~ ito/Chinn-Ito_website.htm.

gen dlgdp = d.lgdp
Descriptive statistics
sum lgdp lrenewable lfossil lco2 lfinancial

After the choice of variables, it is necessary to show the model which will be used in our investigation. The best model to analyze the relationship between financial openness, renewable and nonrenewable consumption, CO_2 emissions, and economic growth in the Latin American countries, is the PVAR. This model was created by Holtz-Eakin, Newey, and Rosen (1988) as an alternative to multivariate simultaneous equation models (Sims, 1980). In the PVAR model, all variables are treated as endogenous, although the existence of restrictions based on statistical procedures may be imposed on disentangling the impact of exogenous shocks onto the system (Abrigo & Love, 2015). This model has been used in multiple applications across the fields. The PVAR model is represented by the following linear equation:

$$Y_{it} = Y_{it-1}e_1 + Y_{it-2}e_2 + \cdots + Y_{it-p+1}e_{p-1} + Y_{it-p}e_p + X_{it}B + u_{it} + \varepsilon_{it}$$

$$(7.1)$$

where, Y_{it} is the vector of dependent variables that are represent by, for example, DLGDP, LRenewable, DLFossil, DLCO2, and DLFinancial, where (L) are variables in the natural logarithms and (D) is the first-differences of the natural logarithms; X_{it} is the vector of exogenous covariates, and ε_{it} are the vectors of the dependent variable in a panel of fixed effects (FE) and idiosyncratic errors, respectively. Moreover the matrices $e_1, e_2, \ldots, e_{p-1}, e_p$ and matrix B are parameters to be estimated.

Before to performing the PVAR model, it is necessary to verify the characteristics of variables. For this, the macroeconometrics literature recommends applying the following preliminary tests:

(1) Variance inflation factor (VIF) to check the existence of multicollinearity between the variables in the panel's data;

(2) Correlations (covariances) of variables or coefficients, to verify the correlations between the variables in the panel's data;

(3) Cross-section dependence (CSD-test) in order to verify the existence of cross-section dependence in the panel data (Pesaran, 2004);

(4) First-generation unit root test that includes the LLC (Levin, Lin, & Chu, 2002), ADF-Fisher (Maddala & Wu, 1999), and ADF-Choi (Choi, 2001) to verify the presence of unit roots. The null hypothesis rejection of LLC is the presence of unit root (common unit root process), and in ADF-Fisher and ADF-Choi, the null hypothesis rejection is the presence of unit root (individual unit root process);

(5) Second-generation unit root test Pesaran's CADF test (Pesaran, 2003), to check the presence of unit roots. The null hypothesis rejection is that the variable is I (1);

(6) Hausman test that determines whether the panel has Random Effects (RE) or FE. The null hypothesis of this test is that the best model is the RE;

(7) PVAR lag-order selection, that reports the model overall coefficient of determination (Hansen, 1982).

To check the proprieties of PVAR model, it is recommended to compute the specification tests. Considering this, some specification tests will be applied, namely:

(1) Granger causality Wald test that analyzes the causal relationship between variables (Abrigo & Love, 2015);

(2) Eigenvalue stability condition that checks the stability condition of PVAR estimates by computing the modulus of each eigenvalue of the model (Abrigo & Love, 2015);

(3) Forecast error varience decomposition (FEVD) that calculates the variance decomposition, which is based on the Cholesky decomposition of the underlying PVAR model. In this test, the standard errors and the confidence intervals are based on Monte Carlos simulation (Abrigo & Love, 2015);

(4) Impulse-response function that computes the plots impulse-response functions (IRF). The confidence bands of IRFs are estimated using Gaussian approximation and base on Monte Carlo simulation (Abrigo & Love, 2015).

The software Stata 15.0 and EViews 10 were used to perform the econometric techniques. Moreover this section shows the database, the model specification, and the preliminary and specification tests that were used in this investigation. In Section 7.4, the results of preliminary tests will be shown, along with the PVAR model and specification tests.

7.4 Results and discussion

This section shows the results of the preliminary test, PVAR model, and specification tests. Table 7.2 shows the results of the correlation test

Table 7.2 Matrices of correlations and variance inflation factor statistics.

Variables	LGDP	LRenewable	LFossil	LCO2	LFinancial
LGDP	1.0000				
LRenewable	0.5146***	1.0000			
LFossil	− 0.0549	0.2207***	1.0000		
LCO2	− 0.0278	0.0222	0.7166***	1.0000	
LFinancial	− 0.1121**	0.0325	− 0.1249**	0.0842*	1.0000
VIF	n.a.	1.11	2.45	2.31	1.10
1/VIF	n.a.	0.9005	0.4075	0.4331	0.9094
Mean VIF			1.74		

Variables	DLGDP	DLRenewable	DLFossil	DLCO2	DLFinancial
DLGDP	1.0000				
DLRenewable	0.0122	1.0000			
DLFossil	0.2688***	0.4971***	1.0000		
DLCO2	0.3118***	− 0.2911***	0.0448	1.0000	
DLFinancial	0.1435***	0.0131	0.0337	0.0874**	1.0000
VIF	n.a.	1.53	1.40	1.16	1.01
1/VIF	n.a.	0.6539	0.7135	0.8604	0.9906
Mean VIF			1.28		

Notes: ***, **, and * denote statically significant at 1%, 5%, and 10% level, respectively; L and D denote variables in the natural logarithms, and the first-differences of the natural logarithms; and n.a. denotes "not available."

and VIF-test, to check the existence of correlation and multicollinearity between the variables in the panel's data.

The results of the correlation test indicate the existence of a high correlation of 70% between "LFossil" and "LCO2" in the natural logarithms. This high correlation is due to the large inclusion of fossil fuels in the Latin American countries' energy matrix and consequently the production of a large amount of emissions (Koengkan, 2018). The result of VIF-test points to the existence of low multicollinearity between the variables in the study. The mean VIF of the variable in the natural logarithms was 1.74, while in the first-differences of the natural logarithms it was 1.23. In fact, both results in the natural logarithms and the first-differences are below the benchmark of 5.

How to do:
Matrices of correlations

    pwcorr lgdp lrenewable lfossil lco2 lfinancial,sig

puvcorr dlgdp dlrenewable dlfossil dlco2 dlfinancial,sig
Variance Inflation Factor
reg lgdp lrenewable lfossil lco2 lfinancial
estat vif
reg dlgdp dlrenewable dlfossil dlco2 dlfinancial
estat vif

In order to verify the presence of cross-section dependence, the CSD-test was applied (Table 7.3).

The result of CSD-test signals for the nonrejection of the null hypothesis in all variables in the natural logarithms and the first-differences of natural logarithms, except for the variable "DLRenewable."

How to do:
Cross-section Dependence
xtcd lgdp lrenewable lfossil lco2 lfinancial
xtcd dlgdp dlrenewable dlfossil dlco2 dlfinancial

In fact, in the presence of cross-section dependence, the econometric literature recommends to verify whether the variables are I(1) or I(0), that is, stationary or nonstationary. For this, the first-generation unit root test that includes the LLC (Levin et al., 2002), ADF-Fisher

Table 7.3 Cross-section dependence test.
Cross-section dependence (CSD-test)

Variables	CD-test	P-value	Corr	Abs (corr)
LGDP	38.19	.000	0.795	0.795
LRenewable	24.15	.000	0.503	0.517
LFossil	44.19	.000	0.919	0.919
LCO2	24.27	.000	0.505	0.541
LFinancial	28.24	.000	0.588	0.614
DLGDP	17.17	.000	0.362	0.362
DLRenewable	− 0.06	.949	− 0.001	0.171
DLFossil	5.36	.000	0.113	0.192
DLCO2	2.67	.008	0.056	0.151
DLFinancial	4.15	.000	0.088	0.166

Notes: L and D denote variables in the natural logarithms, and the first-differences of the natural logarithms; and under the null hypothesis of cross-section independence CD $\sim$ N(0,1).

(Maddala & Wu, 1999), and ADF-Choi (Choi, 2001) to verify the presence of unit roots. The null hypothesis rejection of LLC is the presence of unit root (common unit root process), and in ADF-Fisher and ADF-Choi, the null hypothesis rejection is the presence of unit root (individual unit root process), and the second-generation unit root test (Pesaran's CADF test), to check the presence of unit roots. The null hypothesis rejection is that the variable is I(1). Table 7.4 shows the outcomes of the unit root test of the first-and second-generation.

The LLC, ADF-Fisher, and ADF-Choi tests with lag length (1), and individual intercept and trend were used. The results of the first-generation unit root test indicate that the variables "LGDP, LRenewable, and LFossil" and all variables in the first-differences are I(1). Moreover in the Pesaran's CADF test the variable "LGDP" with "Trend," "LRenewable" without "Trend" and with "Trend," "LFinancial" without "Trend," and all first-differences are I(1).

How to do:

1st Generation unit root tests

  LLC (Levin et al., 2002)

  lgdp.uroot(exog = trend, llc)

  lgdp.uroot(exog = trend, dif = 1, llc)

  ADF-Fisher (Maddala & Wu, 1999) and ADF-Choi (Choi, 2001)

  lgdp.uroot(exog = trend, adf)

  lgdp.uroot(exog = trend, dif = 1, adf)

  2nd Generation unit root tests

  pescadf lgdp if country > = 1 & country < = 12, lags(1)

  pescadf dlgdp if country > = 1 & country < = 12, lags(1)

  pescadf lgdp if country > = 1 & country < = 12, lags(1) trend

  pescadf dlgdp if country > = 1 & country < = 12, lags(1) trend

---

After the realization of the unit root test, it is necessary to verify the presence of RE or FE in the panel's data. The Hausman test of the RE against the FE specification was applied. This test has as null hypothesis that the best model is the RE. The result of this test is statistically significant ($\chi_9^2 = 16.58$) at 5% level, allowing us to reject the null hypothesis, and select the FE model.

Table 7.4 Unit roots tests.

	First-generation unit root tests			Second-generation unit root tests	
				Pesaran's CADF test Z[t-bar]	
	LLC	ADF-Fisher	ADF-Choi	Without trend	With trend
Individual intercept and trend					
LGDP	− 3.5564***	61.4263***	− 2.4129***	− 0.566	− 1.942**
LRenewable	− 3.8550***	60.6989***	− 4.1460***	− 2.507***	− 4.016***
LFossil	− 1.8592**	39.8693***	− 2.3261**	− 3.216***	− 0.560
LCO2	− 0.6640	30.3178	− 1.2148	− 0.270	1.396
LFinancial	0.5747	29.8078	− 0.3388	− 2.492***	− 0.726
DLGDP	− 6.2209***	103.157***	− 7.0754***	− 6.647***	− 5.712***
DLRenewable	− 0.4965***	157.249***	− 10.0711***	− 11.990***	− 10.451***
DLFossil	− 5.0257***	128.117***	− 8.1537***	− 7.663***	− 6.530***
DLCO2	− 7.4484***	151.585***	− 9.4804***	− 11.169***	− 10.031***
DLFinancial	− 5.2389***	106.536***	− 7.5963***	− 8.928***	− 6.924***

Notes: L and D denote variables in the natural logarithms and the first-differences of the natural logarithms; the LLC has H_0: unit root (common unit root process), the test controls for individuals' effects, individual linear trends, has a lag length (1), and Newey–West automatic bandwidth selection and Bartlett kernel were used; the ADF–FISHER and ADF–Choi test has H_0: unit root (individual unit root process), the test controls for individual effects, individual linear trends, has a lag length 1; the Pesaran's CADF test has H_0: series are I(1); and *** and ** denote statistically significant at 1% and 5% level, respectively.

How to do:
Hausman test
  xtreg dlgdp dlrenewable dlfossil dlco2 dlfinancial l.lgdp l.lrenewable l.lfossil l.
lco2 l.lfinancial,fe
    estimates store fixed
    xtreg dlgdp dlrenewable dlfossil dlco2 dlfinancial l.lgdp l.lrenewable l.lfossil l.
lco2 l.lfinancial, re
    estimates store random
    hausman fixed random

Moreover to report the model overall coefficients of determination, the lag-order section was calculated. The overall coefficient of determination (CD), Hansen's J statistic (J), P-value (JP-value), MBIC, MAIC, and MQIC were computed. Table 7.5 shows the results of lag-order selection.

The Panel VAR lag-order selection was used with a maximum of three lags, totalizing 324 observations, 12 panels, and an average of number T of 27.000. The outcome of Hansen's J statistic (J) is higher at one lag, and the MBIC, MAI, and MQIC estimations are lower at one lag.

How to do:
Panel VAR lag-order selection
  pvarsoc dlgdp lrenewable dlfossil dlco2 dlfinancial, maxlag(3) pvaropts(instl (1/6))

After the preliminary tests, the PVAR regression was done. Table 7.6 below shows the outcomes of the PVAR model. The lag length (1), indicated by Panel VAR lag-order selection was used in the PVAR regression.

The results of the PVAR model indicate that as the consumption of renewable energy increases, other areas respond by increasing too: economic growth by 0.0435 in the Latin American countries; fossil fuels consumption by 0.0225, CO_2 emissions by 0.0196, and financial openness by 0.0290. Moreover economic growth increases renewable energy consumption by 0.4961, and CO_2 emissions by 0.1855, while the

Table 7.5 Panel vector auto regression lag-order selection.

Lags	CD	J	JP-value	MBIC	MAIC	MQIC
1	0.9926	128.7039	0.3920	− 593.889	− 121.2961	− 309.9292
2	0.9948	105.1425	0.3429	− 472.9319	− 94.8575	− 245.764
3	0.9933	80.0370	0.3239	− 353.5187	− 69.9629	− 183.1428

Table 7.6 Panel vector auto regression model outcomes.

Response of	Response to				
	DLGDP	LRenewable	DLFossil	DLCO2	DLFinancial
DLGDP	0.2449***	0.4961***	0.3950***	0.0849	− 0.2148**
LRenewable	0.0435***	0.8587***	− 0.0657***	− 0.0182	− 0.0918***
DLFossil	0.0225*	− 0.3721***	0.0256	0.2054***	− 0.1177***
DLCO2	0.0196**	0.1855***	0.0636**	− 0.1943***	− 0.0780***
DLFinancial	0.0290*	− 0.2053***	− 0.0049	0.0931***	0.0291
N. obs			324		
N. panels			12		

Notes: ***, **, and * denote statistical significance level of 1%, 5%, and 10% level, respectively; L and D denote variables in the natural logarithms and the first-differences of the natural logarithms. instruments: l (1/6).

consumption of fossil fuels and financial openness reduce this kind of source by − 0.3721 and − 0.2053, respectively. Economic growth has a positive impact of 0.3950 on the consumption of fossil fuels, and CO_2 emissions of 0.0636, while the consumption of renewable energy reduces the consumption by − 0.0657. The consumption of fossil fuels increases CO_2 emissions by 0.2054 and financial openness by 0.0931. Finally, economic growth, the consumption of renewable energy and fossil fuels, and CO_2 emissions reduces financial openness by − 0.2148, − 0.0918, − 0.1177, and − 0.0780, respectively. In fact, only the variables in the first-differences and the variable LRenewable in the natural logarithms were used in the regression, because the PVAR model requires that all variables be I (1) (see Table 7.4).

How to do:
PVAR model
  pvar dlgdp lrenenewable dlfossil dlco2 dlfinancial, instl(1/6)

The Granger causality Wald test was used to analyze the causal relationship between the variables of the PVAR model. Table 7.7 shows the results of the Granger causality Wald test.

The results point to the existence of a bidirectional relationship between economic growth and the consumption of renewable energy; economic growth and the consumption of fossil fuels; CO_2 emissions and the consumption of fossil fuels; financial openness and economic growth; CO_2 emissions and financial openness; and the consumption of renewable

Table 7.7 Granger causality Wald test.

Equation\Excluded		Chi²	Df.	Prob. > Chi²
DLGDP	LRenewable	24.371	1	***
	DLFossil	2.950	1	*
	DLCO2	3.951	1	**
	DLFinancial	3.328	1	*
	All	26.128	4	***
LRenewable	DLGDP	8.120	1	***
	DLFossil	25.592	1	***
	DLCO2	17.763	1	***
	DLFinancial	13.789	1	***
	All	61.789	4	***
DLFossil	DLGDP	22.389	1	***
	LRenewable	13.801	1	***
	DLCO2	4.279	1	**
	DLFinancial	0.042	1	
	All	48.045	4	***
DLCO2	DLGDP	0.581	1	
	LRenewable	0.474	1	
	DLFossil	25.812	1	***
	DLFinancial	6.814	1	***
	All	43.990	4	***
DLFinancial	DLGDP	4.248	1	**
	LRenewable	20.765	1	***
	DLFossil	19.262	1	***
	DLCO2	12.062	1	***
	All	46.204	4	***

Notes: ***, **, and * denote statistical significance level of 1%, 5%, and 10% level, respectively; L and D denote variables in the natural logarithms and the first-differences of the natural logarithms.

energy and financial openness. Moreover there is a unidirectional nexus between CO_2 emissions and economic growth; consumption of fossil fuels and financial openness, and CO_2 emissions and the consumption of renewable energy. Fig. 7.1 summarizes the statistically significant Granger causalities (dash lines denote P-value < 5% found).

The bidirectional relationship between the consumption of fossil fuels and economic growth is in line with several authors that have studied this nexus previously (e.g., Apergis & Payne, 2010; Chang et al., 2017; Koengkan, 2017a; Koengkan, 2018; Koengkan et al., 2018; Mirza & Kanwal, 2017). With fossil fuels sources being an important input, higher economic growth leads to increases in the consumption of fuels such as coal and petrol to supply the necessary demand (Chang et al., 2017).

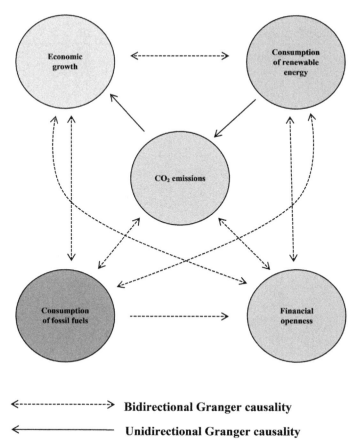

<-------------------> **Bidirectional Granger causality**

<------------------- **Unidirectional Granger causality**

Figure 7.1 Granger causality.

Moreover Mirza and Kanwal (2017) complement that in the Latin America region, fossil fuels sources are the primary inputs for industry and agriculture, and as a consequence influence economic growth.

The bidirectional relationship between the consumption of fossil fuels and CO_2 emissions is confirmed by Fuinhas et al. (2017), Koengkan et al. (2018), Pablo-Romero and Jésus (2016) who studied the same region. The positive influence of the consumption of fossil fuels on environmental degradation in the Latin America region is related to the high economic dependency on this form of energy in most counties of the region (Pablo-Romero & Jésus, 2016). Additionally, Fuinhas et al. (2017) complement that the high economic dependency on fossil fuels in the Latin America region is due to the fact that many countries there are major oil producers, such as Argentina, Brazil, and Venezuela, while others are major importers, such as Uruguay and Paraguay.

The unidirectional nexus between CO_2 emissions and economic growth is confirmed by Azam, Khan, Abdullah, and Qureshi (2016). The unidirectional relationship between emissions to economic growth in the Latin American countries is positive and it implies that these countries are either using green technology or implementing environmental protection agency rules (Azam et al., 2016).

Moreover the bidirectional relationship between consumption of renewable energy and economic growth is confirmed by some studies (e.g., Attiaoui et al., 2017; Destek & Aslan, 2017; Fuinhas et al., 2017; Koengkan, 2017b). The enormous abundance of renewable sources (e.g., biomass, geothermal, hydropower, solar, photovoltaic, wind, and waste) in most countries of the Latin America region stimulates investments and renewable energy technologies and consequently exerts a positive impact on economic growth (Fuinhas et al., 2017).

Moreover the unidirectional nexus between consumption of renewable energy and environmental degradation is in line with Attiaoui et al. (2017) where the increase of environmental degradation stimulates the Latin American countries to converge to a green economy based on renewable energy sources without any pollution, consequently increasing the consumption of green energy.

The bidirectional nexus between consumption of fossil fuels and renewable sources is confirmed by Apergis and Payne (2012). The bidirectionality between consumption of renewable sources and fossil fuels is due to both energy sources being substitutes for each other in the energy matrix in the Latin American countries. The substitutability, between the energy sources, suggests that the development of renewable energy may provide relief from CO_2 emissions generated by the consumption of fossil fuels (Apergis & Payne, 2012).

The founded bidirectional relationship between financial openness and economic growth is in line with several authors (e.g., Ali Bekhet, Matar, & Yasmin, 2017; Işik, Kasimati, & Ongan, 2017; Shahbaz, Khan, & Tahir, 2013). Thus financial openness/development enhances economic growth through investment activities and boosts economic growth and vice versa (Shahbaz et al., 2013). Moreover the bidirectional relationship between financial openness and emissions is confirmed by several authors (e.g., Ali Bekhert et al., 2017; Shahbaz et al., 2013). The bidirectional nexus between emissions and financial openness is related to the positive impact of financial openness on economic growth and energy consumption and consequently on environmental degradation (Ali Bekhet et al., 2017). The unidirectional relationship between financial openness and consumption of fossil fuels is confirmed by some researchers (e.g., Sadorsky, 2010; Shahbaz et al., 2013). Financial openness/development improves banking activities, the stock market, and domestic credit in the private sector and consequently can enhance economic activity and affect energy demand in the long run (Shahbaz et al., 2013). Additionally, Sadorsky (2010) complements that financial openness improves access to financial resources by households and firms that will purchase goods and services and consequently causes a positive impact on energy demand.

Finally the nexus between consumption of renewable energy and financial openness is in line with some studies (e.g., Islam, Shahbaz, Ahmed, & Alam, 2013; Shahbaz et al., 2013). Financial openness facilitates the purchase of renewable energy technologies and energy efficient appliances by households and firms which consequently increase renewable energy consumption, reduces the energy use from fossil fuels, and increases economic growth through new investments in green technologies and energy production (Islam et al., 2013).

How to do:
Granger causality Wald test
pvargranger

Certainly, after the Granger causality Wald test, the eigenvalue stability condition was computed. Table 7.8 displays the graph of Eigenvalue stability condition.

The Eigenvalue-test points that the PVAR model is stable, because all eigenvalues are inside of the unit circle, satisfying the stability condition of the test.

How to do:
Eigenvalue stability condition
pvarstable, graph

The Forecast Error Variance Decomposition (FEVD) needs to be computed after the Eigenvalue-test. Table 7.9 shows the outputs of FEVD test.

Table 7.8 Eigenvalue stability condition.

Eigenvalue			Graph
Real	Imaginary	Modulus	Roots of the companion matrix
0.9220	0.000	0.9220	
− 0.2418	0.000	0.2418	
0.2152	0.000	0.2152	
0.1433	0.000	0.1433	
− 0.0746	0.000	0.0746	

The FEVD test (see Table 7.9) shows that for one period after the shock, the variables themselves explained almost all of the forecast error variance. Fifteen periods after a shock on DLGDP, the variable explains the forecast error variance by 84%, LRenewable explains 15%, DLFossil explains 0.38%, DLCO2 explains 0.36%, and DLFinancial explains 0.45%. The variable LRenewable 15 periods after a shock explains the forecast error variance by 89%, DLGDP explains 6.97%, DLFossil explains 1.79%, DLCO2 explains 0.81%, and DLFinancial explains 1.02%. Moreover one period after a shock on DLFossil, the variables explain the forecast error variance by 86.26%, the variable DLGDP in after five periods explain 11.67%, LRenewable after 15 periods explain 10.24%, DLCO2 explains 0.61%, and DLFinancial 0.15%. The variable DLCO2, one period after the shock explains the forecast error variance by 80.54%, the variable DLGDP after one period explains 0.36%, LRenewable after 15 periods explain 16.03%, DLFossil explains 0.16%, DLFinancial explains 0.57%. Finally, one period after a shock on DLFinancial, the variable explains the forecast error variance by 86.42%, DLGDP after 15 periods explain 4.19%, LRenewable explains 12.38%, DLFossil explains 1.1%, and DLCO2 after one period explains 1.15%.

How to do:
** Forecast error variance decomposition (FEVD-test)**
  pvarfevd, mc(1000) st(15)

Table 7.9 Forecast error variance decomposition.

Response variable and forecast impulse variable horizon	Impulse variable				
	DLGDP	LRenewable	DLFossil	DLCO2	DLFinancial
DLGDP					
0	0	0	0	0	0
1	1	0	0	0	0
5	0.9107	0.0798	0.0023	0.0031	0.0039
10	0.8617	0.1270	0.0033	0.0034	0.0043
15	0.8417	0.1462	0.0038	0.0036	0.0045
LRenewable					
0	0	0	0	0	0
1	0.0260	0.9739	0	0	0
5	0.0619	0.9044	0.0166	0.0074	0.0094
10	0.0680	0.8961	0.0177	0.0080	0.0100
15	0.0697	0.8938	0.0179	0.0081	0.0102
DLFossil					
0	0	0	0	0	0
1	0.0845	0.0528	0.8626	0	0
5	0.1167	0.0869	0.7887	0.0061	0.0013
10	0.1162	0.0977	0.7782	0.0061	0.0015
15	0.1160	0.1024	0.7737	0.0061	0.0015
DLCO2					
0	0	0	0	0	0
1	0.0364	0.1563	0.0017	0.8054	0
5	0.0357	0.1575	0.0167	0.7842	0.0057
10	0.0358	0.1594	0.0167	0.7822	0.0057
15	0.0359	0.1603	0.0167	0.7812	0.0057
DLFinancial					
0	0	0	0	0	0
1	0.0390	0.0744	0.0105	0.0116	0.8642
5	0.0410	0.1092	0.0109	0.0115	0.8272
10	0.0410	0.1092	0.0109	0.0115	0.8272
15	0.0418	0.1238	0.0111	0.0114	0.8117

Note: L and D denote variables in the natural logarithms and the first-differences.

After the application of FEVD test, it is necessary to calculate the impulse-response functions (IRF) of variables. Fig. 7.2 shows the impulse-response functions.

In the long run all variables converge to equilibrium, supporting that the variables of the model are I(1). The impulse-response functions are in concordance with FEVD test.

How to do:
Impulse − Response Functions (IRF)
    pvarirf, mc(1000) oirf byopt(yrescale) st(15)

This section illustrated the empirical results and the possible explanations for the bidirectionality and unidirectionality in the Latin American countries and Section 7.5 will contain the conclusion and policy implications of this study.

7.5 Conclusions and policy implications

The relationship between financial openness, renewable and nonrenewable consumption, CO_2 emissions, and economic growth was assessed for 12 Latin American countries, for the period from 1980 to 2014, by using a PVAR model. The results of preliminary test proved the presence of a high correlation between the consumption of fossil fuels environmental degradation, low multicollinearity, cross-section dependence, unit roots, FE in the PVAR model, and the need to use the lag length (1) in the PVAR model.

The results of PVAR regression showed that the consumption of renewable energy, fossil fuels, CO_2 emissions, and financial openness increase economic growth. Moreover economic growth and emissions increase the consumption of renewable energy, while the consumption of fossil fuels and financial openness reduce this kind of source. Economic growth and CO_2 emissions increase the consumption of fossil fuels, while the consumption of renewable energy substitutes the fossil fuels. Additionally, the consumption of fossil fuels and financial openness increase environmental degradation. Economic growth, consumption of

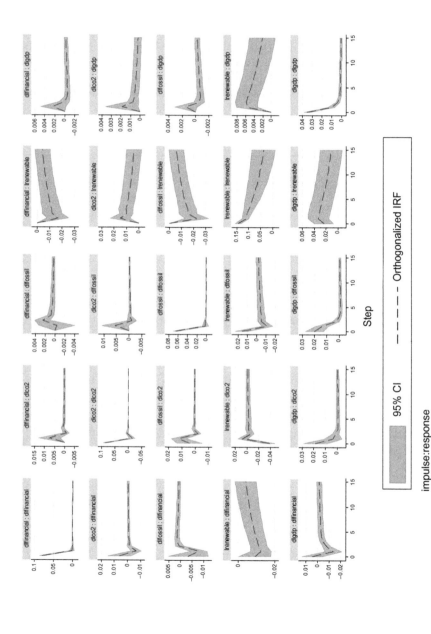

Figure 7.2 Impulse-response functions. Source: *Stata*.

renewable energy and fossil fuels, and environmental degradation reduce financial openness.

The results of specification tests showed the existence of a bidirectional relationship between economic growth and the consumption of renewable energy; economic growth and consumption of fossil fuels; CO_2 emissions and consumption of fossil fuels; financial openness and economic growth; CO_2 emissions and financial openness; and consumption of renewable energy and financial openness. Moreover a unidirectional nexus between CO_2 emissions and economic growth; consumption of fossil fuels and financial openness, and CO_2 emissions and consumption of renewable energy. The PVAR model is stable, that one period after the shock the variables themselves explained almost all the forecast error variance, and all variables converge to equilibrium in the long run, supporting that all variables of the model are I(1).

These findings support that more public policies are needed to encourage the consumption and investment in renewable sources by firms and households. Subsidy policies that stimulate the consumers to purchase appliances with high energy efficiency standards to reduce the energy consumption are needed, and also policies that incentivize the decentralization of generation, where in the Latin America countries they do not receive government support and consideration. These policies need to be implanted to reduce the dependency on fossil fuels, reduce CO_2 emissions, increase the participation of renewable energy sources in energy mix, promote the economic growth and development, and take advantage of the enormous abundance of renewable energy sources in the Latin America region. Finally, this chapter contributes to the demonstration of the application of econometric techniques, which are crucial, not only for the reapplication of these results, but also to assist other researchers in their empirical studies.

References

Abrigo, M. R. M., & Love, I. (2015). *Estimation of panel vector autoregression in Stata: A package of programs*. Department of Economics Working Paper Series, the University of Hawaii at Mānoa. Available at <http://www.economics.hawaii.edu/research/workingpapers/WP_16-02.pdf>.

Ahmed, K. (2017). Revisiting the role of financial development for energy-growth-trade nexus in BRICS economies. *Energy*, *128*(1), 487–495. Available from https://doi.org/10.1016/j.energy.2017.04.055.

Al-Mulali, U. (2011). Oil consumption, CO_2 emission and economic growth in MENA countries. *Energy*, *36*(10), 6165–6171. Available from https://doi.org/10.1016/j.energy.2011.07.048.

Ali Bekhet, H., Matar, A., & Yasmin, T. (2017). CO₂ emissions, energy consumption, economic growth, and financial development in GCC countries: Dynamic simultaneous equation models. *Renewable and Sustainable Energy Reviews, 70*, 117−132. Available from https://doi.org/10.1016/j.rser.2016.11.089.

Apergis, N., & Payne, J. E. (2010). Energy consumption and growth in South America: Evidence from a panel error correction model. *Energy Economics, 32*(6), 1421−1426. Available from https://doi.org/10.1016/j.eneco.2010.04.006.

Apergis, N., & Payne, J. E. (2012). Renewable and non-renewable energy consumption-growth nexus: Evidence from a panel error correction model. *Energy Economics, 34*(3), 733−738. Available from https://doi.org/10.1016/j.eneco.2011.04.007.

Apergis, N., Payne, J. E., Menyah, K., & Wolde-Rufael, Y. (2010). On the causal dynamics between emissions, nuclear energy, renewable energy, and economic growth. *Ecological Economics, 69*(11), 2255−2260. Available from https://doi.org/10.1016/j.ecolecon.2010.06.014.

Asumadu-Sarkodie, S., & Owusu, P. A. (2017). A multivariate analysis of carbon dioxide emissions, electricity consumption, economic growth, financial development, industrialization, and urbanization in Senegal. *Journal Energy Sources, Part B: Economics, Planning, and Policy, 12*(1), 77−84. Available from https://doi.org/10.1080/15567249.2016.1227886.

Attiaoui, I., Toumi, H., Ammouri, B., & Gargouri, I. (2017). Causality links among renewable energy consumption, CO₂ emissions, and economic growth in Africa: Evidence from a panel ARDL-PMG approach. *Environmental Science and Pollution Research, 24*(14), 13036−13048. Available from https://doi.org/10.1007/s11356-017-8850-7.

Azam, M., Khan, A. Q., Abdullah, H. B., & Qureshi, M. E. (2016). The impact of CO₂ emissions on economic growth: Evidence from selected higher CO₂ emissions economies. *Environmental Science and PollutionResearch, 23*(7), 6376−6389. Available from https://doi.org/10.1007/s11356-015-5817-4.

Badeeb, R. A., & Lean, H. H. (2017). Financial development, oil dependence and economic growth: Evidence from the Republic of Yemen. *Studies in Economics and Finance, 34*(2), 281−298. Available from https://doi.org/10.1108/SEF-07-2014-0137.

Behera, S. R., & Dash, D. P. (2017). The effect of urbanization, energy consumption, and foreign direct investment on the carbon dioxide emissions in the SSEA (South and Southeast Asian) region. *Renewable and Sustainable Energy Reviews, 70*, 96−106. Available from https://doi.org/10.1016/j.rser.2016.11.201.

Bekhet, H. A., Matar, A., & Yasmin, T. (2017). CO2 emissions, energy consumption, economic growth, and financial development in GCC countries: Dynamic simultaneous equation models. *Renewable and Sustainable Energy Reviews, 70*, 117−132. Available from https://doi.org/10.1016/j.rser.2016.11.089.

Boden, T. A., Marland, G., & Andres, R.J. (2011). *Global, regional, and national fossil-fuel CO₂ emissions*. Carbon Dioxide Information Analysis Center, Oak Ridge National Laboratory, U.S. Department of Energy, Oak Ridge, Tennessee, USA <https://doi.org/10.3334/CDIAC/00001_V2011>.

Bowden, N., & Payne, J. E. (2010). Sectoral analysis of the causal relationship between renewable and non-renewable energy consumption and real output in the US. *Energy Sources, Part B: Economics, Planning, and Policy, 5*(4), 400−408. Available from https://doi.org/10.1080/15567240802534250.

Chang, T., Deale, D., Gupta, R., Hefer, R., Inglesi-Lotz, R., & Simo-Kengne, B. (2017). The causal relationship between coal consumption and economic growth in the BRICS countries: Evidence from panel-Granger causality tests. *Energy Sources, Part B: Economics, Planning, and Policy, 12*(2), 138−146. Available from https://doi.org/10.1080/15567249.2014.912696.

Choi, I. (2001). Unit root test for panel data. *Journal of International Money and Finance, 20* (1), 249−272.

Destek, M. A., & Aslan, A. (2017). Renewable and non-renewable energy consumption and economic growth in emerging economies: Evidence from bootstrap panel causality. *Renewable Energy, 111*, 757−763. Available from https://doi.org/10.1016/j.renene.2017.05.008.

Fuinhas, J. A., Marques, A. C., & Koengkan, M. (2017). Are renewable energy policies upsetting carbon dioxide emissions? The case of Latin America countries. *Environmental Science and Pollution Research, 24*(17), 15044−15054. Available from https://doi.org/10.1007/s11356-017-9109-z.

Hansen, L. P. (1982). Large sample properties of generalized method of moments estimators. *Econometrica, 50*(4), 1029−1054. Available at <http://www.jstor.org/stable/1912775>.

Holtz-Eakin, D., Newey, W., & Rosen, H. S. (1988). Estimating vector autoregressions with panel data. *Econometrica, 56*(6), 1371−1395.

Işik, C., Kasimati, E., & Ongan, S. (2017). Analyzing the causalities between economic growth, financial development, international trade, tourism expenditure and/on the CO2 emissions in Greece. *Energy Sources, Part B: Economics, Planning, and Policy, 12*(7), 665−673. Available from https://doi.org/10.1080/15567249.2016.1263251.

Islam, F., Shahbaz, M., Ahmed, A. U., & Alam, Md. M. (2013). Financial development and energy consumption nexus in Malaysia: A multivariate time series analysis. *Energy Policy, 38*(5), 2528−2535. Available from https://doi.org/10.1016/j.econmod.2012.09.033.

Jalil, A., & Feridun, M. (2011). The impact of growth, energy and financial development on the environment in China: A cointegration analysis. *Energy Economics, 33*(1), 284−291. Available from https://doi.org/10.1016/j.eneco.2010.10.003.

Jamel, L., & Maktouf, S. (2017). The nexus between economic growth, financial development, trade openness, and CO_2 emissions in European countries. *Journal Cogent Economics & Finance, 5*(1), 1−25. Available from https://doi.org/10.1080/23322039.2017.1341456.

Jebli, M. B., & Belloumi, M. (2017). Investigation of the causal relationships between combustible renewables and waste consumption and CO_2 emissions in the case of Tunisian maritime and rail transport. *Renewable and Sustainable Energy Reviews, 71*, 820−829. Available from https://doi.org/10.1016/j.rser.2016.12.108.

Kasman, A., & Duman, Y. S. (2015). CO2 emissions, economic growth, energy consumption, trade and urbanization in new EU member and candidate countries: A panel data analysis. *Economic Modelling, 44*, 97−103. Available from https://doi.org/10.1016/j.econmod.2014.10.022.

Katircioğlu, S. T., & Taşpinar, N. (2017). Testing the moderating role of financial development in an environmental Kuznets curve: Empirical evidence from Turkey. *Renewable and Sustainable Energy Reviews, 68*(1), 572−586. Available from https://doi.org/10.1016/j.rser.2016.09.127.

Khan, M. T. I., Yaseen, M. R., & Ali, Q. (2017). Dynamic relationship between financial development, energy consumption, trade and greenhouse gas: Comparison of upper middle-income countries from Asia, Europe, Africa and America. *Journal of Cleaner Production, 161*(1), 567−580. Available from https://doi.org/10.1016/j.jclepro.2017.05.129.

Koengkan, M. (2017a). O Nexo entre o Consumo de Energia Primária e o Crescimento Económico nos Países da América da Sul: Uma Análise de Longo Prazo. *Cadernos UniFOA, 34*, 63−74, ISSN: 1982-1816.

Koengkan, M. (2017b). The hydroelectricity consumption and economic growth nexus: A long time span analysis. *Revista Brasileira de Energias Renováveis*, 1−27. Available from https://doi.org/10.5380/rber.v6i4.49181.

Koengkan, M. (2018). The positive impact of trade openness on consumption of energy: Fresh evidence from Andean community countries. *Energy*, *158*(1), 936−943. Available from https://doi.org/10.1016/j.energy.2018.06.091.

Koengkan, M., Losekann, L. D., & Fuinhas, J. A. (2018). The relationship between economic growth, consumption of energy, and environmental degradation: Renewed evidence from Andean community nations. *Environment Systems and Decisions*, 1−13. Available from https://doi.org/10.1007/s10669-018-9698-1.

Komal, R., & Abbas, F. (2015). Linking financial development, economic growth and energy consumption in Pakistan. *Renewable and Sustainable Energy Reviews*, *44*, 211−220. Available from https://doi.org/10.1016/j.rser.2014.12.015.

Levin, A., Lin, C.-F., & Chu, C.-S. J. (2002). Unit root test in panel data: Asymptotic and finite-sample properties. *Journal of Econometrics*, *108*(1), 1−24.

Maddala, G. S., & Wu, S. A. (1999). Comparative study of unit root test with panel data a new simple test. *Oxford Bulletin of Economics and Statistics*, *61*(1), 631−652.

Mirza, F. M., & Kanwal, A. (2017). Energy consumption, carbon emissions and economic growth in Pakistan: Dynamic causality analysis. *Renewable and Sustainable Energy Reviews*, *72*, 1233−1240. Available from https://doi.org/10.1016/j.rser.2016.10.081.

Pablo-Romero, M. D., & Jésus, J. D. (2016). Economic growth, and energy consumption: The energy-environmental Kuznets curve for Latin America and the Caribbean. *Renewable and Sustainable Energy Reviews*, *60*, 1343−1350. Available from https://doi.org/10.1016/j.rser.2016.03.029.

Pesaran, H. (2003). A simple panel unit root test in the presence of cross section dependence. *Cambridge Working Papers in Economics 0346*. Faculty of Economics (DAE), University of Cambridge.

Pesaran, M. H. (2004). General diagnostic tests for cross section dependence in panels. *Cambridge Working Papers in Economics, No. 0435*. Faculty of Economics, University of Cambridge.

Rafindadi, A. A., & Ozturk, I. (2016). Effects of financial development, economic growth and trade on electricity consumption: Evidence from post-Fukushima Japan. *Renewable and Sustainable Energy Reviews*, *54*, 1073−1084. Available from https://doi.org/10.1016/j.rser.2015.10.023.

Sadorsky, P. (2010). The impact of financial development on energy consumption in emerging economies. *Energy Policy*, *38*(5), 2528−2535. Available from https://doi.org/10.1016/j.enpol.2009.12.048.

Saidi, K., & Mbarek, M. B. (2017). The impact of income, trade, urbanization, and financial development on CO2 emissions in 19 emerging economies. *Environmental Science and Pollution Research*, *24*(14), 12748−12757. Available from https://doi.org/10.1007/s11356-016-6303-3.

Salahuddin, M., Alam, K., Ozturk, I., & Sohang, K. (2018). The effects of electricity consumption, economic growth, financial development and foreign direct investment on CO2 emissions in Kuwait. *Renewable and Sustainable Energy Reviews*, *81*(2), 2002−2010. Available from https://doi.org/10.1016/j.rser.2017.06.009.

Sebri, M., & Ben-Salha, O. (2014). On the causal dynamics between economic growth, renewable energy consumption, CO_2 emissions, and trade openness: Fresh evidence from BRICS countries. *Renewable and Sustainable Energy Reviews*, *39*, 14−29. Available from https://doi.org/10.1016/j.rser.2014.07.033.

Shahbaz, M., Hoang, T. H. V., Mahalik, M. K., & Roubaud, D. (2017). Energy consumption, financial development and economic growth in India: New evidence from a nonlinear and asymmetric analysis. *Energy Economics*, *63*, 199—212. Available from https://doi.org/10.1016/j.eneco.2017.01.023.

Shahbaz, M., Hye, Q. M. A., Tiwari, A. K., & Leitão, N. C. (2013). Economic growth, energy consumption, financial development, international trade and CO_2 emissions in Indonesia. *Renewable and Sustainable Energy Reviews*, *25*, 109—121. Available from https://doi.org/10.1016/j.rser.2013.04.009.

Shahbaz, M., Khan, S., & Tahir, M. I. (2013). The dynamic links between energy consumption, economic growth, financial development and trade in China: Fresh evidence from multivariate framework analysis. *Energy Economics*, *40*, 8—21. Available from https://doi.org/10.1016/j.eneco.2013.06.006.

Sims, C. A. (1980). Macroeconomics and reality. *Econometrica*, *48*(1), 1—48.

Wang, S., Li, G., & Fang, C. (2017). Urbanization, economic growth, energy consumption, and CO2 emissions: Empirical evidence from countries with different income levels. *Renewable and Sustainable Energy Reviews*, 1—17. Available from https://doi.org/10.1016/j.rser.2017.06.025.

CHAPTER EIGHT

The interactions between conventional and alternative energy sources in the transport sector: a panel of OECD countries

Sónia Almeida Neves[1], António Cardoso Marques[1] and José Alberto Fuinhas[2]

[1]NECE-UBI and Management and Economics Department, University of Beira Interior, Covilhã, Portugal
[2]NECE-UBI, CeBER, and Faculty of Economics, University of Coimbra, Coimbra, Portugal

Contents

8.1 Introduction

The analysis of the relationship between energy consumption and economic growth has merited the attention of the literature over the last few decades. This milestone on energy economics research starts with the paper of the Kraft and Kraft (1978), who analyzed the effect between energy consumption and Gross National Product for the United States. Thereafter, a lot of papers have focused on this topic, namely by using the empirical approach. Some conclusions could be found for instance in Ozturk (2010). Within the research progress, the traditional energy—growth nexus has been reoriented several times, creating new energy—growth nexus, for instance, electricity, renewable,

The Extended Energy—Growth Nexus.
DOI: https://doi.org/10.1016/B978-0-12-815719-0.00008-5

nuclear, and sectoral. Some conclusions could be found in Omri (2014) and Tiba and Omri (2017).

Recently, the literature has extended their focus namely by including other variables, such as financial development, globalization, trade openness, or CO_2 emissions, creating thus an augmented or extended energy—growth nexus. In fact, the literature supports that the energy—growth nexus is differing from the aggregate analysis to sectoral analysis (Abid & Sebri, 2012). For both, energy consumption is an important variable in the growth explanation (Camarero, Forte, Garcia-donato, Men-, & Ordo, 2015). These evidences have become the sectoral energy—growth nexus attraction, particularly the transport energy—growth nexus. Indeed, the transport sector (henceforth TS) is crucial for the entire dynamics of economies. Moreover, this sector is intensive in terms of fossil fuels consumption, which in turn is highly detrimental to the environment. Therefore to reduce the environmental impacts associated with energy consumption it is fundamental to make changes in the transport energy paradigm, namely by shifting from conventional sources to alternative sources.

Therefore this chapter aims to analyze the augmented TS energy—growth nexus by using TS energy consumption, economic growth, trade openness, and CO_2 emissions. With this approach, the TS energy sources were subdividing into conventional, specifically fossil fuels, use and alternative, that is, electricity and renewable fuels. Consequently, this chapter will present an improvement and contribution to the current literature. First, it analyses the interactions between conventional and alternative TS energy sources. Second, it also analyses the role of these sources in both economic growth and CO_2 emissions. Actually, the analysis of the effects that are resulting from the simultaneous use of both conventional and alternative sources in TS is a point rarely explored by the literature. Some exceptions include (Neves, Marques, & Fuinhas, 2017, 2018) that analyzed the relationships between TS electricity, renewable fuels, fossil fuels, economic growth, and CO_2 emissions. At least, it examines the role of TS energy sources in trade openness. Some literature has analyzed the role of trade openness in the traditional energy—growth nexus (Kasman & Duman, 2015; Kyophilavong, Shahbaz, Anwar, & Masood, 2015; Tiba & Frikha, 2018); however, the effect of this variable in the TS energy—growth nexus has not been explored.

A panel-vector autoregressive (PVAR) approach was used for 19 high-income OECD (Organisation for Economic Cooperation and

Development) countries, from 1971 to 2015. The option to study these countries comes from the fact that energy consumption is crucial to their economic development. In fact, the levels of energy consumption increase when high-income countries are considered. Therefore for internal consistency purposes, the largest group of countries among those countries sharing the same characteristics includes high-income OECD countries. Moreover, these countries are faced with several challenges to achieving sustainable development, namely climate protection (Eppel, 1999).

Thus this chapter corroborates that conventional TS energy sources are contributing to economic growth. In contrast, TS electricity use does not have a relationship with economic growth, while there is a unidirectional causality running from economic growth to TS renewable fuels use. On the one hand, regarding the environmental impacts of the TS energy sources, fossil fuels are increasing CO_2 emissions. On the other hand, there is no statistical evidence of the relationship between TS renewable fuel use and CO_2 emissions, and CO_2 emissions causing TS electricity consumption. However, apparently, the TS renewable fuels have been reducing the TS fossil fuels use. Currently, the TS is in rapid transition toward a low-carbon sector dealing with several challenges. Indeed, understanding what has happened in the past is crucial to providing fundamental guidelines for policymakers right now and mostly for the future.

This chapter is organized as follows. The state-of-the-art is presented in Section 8.2. In Section 8.3, the data and the methodology applied is showed and justified. Subsequently, the results are disclosed in Section 8.4 and discussed in Section 8.5. Finally, the conclusions are presented in Section 8.6.

8.2 Literature review

In the last few decades, the analysis of the relationships between energy consumption and economic growth had stimulated the literature in go further. The results obtained are far from consensual (Omri, 2014; Ozturk, 2010; Payne, 2010; Tiba & Omri, 2017), which has inspired the literature, to define four main hypotheses to explain these relationships.

Under the growth hypothesis energy consumption incentivizes economic growth, that is, there is a unidirectional causality running from energy consumption to economic growth (Chang, 2010; Wang, Wang, Zhou, Zhu, & Lu, 2011). According to the conservation hypothesis, economic growth stimulates energy consumption, which means that there is a unidirectional causality running from economic growth to energy consumption (Bartleet & Gounder, 2010; Zhang & Cheng, 2009). Based on the feedback hypothesis energy consumption encourages economic growth and vice versa, signifying that, there is a bidirectional causality between energy consumption and economic growth (Dagher & Yacoubian, 2012; Zhixin & Xin, 2011). Lastly, following the neutrality hypothesis, energy consumption has no effect on economic growth or vice versa, which indicates that there is no causal relationship between energy consumption and economic growth (Halicioglu, 2009; Soytas & Sari, 2009).

The growth of research into the energy—growth nexus has enthused the scientific community to include others explanatory variables in this framework, creating the new concept: augmented energy—growth nexus. This means that, to the traditional energy—growth nexus, additional explanatory variables have been included such as globalization or trade openness. For instance, on the one hand, Marques, Fuinhas, and Marques (2017) analyzed the augmented energy—growth nexus with the globalization for 43 countries comprising the time span 1971 to 2013 by applying an autoregressive distributed lag approach. Their results support the existence of the feedback hypothesis between energy consumption and economic growth. Additionally, they also found that globalization promotes both economic growth and energy consumption in the long run. On the other hand, Tiba and Frikha (2018) analyzed the relationships between gross domestic product (GDP), trade openness and energy consumption for 12 high-income countries and 12 middle-income countries from 1990 to 2011. Their results advise that there is bidirectional causality between both energy consumption and economic growth and trade openness and economic growth for high- and middle-income countries. Furthermore, there is a unidirectional causality running from energy consumption to trade openness.

Notwithstanding, also in recent years, the literature had reoriented the traditional energy—growth nexus, creating a new nexus such as electricity, renewables, nuclear, or sectoral. Some conclusions could be found, for instance, in Omri (2014) and Tiba and Omri (2017). Coherently, the results of the traditional energy—growth nexus could be differing from the traditional to sectoral energy—growth nexus. In both, energy consumption is an important variable to explain economic growth (Camarero et al., 2015). In this sense, the transport energy—growth nexus has attracted the attention of the specialized literature not only for its importance for the entry dynamics of economies but also for its intensity in fossil fuels consumption which has highly harmful effects on the environment.

As with the traditional energy—growth nexus, the relationships between transport, energy consumption and economic growth are also not consensual within the literature. The traditional hypothesis formulated for the energy—growth nexus was also verified when considering the transport energy—growth nexus. For example, Saboori, Sapri, and bin Baba (2014) confirms the existence of the feedback hypothesis for 27 OECD countries, and Liddle and Lung (2013) found a conservation hypothesis for 107 countries. Ibrahiem (2017) validates the growth hypothesis for Egypt, while Alshehry and Belloumi (2017) support the existence of the neutrality hypothesis in Saudi Arabia.

With the TS being intensive in fossil fuels use, namely oil, the relationships between TS energy consumption and CO_2 emissions have stimulated the literature in going further. On this point, the literature has shown consensual effects. In fact, TS energy consumption is highly detrimental for the environment (Alshehry & Belloumi, 2017; Ben Abdallah, Belloumi, & De Wolf, 2013; Chandran & Tang, 2013; Saboori et al., 2014). Following the aforementioned, Chandran and Tang (2013) examined the short- and long-run relationships between road energy consumption, CO_2 emissions, GDP, and foreign direct investment for five ASEAN (Association of Southeast Asian Nations) countries from 1971 to 2008 by applying a vector error correction model Granger causality test. Their findings are not unanimous for the analyzed countries. There is a long-run bidirectional causality between road energy consumption and CO_2 emissions for Malaysia and Thailand, and a short- and long-run bidirectional causality between GDP and road energy consumption for Malaysia. In contrast, there is a unidirectional causality running from road energy use to economic growth in the long run for Indonesia and Thailand. Meanwhile, the conservation hypothesis is validated in the short run for the Philippines once there is a unidirectional causality running from economic growth to the road energy use. Additionally, the feedback hypothesis between transport energy use and economic growth is verified for the 27 OECD countries by using Fully Modified Ordinary Least squares (FMOLS) (Saboori et al., 2014), and for 107 countries by using a heterogeneous panel causality test (Liddle & Lung, 2013).

To sum up, briefly, the energy—growth nexus has been a topic with great potential within the scientific community. There are a vast number of papers published in this area. The dearth of consensus could be attributed to the use of the different methods, variables, countries, and time period (Omri, 2014; Ozturk, 2010; Payne, 2010; Tiba & Omri, 2017). Recently, the augmented energy—growth nexus, as well as the sectoral energy—growth nexus has stimulated the literature. Thus this chapter aims to contribute to these two hot topics, by analyzing the augmented TS energy—growth nexus. To do that, it analyses the transport energy—growth nexus by disaggregating the energy sources. Additionally, the TS being vital for the entry dynamics of the economies as well as highly detrimental for the environment, it also analyses the role of the trade openness and CO_2 emissions on this framework.

8.3 Data and methodology

This study uses annual panel data from 1971 to 2015 for 19 high-income OECD countries. These countries were selected in accordance with the data availability criteria for all the variables. The countries considered are: Australia, Austria, Belgium, Canada, Denmark, Finland, France, Germany, Greece, Ireland, Italy, Luxembourg, the Netherlands, Norway, Portugal, Spain, Sweden, the United Kingdom, and the United States. The variables used as well as their description and statistics descriptive are shown in Table 8.1.

Good econometrics practices predict that the features of both crosses and variables should be checked to produce robust estimations. To do that, the adopted procedure includes: (1) cross-section dependence test (CD-test) (Table 8.2); (2) panel unit root test namely, cross-sectionally augmented Im, Pesaran and Shin (CIPS) (see Table 8.2); (3) correlation matrix values; and (4) variance inflation factors (VIFs). The procedure adopted by using the STATA 14.0 software is described as follows:

Table 8.1 Variables' definition and descriptive statistics.

Variable	Description	Obs.	Mean	Std. Dev.	Min.	Max.	Source
LGDP_PC	The ratio between GDP (constant LCU) and population	855	10.5313	1.0089	8.8667	13.2245	WDI
LFF_PC	The ratio between transports' fossil fuels consumption and population (kg/person)	855	6.6036	0.5453	5.0122	8.5303	IEA
LELE_PC	The ratio between transports' electricity consumption and population (kg/person)	855	2.0993	0.8323	0	3.7428	IEA
LRES_PC	The ratio between transports' renewable fuels consumption and population (kg/person)	855	0.8422	1.3903	0	4.9842	IEA
LEN_PC	The ratio between total energy consumption (except in TS) and population (kg/person)	855	7.6818	0.5056	6.0696	8.9311	OECD statistics
LTRADE	Sum of exports and imports of the goods and services (% of the GDP)	855	4.1394	0.5586	2.3731	6.0391	WDI
LCO2_PC	The ratio between total CO_2 emissions from fuel consumption and population (kg/person)	855	9.1189	0.5046	7.4181	10.8145	IEA

Note: WDI stands for World Development Indicators (available from http://databank.worldbank.org/data/source/world-development-indicators); IEA stands for International Energy Agency (IEA Headline Global Energy Data, 2016 edition) (available from https://www.iea.org/statistics/); and LCU stands for Local Currency Unit.

Table 8.2 Cross-section dependence test and second-generation unit root test (CIPS).

| | CD-test | | | | CIPS | |
	CD-Test	Corr.	Abs (corr.)	Lags	Without trend	With trend
LGDP_PC	85.24***	0.972	0.972	1	− 2.297**	− 0.540
				2	− 1.718**	0.517
LFF_PC	70.81***	0.807	0.807	1	− 3.153***	− 0.215
				2	− 1.643*	0.261
LELE_PC	50.57***	0.576	0.611	1	− 2.080**	− 0.779
				2	− 1.607*	− 0.144
LRES_PC	79.14***	0.902	0.902	1	− 0.989	− 2.674***
				2	3.241	1.373
LCO2_PC	16.36***	0.187	0.554	1	− 0.248	− 0.212
				2	0.778	1.368
LTRADE	63.53***	0.724	0.789	1	− 3.367***	− 2.296**
				2	− 1.620	− 0.244
LEN_PC	16.60***	0.189	0.563	1	− 0.259	− 1.105
				2	0.167	0.059
DLGDP_PC	43.11***	0.497	0.497	1	− 9.077***	− 8.415***
				2	− 6.797***	− 5.478***
DLFF_PC	32.11***	0.370	0.371	1	− 11.573***	− 10.281***
				2	− 9.595***	− 8.972***
DLELE_PC	1.52	0.018	0.116	1	− 12.284***	− 11.563***
				2	− 8.337***	− 7.678***
DLRES_PC	20.66***	0.238	0.261	1	− 13.891***	− 12.667***
				2	− 10.853***	− 9.333***
DLCO2_PC	26.13***	0.301	0.322	1	− 13.705***	− 12.667***
				2	− 9.325***	− 8.138***
DLTRADE	46.15***	0.532	0.548	1	− 12.054***	− 10.216***
				2	− 7.927***	− 5.590***
DLEN_PC	34.37***	0.396	0.398	1	− 14.797***	− 13.797***
				2	− 10.598***	− 9.380***

Note: CD-test was performed according to the null hypothesis of the cross-sectional independence; the second-generation unit root test was performed under the null hypothesis wherein the variables are $I(1)$; and ***, **, and * denote statistical significance level at 1%, 5%, and 10%, respectively.

How to do
CD-test
    xtcd lgdp_pc lff_pc lele_pc
    xtcd lres_pc lco2_pc ltrade len_pc
    xtcd dlgdp_pc dlff_pc dlele_pc
    xtcd dlres_pc dlco2_pc dltrade dlen_pc
    second generation unit root test

multipurt lgdp_pc lff_pc lele_pc lres_pc lco2_pc ltrade len_pc, lags(2)

multipurt dlgdp_pc dlff_pc dlele_pc dlres_pc dlco2_pc dltrade dlen_pc, lags(2)

correlation matrix

corr lgdp_pc lff_pc lele_pc lres_pc lco2_pc ltrade len_pc

corr dlgdp_pc dlff_pc dlele_pc dlres_pc dlco2_pc dltrade dlen_pc

**VIF*

reg lgdp_pc lff_pc lele_pc lres_pc lco2_pc ltrade len_pc

vif

reg dlgdp_pc dlff_pc dlele_pc dlres_pc dlco2_pc dltrade dlen_pc

vif

The results from the CD-test, disclosed in Table 8.2 suggest the presence of the cross-section dependence for all the variables, except *DLELE_PC*. In fact, when this phenomenon is present the first-generation unit root tests are not reliable. As such, the second-generation unit root tests CIPS, proposed by Pesaran (2007) were performed. The results of the CIPS test indicate that the variables are stationary at first-differences. For *DLELE_PC* both first- and second-generation unit root tests were performed. The results of the first-generation unit root test, suggested by Maddala and Wu (1999) are in accordance with those obtained in CIPS unit root test, that is, the *DLELE_PC* is stationary.

The use of the PVAR, proposed by Love and Zicchino (2006) is appropriated for this research once it deals with variables that are potentially endogenous. The results disclosed in the Section 8.4 evidence the presence of the endogeneity. In fact, this estimator supports stationary endogenous variables and unobserved individual heterogeneity.

Remembering that the main objective is to analyze the interactions between TS fossil fuels consumption, TS electricity use, TS renewable fuels, economic growth, CO_2 emissions, trade openness, and total energy consumption, except that which is consumed by TS, a PVAR was estimated. Please note that, the inclusion of the last variable aims to increase the explicative power of the models, once the energy use is an important variable to explain the growth (Camarero et al., 2015). Therefore the estimated PVAR functional form is explained as follows:

$$Z_{it} = \Gamma_0 + \Gamma_1 Z_{it-1} + f_i + d_{c,t} + \varepsilon_t \tag{8.1}$$

where, Z_{it} denotes the vector of the endogenous variables used (*DLGDP_PC*, *DLFF_PC*, *DLELE_PC*, *DLRES_PC*, *DLCO2_PC*, *DLTRADE* and *DLEN_PC*). $\Gamma_1 Z_{it-1}$ denotes the polynomial matrix, f_i

embodies the fixed effects, $d_{c,t}$ represents the time effects, and ε_t denotes the error term.

The existence of the fixed effects raises correlation problems between the regressors. So, when they are present, this method permits the removal of them by using the *Hermelet procedure* as proposed by Arellano and Bover (1995). Indeed, the presence of the fixed effects was tested by using the Hausman test which test fixed effects against random effects. The Hausman test was performed considering all the variables as dependent variables and the others as an independent. The results show that when the *DLELE_PC* was tested as the dependent variable; the existence of the fixed effects is proven.

Therefore in this estimator, the regressors lagged were used as instrumental variables on the system estimations based on generalized method of moments (GMM). The validity of the instrumental variables used was checked by using the Hansen test of overidentifying restrictions, and under the null hypothesis of the overidentifying restrictions, they are valid.

To ascertain the causal relationships between the variables, the Granger causality test was performed. The null hypothesis predicts the inexistence of the causality. Furthermore, the impulse response functions (IRFs) were estimated by using a Gaussian approximation based on the Monte Carlo simulations, showing the reaction of one variable to the shock of another variable. The orthogonalized IRFs are based on the Cholesky decomposition, and the standard errors and the confidence intervals were estimated according to the 1000 Monte Carlo simulations. After that, the forecast error variance decomposition (FEVD) was performed, based on a Cholesky decomposition of the residual covariance matrix, using 1000 Monte Carlo simulations, and for 15 periods. The FEVD shows us the percentage that each independent variable explains the forecast error variance of the other variable. In both IRF and FEVD estimations the VAR—Cholesky ordering of variables was used, by placing the variables in the decreasing order of the exogeneity.

8.4 Results

In order to choose the optimal number of lags that will be used, the three lags selection criteria was followed, namely Bayesian information

Table 8.3 Lag order selection criteria and Hansen test of overidentifying restriction.

Lag	CD	J	J-P value	MBIC	MAIC	MQIC
1	0.6287	200.4493	0.0022	− 770.9268	− 93.5507	− 354.7054
2	0.6996	105.8123	0.2772	− 541.7718	− 90.1877	− 264.2908
3	0.7387	73.5971	0.0130	− 250.1949	− 24.4029	− 111.4545
4	0.6852	−	−	−	−	−

Hansen test Chi^2: 105.8123

criteria (MBIC), Akaike information criteria (MAIC), and Hannan and Quinn (MQIC), proposed by Andrews and Lu (2001). The optimal lags number is the one that minimizes the lags selection criteria. The results disclosed in Table 8.3 show that the optimal lags are one for both the estimated PVAR. In this chapter, it was opted to use the optimal lag number plus one, that is, two lags. First, the inclusion of the two lags in the PVAR estimation allows the used instruments (the lagged endogenous variables) be valid. Second, the analysis of the results of the PVAR shows us that the second lag in the PVAR estimation has a significance level for a set of the endogenous variables used.

The results in Table 8.3 were calculated by using the software STATA 14.0. To do that, the procedure adopted to determine both the optimal lag number, and the PVAR estimation uses the commands described as follows:

How to do

Lag order selection criteria

    pvarsoc dlen_pc dlele_pc dlres_pc dlco2 dltrade dlgdp_pc dlff_pc, maxlag(4) pvaropts(instl(1/4)

    PVAR

    pvar dlen_pc dlele_pc dlres_pc dlco2 dltrade dlgdp_pc dlff_pc, instl (1/4) lags(2) overid

---

The second-order PVAR was estimated based on the GMM and using the regressors lagged as instrumental variables. The results of the Hansen test, disclosed in Table 8.3, support that the instrumental variables used are valid.

So that the results of the IRF and FEVD have a known interpretation, the PVAR must be stable (Abrigo & Love, 2015). The results of the PVAR stability test are shown in Table 8.4, revealing that the stability conditions are verified once the values are inside the circle.

Table 8.4 Eigenvalue stability condition.
Eigenvalue

Real	Imaginary	Modulus
0.6960	0	0.6960
0.3891	-0.1158	0.4060
0.3891	-0.1158	0.4060
-0.1372	0.3695	0.3942
-0.1372	-0.3695	0.3942
-0.0870	0.3726	0.3826
-0.0870	-0.3726	0.3826
-0.3392	0	0.3392
0.0962	0.2927	0.3092
0.0962	-0.2927	0.3092
0.1199	0.2317	0.2609
0.1199	-0.2317	0.2609
-0.1509	-0.1705	0.2277
-0.1509	0.1705	0.2277

Roots of the companion matrix

Note: All the eigenvalues lie inside the unit circle; pVAR satisfies stability condition.

The results of the Granger causality test are displayed in Table 8.5. A sum of the causalities found are: $DLRES\_PC \rightarrow DLELE\_PC$, $DLTRADE \rightarrow DLEN\_PC$, $DLGDP\_PC \rightarrow DLEN\_PC$, $DLFF\_PC \rightarrow DLEN\_PC$, $DLRES\_PC \leftrightarrow DLELE\_PC$, $DLCO2\_PC \rightarrow DLELE\_PC$, $DLELE\_PC \neq DLTRADE$, $DLELE\_PC \neq DLGDP\_PC$, $DLFF\_PC \rightarrow DLELE\_PC$, $DLRES\_PC \neq DLCO2\_PC$, $DLRES\_PC \rightarrow DLTRADE$, $DLGDP\_PC \rightarrow DLRES\_PC$, $DLRES\_PC \rightarrow DLFF\_PC$, $DLTRADE \rightarrow DLCO2\_PC$, $DLGDP\_PC \leftrightarrow DLCO2\_PC$, $DLCO2\_PC \leftrightarrow DLFF\_PC$, $DLTRADE \leftrightarrow DLGDP\_PC$, $DLFF\_PC \leftrightarrow DLTRADE$, and, $DLFF\_PC \leftrightarrow DLGDP\_PC$.

Regarding the effects between TS energy sources and economic growth, there is a bidirectional causality between TS fossil fuels consumption and economic growth. Economic growth causes an increase in the use of renewable fuels. Additionally, there is no relationship between TS electricity use and economic growth.

Concerning the effects of TS energy sources on CO_2 emissions, the renewable fuels show no causal relationship with CO_2 emission.

Table 8.5 Granger causality test.

	DLEN_PC	DLELE_PC	DLRES_PC	DLCO2_PC	DLTRADE	DLGDP_PC	DLFF_PC
DLEN_PC does not cause	–	3.396	0.801	4.482	4.020	2.360	0.479
DLELE_PC does not cause	1.494	–	11.636***	3.724	0.302	0.807	0.641
DLRES_PC does not cause	5.888*	9.791***	–	0.450	9.520***	1.437	17.128***
DLCO2_PC does not cause	0.309	8.457**	1.036	–	1.092	9.992***	5.942*
DLTRADE does not cause	47.788***	3.160	0.455	16.095***	–	13.149***	21.106***
DLGDP_PC does not cause	6.844**	2.438	7.019**	5.464*	13.775***	–	29.336***
DLFF_PC does not cause	8.426**	6.500**	3.890	30.479***	10.398***	33.102***	–
ALL	105.505***	32.531***	40.463***	94.871***	60.003***	58.780***	82.012***

Note: ***, **, and * denotes statistical significance at 1%, 5%, and 10%, respectively.

Furthermore, much as expected, there is a bidirectional causality between TS fossil fuels use and CO_2 emissions and there is a unidirectional causality running from CO_2 emissions to TS electricity use.

By using the package of the commands by STATA software proposed by Abrigo and Love (2015) the PVAR postestimations commands used to verify the stability of the PVAR estimated as well as the Granger causality test are *pvarstable* and *pvargranger*, respectively.

The Granger causality test is not able to show us all the knowledge about the relationships between the variables. To overcome this obstacle, the IRF and FEVD were estimated. On the one hand, the IRFs show how one endogenous variable respond faced with a shock or innovation in another endogenous variable. On the other hand, the FEVD shows how much each one endogenous variable explains of the forecast error variance of the other endogenous variable. Therefore the methodology followed in this chapter finishes with the estimation of the IRF and FEVD. The postestimation commands used after running a PVAR is the following:

```
**IRF**
    pvarirf, mc(1000) oirf byopt(yrescale) st(15)
    **FEVD**
    pvarfevd, mc(1000) st(15)
```

The results of the IRF are shown in Fig. 8.1. All the IRFs return to the equilibrium point, which is a clear sign of the stationarity of the variables. Overall, the return to the equilibrium occurs approximately at five/seven periods. Faced with a shock in both renewable fuels and TS electricity use, CO_2 emissions respond negatively. However, the return to the equilibrium point occurs more quickly in the electricity than in the renewable fuels. Regarding the effects of the TS energy sources on economic growth, it handles positively when it is confronted with the shock in both TS fossil fuels consumption and TS electricity consumption. On the contrary, faced with a shock in TS renewable fuels consumption, economic growth responds negatively. Trade openness responds positively when faced with a shock in both TS fossil fuels use and TS renewable fuels consumption.

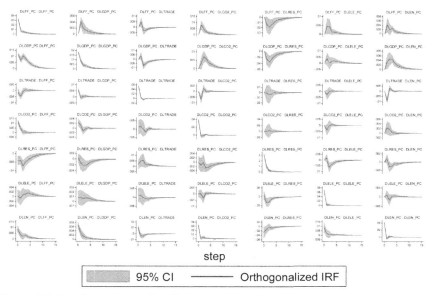

Figure 8.1 Impulse response functions.

The results of the FEVD are displayed in Table 8.6. Regarding the FEVD in the total energy consumption on the economy, except that which is consumed by the TS, in the second period, 93.338% of the FEVD is self-explained and 4.59% is explicated by *DLTRADE*. The percentage that is explained by the other variables is negligible. In the 10th year, to the equilibrium point, 88.20% of the forecast error variance is self-explained, while the *DLGDP_PC* explains 3.51% and *DLTRADE* justifies 4.71%.

The largest part of the forecast error variance of both the TS electricity and renewable fuel consumption is self-explained over the 15 periods. In the first, 98.34% of the DLELE_PC forecast error variance is self-explained and 99.23% of the variance in DLRES_PC also is explained by itself. The equilibrium is achieved in the 10th period for both. At this point, DLELE_PC explains 95.13%, *DLRES_PC* and *DLEN_PC* explain 1.23% and 1.73% of the forecast error variance in the *DLELE_PC*.

Concerning the forecast error variance of the DLCO2_PC, as expected, the variables that contribute with the largest part to the equilibrium point are the *DLCO2_PC*, *DLEN_PC*, *DLGDP_PC*, and *DLFF_PC*. In fact, in the 10th period, each one of these variables contributes by 0.5254%, 36.73%, 3.42%, and 4.26%, respectively.

Table 8.6 Forecast error variance decomposition.

Response variable	Forecast horizon		Impulse variable					
		DLEN_PC	DLELE_PC	DLRES_PC	DLCO2_PC	DLTRADE	DLGDP_PC	DLFF_PC
DLEN_PC	1	1	0	0	0	0	0	0
	2	0.9338	0.0006	0.0020	0.0030	0.0449	0.0064	0.0100
	5	0.8874	0.0022	0.0111	0.0044	0.0474	0.0320	0.0155
	10	0.8820	0.0025	0.0127	0.0044	0.0471	0.0351	0.0161
	15	0.8819	0.0025	0.0128	0.0044	0.0471	0.0352	0.0161
DLELE_PC	1	0.0166	0.9834	0	0	0	0	0
	2	0.0174	0.9705	0.0006	0.0028	0.0017	0.0027	0.0043
	5	0.0173	0.9532	0.0123	0.0029	0.0017	0.0042	0.0084
	10	0.0174	0.9513	0.0129	0.0029	0.0017	0.0052	0.0086
	15	0.0174	0.9513	0.0129	0.0029	0.0017	0.0052	0.0086
DLRES_PC	1	0.0071	0.0006	0.9923	0	0	0	0
	2	0.0083	0.0091	0.9754	0.0000	0.0000	0.0055	0.0016
	5	0.0087	0.0178	0.9424	0.0001	0.0002	0.0239	0.0069
	10	0.0089	0.0181	0.9392	0.0001	0.0002	0.0260	0.0074
	15	0.0089	0.0181	0.9391	0.0001	0.0002	0.0261	0.0075
DLCO2_PC	1	0.4089	0.0000	0.0000	0.5911	0.0000	0	0
	2	0.3892	0.0000	0.0007	0.5641	0.0176	0.0039	0.0245
	5	0.3698	0.0044	0.0049	0.5297	0.0189	0.0385	0.0336
	10	0.3673	0.0048	0.0068	0.5254	0.0188	0.0426	0.0342
	15	0.3672	0.0048	0.0069	0.5253	0.0188	0.0427	0.0343
DLTRADE	1	0.0364	0.0006	0.0009	0.0003	0.9618	0	0
	2	0.0378	0.0010	0.0079	0.0012	0.9402	0.0044	0.0075
	5	0.0420	0.0014	0.0184	0.0020	0.8946	0.0291	0.0125
	10	0.0421	0.0016	0.0194	0.0020	0.8909	0.0311	0.0129
	15	0.0421	0.0016	0.0195	0.0020	0.8908	0.0311	0.0129
DLGDP_PC	1	0.1178	0.0016	0.0005	0.0147	0.0823	0.7831	0
	2	0.1163	0.0024	0.0029	0.0145	0.0646	0.7660	0.0333
	5	0.1124	0.0046	0.0223	0.0159	0.0589	0.7453	0.0406
	10	0.1116	0.0055	0.0257	0.0157	0.0582	0.7419	0.0414
	15	0.1116	0.0055	0.0258	0.0157	0.0582	0.7418	0.0414
DLFF_PC	1	0.0513	0.0001	0.0125	0.0938	0.0008	0.0973	0.7443
	2	0.0551	0.0003	0.0205	0.0961	0.0146	0.1175	0.6959
	5	0.0542	0.0026	0.0628	0.0779	0.0123	0.2018	0.58842
	10	0.0541	0.0041	0.0686	0.0757	0.0120	0.2107	0.5748
	15	0.0541	0.0041	0.0688	0.0756	0.0120	0.2109	0.5745

With regard the FEVD in economic growth, at first year, 78.31% is self-explained, 11.78% is explained by $DLEN\_PC$, 8.23% by the trade openness, and 3.33% by the TS fossil fuels consumption. The equilibrium point occurs in the 10th period, whereupon the variance of the $DLGDP\_PC$ is explained in 11.16% by $DLEN\_PC$, 5.82% by $DLTRADE$, 4.14% by $DLFF\_PC$, 2.57% by $DLRES\_PC$ and 74.19% by the variable itself.

8.5 Discussion

The analysis of the relationships between energy consumption and economic growth has merited the attention of the literature. This chapter contributes to this current and intense debate around the interactions between economic growth, CO_2 emissions, trade openness, and TS energy consumption, by subdividing it into fossil fuels, electricity, and renewable fuels.

As is expected, TS fossil fuels use contributes to economic growth and vice versa. Indeed, it is a usual outcome found in the literature that shows us the importance of the TS for economies as a whole, and the intensity of this sector in fossil fuels use. It is well known, that the use of this kind energy source is detrimental to the environment, and, as such, environmental sustainability remains entirely dependent on the reduction of fossil fuels use namely in the TS. The penetration of alternative energy sources on the TS energy paradigm aims to contribute to achieving this goal. However, this concern is a quite recent topic on the political agenda, and considering the sample analyzed, the desired effects could remain far from being achieved.

This chapter evidences that environmental awareness is crucial for electricity deployment in the TS; however, apparently, electricity use in the TS has not had an effect on CO_2 emissions. This outcome could be explained twofold. First, electricity used by any TS is mainly associated with railways and, could not be significant in CO_2 emissions reduction. In fact, the penetration of electricity in the road system is a recent concern. Currently, electric vehicles remain faced with several challenges that allow their intensive use, such as technological progress and social acceptance. Second, the variable of CO_2 emissions used in this chapter comprises all the CO_2 emissions from fuel combustion. This could indicate that the CO_2 savings achieved by the use of electricity in the TS are compensated with an increase in the CO_2 emissions caused in the electricity generation process. This could indicate that the environmental benefits associated with TS electricity use could only be achieved if it uses electricity generated using renewable energies, such as noted in the literature (Ajanovic & Haas, 2016). Furthermore, there is no relationship between TS electricity consumption and economic growth. This supports that electricity penetration within the TS energy paradigm is a political decision and does not remain dependent on economic performance. Accordingly, electricity use has not had an effect on economic activity, neither stimulating nor obstructing it. This unexpected outcome could be a result of the time period chosen by this chapter. Indeed, following the results of the Neves et al. (2017) that analyze the role of alternative energy sources on economic growth from 1995 to 2014, TS electricity use hampers economic growth, which could be a clear sign of the elevated costs that the transition from fossil fuels to electricity has on economies.

Concerning renewable fuels use in TS, it is caused by economic growth, but the opposite is not true. Additionally, this alternative source is not causing CO_2 emissions either and vice versa. This means that in the period under analysis, the renewable fuels use in the TS has not contributed to reducing or stimulating CO_2 emissions, suggesting that renewable fuels use has been insufficient to accomplish the reduction in CO_2 emissions. Furthermore, renewable fuels use in TS causes TS fossil fuels consumption. Apparently, this causality occurs in negative basis. This could indicate that the penetration of renewable fuels has to contribute to reducing TS fossil fuels consumption. In fact, it is the desired effect under the perspective of TS decarbonization. Although it does not contribute to CO_2 emissions, their penetration is reducing the need for fossil fuels, which consequently must lead to a reduction in CO_2 emissions. Additionally, economic growth causes TS renewable fuels use.

To sum up, the TS is crucial for economies as a whole. TS fossil fuels use is a driver of economic growth, also driving CO_2 emissions. Therefore environmental sustainability remains dependent upon a shift in the TS energy paradigm. To achieve this goal, the policymakers should incentivize the use of alternative energy sources in the TS, such as electricity and renewable fuels. Regarding TS electricity use, this chapter found evidence of the neutrality hypothesis, meaning that there is no relationship between TS electricity use and economic growth. Concerning renewable fuels, there is evidence of the conservation hypothesis and in addition the feedback hypothesis is verified between TS fossil fuels use and economic growth.

8.6 Conclusion

The analysis of the interactions between TS energy consumption, economic growth, and CO_2 emissions has stimulated a growing branch of literature. However, the promotion of the alternative TS energy sources has been accomplished in order to reduce the environmental impacts associated with this sector. Therefore this chapter aims to provide crucial guidelines for policymaking to identify the effects that the simultaneous use of the both conventional and alternative TS energy sources are having on economic growth, CO_2 emissions, and trade openness. To do that, an annual panel VAR was estimated by using data from 1971 to 2015 for 19 OECD countries.

The policymakers should incentivize the use of alternative TS energy sources to decarbonize this sector. Environmental awareness has been crucial for the deployment of electricity in the TS energy paradigm; however, it has not had a direct effect on CO_2 emissions. This could indicate that electricity use in the TS must be from renewable sources in order to capture advantages of the electricity use in this area. Also, there is no relationship between TS renewable fuels use and CO_2 emissions.

There is no causal relationship between electricity use in the TS and economic growth, which could indicate that electricity consumption in the TS has been a question of policymaking, rather than being dependent on economic performance. At the same time, the increasing use of renewable fuels has been caused by economic growth, but the opposite is not true. To make TS alternative energy sources compatible with economic growth, their cost-effectiveness must be improved. On the one hand, the social acceptance of electric mobility by the users must be enlarged, and the technological improvements in their batteries, namely regarding their costs and range must be stimulated to make it more attractive. On the other hand, the cost-effectiveness of renewable fuels in areas like octane number must be improved to increase social acceptance and reduce the need for them to be mixed with a traditional fuel, such as gasoline.

Acknowledgments

This research was supported by NECE, R&D unit and funded by the FCT—Portuguese Foundation for the Development of Science and Technology, Ministry of Science, Technology and Higher Education, project UID/GES/04630/2019.

References

Abid, M., & Sebri, M. (2012). Energy consumption-economic growth nexus: Does the level of aggregation matter?. *International Journal of Energy Economics and Policy*, *2*(2), 55−62. Available from www.econjournals.com.

Abrigo, M.R.M., & Love, I. (2015). Estimation of panel vector autoregression in stata: A package of programs, February, 28. https://doi.org/10.1017/CBO9781107415324.004

Ajanovic, A., & Haas, R. (2016). Dissemination of electric vehicles in urban areas: Major factors for success. *Energy*. Available from https://doi.org/10.1016/j.energy.2016.05.040.

Alshehry, A. S., & Belloumi, M. (2017). Study of the environmental Kuznets curve for transport carbon dioxide emissions in Saudi Arabia. *Renewable and Sustainable Energy Reviews*, *75*, 1339−1347. Available from https://doi.org/10.1016/j.rser.2016.11.122.

Andrews, D. W. K., & Lu, B. (2001). Consistent model and moment selection procedures for GMM estimation with application to dynamic panel data models. *Journal of Econometrics*, *101*(1), 123−164. Available from https://doi.org/10.1016/S0304-4076(00)00077-4.

Arellano, M., & Bover, O. (1995). Another look at the instrumental variable estimation of error-components models. *Journal of Econometrics*, *68*(1), 29−51. Available from https://doi.org/10.1016/0304-4076(94)01642-D.

Bartleet, M., & Gounder, R. (2010). Energy consumption and economic growth in New Zealand: Results of trivariate and multivariate models. *Energy Policy*, *38*(7), 3508−3517. Available from https://doi.org/10.1016/j.enpol.2010.02.025.

Ben Abdallah, K., Belloumi, M., & De Wolf, D. (2013). Indicators for sustainable energy development: A multivariate cointegration and causality analysis from Tunisian road transport sector. *Renewable and Sustainable Energy Reviews*, *25*, 34−43. Available from https://doi.org/10.1016/j.rser.2013.03.066.

Camarero, M., Forte, A., Garcia-donato, G., Men-, Y., & Ordo, J. (2015). Variable selection in the analysis of energy consumption-growth nexus. *Energy Economics*. Available from https://doi.org/10.1016/j.eneco.2015.10.012.

Chandran, V. G. R., & Tang, C. F. (2013). The impacts of transport energy consumption, foreign direct investment and income on CO_2 emissions in ASEAN-5 economies. *Renewable and Sustainable Energy Reviews*, *24*, 445−453. Available from https://doi.org/10.1016/j.rser.2013.03.054.

Chang, C.-C. (2010). A multivariate causality test of carbon dioxide emissions, energy consumption and economic growth in China. *Applied Energy*, *87*(11), 3533−3537. Available from https://doi.org/10.1016/j.apenergy.2010.05.004.

Dagher, L., & Yacoubian, T. (2012). The causal relationship between energy consumption and economic growth in Lebanon. *Energy Policy*, *50*, 795−801. Available from https://doi.org/10.1016/j.enpol.2012.08.034.

Eppel, J. (1999). Sustainable development and environment: A renewed effort in the OECD. *Environment, Development and Sustainability*, *1*(1), 41−53. Available from https://doi.org/10.1350/enlr.2007.9.1.41.

Halicioglu, F. (2009). An econometric study of CO_2 emissions, energy consumption, income and foreign trade in Turkey. *Energy Policy*, *37*(3), 1156−1164. Available from https://doi.org/10.1016/j.enpol.2008.11.012.

Ibrahiem, D. M. (2017). Road energy consumption, economic growth, population and urbanization in Egypt: Cointegration and causality analysis. *Environment, Development and Sustainability*, *20*(3), 1053−1066. Available from https://doi.org/10.1007/s10668-017-9922-z.

Kasman, A., & Duman, Y. S. (2015). CO_2 emissions, economic growth, energy consumption, trade and urbanization in new EU member and candidate countries: A panel data analysis. *Economic Modelling*, *44*, 97−103. Available from https://doi.org/10.1016/j.econmod.2014.10.022.

Kraft, J., & Kraft, A. (1978). On the relationship between energy and GNP. *The Journal of Energy and Development*, *3*, 401−403.

Kyophilavong, P., Shahbaz, M., Anwar, S., & Masood, S. (2015). The energy-growth nexus in Thailand: Does trade openness boost up energy consumption? *Renewable and Sustainable Energy Reviews*, *46*, 265−274. Available from https://doi.org/10.1016/j.rser.2015.02.004.

Liddle, B., & Lung, S. (2013). The long-run causal relationship between transport energy consumption and GDP: Evidence from heterogeneous panel methods robust to cross-sectional dependence. *Economics Letters*, *121*, 524−527. Available from https://doi.org/10.1016/j.econlet.2013.10.011.

Love, I., & Zicchino, L. (2006). Financial development and dynamic investment behavior: Evidence from panel VAR. *Quarterly Review of Economics and Finance*, *46*(2), 190−210. Available from https://doi.org/10.1016/j.qref.2005.11.007.

Maddala, G. S., & Wu, S. (1999). A comparative study of unit root tests with panel data and a new simple test. *Oxford Bulletin of Economics and Statistics*, *61*(S1), 631−652. Available from https://doi.org/10.1111/1468-0084.0610s1631.

Marques, L. M., Fuinhas, J. A., & Marques, A. C. (2017). Augmented energy-growth nexus: Economic, political and social globalization impacts. *Energy Procedia*, *136*, 97−101. Available from https://doi.org/10.1016/j.egypro.2017.10.293.

Neves, S. A., Marques, A. C., & Fuinhas, J. A. (2017). Is energy consumption in the transport sector hampering both economic growth and the reduction of CO_2 emissions? A disaggregated energy consumption analysis. *Transport Policy*, *59*(July), 64−70. Available from https://doi.org/10.1016/j.tranpol.2017.07.004.

Neves, S. A., Marques, A. C., & Fuinhas, J. A. (2018). Could alternative energy sources in the transport sector decarbonise the economy without compromising economic growth? *Environment, Development and Sustainability*, *20*(1), 23−40. Available from https://doi.org/10.1007/s10668-018-0153-8.

Omri, A. (2014). An international literature survey on energy-economic growth nexus: Evidence from country-specific studies. *Renewable and Sustainable Energy Reviews*, *38*, 951−959. Available from https://doi.org/10.1016/j.rser.2014.07.084.

Ozturk, I. (2010). A literature survey on energy−growth nexus. *Energy Policy*, *38*(1), 340−349. Available from https://doi.org/10.1016/j.enpol.2009.09.024.

Payne, J. E. (2010). A survey of the electricity consumption-growth literature. *Applied Energy*, *87*(3), 723−731. Available from https://doi.org/10.1016/j.apenergy.2009.06.034.

Pesaran, M. H. (2007). A simple panel unit root test in the presence of cross-section dependence. *Journal of Applied Econometrics*, *22*(2), 265−312. Available from https://doi.org/10.1002/jae.951.

Saboori, B., Sapri, M., & bin Baba, M. (2014). Economic growth, energy consumption and CO_2 emissions in OECD (Organization for Economic Co-operation and

Development)'s transport sector: A fully modified bi-directional relationship approach. *Energy*, *66*, 150−161. Available from https://doi.org/10.1016/j.energy.2013.12.048.

Soytas, U., & Sari, R. (2009). Energy consumption, economic growth, and carbon emissions: Challenges faced by an EU candidate member. *Ecological Economics*, *68*(6), 1667−1675. Available from https://doi.org/10.1016/j.ecolecon.2007.06.014.

Tiba, S., & Frikha, M. (2018). Income, trade openness and energy interactions: Evidence from simultaneous equation modeling. *Energy*, *147*, 799−811. Available from https://doi.org/10.1016/j.energy.2018.01.013.

Tiba, S., & Omri, A. (2017). Literature survey on the relationships between energy, environment and economic growth. *Renewable and Sustainable Energy Reviews*, *69*(August 2015), 1129−1146. Available from https://doi.org/10.1016/j.rser.2016.09.113.

Wang, Y., Wang, Y., Zhou, J., Zhu, X., & Lu, G. (2011). Energy consumption and economic growth in China: A multivariate causality test. *Energy Policy*, *39*(7), 4399−4406. Available from https://doi.org/10.1016/j.enpol.2011.04.063.

Zhang, X.-P., & Cheng, X.-M. (2009). Energy consumption, carbon emissions, and economic growth in China. *Ecological Economics*, *68*(10), 2706−2712. Available from https://doi.org/10.1016/j.ecolecon.2009.05.011.

Zhixin, Z., & Xin, R. (2011). Causal relationships between energy consumption and economic growth. *Energy Procedia*, *5*, 2065−2071. Available from https://doi.org/10.1016/j.egypro.2011.03.356.

CHAPTER NINE

Daily management of the electricity generation mix in France and Germany

Diogo Santos Pereira[1,*], António Cardoso Marques[1,*] and José Alberto Fuinhas[2,*]

[1]NECE-UBI and Management and Economics Department, University of Beira Interior, Covilhã, Portugal
[2]NECE-UBI, CeBER and Faculty of Economics, University of Coimbra, Coimbra, Portugal

Contents

9.1 Introduction

In the past countries have chosen fossil fuels to fulfill the increasing demand for electricity. Indeed, electricity use has been a major driver of economic growth, while at the same time, economic growth has led to an increase in electricity consumption (Hamdi, Sbia, & Shahbaz, 2014; Omri, 2014; Tiba & Omri, 2017). The increasing electricity demand has been provoked by several factors namely economic activity or industrial activity, the electrification of the industrial, residential, services, and

* This research was supported by NECE, R&D unit and funded by the FCT — Portuguese Foundation for the Development of Science and Technology, Ministry of Science, Technology and Higher Education, project UID/GES/04630/2019.

transports sector, and population expansion. However, environmental problems often caused by pollution produced during electricity production has led countries to rethink their energy mix and begin to include renewable energy sources (RES), in the largest part, wind power and solar photovoltaic (PV). Within a context of increasing electrification of economies, countries have been obliged to shift their traditional sources, namely fossil fuels and nuclear power toward a portfolio of several RES. This energy transition has faced several barriers, namely the intermittency of wind power and solar PV, the lack of controllable RES, and energy storage systems. Nevertheless, it is essential that the diversification of the electricity mix is not merely a theoretical goal. Thus research about how to increase the RES installed capacity, how to accommodate accurately their production, and how they interact with economic growth and activity is mandatory to understanding the conditions to achieve a successful diversification.

The literature has previously analyzed the electricity—growth nexus along with the interactions between electricity sources, but only utilizing annual and monthly data (Apergis & Payne, 2011; Tiba & Omri, 2017). Notwithstanding, when electricity supply and demand are analyzed using monthly and annual data, the real-time relationships are attenuated in the mean values and econometric procedures. In fact, normally factors such as forecasts of electricity generation from wind power and solar PV, electricity consumption, capacity factors, temperatures, and wind velocity are carried out on a daily and hourly basis. Thus the influence of these prediction factors and the interactions for electricity mix adjustments are not captured by econometric techniques using low frequency data (annual and monthly). The emergence of hourly, daily, and weekly data of electricity supply and demand allows a trustworthy evaluation of the interactions of electricity systems management. Besides, the availability of high-frequency data for financial markets could make it possible to model daily economic activity and to study its relationship with electricity supply and demand. This research aims to fill these gaps in the existing literature, by analyzing (1) the interactions between electricity sources; and (2) the relationship of them with financial or economic activity. To the best of our knowledge, no other research has tried to study the electricity—growth nexus and the interactions between electricity sources using daily data.

It is crucial to understand the transformation that must occur, in supply, to make feasible higher penetration of RES, and consequently, a positive impact of RES and electricity mix on economic activity. So this chapter will focus: (1) on the explanation of econometric procedures to study daily data of the electricity—growth nexus; (2) on the setting of financial data to model daily economic activity, and study its relationship with electricity sources; (3) on the French and German electricity mix, and on their nuclear phase-out; (4) on the appropriateness of the daily and disaggregated analysis of electricity sources interactions; and (5) on the empirical evidence of daily data to provide ley factors to successfully integrate RES with a positive impact on economic activity.

In this chapter Vector Autoregressive (VAR) models were used to reveal the French and German relationships between electricity sources and economic activity from 1 January 2015 to 30 April 2018. This chapter has a main aim of answering the following questions: (1) what has been the daily role of fossil fuels in the electricity production systems? (2) how effective has wind power and solar PV been in substituting fossil fuels? (3) how effective has controllable RES (hydropower, biomass, waste, and geothermal) been in substituting the backup role played by fossil fuels? (4) what have been the consequences of the daily electricity mix on economic activity? and (5) how has economic activity contributed to the diversification of the electricity mix?

This chapter is described as follows: Section 9.2 covers the literature on the electricity—growth nexus. Section 9.3 presents the data and the methodology used. The results and the explanation of how to get them in EViews (econometric software), by the graphic ambient and by the command line are presented in Section 9.4. Section 9.5 discusses the results obtained and Section 9.6 concludes.

9.2 Literature review

The study of the electricity—growth nexus has been stimulated by two trends. First, the electrification of several economic sectors, such as industrial, residential, services, and transports sectors, and the increasing pressure to rethink and closely analyze the consequences of them on economies. Second, RES penetration, motivated by the political will and environment preoccupation, has revealed the necessity to understand the effects of each source on economic activity and vice versa.

In earlier studies, as happened in the tradition energy—growth nexus, the electricity—growth nexus has been analyzed through both specific countries and panels of countries, recurring to several economic and econometric techniques (Omri, 2014; Rüstemoğlu & Andrés, 2016). The literature has defined four main hypotheses to describe the relationships between electricity consumption/production and economic growth, namely the *Growth hypothesis*; the *Conservation hypothesis*; the *Feedback hypothesis*; and the *Neutrality hypothesis*.

The literature of electricity—growth nexus has evolved, and gradually corroborated the necessity to analyze the nexus by electricity source. Indeed, electricity generation technologies are not identical. In contrast, if the exploitation of endogenous and green resources by economies is highly dependent on primary energy from exterior sources, this could transform the nature of the nexus because of the potential they have on economic activity. Thus the evaluation of the interactions between electricity sources, such as RES, fossil fuels, and nuclear power, has been very attractive to the energy economics community. Indeed, the electricity—growth nexus has become richer, allowing the assessment of the relationships between the technological characteristics of each source and economic activity, as well as the interactions between the various electricity sources themselves (Marques, Fuinhas, & Menegaki, 2014). Furthermore, this has led the literature to coin new terms to describe the relationships between electricity sources, namely the *baseload role*, the *backup role*, the *substitution effect*, and the *complementary effect*.

The literature has not yet unequivocally proved the substitution effect of RES on nonrenewable energy sources (NRES) use to generate electricity. The literature frequently reveals that RES provokes fossil fuels burning to generate electricity (Cerdeira Bento & Moutinho, 2016; Marques et al., 2014). Nevertheless, the unidirectional causality from NRES to RES has been poorly proved (Ben Jebli & Ben Youssef, 2015). The nonconsensuality of literature results and conclusions about the effects of RES has led some authors to argue that RES have not had the anticipated effect, and they could continue to hamper the desired benefits (Flora, Marques, & Fuinhas, 2014; Glasnovic & Margeta, 2011; Nel & Cooper, 2009). Besides, the literature often proves that NRES have a positive impact on economic growth (Apergis & Payne, 2012; Dogan, 2015; Salim, Hassan, & Shafiei, 2014). While, RES have been a negative impact on economic growth and activity (Marques & Fuinhas, 2016).

When RES are analyzed separately, mainly the intermittent RES, the results are differentiated. On the one hand, solar PV raises both economic activity and growth, even small-scale PV installations. On the other hand, wind power restricts economic growth. The main reason provided by the literature regarding this result is the high subsidies provided to new wind farms. So the need to understand how to integrate intermittent RES into electricity systems, as well as their repercussions for economies and for maintaining fossil fuels, has received a good deal of attention. The difficulties in attempting to match the intermittent generation of RES with an uncertain demand, and the unavailability of large electricity storage to defer RES generation, has also stimulated the study of demand-side management (DSM) policies and measures. Through these the demand side could be able to add flexibility to electricity management systems, and harness intermittent production more accurately, which could lead to a positive impact and multiplier effects on economies (Auer & Haas, 2016).

9.3 Data and methodology

This chapter focuses on both the French and German electricity systems, revealing the relationships between electricity sources generation and financial activity. This research uses daily data from January 1, 2015 to April 30, 2018 only focusing on weekdays, excluding holidays, which makes a total of 1216 observations for both countries. All the electricity supply data for both countries has been obtained from the European Network of Transmission System Operators (ENTSO-E) transparency platform.[1] The ENTSO-E provides data on the electricity generated hourly and daily from each source, namely biomass, coal, oil, natural gas, geothermal, hydropower (pumped storages, run-of-river, and water reservoirs), marine, nuclear, solar PV, wastes, and wind (onshore and offshore), as well as the electricity used in pumping, electricity exchanged in cross-border markets, and electricity consumption. The daily low, high, and close prices and volume of exchanged actions of CAC40 (for France) and DAX30 (for Germany) were obtained from

---

[1] Available at: https://www.entsoe.eu/data/power-stats/.

the Yahoo finance database.[2] Afterwards the daily Gross Cash Flow (GCF) was calculated by using the typical price and the volume of daily actions transactions, following Eq. (9.1).

$$GCF = Price_{typical} \times Volume$$
$$\Leftrightarrow GCF = \left[\frac{Price_{low} + Price_{high} + Price_{close}}{3} \right] \times Volume \qquad (9.1)$$

where $Price_{low}$ is the lowest price of actions of the day, $Price_{high}$ is the highest price of actions in a specific day, $Price_{close}$ is the final price at which an action is traded on a given trading day, and volume is the number of actions exchanged in a day. The GCF defines the financial volume of money traded on a given trading day.

The econometric techniques using daily data carries several challenges, specifically white noise and extreme values, which has led some authors to argue that it generates outliers, provoking bias results (Aït-Sahalia & Xiu, 2017; At-Sahalia, Mykland, & Zhang, 2011; Cao & Tay, 2001; Li, Todorov, & Tauchen, 2017; Zhong & Enke, 2017). Nevertheless it is incorrect to call the extreme values outliers when analyzing the electricity generation by each source. Indeed, they are a genuine concern for electricity systems management services, because they occur every day, and management services must respond to them. Thus the exclusion of extreme values could produce erroneous results, and it is essential to include them to reflect the pressures experienced in the daily management of electricity systems. Seasonality effects are also expected in the series. However, the seasonality parameters are similar in all years, and they also constitute a concern for electricity systems management services.

The management of electricity systems is performed in real time. So one expects that all electricity sources interact with each other, which could provoke an effect of an endogenous adjustment. In fact the decision of use some sources during the day is contingent from the availability of other sources. Therefore the VAR technique is required to handle this data feature, as well as to deal with multiple seasonality parameters (Ghysels & Osborn, 2001; Sims, 1980). The VAR model treats all variables as potentially endogenous,

---

[2] Available at: https://finance.yahoo.com/.

and it measures the relationships without requiring the necessity to distinguish the series in endogenous and exogenous. Accordingly the VAR models are specified as follows:

$$Y_t = \sum_{j=1}^{\alpha} \gamma \times Y_{t-1} + \varphi \times X_t + \omega_t, \qquad (9.2)$$

where Y_t denotes the vector of the endogenous variables, X_t the vector of the exogenous variables, γ the coefficient matrix of endogenous variables, φ the coefficient matrix of exogenous variables, ω_t the residuals, and α means the optimal number of lags. The basis procedures followed in the VAR estimations were to: (1) assess the endogenous and exogenous series; (2) choose the optimal number of lags, through the lag order selection criteria and the exclusion tests of lag number; (3) test the stability condition of the models; (4) execute the residual diagnostic tests, to evaluate the normality, autocorrelation, and heteroskedasticity; (5) perform the Granger causality and block of exogeneity test estimation; (6) compute the impulse response functions (IRF); and (7) estimate the variances decomposition (VDC).

The Granger causality test permits to identify the causal link between the series, which occurs when a specific series in the past or in the present is helpful to predict the future values of another series (Granger, 1969). The IRF allows the realization of the behavior of the variable to an existing impulse in another variable, that is, ceteris paribus. Thus the IRF displays the impact that a shock in the error term, in a given period, has on the values of current and future endogenous series. The forecast error variance decomposition or VDC assesses how a series responds to shock in another, in percentage.

9.4 Results

The empirical application in this chapter focuses on both the French and German electricity generation systems, revealing the dynamics among the diverse electricity sources used and financial activity therein. Furthermore, this work analyzes electricity management in two different ways. On the one hand, this chapter analyzes an electricity mix highly dependent on nuclear power, the French case, on the other hand, it studies an electricity mix traditionally less dependent on nuclear source, the German case. As is well-known, Germany and France have set out ambitious targets to replace their nuclear sources. However, France still has a low RES share, and nuclear power is still playing a crucial role in electricity supply. Accordingly, both France and Germany were replacing a strong a rigid baseload source with a mix of sources, namely RES, with notorious different characteristics, which makes the analysis of this chapter highly exciting. The results of France and Germany will be presented separately. France's results will be explained and presented among indications through the EViews graphic framework. While, Germany's results will be displayed together with the EViews commands that could be used to create a program file, or simply to put them in the command window.

9.4.1 French results

First, a visual inspection of the series among an examination of descriptive statistics should be made. In order to get the descriptive statistics (see Table 9.1):

How to do:

Go to menu quick ⇒ group statistics ⇒ descriptive statistics ⇒ common sample ⇒ introduce all variables names in study ⇒ OK

It is important to note that the electricity series is measured in megawatts (MW). It can be seen by both the descriptive statistics and by the series graphics that all variables have extreme values, and seasonality effects. As the *WASTE* series has three means, that is, the mean value is different in three periods, so, it is expected that this series are I(1). Afterwards, all variables have been transformed in their natural logarithms, represented by the "L" prefix, the "D" prefix denotes the first differences of variables.

To perform the graphics of the series (see Fig. 9.1):

How to do:

Go to menu quick ⇒ graph ⇒ introduce all variables names in study ⇒ OK ⇒ in multiple series option choose multiple graphs ⇒ OK.

Table 9.1 Descriptive statistics.

Variable	Mean	Median	Max.	Min.	Std. Dev.	Skewness	Kurtosis	Jarque–Bera	Obs.
WINDON	59479.39	45887.00	220220.0	8708.000	39971.22	1.421990	4.742201	370.7829***	800
SOL	22287.13	22340.50	45279.00	4987.000	9777.473	0.181188	2.058603	33.91820***	800
HYDRO	173968.6	176017.0	293124.0	68838.00	48488.20	0.037320	2.016337	32.43879***	800
PUMP	12583.18	12099.00	36551.00	59.00000	4344.680	1.008953	5.639459	367.9563***	800
BIO	7238.908	6774.000	14295.00	3029.000	2301.269	1.515210	4.566262	387.8872***	800
WASTE	5046.104	5560.500	7303.000	1227.000	1594.170	−1.034687	2.941322	142.8585***	800
COAL	25483.36	24254.50	73888.00	1.000000	18743.06	0.278504	2.104228	37.08879***	800
NGAS	103470.4	102142.5	220790.0	13120.00	57605.72	0.139344	1.904348	42.60397***	800
OIL	7045.264	5290.500	66576.00	2433.000	6974.381	4.888527	33.69485	34592.14***	800
NUC	1092774.	1067222.	1417069.	805315.0	146693.4	0.319677	2.080387	41.81543***	800
RXM	1.535244	1.132323	35.61395	1.000000	1.757263	11.07835	186.4166	1137752.***	800
GCF	5.03E + 11	4.75E + 11	1.71E + 12	0.000000	1.70E + 11	1.628021	9.790743	1890.533***	800

Notes: WINDON is the electricity generation from onshore wind power; *SOL* is the electricity generation from solar PV; *HYDRO* is the electricity generation from hydropower; *PUMP* is the electricity consumed in pumping systems; *BIO* is the electricity generation from biomass; *WASTE* is the electricity generation from wastes; *COAL* is the electricity generation from coal; *NGAS* is the electricity generation from natural gas; *OIL* is the electricity generation from oil; *NUC* is the electricity generation from nuclear; *RXM* is the coverage ratio of electricity imports by exports; and *GCF* is the gross cash flow.

How it looks like

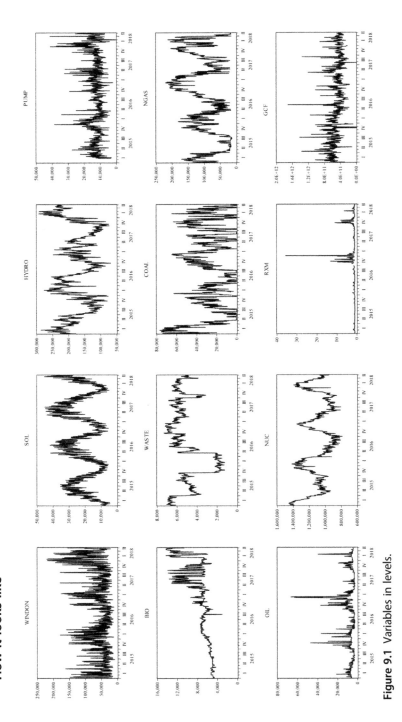

Figure 9.1 Variables in levels.

The augmented Dickey–Fuller (ADF) test (Dickey & Fuller, 1981), the Phillips and Perron (PP) test (Phillips & Perron, 1988), and the Kwiatkowski–Phillips–Schmidt–Shin (KPSS) test (Kwiatkowski, Phillips, Schmidt, & Shin, 1992) were executed to evaluate the integration order of the series. The ADF tests were performed under the null hypothesis of unit root, subsequent the Schwartz information criterion. The KPSS and the PP tests are executed by the Bartlett Kernel Spectral estimation method and the Newey-West bandwidth. The null hypothesis of the PP test is the existence of a unit root. Conversely the null hypothesis of KPSS is the nonexistence of a unit root. To perform the integration order tests:

How to do:

Go to menu quick ⇒ series statistics ⇒ unit root test ⇒ introduce the variable name ⇒ OK ⇒ choose the type of the test ⇒ choose the lag length criterion ⇒ choose test unit root for level, first or second differences ⇒ choose the inclusion of constant, constant and trend, or none of both ⇒ OK

   To make a different test:

Go to menu view ⇒ unit root test ⇒ choose the options ⇒ OK

How ADF test looks like

Null hypothesis: LSOL has a unit root
Exogenous: Constant
Lag Length: 6 (Automatic—based on SIC, maxlag = 20)

	t-statistic	Prob.[a]
Augmented Dickey–Fuller test statistic	− 2.783620	0.0610
Test critical values:	1% level	− 3.437721
	5% level	− 2.864683
	10% level	− 2.568497

[a]MacKinnon (2008) one-sided P-values.

Augmented Dickey–Fuller Test Equation
Dependent variable: D(LSOL)
Method: Least squares
Sample (adjusted): 1/12/2015 4/30/2018
Included observations: 861 after adjustments

Variable	Coefficient	Std. error	t-statistic	Prob.
LSOL(−1)	− 0.043687	0.015694	− 2.783620	0.0055
D(LSOL(−1))	− 0.443433	0.035841	− 12.37225	0.0000
D(LSOL(−2))	− 0.340057	0.038281	− 8.883133	0.0000

Variable	Coefficient	Std. error	t-statistic	Prob.
D(LSOL(−3))	− 0.237208	0.039094	− 6.067639	0.0000
D(LSOL(−4))	− 0.210975	0.038824	− 5.434072	0.0000
D(LSOL(−5))	− 0.169618	0.037269	− 4.551165	0.0000
D(LSOL(−6))	− 0.142122	0.033972	− 4.183441	0.0000
C	0.435521	0.155001	2.809790	0.0051
R-squared	0.216719	Mean dependent var		0.001651
Adjusted R-squared	0.210291	S.D. dependent var		0.250946
S.E. of regression	0.223005	Akaike info criterion		− 0.153997
Sum squared resid	42.42074	Schwarz criterion		− 0.109787
Log likelihood	74.29571	Hannan−Quinn criter.		− 0.137073
F-statistic	33.71550	Durbin−Watson stat		2.000834
Prob(F-statistic)	0.000000			

How PP test looks like

Null hypothesis: LSOL has a unit root
Exogenous: Constant
Bandwidth: 3 (Newey-West automatic) using Bartlett kernel

		Adj. t-stat	Prob.[a]
Phillips−Perron test statistic		− 5.900422	0.0000
Test critical values:	1% level	− 3.437669	
	5% level	− 2.864660	
	10% level	− 2.568485	

[a]MacKinnon (2008) one-sided P-values.

Residual variance (no correction)	0.059019
HAC corrected variance (Bartlett kernel)	0.035751

Phillips−Perron test equation
Dependent variable: D(LSOL)
Method: Least squares
Sample (adjusted): 1/02/2015 4/30/2018
Included observations: 867 after adjustments

Variable	Coefficient	Std. error	t-statistic	Prob.
LSOL(−1)	− 0.114835	0.015766	− 7.283673	0.0000
C	1.133882	0.155728	7.281171	0.0000
R-squared	0.057787	Mean dependent var		0.001207

Variable	Coefficient	Std. error	t-statistic	Prob.
Adjusted R-squared	0.056698	S.D. dependent var		0.250421
S.E. of regression	0.243218	Akaike info criterion		0.012589
Sum squared resid	51.16916	Schwarz criterion		0.023581
Log likelihood	− 3.457177	Hannan−Quinn criter.		0.016795
F-statistic	53.05189	Durbin−Watson stat		2.495777
Prob(F-statistic)	0.000000			

How KPSS test looks like

Null Hypothesis: LSOL is stationary
Exogenous: Constant
Bandwidth: 23 (Newey-West automatic) using
Bartlett kernel

		LM-Stat.
Kwiatkowski−Phillips−Schmidt−Shin test statistic		0.148667
Asymptotic critical values[a]:	1% level	0.739000
	5% level	0.463000
	10% level	0.347000

[a]Kwiatkowski−Phillips−Schmidt−Shin (1992, Table 9.1)

Residual variance (no correction)	0.274321
HAC corrected variance (Bartlett kernel)	5.150397

KPSS test equation
Dependent variable: LSOL
Method: Least squares
Sample: 1/01/2015 4/30/2018
Included observations: 868

Variable	Coefficient	Std. error	t-statistic	Prob.
C	9.863932	0.017788	554.5367	0.0000
R-squared	0.000000	Mean dependent var		9.863932
Adjusted R-squared	− 0.000000	S.D. dependent var		0.524058
S.E. of regression	0.524058	Akaike info criterion		1.546724
Sum squared resid	238.1104	Schwarz criterion		1.552215
Log likelihood	− 670.2782	Hannan−Quinn criterion		1.548825
Durbin−Watson stat	0.228082			

In the ADF test the results to take into account are the *t*-statistic and the probability (Prob.*) of the null hypothesis. The null hypothesis of the tests is displayed in the first line. In the example, the null hypothesis is that *LSOL* has a unit root test, as the probability is between 0.1 and 0.05, the null hypothesis is rejected with 10% level of significance. So to complete the table of unit roots, transcribe the *t*-statics value, -2.7836, with one "*." The PP test interpretation is similar to the ADF, the null hypothesis is that *LSOL* has a unit root, as the probability is lower than .01, this means that the null hypothesis is rejected with 1% level of significance. Accordingly, in the table should appear -4.1866***. The KPSS test is a unilateral right test, to accept the null hypothesis the LM-stat has to be lower than the 10% critical value, and to reject, the LM-stat has to be higher than the 1% critical value. In the example, as the LM-stat is 0.0899 lower than 0.347 (the critical value at 10% level of significance), so the null hypothesis that *LSOL* is stationary is accepted.

Table 9.2 discloses the results of the unit roots tests. Even with the lack of consensus from the KPSS test, in general, the tests support that all series excluding *LWASTE* and *LNUC* are I(0) in their levels with intercept and with intercept and trend. Thus all variables are stationary in their levels, except *LWASTE* and *LNUC* which contains a unit root in level, that is, they are I(1). The KPSS test is not robust in the presence of extreme values, so, in daily data, their lack of consensus could provoke erroneous results. Therefore, from now on attention should be paid to the fact that all the tests should be made with *LWASTE* and *LNUC* series in first differences, even the VAR model, because of VAR estimation require that all variables are I(0).

Afterwards, both the collinearity and multicollinearity should be checked. To do that it is indispensable to inspect the correlation matrix (see Table 9.3) and the Variance Inflation Factors (VIF) statistics. To compute the correlation matrix:

How to do:
Go to menu quick ⇒ group statistics ⇒ correlations ⇒ introduce the variables names ⇒ OK

Table 9.2 Integration order tests.

Variable	ADF		PP		KPSS	
	c	ct	c	ct	C	Ct
LGCF	− 6.579126***	− 8.06689***	− 18.29670***	− 19.24040***	2.162717***	0.219024***
LWINDON	− 15.30500***	− 15.70612***	− 16.05039***	− 16.17774***	0.754023***	0.251003***
LSOL	− 2.783620*	− 2.766836	− 5.900422***	− 5.931670***	0.148667	0.093646
LHYDRO	− 4.636255***	− 4.625616***	− 4.851955***	− 4.847446***	0.174440	0.147858**
LPUMP	− 17.88547***	− 17.90312***	− 19.25496***	− 19.26821***	0.133279	0.098468
LBIO	− 4.636430***	− 8.703800***	− 4.653065***	− 7.844840***	2.881021***	0.077498
LWASTE	− 2.804900*	− 3.013863	− 2.509655	− 2.761664	0.714593**	0.303672***
DLWASTE	− 30.23309***	− 30.21924***	− 30.87332***	− 30.86285***	0.069600	0.054115
LCOAL	− 6.976945***	− 6.964236***	− 7.927305***	− 7.912721***	0.083730	0.077595
LNGAS	− 3.026785**	− 3.487904**	− 4.961230***	− 5.794079***	0.704396**	0.148173**
LOIL	− 6.758553***	− 6.778314***	− 10.14219***	− 10.17720***	0.114708	0.086956
LNUC	− 2.588393*	− 2.525395	− 4.002243***	− 3.232834*	0.364503*	0.169352**
DLNUC	− 14.95924***	− 14.96355***	− 43.08451***	− 43.07485***	0.070547	0.059441
LRXM	− 8.601303***	− 8.934967***	− 8.180997***	− 8.571252***	0.649730**	0.106467

Notes: C means constant, and CT means constant and trend; ***, **, and * indicate that the statistic is significant at 1%, 5%, and 10%, respectively.

Table 9.3 Correlation matrix.

	LWINDON	LSOL	LHYDRO	LPUMP	LBIO	DLWASTE	LCOAL	LNGAS	LOIL	DLNUC	LRXM	LGCF
LWINDON	1.0000	− 0.3883	0.1241	0.2069	0.1420	− 0.0394	− 0.0050	0.1269	0.1413	0.0042	− 0.0657	0.0037
LSOL	− 0.3883	1.0000	− 0.0590	− 0.2142	0.1618	0.0442	− 0.3234	− 0.5132	− 0.5430	− 0.0446	− 0.2819	− 0.0501
LHYDRO	0.1241	− 0.0590	1.0000	− 0.1053	0.0884	0.0255	− 0.0150	0.0500	0.1939	− 0.0112	0.0013	0.2030
LPUMP	0.2069	− 0.2142	− 0.1053	1.0000	− 0.0427	− 0.0120	− 0.1600	− 0.0949	− 0.1250	− 0.0673	− 0.1522	− 0.0285
LBIO	0.1420	0.1618	0.0884	− 0.0427	1.0000	0.0170	0.0507	0.2086	− 0.0938	− 0.0172	0.1390	− 0.2787
DLWASTE	− 0.0394	0.0442	0.0255	− 0.0120	0.0170	1.0000	− 0.0141	− 0.0230	− 0.0045	0.0531	0.0140	0.0299
LCOAL	− 0.0050	− 0.3234	− 0.0150	− 0.1600	0.0507	− 0.0141	1.0000	0.6631	0.4045	0.0398	0.3199	0.1156
LNGAS	0.1269	− 0.5132	0.0500	− 0.0949	0.2086	− 0.0230	0.6631	1.0000	0.5132	0.0625	0.4592	− 0.1046
LOIL	0.1413	− 0.5430	0.1939	− 0.1250	− 0.0938	− 0.0045	0.4045	0.5132	1.0000	− 0.0049	0.5514	0.1281
DLNUC	0.0042	− 0.0446	− 0.0112	− 0.0673	− 0.0172	0.0531	0.0398	0.0625	− 0.0049	1.0000	0.0135	0.0324
LRXM	− 0.0657	− 0.2819	0.0013	− 0.1522	0.1390	0.0140	0.3199	0.4592	0.5514	0.0135	1.0000	− 0.1157
LGCF	0.0037	− 0.0501	0.2030	− 0.0285	− 0.2787	0.0299	0.1156	− 0.1046	0.1281	0.0324	− 0.1157	1.0000

In order to perform the VIF statistics:

How to do:

Go to menu quick $\Rightarrow$ estimate equation $\Rightarrow$ introduce the variables names and the constant (C) $\Rightarrow$ OK $\Rightarrow$ go to menu view $\Rightarrow$ coefficient diagnostics $\Rightarrow$ variance inflation factors

How VIF statistics looks like

Variance inflation factors
Sample: 1/01/2015 4/30/2018
Included observations: 797

Variable	Coefficient Variance	Uncentered VIF	Centered VIF
LSOL	0.002894	777.6399	1.988303
LHYDRO_ALL	0.004833	1912.675	1.157488
LHYDRO_PUMP	0.002674	643.6727	1.221190
LBIO	0.006278	1344.500	1.317049
D(LWASTE)	0.057937	1.008241	1.008096
LCOAL	0.000193	48.00292	1.984947
LNGAS	0.001874	660.0151	2.827207
LOIL	0.002539	521.4418	2.257218
D(LNUC)	0.342459	1.021047	1.020633
LRXM	0.003268	2.313807	1.656434
LGCF	0.004668	9236.301	1.263611
C	5.344434	14614.85	NA

In the correlation matrix, as the values are below 0.8 it could be argued that problems of correlation do not exist. In fact, correlation values above 0.8 could bring correlation problems to model estimation. Thus, the series with a correlation value higher than 0.8 could not be estimated in the same model. The VIF statistics (in EViews the Centred VIF) should not be higher than 10; if higher than 10, problems exist of collinearity or multicollinearity. The most suitable estimators are those where VIF statistics are lower than 6.

In the correlation matrix, the highest value is between $LNGAS$ and $LCOAL$, 0.6631. Accordingly, there are problems of correlation between variables. The highest value in the VIF statistics are 2.8272, so any doubts about collinearity and multicollinearity were set aside. To carry out the VAR estimation, first, it is important to choose the optimal lag structure throughout the sequential modified LR, the final prediction error, Akaike, Schwarz, and Hannan—Quinn information criterions. To estimate the VAR model:

How to do:

Go to menu quick ⇒ estimate VAR ⇒ introduce the variables names in endogenous variables, and introduce C (the constant) in exogenous variables ⇒ OK

After, to compute the lag order selection criteria:

How to do:

Go to menu view ⇒ lag structure ⇒ lag length criteria ⇒ introduce the maximum lag to be tested, in our case 27 ⇒ OK

How the Lag order section criteria looks like

VAR lag order selection criteria
Endogenous variables: LWINDON LSOL LHYDRO LPUMP LBIO
D(LWASTE) LCOAL LNGAS LOIL D(LNUC) LRXM LGCF
Exogenous variables: C
Sample: 1/01/2015 4/30/2018
Included observations: 397

Lag	LogL	LR	FPE	AIC	SC	HQ
0	− 911.9159	NA	1.71e−13	4.654488	4.774910	4.702191
1	1300.108	4279.180	5.10e−18[a]	− 5.763769	− 4.198293[a]	− 5.143637[a]
2	1444.063	269.7783	5.11e−18	− 5.763539	− 2.753008	− 4.570977
3	1545.122	183.2815	6.37e−18	− 5.547214	− 1.091627	− 3.782222
4	1669.149	217.4382	7.10e−18	− 5.446595	0.454046	− 3.109173
5	1773.943	177.3843	8.78e−18	− 5.249084	2.096612	− 2.339232
6	1863.541	146.2454	1.18e−17	− 4.975018	3.815733	− 1.492737
7	1946.622	130.5852	1.65e−17	− 4.668119	5.567687	− 0.613408
8	2041.713	143.7153	2.20e−17	− 4.421730	7.259131	0.205411
9	2139.688	142.1491	2.92e−17	− 4.189862	8.936054	1.009709
10	2248.283	150.9936	3.74e−17	− 4.011500	10.55947	1.760501

Lag	LogL	LR	FPE	AIC	SC	HQ
11	2370.135	162.0600	4.54e-17	− 3.899922	12.11610	2.444508
12	2509.209	176.5574	5.15e-17	− 3.875106	13.58597	3.041754
13	2625.184	140.2217	6.70e-17	− 3.733923	15.17221	3.755367
14	2739.875	131.7358	9.00e-17	− 3.586271	16.76492	4.475449
15	2899.890	174.1229	9.89e-17	− 3.666954	18.12929	4.967196
16	3061.188	165.7667	1.12e-16	− 3.754095	19.48721	5.452484
17	3208.713	142.6946	1.40e-16	− 3.771855	20.91450	6.007154
18	3371.489	147.6052	1.69e-16	− 3.866443	22.26497	6.484996
19	3557.890	157.7602	1.91e-16	− 4.080051	23.49641	6.843818
20	3761.451	159.9772	2.09e-16	− 4.380105	24.64142	7.116193
21	3942.012	130.9865	2.76e-16	− 4.564293	25.90228	7.504436
22	4204.593	174.6129	2.60e-16	− 5.161677	26.74995	7.479481
23	4425.224	133.3787	3.33e-16	− 5.547726	27.80896	7.665862
24	4744.105	173.4971[a]	2.92e-16	− 6.428740	28.37300	7.357278
25	5070.708	157.9544	2.85e-16	− 7.348657	28.89814	7.009791
26	5436.488	154.7885	2.75e-16	− 8.465936	29.22591	6.464941
27	5849.953	149.9721	2.67e-16	− 9.823441[a]	29.31346	5.679866

Notes: LR: sequential modified LR test statistic (each test at 5% level); FPE: final prediction error; AIC: Akaike information criterion; SC: Schwarz information criterion; and HQ: Hannan−Quinn information criterion.
[a]Indicates lag order selected by the criterion.

The values with "*" are the optimal lags number chosen by each information criterion. The FPE, SC, and HQ criterions has chosen one has the optimal number of lags, the LR and the AIC are the only nonconsensual, choosing 24 and 27, respectively. To overcome the nonconsensuality of criterions, it is even possible perform a lag exclusion test. However, before applying the lag exclusion test, it is advisable to check the residuals and the Granger causalities, to conclude about the necessity to include dummies to correct errors, and to determine the exogenous and endogenous variables. As the optimal number of lags is 1, it is necessary re-estimate the VAR model, go to estimate menu ⇒ in the lag intervals for endogenous, change "1 2" by "1 1" ⇒ OK. The next step is computing the Granger causalities and the blocks of exogeneity:

How to do:

Go to menu view ⇒ lag structure ⇒ Granger causality/block exogeneity tests

What a block of exogeneity looks like:

Dependent variable: D(LWASTE)

Excluded	Chi-sq	df	Prob.
LWINDON	23.96448	1	0.2439
LSOL	18.93951	1	0.5258
LHYDRO	21.90444	1	0.3457
LPUMP	10.12227	1	0.9659
LBIO	13.43187	1	0.8581
LCOAL	24.97328	1	0.2025
LNGAS	11.91792	1	0.9189
LOIL	21.38199	1	0.3750
D(LNUC)	18.73310	1	0.5392
LRXM	15.56840	1	0.7430
LGCF	19.11210	1	0.5146
All	190.3295	1	0.9267

Dependent variable: LNGAS

Excluded	Chi-sq	df	Prob.
LWINDON	14.05813	1	0.0002
LSOL	0.152863	1	0.6958
LHYDRO	1.565394	1	0.2109
LPUMP	13.06402	1	0.0003
LBIO	0.000139	1	0.9906
D(LWASTE)	5.249106	1	0.0220
LCOAL	2.794093	1	0.0946
LOIL	2.643396	1	0.1040
D(LNUC)	10.37572	1	0.0013
LRXM	5.705183	1	0.0169
LGCF	11.27390	1	0.0008
All	88.50979	11	0.0000

The null hypothesis is that the independent variable does not cause the dependent. In the right-side example, the independent variables do not cause $DWASTE$, neither all variables together cause $DLWASTE$. In the left-side example, the null hypothesis that $DLWASTE$ does not cause $LNGAS$ is rejected at a 5% level of significance. So it can be concluded that $DLWASTE$ is an exogenous variable, because it is not caused, but causes others. As title example, if the $DLWASTE$ does not cause another variable, it should be excluded from the model estimation. Once again, it is necessary to re-estimate the VAR model, changing the $DLWASTE$ from endogenous variables to exogenous variables. Next, check the residuals:

How to do:

Go to menu resides

How residuals graph looks like

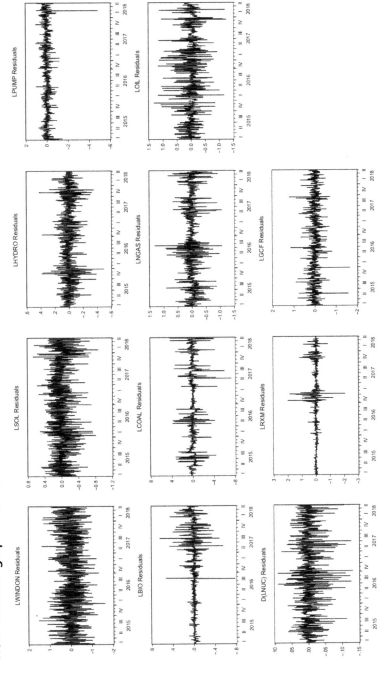

It could be observable in the residual's graphics, that *LPUMP*, *LBIO*, and *LGCF* seems to have outliers in residuals. As such, one generates dummies to check the necessity to correct these residuals. In order to generate an impulse dummy, which it will take value 1 in a specific day and 0 in the remaining:

How to do:

Go to add-ins menu ⇒ generate dummy variables ⇒ choose impulse ⇒ Ok ⇒ introduce the date, in our case 8/17/2016 ⇒ OK

Now go to the VAR estimation, and introduce the dummy variable as an exogenous variable:

How to do:

Estimate menu ⇒ introduce the dummy variable name, d_8_17_2016, in the exogenous variables ⇒ OK

Go check again the residuals, going to menu residuals. In this case, with the introduction of this dummy, all residuals have been corrected. Indeed, in France several biomass plants were shut down for maintenance (ENTSOE-E), which has caused this disruption in the model. So far the endogenous and exogenous variables have been distinguished, and the residuals corrected. Afterwards, it is necessary to check again the lag order selection, the SC and HQ have chosen 1, FPE choose 2, LR choose 16, and AIC choose 27 as optimal number of lags. As the tests are not consensual, it is necessary to perform the lag exclusion test:

How to do:

Re-estimate the VAR model with 27 lags (in lag intervals for endogenous introduce 1 27), go to menu view ⇒ lag structure ⇒ lag exclusion tests.

How the lag exclusion test looks like

VAR lag exclusion Wald tests
Sample: 1/01/2015 4/30/2018
Included observations: 397
Chi-squared test statistics for lag exclusion:
Numbers in [ ] are P-values

	LWINDON	LSOL	LHYDRO	LPUMP	LBIO	LCOAL	LNGAS	LOIL	D(LNUC)	LRXM	LGCF	Joint
Lag 1	32.98428	26.74188	46.46484	36.88965	102.0007	37.01285	102.5890	39.62669	28.78608	122.1917	26.74005	636.8107
	[.000529]	[.005026]	[2.68e-06]	[.000120]	[1.11e-16]	[.000115]	[.000000]	[4.14e-05]	[.002450]	[.000000]	[.005029]	[.000000]
Lag 2	8.729137	15.94802	8.580064	23.20513	6.304213	12.55500	13.10216	12.75569	14.36627	15.17614	10.08798	153.7874
	[.646878]	[.143072]	[.660591]	[.016534]	[.852315]	[.323402]	[.286701]	[.309593]	[.213385]	[.174575]	[.522491]	[.023592]
Lag 3	11.67461	13.80451	5.849007	6.969131	4.851774	10.91301	9.343777	27.65017	23.63448	10.30935	6.518192	141.7069
	[.388592]	[.244000]	[.883246]	[.801578]	[.938132]	[.450579]	[.590193]	[.003661]	[.014365]	[.502794]	[.836653]	[.096077]
Lag 4	11.10847	15.88679	5.022005	12.90436	3.958314	13.97641	8.838264	26.08616	16.49262	15.74669	6.730637	160.1084
	[.434221]	[.145386]	[.930096]	[.299622]	[.971121]	[.234302]	[.636818]	[.006301]	[.123805]	[.150799]	[.820459]	[.009988]
Lag 5	10.49329	9.125192	8.047021	18.51501	7.528172	17.01210	4.903135	26.15434	13.32270	9.340023	4.508898	131.3660
	[.486636]	[.610338]	[.709086]	[.070374]	[.754842]	[.107518]	[.935767]	[.006155]	[.272758]	[.590538]	[.952605]	[.244847]
Lag 27	14.16004	9.941940	7.937549	17.16153	4.114286	14.93297	18.11614	10.33193	29.44409	8.168021	8.630077	162.3883
	[.224264]	[.535617]	[.718887]	[.103188]	[.966454]	[.185586]	[.079925]	[.500800]	[.001936]	[.698178]	[.655995]	[.007182]

The null hypothesis of the lag exclusion test is that a given series with a given lag number is nonsignificant to the model estimation. It can be seen that the null hypothesis is only rejected to all variables with one lag, with two lags the null hypothesis is only rejected in one variable and in the joint test, with 5% level of significance. So the optimal number of lags is one, that is, VAR(1) is the optimal. This result is a sign of the absence of omitted-variables bias. Re-estimate the VAR model with one lag, check if all variables are endogenous. Indeed, all variables are endogenous in the French model. The endogeneity of *DLWASTE was tested again*, but the series continued to be exogenous even with the introduction of the dummy.

What the LM test looks like:

VAR residual serial correlation LM tests
Null hypothesis: no serial correlation at lag order h
Sample: 1/01/2015 4/30/2018
Included observations: 776

Lags	LM–Stat	Prob
1	275.1645	0.0000
2	147.5157	0.0509
3	111.8821	0.7117
4	181.5740	0.0003
5	201.4155	0.0000
6	155.9499	0.0177
7	137.7107	0.1421
8	127.0430	0.3355
9	129.7223	0.2775
10	181.1548	0.0003

To compute the White test:

How to do:

Go to view menu ⇒ residuals tests ⇒ white heteroskedasticity (no cross terms)

What the White test looks like:

VAR residual heteroskedasticity tests: no
cross terms (only levels and squares)
Sample: 1/01/2015 4/30/2018

Included observations: 776
Joint test:

Chi-sq	Df	Prob.
2829.505	1650	0.0000

To execute the Jarque—Bera test:

How to do:

Go to view menu ⇒ residuals tests ⇒ normality test ⇒ choose Cholesky of covariance option ⇒ OK

How normality test looks like

VAR residual normality tests
Orthogonalization: Cholesky (Lutkepohl)
Null hypothesis: residuals are multivariate normal
Sample: 1/01/2015 4/30/2018
Included observations: 776

Component	Skewness	Chi-sq	Df	Prob.
1	0.051556	0.343768	1	0.5577
2	− 0.532780	36.71179	1	0.0000
3	− 0.328292	13.93894	1	0.0002
4	− 4.166734	2245.443	1	0.0000
5	0.658583	56.09599	1	0.0000
6	− 1.033681	138.1921	1	0.0000
7	− 0.165888	3.559099	1	0.0592
8	0.379700	18.64627	1	0.0000
9	− 1.094821	155.0232	1	0.0000
10	1.561250	315.2500	1	0.0000
11	0.087636	0.993290	1	0.3189
Joint		2984.197	11	0.0000

The stability of models, given by the AR roots test, is supported once the P-values are inside the circle, that is, the values are below one. In the LM test the null hypothesis of no serial correlation is only accepted in 3, 7, 8, and 9 lags, the White test rejects the hypothesis that the model is homoscedastic, and the normality test rejects the hypothesis of normality, except in model one (wind power model). In fact the VAR model fails all relevant diagnostic tests, namely there is strong evidence of the presence of heteroskedasticity, nonnormality of residuals, and autocorrelation, which is not new when working with this high-frequency data. These violations are of minor concern when in the presence of numerable observations, as is the case under research. Financial econometrics suggest that it is problematic to separate underlying trends and patterns from random features, which are mainly persistent in high-frequency data analysis (Brooks, 2008). Furthermore, the data used is not normally distributed (see descriptive statistics table), as it is in high-frequency financial econometrics data studies, although most econometric techniques assume that data it is (Brooks, 2008). Thus it was expected, but not desired, that the VAR model employed would fail to reject the null hypothesis of the diagnostic tests. Nevertheless, the literature argues that it is feasible to estimate a VAR model with high-frequency data that does not assume normality, homoscedasticity, and nonautocorrelation (Brooks, 2008). Indeed, it is often proved that, when the sample contains a great deal of information, the violation of a diagnostic test is virtually inconsequential (Brooks, 2008). This argument is often corroborated by the central limit theorem, which states that high-frequency data statistics, and econometric procedures using them, will asymptotically follow the appropriate distribution, even when diagnostic tests are rejected (Brooks, 2008). Therefore the violation and nonrejection of the null hypothesis of diagnostic tests are a minor concern and inconsequential in the assessment of large samples, such as the one used in the French research containing 776 daily observations after adjustments. After the diagnostic tests compute the granger causalities IRF:

How to do:

menu view ⟹ lag structure ⟹ granger causality/ block exogeneity tests), the IRF and the VDC.

What Granger causalities for wind looks like:

VAR Granger causality/block
exogeneity Wald tests
Sample: 1/01/2015 4/30/2018
Included observations: 776
Dependent variable: LWINDON

Excluded	Chi-sq	df	Prob.
LSOL	8.410187	1	0.0037
LHYDRO	4.012810	1	0.0452
LPUMP	4.120435	1	0.0424
LBIO	6.870012	1	0.0088
LCOAL	2.149447	1	0.1426
LNGAS	3.767500	1	0.0523

Excluded	Chi-sq	df	Prob.
LOIL	0.578499	1	0.4469
D(LNUC)	0.199714	1	0.6550
LRXM	1.436770	1	0.2307
LGCF	0.683556	1	0.4084
All	48.08574	10	0.0000

Remember that, the null hypothesis is that the independent series does not cause the dependent. Analyzing onshore wind power as the dependent variable, the *LHYDRO* and *LPUMP* causes *LWINDON* with 5% level of significance, *LSOL* and *LBIO* causes *LWINDON* with 1% level of significance, and *LNGAS* causes *LWINDON* with 10% level of significance. So, the table of causalities looks like Table 9.4.

The relatively large number of Granger causalities founded, emphasizes that endogeneity is present in the interactions between French electricity sources and financial activity, and it also could be seen as further enhancing confidence in the robustness of the results. In order to compute the VDC (see Table 9.5):

How to do:

Go to view menu ⇒ variance decomposition ⇒ choose the option table, and the periods under analysis (30 in this case)

The VDC reveals how a variable responds to a shock in another series. For example, see the VDC of *LSOL*, after a 2-day gag, shocks to *LSOL* explain around 92.6553% of the forecast error variance. This impact is reduced to 63.7021% after 30 days. Comparing the shocks to *LNGAS* and *LHYDRO*, the shocks to *LNGAS* explain a larger percentage of the forecast error variance than the shocks to *LHYDRO*, about 10% and 6%, respectively after 30 days. It is worth highlight that, shocks to *LNGAS* has gained strength consistently, and jump from about 1% to 10% in the explanation of the *LSOL* forecast error variance. Regarding to *LGCF*, shocks to *LHYDRO* and *LBIO* explain around 6% of the forecast error variance at the end of 30-day lag. While *LCOAL*, *LGAS*, and *LOIL* explain a lower percentage of the forecast error variance in *LGCF*, around 5%, 3%, and 2% at the end of 30-day lag. Finally, to estimate the IRF:

How to do:

Go to menu view ⇒ impulse response ⇒ choose multiple graphs, analytic (asymptotic), and introduce 30 periods.

Table 9.4 Granger causalities.

	LWINDON	LSOL	LHYDRO	LPUMP	LBIO	LCOAL	LNGAS	LOIL	DLNUC	LRXM	LGCF
LWINDON	–	1.802	20.9556***	1.8928	0.2834	0.3315	15.0202***	3.0658*	5.9404**	1.1563	0.9157
LSOL	8.4102***	–	0.5148	23.0594***	1.1176	0.2078	0.0872	13.4919***	1.586	0.0048	0.1752
LHYDRO	4.0128**	3.6219*	–	0.0139	0.8038	1.8225	1.4528	1.2459	3.4347*	3.5131*	6.9824***
LPUMP	4.1204**	0.5062	17.6132***	–	1.3629	0.2181	12.8629***	0.0037	0.2419	0.2091	0.4058
LBIO	6.87***	5.0642**	0.4966	0.9963	–	1.0141	0.0101	3.1067*	3.0416*	2.3955	12.4631***
LCOAL	2.1494	0.9723	4.1145**	3.5173*	0.3373	–	3.1539*	5.4488**	0.0279	0.1089	22.5042***
LNGAS	3.7675*	11.2595***	5.0908**	0.0103	6.0795**	19.7022***	–	0.1021	1.2659	1.2283	15.0668***
LOIL	0.5785	10.36***	0.369	3.7835*	1.36	1.1221	2.7919*	–	0.0354	2.2935	5.3389**
DLNUC	0.1997	3.2765*	3.0517*	2.9759*	0.0009	1.6334	11.1498***	0.8911	–	0.1216	0.7574
LRXM	1.4368	1.9071	0.5886	1.8586	0.0288	0.0133	5.5984**	15.7746***	3.1359*	–	1.1572
LGCF	0.6836	1.5569	1.1319	2.7604*	2.7294*	0.0879	12.1202***	1.6858	9.5116***	2.4279	–
All	48.0857***	56.1823***	70.4275***	38.0227***	13.8342	45.0584***	83.0708***	70.4827***	36.0317***	23.4072***	58.4087***

Notes: "All" denotes the causality test set for all independent variables; ***, **, and * denote statistical significance at 1%, 5%, and 10%, respectively.

Table 9.5 Variances decomposition.

Period	S.E.	LWINDON	LSOL	LHYDRO	L_PUMP	LBIO	LCOAL	LNGAS	LOIL	DLNUC	LRXM	LGCF
Variance decomposition of LWINDON:												
2	0.5641	98.5497	0.4216	0.2492	0.3455	0.1117	0.0659	0.1021	0.0252	0.0045	0.0694	0.0552
15	0.6148	88.9892	3.4723	2.0927	0.5547	1.3873	0.1785	2.1418	0.6377	0.0294	0.3517	0.1647
30	0.6247	86.1720	3.9358	2.1825	0.5485	1.7653	0.2547	3.3338	0.8234	0.0546	0.6669	0.2624
Variance decomposition of LSOL:												
2	0.2957	6.0595	92.6553	0.0253	0.0001	0.0744	0.0000	0.2232	0.5974	0.2136	0.0540	0.0973
15	0.4570	4.3396	71.5773	0.2149	0.3122	2.0490	0.6751	6.8414	9.1800	0.1631	4.4123	0.2352
30	0.4908	3.8510	63.7021	1.5033	0.5593	2.1141	1.0234	10.4520	10.1246	0.1968	6.0317	0.4416
Variance decomposition of LHYDRO:												
2	0.1332	3.6474	0.4699	94.2951	1.1296	0.0044	0.0635	0.0914	0.0022	0.2089	0.0226	0.0651
15	0.2693	2.7846	4.9924	85.7751	4.1533	1.1921	0.2561	0.5587	0.1184	0.1242	0.0143	0.0309
30	0.2991	2.9617	6.5352	83.0134	4.3039	2.1073	0.2865	0.4931	0.1026	0.1185	0.0426	0.0352
Variance decomposition of LPUMP:												
2	0.3911	4.5616	1.3292	9.7074	83.1171	0.0242	0.1335	0.0000	0.4483	0.3424	0.1025	0.2338
15	0.4103	4.8695	4.5327	9.3103	77.9924	0.1476	0.7273	0.0053	0.8673	0.4390	0.4813	0.6273
30	0.4106	4.8634	4.5437	9.3048	77.8900	0.2296	0.7269	0.0055	0.8842	0.4386	0.4860	0.6273
Variance decomposition of LBIO:												
2	0.1287	0.0021	0.6471	0.0091	0.3619	98.6522	0.0016	0.0974	0.0765	0.0035	0.0000	0.1486
15	0.2478	0.0011	1.1281	0.0309	1.2043	91.2874	0.1493	3.5427	1.3846	0.0984	0.0328	1.1402
30	0.2668	0.0042	1.0092	0.1302	1.3340	89.2268	0.1423	5.2196	1.4243	0.1373	0.0360	1.3360

(*Continued*)

Table 9.5 (Continued)

Period	S.E.	LWINDON	LSOL	LHYDRO	L_PUMP	LBIO	LCOAL	LNGAS	LOIL	DLNUC	LRXM	LGCF
Variance decomposition of LCOAL:												
2	1.2799	3.2638	0.2235	0.3717	1.5777	0.1164	93.8520	0.3923	0.0901	0.1062	0.0007	0.0056
15	1.8063	3.6723	2.6583	0.5113	1.3585	0.1231	74.7621	12.2769	2.3352	0.3136	1.4779	0.5108
30	1.9236	3.3534	3.3428	1.6352	1.3691	0.1140	66.4326	16.3477	3.4109	0.3520	2.8628	0.7796
Variance decomposition of LNGAS:												
2	0.3278	9.0001	1.3088	1.9347	1.4622	0.5123	7.5694	76.0480	0.3423	0.8932	0.2213	0.7076
15	0.6352	2.8307	6.7698	0.7587	0.4204	1.6418	6.9786	67.8072	3.8993	1.0772	4.9568	2.8596
30	0.7250	2.2913	7.2654	1.7787	0.4357	2.1472	6.0551	64.0756	5.1069	1.0113	6.7915	3.0413
Variance decomposition of LOIL:												
2	0.3998	0.7196	1.5953	6.0798	0.8867	0.4334	0.2951	0.0978	89.1581	0.0147	0.6048	0.1147
15	0.5473	0.4012	10.7310	5.1466	0.8890	0.9033	2.1279	3.9114	67.1352	0.0924	8.0795	0.5824
30	0.5757	0.4050	11.0712	5.1115	0.9145	0.8317	2.2753	7.2943	62.1463	0.1402	9.0478	0.7623
Variance decomposition of DLNUC:												
2	0.0305	2.2190	2.1902	1.7066	0.3955	0.2221	1.2570	0.0402	2.0426	88.8283	0.2073	0.8912
15	0.0307	2.2547	2.3215	1.9419	0.4340	0.2771	1.3199	0.0661	2.1131	87.8801	0.4483	0.9433
30	0.0308	2.2568	2.3174	2.0732	0.4465	0.2911	1.3172	0.0870	2.1222	87.6851	0.4615	0.9421
Variance decomposition of LRXM:												
2	0.2985	5.5110	0.1642	1.8069	0.0596	0.0471	0.0172	0.0652	7.9802	0.6878	83.5109	0.1499
15	0.4163	4.0268	0.8284	1.6684	0.1333	1.7220	0.1392	3.5794	10.6184	0.7307	75.3015	1.2518
30	0.4335	3.8174	0.9175	2.8482	0.1860	2.4298	0.2098	6.6804	10.2789	0.7252	70.4495	1.4572
Variance decomposition of LGCF:												
2	0.2783	0.1007	0.0173	3.2734	0.0076	0.5527	1.5112	0.3571	0.6335	1.6539	0.5293	91.3632
15	0.3124	0.1360	0.5227	5.2551	0.0482	5.1702	5.4492	2.4860	1.5151	1.4175	0.7267	77.2733
30	0.3154	0.1495	0.6659	5.5038	0.0481	6.1047	5.3736	2.6735	1.5330	1.3934	0.7141	75.8403

What IRF looks like:

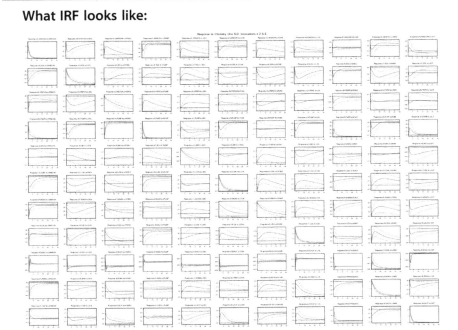

The IRF analyses the behavior of a series according to an existing impulse in another variable. For example, see *LGCF* IRF's, a positive and standard shock to *LHYDRO* leads to a rise of 4% points in the growth rate of *LGCF*. Furthermore, a positive and standard shock to *LNGAS* leads to a drop of 2% points in the growth rate of *LGCF*.

9.4.2 German results

In order to get the descriptive statistics (see Table 9.6), the command lines are: group GROUPNAME VARNAME's ⇒ GROUPNAME.stats, to display the graphics, GROUPNAME.line(m). It should be noted that, when it says GROUPNAME it means substitute using a name for the variables group, and when it says VARNAME it means input the variable or the variables name. Afterwards, all variables have been transformed in their natural logarithms, represented by the "L" prefix.

In order to evaluate the integration order of the series the most usual integration order test of ADF, PP, and KPSS were performed (see Table 9.8). Table 9.7 summarizes the commands to perform the ADF, PP, and KPSS tests in levels and first differences, with constant, constant

Table 9.6 Descriptive statistics.

	Mean	Median	Max.	Min.	Std. Dev.	Skewness	Kurtosis	Jarque–Bera	Obs.
WINDOFF	143759.3	125275.0	428056.0	0.000000	105320.5	0.571949	2.340144	61.25496***	843
WINDON	822137.5	613950.0	3347679.	0.000000	640856.9	1.174926	3.741434	213.2623***	843
SOL	379753.3	371210.0	951367.0	0.000000	248179.8	0.298207	1.887253	55.98626***	843
GEO	564.6963	480.0000	1248.000	0.000000	256.4359	0.838457	2.983798	98.78217***	843
HYDRO	250919.9	251352.0	388662.0	5817.000	50384.79	0.187037	4.232707	58.28980***	843
PUMP	74186.93	73638.00	164002.0	0.000000	18918.33	0.391600	4.670937	119.6158***	843
BIO	394970.5	395326.00	460958.0	0.000000	43158.30	− 3.873976	34.42787	36801.93***	843
WASTE	32412.74	26532.00	68197.00	0.000000	18013.23	0.408817	2.345695	38.51947***	843
COAL	2480262.	2509560.	3567694.	0.000000	512236.5	− 0.51817	3.520209	47.22969***	843
NUC	861736.4	880142.0	1098514.	0.000000	149782.0	− 1.007598	5.422375	348.7531***	843
OIL	20496.78	19192.00	169625.0	0.000000	17869.46	2.769801	14.25253	5525.392***	843
NGAS	177392.3	149728.0	688724.0	0.000000	117228.1	1.086786	4.063330	205.6599***	843
RXM	1.314324	1.257902	3.115948	1.002883	0.232100	1.944673	9.585453	2054.644***	843
GCF	1.09E + 12	1.03E + 12	3.09E + 12	3.39E + 11	3.38E + 11	1.737853	8.837871	1621.414***	843

Notes: WINDOFF is the electricity generation from offshore wind power; WINDON is the electricity generation from onshore wind power; SOL is the electricity generation from solar PV; GEO is the electricity generation from geothermal; HYDRO is the electricity generation from hydropower; PUMP is the electricity consumed in pumping systems; BIO is the electricity generation from biomass; WASTE is the electricity generation from wastes; COAL is the electricity generation from coal; NUC is the electricity generation from nuclear; OIL is the electricity generation from oil; NGAS is the electricity generation from natural gas; RXM is the coverage ratio of electricity imports by exports; and GFC is the gross cash flow.

and trend, and none, the information criterions will be chosen automatically. It is necessary to substitute VARNAME by the name of the variable that will be tested.

How to do:

Table 9.7 Unit roots commands (Eviews).

	Level	First differences
ADF test, C	VARNAME.uroot	VARNAME.uroot(dif = 1)
ADF test, CT	VARNAME.uroot (exog = trend)	VARNAME.uroot (exog = trend, dif = 1)
ADF test, N	VARNAME.uroot (exog = none)	VARNAME.uroot (exog = none, dif = 1)
PP test, C	VARNAME.uroot(pp)	VARNAME.uroot(dif = 1, pp)
PP test, CT	VARNAME.uroot (exog = trend, pp)	VARNAME.uroot (exog = trend, dif = 1, pp)
PP test, N	VARNAME.uroot (exog = none, pp)	VARNAME.uroot (exog = none, dif = 1, pp)
KPSS test, C	VARNAME.uroot(kpss)	VARNAME.uroot(dif = 1, kpss)
KPSS test, CT	VARNAME.uroot (exog = trend, kpss)	VARNAME.uroot (exog = trend, dif = 1, kpss)

Notes: VARNAME is the correspond name of the variable to be tested; C means constant; CT means constant and trend; and N denotes without constant and trend; the ADF test uses the Schwarz information criterion as definition; and PP and KPSS used the Barlett kernel and Newey-west bandwidth as standard definition.

The descriptive statistics and the series graphics highlight that series have extreme values and seasonality effects. Besides the German electricity generation database has some failures. In 4 days the dataset gives a value zero to certain sources but the correct method is to state them as missing values.

Overall the integration order tests reveal that all the series are I(0) in their levels, with intercept, and with intercept and trend. The next step is checking the collinearity and multicollinearity through the correlation matrix and VIF statistics (see Table 9.9). To perform a correlation matrix exists two possible commands: (1) group GROUPNAME VARNAME's ⇒ cor GROUPNAME; or (2) cor VARNAME's. To execute the VIF statistics.

How to do:
equation EQNAME.ls VARNAME's (including constant)
    EQNAME.results
    EQNAME.varinf
    Notes: EQNAME should be substituted by a name to the equation.

Table 9.8 Integration order tests.

	ADF		PP		KPSS	
	c	ct	c	ct	c	ct
LWINDOFF	− 11.35618***	− 20.43044***	− 21.19625***	− 20.91531***	2.303253***	0.186574**
LWINDON	− 20.19740***	− 20.50475***	− 21.20576***	− 21.14702***	0.807770***	0.244360***
LSOL	− 4.18644***	− 4.204219***	− 25.27426***	− 25.26051***	0.089892	0.081279
LGEO	− 4.43424***	− 5.923874***	− 23.35064***	− 26.59518***	2.237652***	0.153779**
LHYDRO	− 5.914171***	− 6.403277***	− 27.49800***	− 28.11090***	0.811834***	0.139646*
LPUMP	− 26.82787***	− 26.81253***	− 27.92808***	− 27.91496***	0.310484	0.310004***
LBIO	− 28.50507***	− 28.67830***	− 28.51442***	− 28.67830***	0.558095**	0.083947
LWASTE	− 8.728522***	− 9.528532***	− 10.58520***	− 11.59092***	1.290301***	0.244238***
LCOAL	− 26.38176***	− 26.60156***	− 26.76051***	− 26.83905***	0.665070**	0.063380
LNUC	− 28.02572***	− 28.20250***	− 28.48764***	− 28.50110***	0.757982***	0.320880***
LOIL	− 3.787232***	− 3.866087**	− 8.096534***	− 8.275677***	0.463232**	0.202950**
LNGAS	− 7.157022***	− 7.512342***	− 24.14961***	− 24.4447***	0.893977***	0.181301**
LRXM	− 6.390960***	− 6.660420***	− 17.85949***	− 18.27273***	0.536020**	0.058055
LGCF	− 16.02139***	− 16.34745***	− 18.28009***	− 18.42736***	0.887944***	0.377923***

Notes: C means constant; CT means constant and trend; None denotes without constant and trend; ***, **, and * indicate that the statistic is significant at 1%, 5%, and 10%, respectively.

Table 9.9 Correlation matrix and variance inflation factors statistics.

	LWINDOFF	LWINDON	LSOL	LGEO	LHYDRO	LPUMP	LBIO	LWASTE	LCOAL	LNUC	LOIL	LNGAS	LRXM	LGCF
LWINDOFF	1.0000	0.7776	0.1474	0.1415	0.2757	0.5148	0.4374	0.2989	0.1951	0.4340	0.1191	0.3354	−0.3467	0.1131
LWINDON	0.7776	1.0000	0.1998	0.2812	0.2941	0.6751	0.5037	0.2791	0.2578	0.5955	0.1190	0.3038	−0.3470	0.1017
LSOL	0.1474	0.1998	1.0000	0.3310	0.6461	0.4618	0.4621	0.2354	0.3627	0.5043	−0.0804	0.1105	0.1230	−0.0369
LGEO	0.1415	0.2812	0.3310	1.0000	0.2563	0.5389	0.6265	0.0939	0.4486	0.5702	−0.1573	0.2355	0.1090	−0.0418
LHYDRO	0.2757	0.2941	0.6461	0.2563	1.0000	0.5403	0.6479	0.3357	0.4363	0.6139	0.0715	0.4049	0.1387	0.0175
LPUMP	0.5148	0.6751	0.4618	0.5389	0.5403	1.0000	0.7474	0.3679	0.6000	0.7809	0.1332	0.5805	−0.0413	0.0630
LBIO	0.4374	0.5037	0.4621	0.6265	0.6479	0.7474	1.0000	0.4915	0.5649	0.7754	0.1328	0.5678	0.0061	0.0211
LWASTE	0.2989	0.2791	0.2354	0.0939	0.3357	0.3679	0.4915	1.0000	0.2502	0.3609	0.0748	0.2938	−0.0341	0.0597
LCOAL	0.1951	0.2578	0.3627	0.4486	0.4363	0.6000	0.5649	0.2502	1.0000	0.6829	0.1495	0.5730	−0.0279	0.0586
LNUC	0.4340	0.5955	0.5043	0.5702	0.6139	0.7809	0.7754	0.3609	0.6829	1.0000	0.1593	0.6357	−0.0316	0.0319
LOIL	0.1191	0.1190	−0.0804	−0.1573	0.0715	0.1332	0.1328	0.0748	0.1495	0.1593	1.0000	0.4078	−0.2041	−0.0733
LNGAS	0.3354	0.3038	0.1105	0.2355	0.4049	0.5805	0.5678	0.2938	0.5730	0.6357	0.4078	1.0000	−0.1185	0.0422
LRXM	−0.3467	−0.3470	0.1230	0.1090	0.1387	−0.0413	0.0061	−0.0341	−0.0279	−0.0316	−0.2041	−0.1185	1.0000	−0.0692
LGCF	0.1131	0.1017	−0.0369	−0.0418	0.0175	0.0630	0.0211	0.0597	0.0586	0.0319	−0.0733	0.0422	−0.0692	1.0000
VIF statistics	1.7711	2.7299	2.2193	2.71	2.9289	5.9622	5.0446	1.4986	2.1839	7.1091	1.387	2.7708	1.3729	1.0479

In the correlation matrix the highest value is 0.78, and in the VIF statistics the highest value is 7, the others are below 6. The *LNUC* VIF statistics is high but is not above 10, so, any doubts about collinearity and multicollinearity were set aside. Consequently, let us move on to the VAR estimation, the command is: var VARNAME.ls 1 2 ENDOVARNAME @ EXOVARNAME ⇒ VARNAME.results, ENDOVARNAME should be substituted by the endogenous variables name, and the EXOVARNAME substituted by exogenous variables name, in this first attempt a constant. After, the lag order selection criteria command is VARNAME.laglen(27), 27 is the number of lags maximum to be tested. The FPE, SC and HQ choose 1, and LR choose 7 as optimal number of lags, therefore, re-estimate VAR with 1 lag, var VARNAME. ls 1 1 ENDOVARNAME @ EXOVARNAME ⇒ VARNAME.results. Next, it is necessary to check if exogenous variables exist (VARNAME. testexog), and the residuals (VARNAME.resids). The blocks of exogeneity reveal that none of the series are exogenous, and the residuals demonstrate that the database problems generate outliers in the residuals (see Fig. 9.1). These outliers in the residuals have been provoked by the zero values that should be missing values, in the dates 13/1/2015, 1/6/2016, 28/10/2016, and 9/12/2016, to generate the dummy variables the command is series DUMMYNAME = @recode(@date = @dateval("mm/dd/ aaaa"),1,0), DUMYNAME is a given name for the dummy, mm/dd/aaaa substitute by the month, day, and year, respectively, and the variable will take the value 1 in the given day and zero in the remaining. As an example, let us generate the dummy variable for 13/1/2015, series d_1_13_2015 = @recode(@date = @dateval("1/13/2015"),1,0).   Re-estimating the VAR with the dummy variables, var bvar.ls 1 1 LWINDOFF LWINDON LSOL LGEO LHYDRO LPUMP LBIO LWASTE LCOAL LNUC LOIL LNGAS LRXM LGCF @ c d_1_13_2015 d_6_1_2016 d_10_28_2016 d_12_09_2016, after the introduction of the dummies the residuals reveals consistency (Fig. 9.2).

After the introduction of the dummies, the optimal numbers of lags have been tested once again, the FPE, AIC, SC, and HQ points to one, and LR to 7 as the optimal number of lags. Thus it is not necessary perform the lag exclusion tests, but if needed the commands are (to test 7 as maximum lags) var VARNAME.ls 1 7 ENDOVARNAME @ EXOVARNAME ⇒ VARNAME.testlags. In order to perform the diagnostic tests, the command are: (1) AR roots test: VARNAME.arroots (graph); (2) LM test: VARNAME.arlm(10), 10 is the number of lags

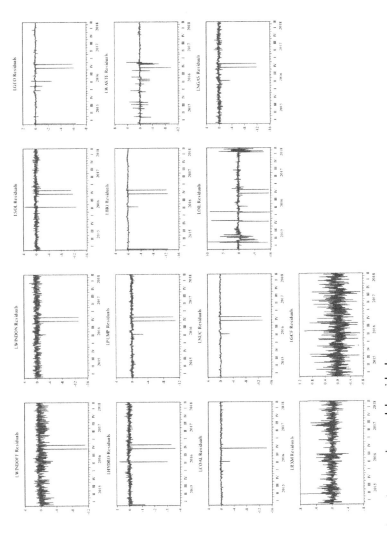

Figure 9.2 Vector autoregressive model residuals.

maximum; (3) White test: VARNAME.white; and (4) Jarque—Bera test: VARNAME.jbera. The stability of models is supported by the AR roots test, but the French VAR model also fails to reject the null hypothesis of diagnostic tests, revealing serial correlation, heteroskedasticity, and non-normality. However, the results are as expected, (please see the justification given in French results), and it does not have interference in the model estimation once the number of the observation is 825. After the diagnostic test, it is necessary to compute the Granger causalities, the command is:

How to do:
VARNAME.testexog

The large number of causalities found highlights that endogeneity is highly present in the relationships of German electricity sources and financial activity (see Tabe 9.10). However, only pump, oil, natural gas, and the electricity exchanged in cross-border markets drives financial activity. Further, to compute the VDC the command is:

How to do:
VARNAME.decomp(31, t)
Notes: Decomposes the variance in 31 periods and displays it in tables.

Regarding the GCF, after a 2-day lag, shocks to *LGCF* explain around 94% of the forecast error variance. This impact is slightly decreased to 90% after 30 days (see Table 9.11). This implies that the French electricity mix has a reduced impact on French financial activity. Comparing the shocks to both *LPUMP* and *LOIL*, the shocks to *LOIL* explains a larger percentage of the forecast error variance than the shocks to *LPUMP*, about 2.13% and 1.39%, respectively after 30 days. Lastly, to compute the IRF the command is (Fig. 9.3):

How to do:
VARNAME.impulse(31, se = a)

Table 9.10 Granger causalities.

	LWINDOFF	LWINDON	LSOL	LGEO	LHYDRO	LPUMP	LBIO	LWASTE	LCOAL	LNUC	LOIL	LNGAS	LRXM	LGCF
LWINDOFF	–	2.8249*	0.5578	0.9035	0.005021	2.333	0.2206	2.1721	4.8423**	7.8811***	0.8118	0.1198	0.0706	1.2896
LWINDON	0.0147	–	7.3364***	4.3868**	0.015554	0.2528	5.0985***	0.0127	45.0609***	65.4187***	1.4983	0.1638	6.9685***	0.5499
LSOL	4.6826**	9.1735***	–	41.8831***	12.17891***	40.6961***	40.7051***	0.0378	7.0119***	290.6705***	2.8214*	30.2039***	3.6417*	0.0043
LGEO	3.504*	0.2333	13.0551***	–	72.75209***	7.7257***	79.3025***	12.8908***	23.5968***	28.7758***	4.7979**	0.0807	0.2568	1.4246
LHYDRO	0.0065	0.6067	1.2209	38.6451***	–	0.0122	2.3952	8.8679***	20.9419***	5.2251**	0.1959	3.5379*	0.0031	0.0409
LPUMP	0.03269	0.1404	0.8158	0.6045	7.328843***	–	2.1613	3.4891*	0.7596	135.9959***	4.6332**	14.1843***	1.7796	2.8645*
LBIO	1.7643	0.0005	17.1096***	1491.453***	5.537378***	8.1106***	–	20.9074***	1.9876	59.4675***	0.8063	0.6479	0.0531	0.0591
LWASTE	0.0925	0.0934	0.2906	12.8893***	4.640287**	4.2605**	0.0215	–	0.5177	6.1158**	0.8505	0.3598	0.2177	0.3294
LCOAL	0.0448	0.4198	12.3838***	0.0686	2.901686*	0.0132	5.1362**	29.1851***	–	38.0419***	0.0289	0.0537	0.9614	0.3698
LNUC	13.9424***	9.5744***	15.4427***	0.0712	9.027282***	50.3133***	164.9821***	2.7835*	3.1171*	–	2.7321*	64.6783***	8.0712***	1.6458
LOIL	1.2298	0.0029	1.5072	4.4288**	2.787405*	2.3488	0.1997	1.4636	2.2365	0.0282	–	5.5376**	1.377573	12.1629***
LNGAS	4.1232**	0.2542	48.3237***	6.0643**	43.71322***	0.2663	21.8843***	0.1776	25.1145***	86.3507***	4.9602**	–	2.6771	3.0019*
LRXM	0.3029	0.0467	1.6833	3.3712*	0.055227	4.7586**	2.8587*	1.9548	34.3089***	195.3159***	2.6379	30.867***	–	5.9755**
LGCF	0.0015	0.5963	0.593	0.2122	0.206684	0.3005	5.6233***	0.0677	2.7079*	12.3299***	4.6889**	0.1737	1.14E-06	–
ALL	103.7850***	138.7298***	696.7313***	7195.388***	772.3605***	230.3245***	726.87***	423.6425***	403.4022***	1565.803***	115.0536***	1021.853***	47.0287***	26.3437***

Notes: "All" denotes the causality test set for all independent variables; ***, **, and * denote statistical significance at 1%, 5%, and 10%, respectively.

Table 9.11 Variances decomposition.

Period	S.E.	LWINDOFF	LWINDON	LSOL	LGEO	LHYDRO	LPUMP	LBIO	LWASTE	LCOAL	LNUC	LOIL	LNGAS	LRXM	LGCF
Variance decomposition of LWINDOFF:															
2	0.9594	99.4412	0.0003	0.2109	0.0056	0.0004	0.0008	0.0101	0.0022	0.0070	0.1399	0.0331	0.1344	0.0140	0.0001
15	1.0283	94.3451	0.0013	1.0705	0.4321	0.0928	0.0439	0.1889	0.1215	0.1933	0.4582	0.1892	2.7925	0.0638	0.0069
30	1.0339	93.3578	0.0061	1.0697	0.8697	0.1679	0.0547	0.2687	0.1916	0.1995	0.4736	0.3091	2.9455	0.0774	0.0088
Variance decomposition of LWINDON:															
2	0.7817	48.0943	51.4236	0.2660	0.0002	0.0270	0.0066	0.0002	0.0011	0.0080	0.1245	0.0004	0.0076	0.0011	0.0394
15	0.8329	48.7681	48.4793	1.1811	0.0051	0.0508	0.0477	0.0189	0.0082	0.1170	0.2562	0.0800	0.8580	0.0438	0.0860
30	0.8340	48.6416	48.3509	1.2033	0.0148	0.0513	0.0547	0.0236	0.0098	0.1232	0.2555	0.1562	0.9625	0.0647	0.0878
Variance decomposition of LSOL:															
2	0.5857	1.2713	3.1327	93.2317	0.0351	0.0940	0.0213	0.0011	0.0045	0.3569	0.4116	0.0703	1.2768	0.0595	0.0334
15	0.8212	1.7726	2.1026	71.4215	0.8371	0.2925	0.8855	0.0047	0.0901	1.3498	1.2550	3.3091	12.1376	4.4339	0.1081
30	0.8415	1.6918	2.0488	68.6750	1.3574	0.4979	0.9826	0.0356	0.1072	1.3684	1.3251	4.2737	12.7594	4.7441	0.1331
Variance decomposition of LGEO:															
2	0.1205	0.0144	0.2696	1.7131	92.7807	1.0004	0.0352	3.5097	0.2310	0.0226	0.0079	0.1338	0.1597	0.1113	0.0105
15	0.2666	1.0851	0.8996	0.8667	70.9049	10.1304	0.1884	8.1249	3.7748	0.0429	1.6920	1.1623	0.7975	0.2896	0.0410
30	0.3322	1.5236	1.0580	1.1113	67.2945	11.3287	0.1320	8.3121	4.8054	0.0278	2.4098	1.0109	0.6655	0.2922	0.0282
Variance decomposition of LHYDRO:															
2	0.1374	2.9825	5.2197	0.3460	2.6740	86.5555	0.3675	0.0001	0.0877	0.1483	0.2816	0.1112	1.2116	0.0017	0.0126
15	0.1755	1.8975	3.5471	1.3106	7.1050	70.5964	0.4918	0.5062	0.9164	0.4840	0.9722	2.1048	8.5932	1.3884	0.0863
30	0.1837	1.8230	3.3773	1.7780	10.8308	65.7742	0.4989	0.9770	1.0352	0.4727	1.2720	2.2401	8.2646	1.5570	0.0992

Variance decomposition of LPUMP:

2	0.2378	4.2684	5.9832	1.0269	0.0722	1.3299	86.1509	0.0146	0.1310	0.0096	0.6538	0.0689	0.0206	0.2481	0.0218
15	0.2511	3.9541	5.8117	3.4298	0.9526	1.4386	80.3358	0.0686	0.6962	0.1326	0.9056	0.2261	1.6220	0.3323	0.0941
30	0.2522	3.9218	5.7717	3.4880	1.3342	1.5630	79.6127	0.1104	0.6980	0.1374	0.9340	0.2575	1.7080	0.3682	0.0952

Variance decomposition of LBIO:

2	0.0672	2.1100	1.3075	5.0370	4.1416	0.3727	0.1589	83.1974	0.0036	0.3694	1.9296	0.0000	0.8122	0.1216	0.4385
15	0.0760	3.4697	1.4103	6.2455	6.7526	1.3865	0.5290	66.2707	0.2765	1.0166	2.7319	0.8119	8.3833	0.2728	0.4429
30	0.0783	3.4213	1.3681	5.8984	9.2430	1.8827	0.5363	62.9391	0.5757	0.9813	2.7178	1.2740	8.4488	0.2897	0.4237

Variance decomposition of LWASTE:

2	0.6751	0.2846	0.2495	0.2386	0.1717	0.5170	0.0745	0.0690	97.9990	0.2625	0.0207	0.0394	0.0014	0.0688	0.0033
15	1.0565	2.4468	0.6456	0.1642	1.6846	1.5197	0.2727	0.1209	90.8774	0.5521	0.0734	0.8520	0.0062	0.6997	0.0847
30	1.0843	2.5676	0.6946	0.2385	3.3123	1.5590	0.2598	0.3145	88.5567	0.5396	0.1608	0.9338	0.0065	0.7633	0.0929

Variance decomposition of LCOAL:

2	0.1862	19.0927	19.7204	2.5570	0.0529	1.6945	0.6620	1.2131	0.3710	51.3078	0.2901	0.1689	1.0402	1.6344	0.1951
15	0.2081	18.4633	17.4342	3.0688	1.1437	2.6533	1.1048	1.0502	0.4237	41.4265	1.4906	2.0028	4.2856	5.2400	0.2125
30	0.2107	18.0260	17.0367	3.2116	2.1100	2.8857	1.1101	1.1330	0.4699	40.4060	1.5742	2.1905	4.3694	5.2611	0.2157

Variance decomposition of LNUC:

2	0.1236	0.9566	0.0382	6.2563	1.7498	0.1343	5.9222	0.0813	0.1542	0.2491	74.9080	0.0338	1.5331	7.2904	0.6927
15	0.1593	1.7579	0.0622	8.6288	2.7674	0.7502	8.0953	0.4482	0.4110	0.1558	56.2149	0.3529	2.5383	16.4156	1.4016
30	0.1625	1.7719	0.1106	8.4354	4.9418	1.3264	7.7868	0.7561	0.4902	0.1498	54.2441	0.3426	2.4387	15.8593	1.3462

(Continued)

Table 9.11 (Continued)

Period	S.E.	LWINDOFF	LWINDON	LSOL	LGEO	LHYDRO	LPUMP	LBIO	LWASTE	LCOAL	LNUC	LOIL	LNGAS	LRXM	LGCF
Variance decomposition of LOIL:															
2	1.8092	0.2493	0.1193	0.0697	0.0614	0.0001	0.1850	0.0212	0.2520	0.0677	0.1176	98.3563	0.1447	0.1149	0.2410
15	2.7454	0.1514	0.0596	1.1885	1.2189	0.1430	1.2837	0.3882	0.1644	0.2171	0.0806	88.0964	4.3739	1.5517	1.0825
30	2.8299	0.1806	0.0584	1.3147	2.1796	0.3521	1.3503	0.6079	0.1683	0.2792	0.0917	85.2468	5.3240	1.7771	1.0693
Variance decomposition of LNGAS:															
2	0.4627	5.9976	9.9461	7.1039	0.0018	1.2808	1.3087	0.4625	0.0242	2.7816	1.1029	0.4219	68.3690	1.1896	0.0096
15	0.6762	3.0676	5.4846	9.3529	0.2641	0.6234	2.2047	0.7553	0.1491	3.1695	0.5235	7.4791	61.7676	4.9054	0.2533
30	0.6948	2.9468	5.1979	9.2569	0.5572	0.6173	2.2550	0.8269	0.1808	3.1037	0.4973	8.9666	60.2359	5.0738	0.2839
Variance decomposition of LRXM:															
2	0.1414	19.6746	10.6945	1.6300	0.6588	0.2007	0.0773	0.4335	0.0464	1.4696	1.2576	0.3889	0.8786	62.5895	0.0000
15	0.1611	15.4811	8.3594	1.9670	0.8222	0.1586	1.1403	0.4672	0.2295	1.4504	2.6649	2.4528	2.2849	62.5189	0.0028
30	0.1617	15.3644	8.2958	2.0215	0.8379	0.1580	1.1704	0.4725	0.2420	1.4500	2.6536	2.7376	2.4516	62.1382	0.0069
Variance decomposition of LGCF:															
2	0.2686	0.8029	0.3801	0.1378	0.0308	0.0430	1.0814	0.2253	0.3282	1.3923	0.3305	0.3170	0.1040	0.3890	94.4377
15	0.2848	0.8514	0.6416	0.2253	0.0811	0.0436	1.3949	0.2760	0.5030	1.6275	0.2989	2.1222	0.7427	1.0084	90.1833
30	0.2849	0.8554	0.6419	0.2256	0.1058	0.0449	1.3936	0.2789	0.5467	1.6260	0.2996	2.1328	0.7437	1.0080	90.0971

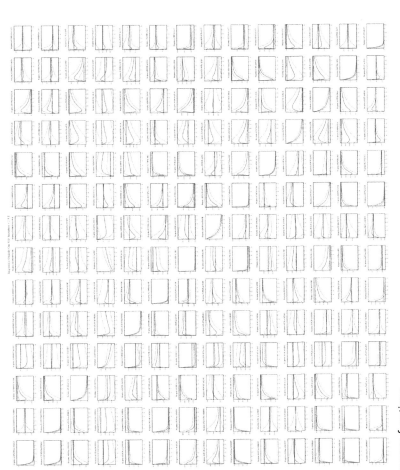

Figure 9.3 Impulse response functions.

As all IRF converges to zero, this corroborates the Integration order tests confidence. Regarding the *LGCF*, a positive and standard shock to *LPUMP* leads to a rise of 2 percentage points in the growth rate of *LGCF*, whereas a positive and standard shock to *LOIL* leads to a drop of 2 percentage points in the growth rate of LGCF. A positive and standard shock to *LGCF* provokes a rise of 0.4 percentage points in the growth rate of *LBIO*. While, a positive and standard shock to *LGCF* generates a drop of 10 percentage points in the growth rate of *LOIL*.

9.5 Discussion

The evaluation of the daily electricity—growth nexus and the inter-actions between electricity sources, in countries where the energy transition and the nuclear phase-out has been implemented with different rhythms has been a revealing experience. On the one hand, France is still highly dependent on nuclear power, and RES have been only slowly integrated into the electricity mix. On the other hand, German is very much less dependent on nuclear than France, and it has been a model country in terms of RES implementation, implementing high capacity levels. Germany have at their disposable diverse renewable technologies, the intermittent, namely both onshore and offshore wind power and solar PV, and the controllable such as geothermal, biomass, and hydropower. In contrast, France only has at its disposable onshore wind power, solar PV, biomass, and hydropower. For France, there is strong evidence for: (1) a growth hypothesis for coal, oil, and hydropower; (2) a feedback hypothesis for natural gas and biomass; and (3) a conservation hypothesis for nuclear. For Germany, there is strong evidence for: (1) a growth hypothesis for natural gas; (2) a feedback hypothesis for oil; and (3) a conservation hypothesis for nuclear, coal, and biomass.

The feedback hypothesis for natural gas and biomass is verified in France, and is of particular interest, deserving further and careful discussion. In fact, the relationship of both natural gas and biomass with financial activity, and vice versa, is negative. Biomass and natural gas have been key energy sources during the transition toward RES, widely used to backup intermittency of RES and fulfilling demand peaks. It is a fact that French electricity systems have been relatively closed to the exterior, although the cross-border countries do exert pressure for greater openness, managing the surplus of electricity through pumping, and in scarcity recurring to biomass, natural gas, and hydropower. However, any direct access to Germany could allow the importation of RES production at lower prices, instead of resorting to fossil fuels. Thus if backup can be provided through imports this could provoke beneficial conditions for the economy of France.

The feedback hypothesis for oil, in Germany is also verified and is curious given that the relationships are negative. So this result raises an interesting question; why policymakers and electricity systems do not shut down and dismantle oil powered thermal plants? Furthermore why not when electricity production through oil is the most direct and indirect polluting method? Besides the results reveal the substitution effect between oil and both the solar PV, geothermal, and hydropower. Thus given that oil has been substituted by RES, Germany should consider shutting down the oil plants, an action which will also subsequently contribute positively to the environment.

In contrast with France the German backup systems, powered by natural gas and pumping have been beneficial to economic activity. In fact, even with two wind technologies, the German electricity systems seems to be carefully designed, given that intermittent RES have been substituting the polluting oil and coal sources, and also the nuclear usage. At the same time, hydropower, geothermal, and biomass have been substituting natural gas in the backup. Thus this could be a signal of maturity of RES technologies, and high efficiency in the accommodation of them into the electricity system. These facts support that the decision to replace nuclear power by a portfolio of intermittent and controllable RES is appropriate. Besides, given that all RES impact negatively on nuclear electricity generation, the rational for its replacement is based on historical data.

Overall, one gets the idea that Germany could be less dependent upon nuclear power. In fact it seems that the transition of nuclear toward RES has been prepared over the years. It is very remarkable, in the daily data, that nuclear phase-out and replacement by RES is in process. Moreover it was believed that France has been planning its energy transition from nuclear to RES because of external and internal factors, such as the Fukushima accident, and the pending long-term safety reviews of nuclear facilities. The French electricity supply reveals a capacity to substitute their rigid baseload source, by a portfolio of intermittent and controllable RES. However, France still has several barriers and challenges in its path, so the transmission system operators, electricity producers, and policymakers should together create a proper political framework to do that.

Germany has at its disposable singular conditions to make a successful energy transition, without compromising its economy. In contrast the results of this research reveal that France needs to develop and evolve their energy transition plan. There seems to be an overall rationality in the German system, and the access to the Nord Pool is a crucial piece. So French electricity systems and government should rethink their insularity, and open their electricity market to the Iberian Market and to the Nord Pool, benefiting from key factors available to manage the surplus and excess of electricity. In conclusion it seems that a widespread daily adaptation of supply with a high availability of green and endogenous resources, should guarantee lower electricity prices, and a healthier economy.

9.6 Conclusion

This chapter is focused on two pertinent exciting energy economics research topics, which are the composition of the electricity mix in the energy transition era, and their relationship with economic activity, that is, the electricity—growth nexus. The chapter briefly reviews the literature about the electricity—growth nexus. The main focus of this chapter is the study of electricity—growth nexus and electricity sources interactions with daily data, through a disaggregated analysis of electricity sources. To do that, the data sources are revealed, and largely explained in the methodology, and the procedural steps in EViews (econometric software) to obtain the results shared, as well as how to diagnose the results obtained.

The electricity—growth nexus along with the interactions of electricity sources, with daily data from January 1, 2015 to April 30, 2018 through a VAR model was examined. The VAR methodology was required to handle the endogeneity present in both French and German electricity systems and economic activity. Thus the large number of Granger causalities provided new insights into the conditions needed to achieve a suitable energy transition, from both fossil fuels and nuclear power toward a portfolio of intermittent and controllable RES, without compromising economic growth and activity.

In both countries there is a strong empirical evidence to support the growth, feedback, and conservation hypothesis distinguished by electricity sources. The results highlight that both countries have suitable conditions to substitute their electricity sources without hampering their economic growth. However, Germany has more potential to substitute nuclear power with RES than France. France is still highly dependent on nuclear power with a very low RES implementation. As the results revealed, German nuclear substitution has been accurately made and France should follow their policy framework, namely because of their success and because of the similarities between both countries.

Further research is needed to help in the daily management of both the RES intermittency and electricity demand oscillations. It should be mandatory to analyze high-frequency data, namely daily and hourly, to increase the framework of policymakers and transmission system operators to accommodate accurately RES production. Besides, it is crucial to analyze the interactions between the many periods of electricity demand, to help policymakers smooth the nonguided electricity demand to achieve the shift to electrification through RES production. What is more, energy storage and cross-border markets should be studied so that electricity production systems can efficiently manage the excess and the scarcity of RES production without resorting to fossil fuels.

References

Aït-Sahalia, Y., & Xiu, D. (2017). Using principal component analysis to estimate a high dimensional factor model with high-frequency data. *Journal of Econometrics*, *201*, 384–399. Available from: https://doi.org/10.1016/j.jeconom.2017.08.015.

Apergis, N., & Payne, J. E. (2011). The renewable energy consumption-growth nexus in Central America. *Applied Energy*, *88*(1), 343–347. Available from: https://doi.org/10.1016/j.apenergy.2010.07.013.

Apergis, N., & Payne, J. E. (2012). Renewable and non-renewable energy consumption-growth nexus: Evidence from a panel error correction model. *Energy Economics*, *34*(3), 733–738. Available from: https://doi.org/10.1016/j.eneco.2011.04.007.

At-Sahalia, Y., Mykland, P. A., & Zhang, L. (2011). Ultra high frequency volatility estimation with dependent microstructure noise. *Journal of Econometrics*, *160*(1), 160–175. Available from: https://doi.org/10.1016/j.jeconom.2010.03.028.

Auer, H., & Haas, R. (2016). On integrating large shares of variable renewables into the electricity system. *Energy*, *115*, 1592–1601. Available from: https://doi.org/10.1016/j.energy.2016.05.067.

Ben Jebli, M., & Ben Youssef, S. (2015). The environmental Kuznets curve, economic growth, renewable and non-renewable energy, and trade in Tunisia. *Renewable and Sustainable Energy Reviews*, *47*, 173–185. Available from: https://doi.org/10.1016/j.rser.2015.02.049.

Brooks, C. (2008). Introductory econometrics for finance. *The Economic Journal*, *113*(488), F397–F398. Available from: https://doi.org/10.1111/1468-0297.13911.

Cao, L., & Tay, F. E. H. (2001). Financial forecasting using support vector machines. *Neurocomputing*, *1*(2), 1–36. Available from: https://doi.org/10.1080/14697688.2015.1032546.

Cerdeira Bento, J. P., & Moutinho, V. (2016). CO_2 emissions, non-renewable and renewable electricity production, economic growth, and international trade in Italy. *Renewable and Sustainable Energy Reviews*, *55*, 142–155. Available from: https://doi.org/10.1016/j.rser.2015.10.151.

Dickey, B. Y. D. A., & Fuller, W. A. (1981). Likelihood ratio statistics for autoregressive time series with a unit root. *Econometrica*, *49*(4), 1057–1072.

Dogan, E. (2015). The relationship between economic growth and electricity consumption from renewable and non-renewable sources: A study of Turkey. *Renewable and Sustainable Energy Reviews*, *52*, 534–546. Available from: https://doi.org/10.1016/j.rser.2015.07.130.

Flora, R., Marques, A. C., & Fuinhas, J. A. (2014). Wind power idle capacity in a panel of European countries. *Energy*, *66*, 823–830. Available from: https://doi.org/10.1016/j.energy.2013.12.061.

Ghysels, E., & Osborn, D. (2001). *The econometric analysis of seasonal time series*. Cambridge University Press. Available from: https://econpapers.repec.org/RePEc:cup:cbooks:9780521565882.

Glasnovic, Z., & Margeta, J. (2011). Vision of total renewable electricity scenario. *Renewable and Sustainable Energy Reviews*, *15*(4), 1873–1884. Available from: https://doi.org/10.1016/j.rser.2010.12.016.

Granger, C. W. J. (1969). Investigating causal relations by econometric models and cross-spectral methods. *Econometrica*, *37*(3), 424–438. Available from: https://doi.org/10.2307/1912791.

Hamdi, H., Sbia, R., & Shahbaz, M. (2014). The nexus between electricity consumption and economic growth in Bahrain. *Economic Modelling*, *38*, 227–237. Available from: https://doi.org/10.1016/j.econmod.2013.12.012.

Kwiatkowski, D., Phillips, P. C. B., Schmidt, P., & Shinb, Y. (1992). Testing the null hypothesis of stationary against the alternative of a unit root. *Journal of Econometrics*, *54*(1), 159–178.

Li, J., Todorov, V., & Tauchen, G. (2017). Adaptive estimation of continuous-time regression models using high-frequency data. *Journal of Econometrics*, *200*(1), 36–47. Available from: https://doi.org/10.1016/j.jeconom.2017.01.010.

Mackinnon, J. G., Econometrics, A., & Dec, N. N. (2008). *Numerical Distribution Functions for Unit Root*, *11*(6), 601–618.

Marques, A. C., & Fuinhas, J. A. (2016). How electricity generation regimes are interacting in Portugal. Does it matter for sustainability and economic activity? *Journal of Renewable and Sustainable Energy*, *8*(2), 25902. Available from: https://doi.org/10.1063/1.4944959.

Marques, A. C., Fuinhas, J. A., & Menegaki, A. N. (2014). Interactions between electricity generation sources and economic activity in Greece: A VECM approach. *Applied Energy*, *132*, 34–46. Available from: https://doi.org/10.1016/j.apenergy.2014.06.073.

Nel, W. P., & Cooper, C. J. (2009). Implications of fossil fuel constraints on economic growth and global warming. *Energy Policy*, *37*(1), 166–180. Available from: https://doi.org/10.1016/j.enpol.2008.08.013.

Omri, A. (2014). An international literature survey on energy-economic growth nexus: Evidence from country-specific studies. *Renewable and Sustainable Energy Reviews*, *38*, 951–959. Available from: https://doi.org/10.1016/j.rser.2014.07.084.

Phillips, P. C. B., & Perron, P. (1988). Testing for a unit root in time series regression. *Biometrika*, *75*(2), 335–346.

Rüstemoğlu, H., & Andrés, A. R. (2016). Determinants of CO_2 emissions in Brazil and Russia between 1992 and 2011: A decomposition analysis. *Environmental Science and Policy*, *58*, 95–106. Available from: https://doi.org/10.1016/j.envsci.2016.01.012.

Salim, R. A., Hassan, K., & Shafiei, S. (2014). Renewable and non-renewable energy consumption and economic activities: Further evidence from OECD countries. *Energy Economics*, *44*, 350–360. Available from: https://doi.org/10.1016/j.eneco.2014.05.001.

Sims, C. A. (1980). Macroeconomics and reality. *Econometrica*, *48*(1), 1–48. Available from: https://doi.org/10.2307/1912017.

Tiba, S., & Omri, A. (2017). Literature survey on the relationships between energy, environment and economic growth. *Renewable and Sustainable Energy Reviews*, *69*(August 2015), 1129–1146. Available from: https://doi.org/10.1016/j.rser.2016.09.113.

Zhong, X., & Enke, D. (2017). A comprehensive cluster and classification mining procedure for daily stock market return forecasting. *Neurocomputing*, *267*, 152–168. Available from: https://doi.org/10.1016/j.neucom.2017.06.010.

Index

Note: Page numbers followed by "*f*" and "*t*" refer to figures and tables, respectively.

Printed in the United States
By Bookmasters